Shojo Beat

The Cain Saga

the seal of the red ram · Part 1

Earl Cain Series 4

Story & Art by **Kaori Yuki**

Read Kaori Yuki's entire
Earl Cain Series

Series 1:
The Cain Saga: Forgotten Juliet

Series 2:
The Cain Saga: The Sound of a Boy Hatching

Series 3:
The Cain Saga: Kafka

Series 4:
The Cain Saga: The Seal of the Red Ram, Parts 1 & 2

Series 5:
Godchild, Volumes 1-8

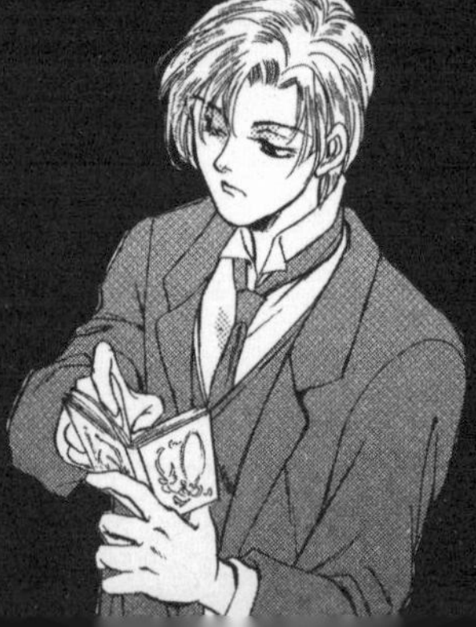

Essentially the story that links *The Cain Saga* with its sequel, *Godchild, The Seal of the Red Ram* is a two-part tale that sheds more light on the early life of Cain and his fractured family – and sets the stage for the deeper drama of *Godchild*. If you're trying to figure it all out, *Red Ram* really is the piece of the puzzle you simply can't be without when you put the whole thing together!

Enjoy,
Joel Enos
Editor
Earl Cain Series

Contents

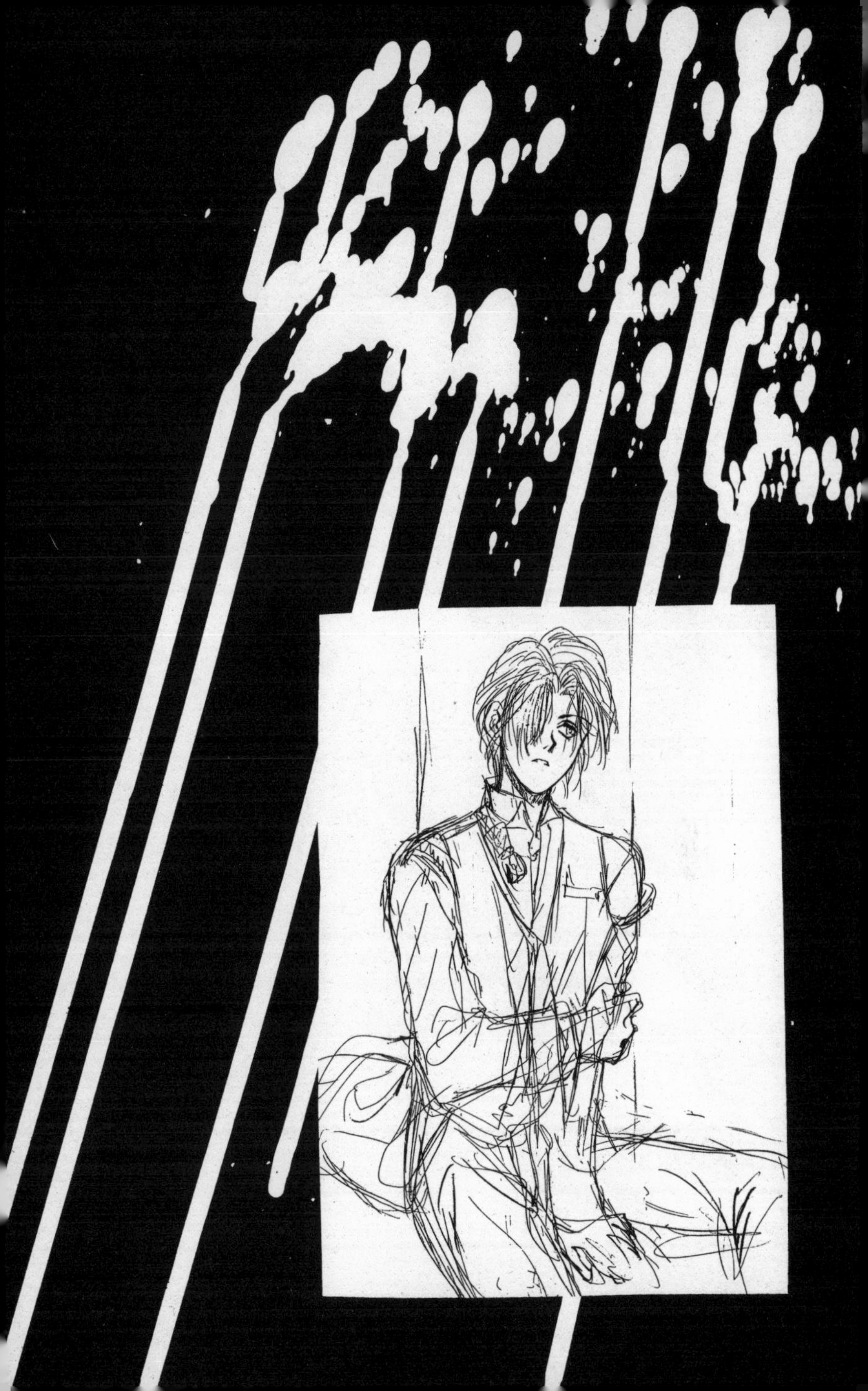

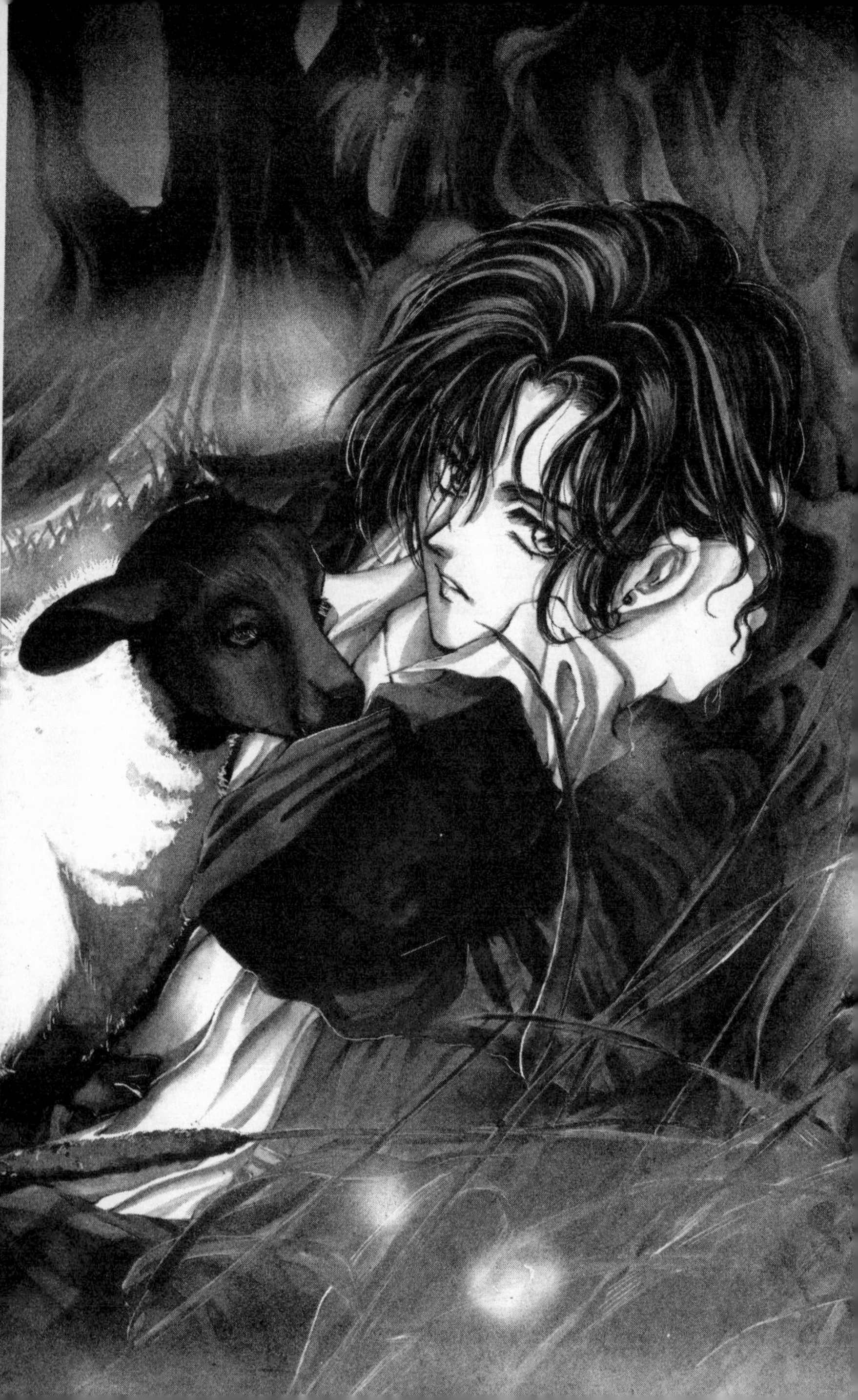

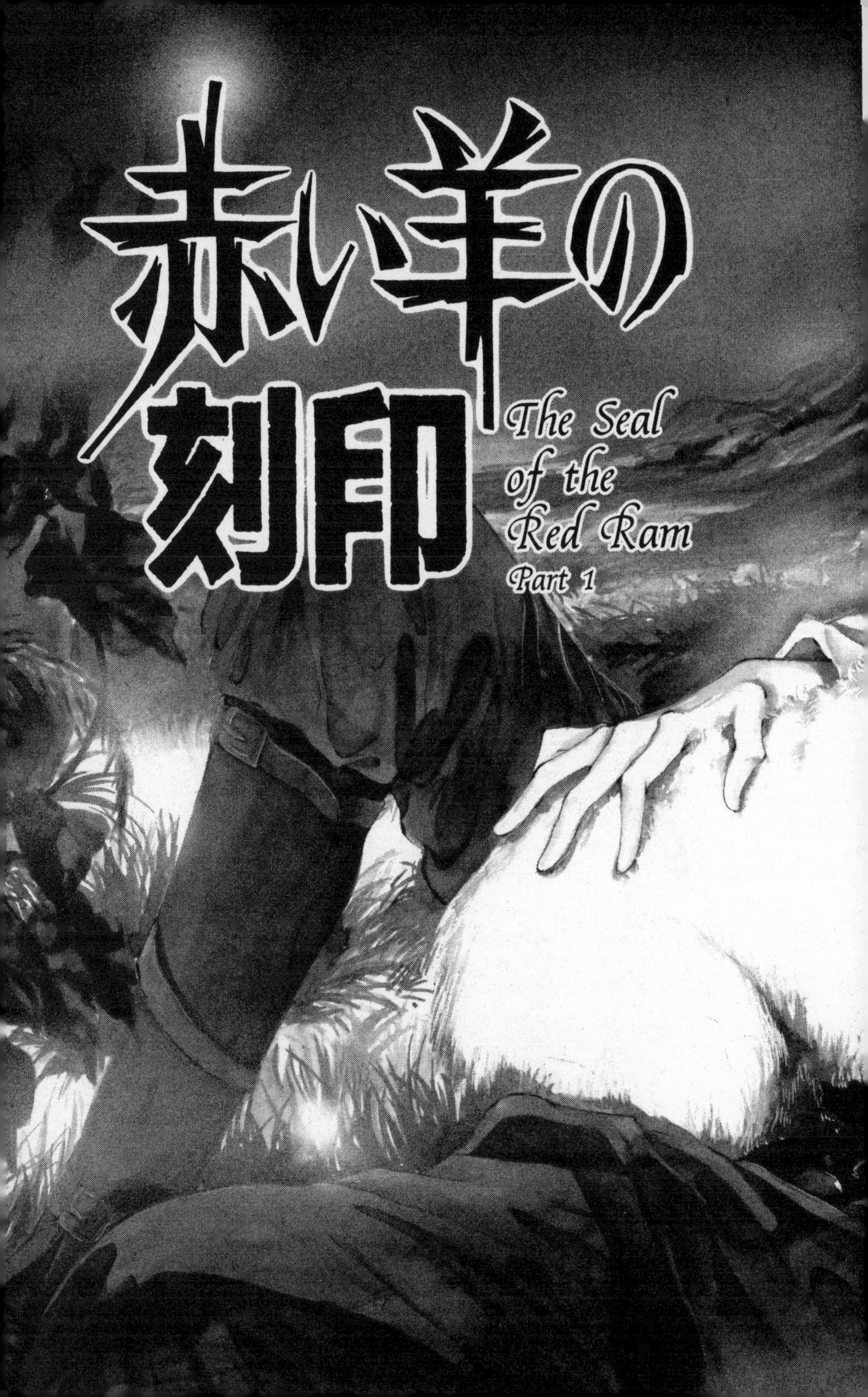
赤い羊の刻印
The Seal of the Red Ram
Part 1

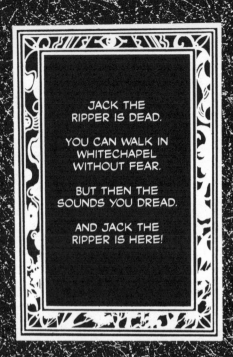

JACK THE
RIPPER IS DEAD.

YOU CAN WALK IN
WHITECHAPEL
WITHOUT FEAR.

BUT THEN THE
SOUNDS YOU DREAD.

AND JACK THE
RIPPER IS HERE!

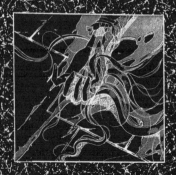

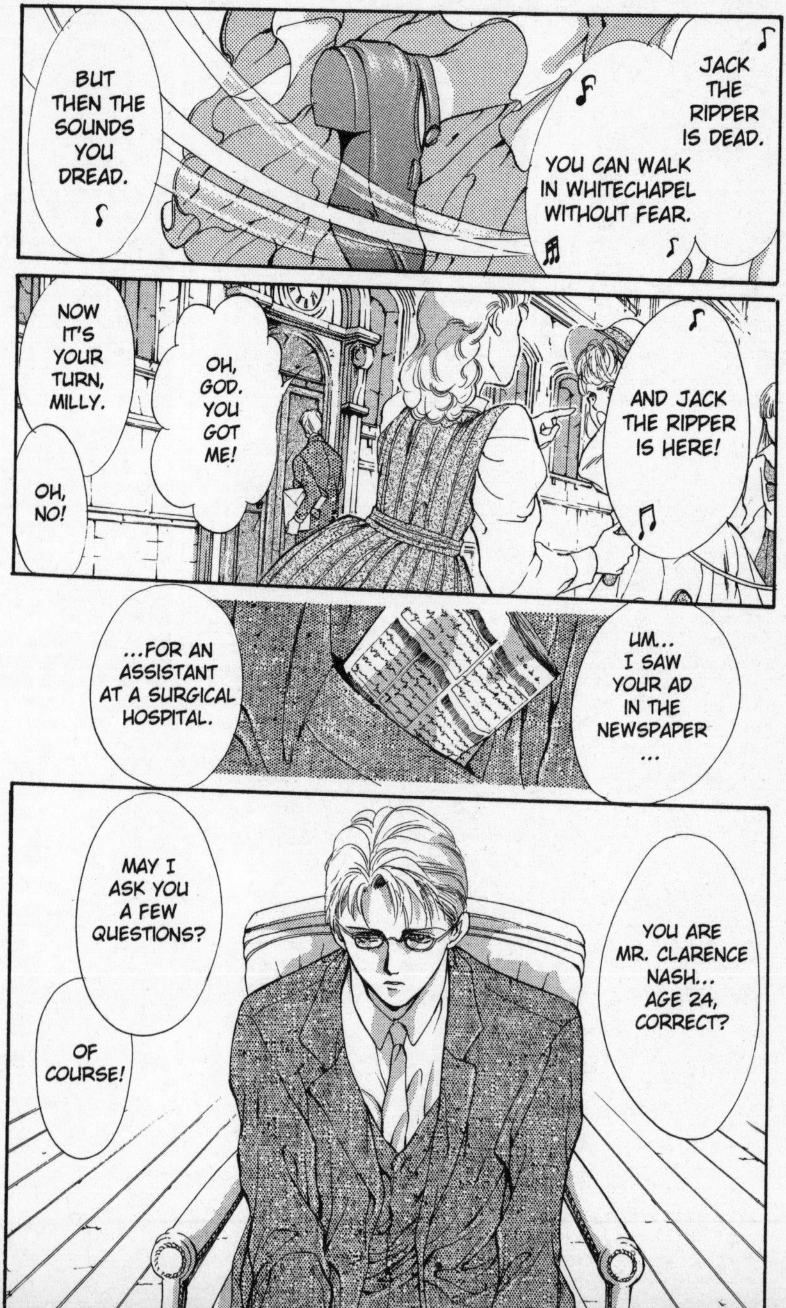
JACK THE RIPPER IS DEAD.
YOU CAN WALK IN WHITECHAPEL WITHOUT FEAR.
BUT THEN THE SOUNDS YOU DREAD.
AND JACK THE RIPPER IS HERE!
OH, GOD. YOU GOT ME!
NOW IT'S YOUR TURN, MILLY.
OH, NO!
UM... I SAW YOUR AD IN THE NEWSPAPER ...
...FOR AN ASSISTANT AT A SURGICAL HOSPITAL.
YOU ARE MR. CLARENCE NASH... AGE 24, CORRECT?
MAY I ASK YOU A FEW QUESTIONS?
OF COURSE!

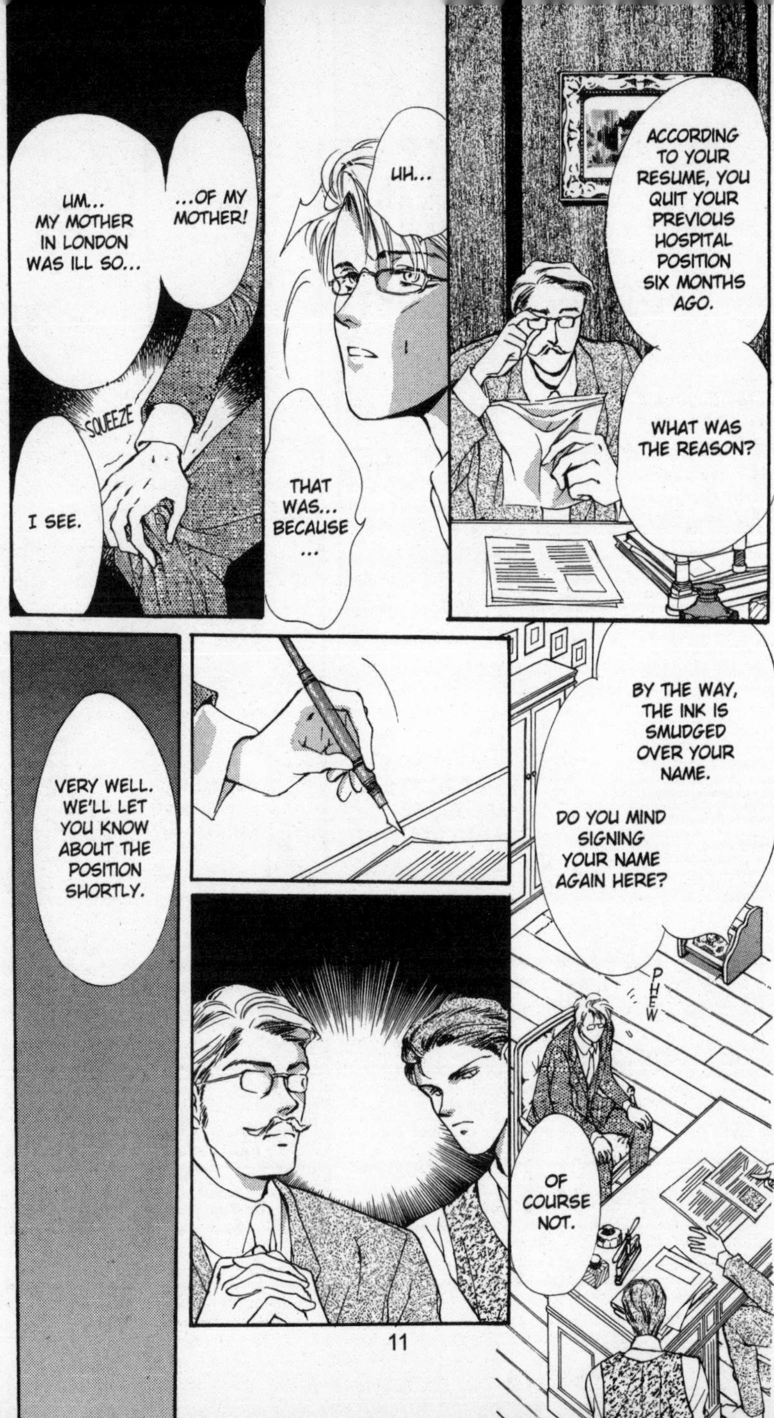

ACCORDING TO YOUR RESUME, YOU QUIT YOUR PREVIOUS HOSPITAL POSITION SIX MONTHS AGO.
WHAT WAS THE REASON?
UH...
THAT WAS... BECAUSE ...
...OF MY MOTHER!
UM... MY MOTHER IN LONDON WAS ILL SO...
SQUEEZE
I SEE.
BY THE WAY, THE INK IS SMUDGED OVER YOUR NAME.
DO YOU MIND SIGNING YOUR NAME AGAIN HERE?
PHEW
OF COURSE NOT.
VERY WELL. WE'LL LET YOU KNOW ABOUT THE POSITION SHORTLY.

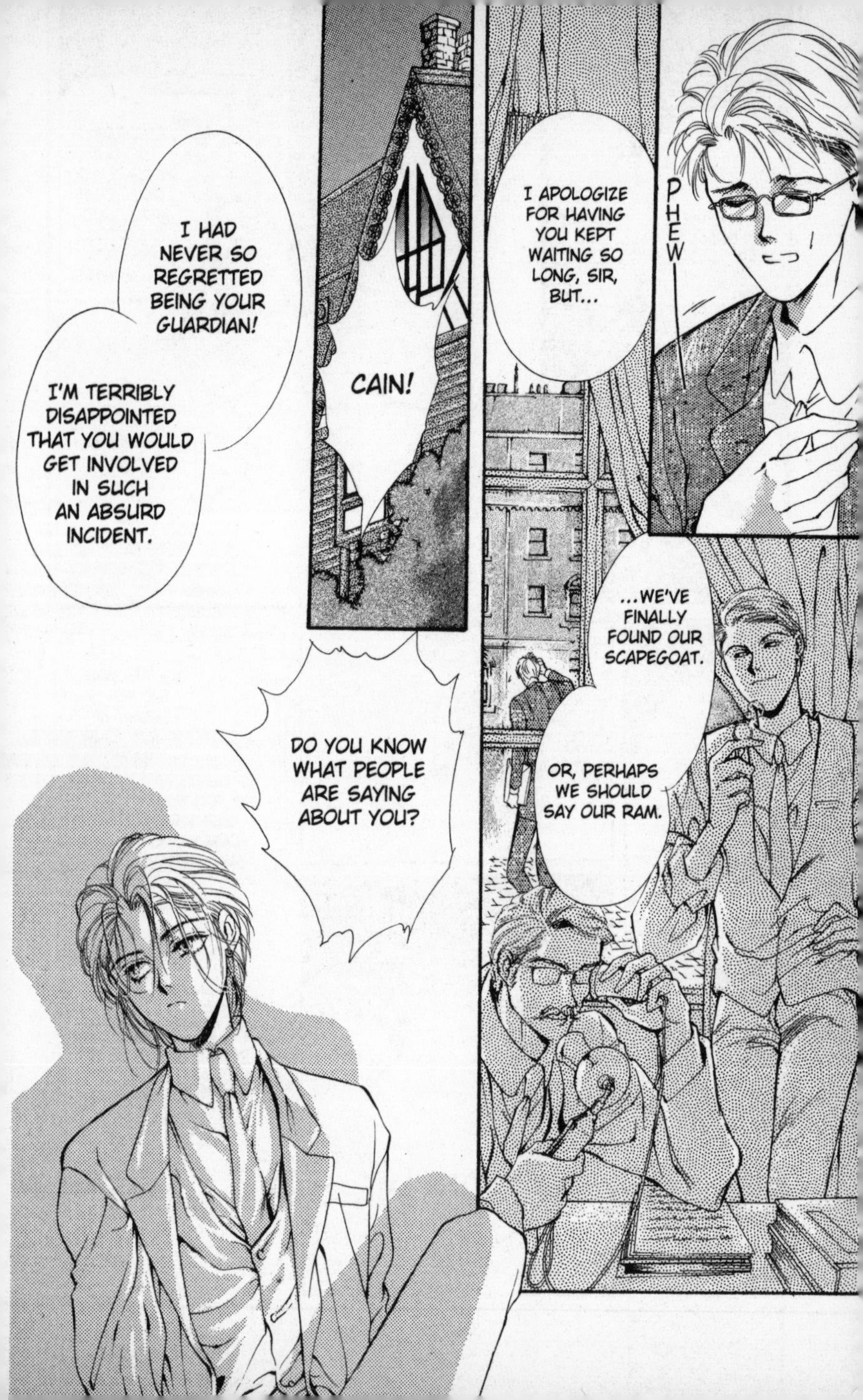
PHEW
I APOLOGIZE FOR HAVING YOU KEPT WAITING SO LONG, SIR, BUT...
...WE'VE FINALLY FOUND OUR SCAPEGOAT.
OR, PERHAPS WE SHOULD SAY OUR RAM.
CAIN!
I HAD NEVER SO REGRETTED BEING YOUR GUARDIAN!
I'M TERRIBLY DISAPPOINTED THAT YOU WOULD GET INVOLVED IN SUCH AN ABSURD INCIDENT.
DO YOU KNOW WHAT PEOPLE ARE SAYING ABOUT YOU?

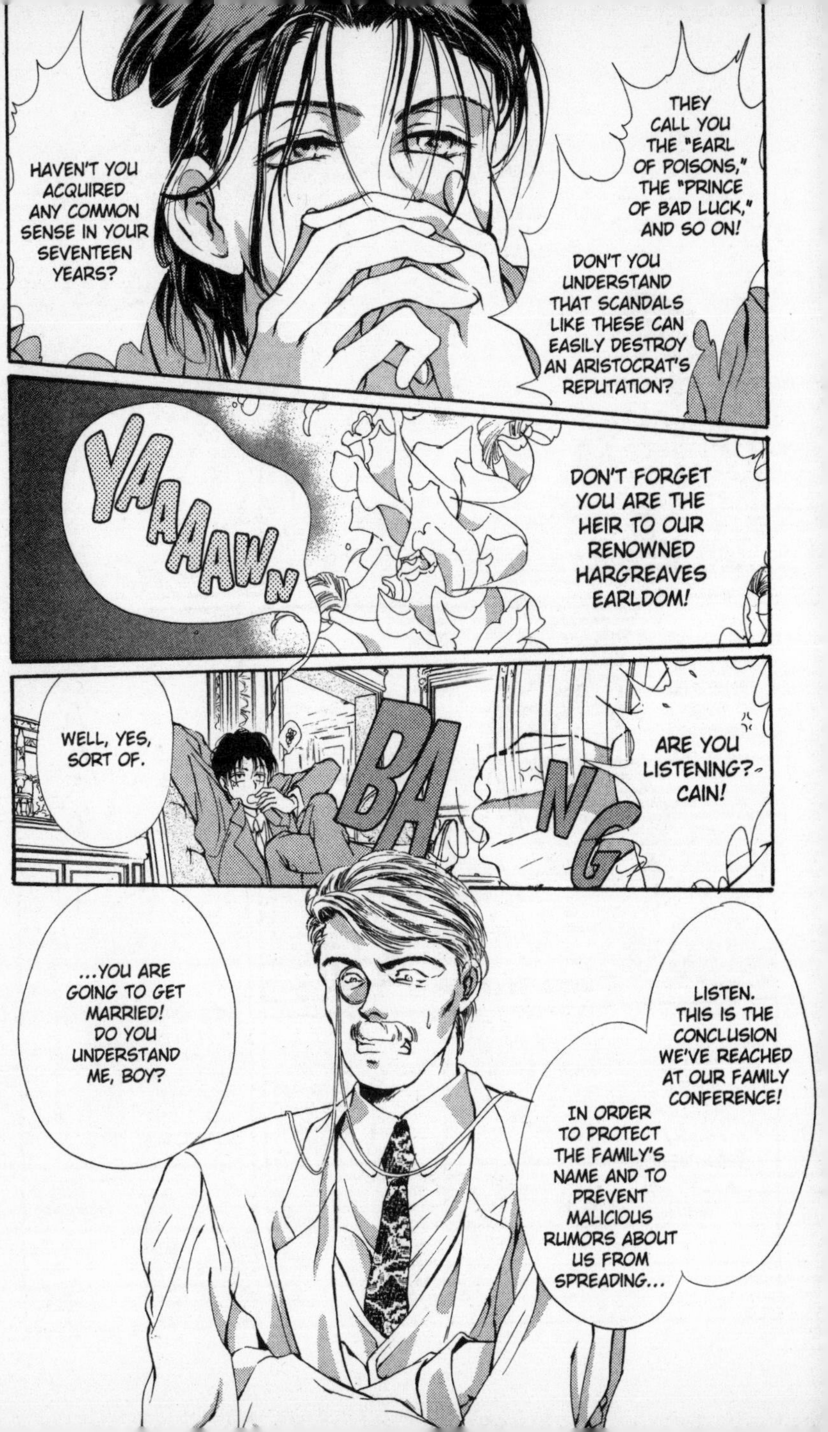
THEY CALL YOU THE "EARL OF POISONS," THE "PRINCE OF BAD LUCK," AND SO ON!
DON'T YOU UNDERSTAND THAT SCANDALS LIKE THESE CAN EASILY DESTROY AN ARISTOCRAT'S REPUTATION?
HAVEN'T YOU ACQUIRED ANY COMMON SENSE IN YOUR SEVENTEEN YEARS?
DON'T FORGET YOU ARE THE HEIR TO OUR RENOWNED HARGREAVES EARLDOM!
YAAAAAWN
ARE YOU LISTENING? CAIN!
BANG
WELL, YES, SORT OF.
LISTEN. THIS IS THE CONCLUSION WE'VE REACHED AT OUR FAMILY CONFERENCE!
IN ORDER TO PROTECT THE FAMILY'S NAME AND TO PREVENT MALICIOUS RUMORS ABOUT US FROM SPREADING...
...YOU ARE GOING TO GET MARRIED! DO YOU UNDERSTAND ME, BOY?

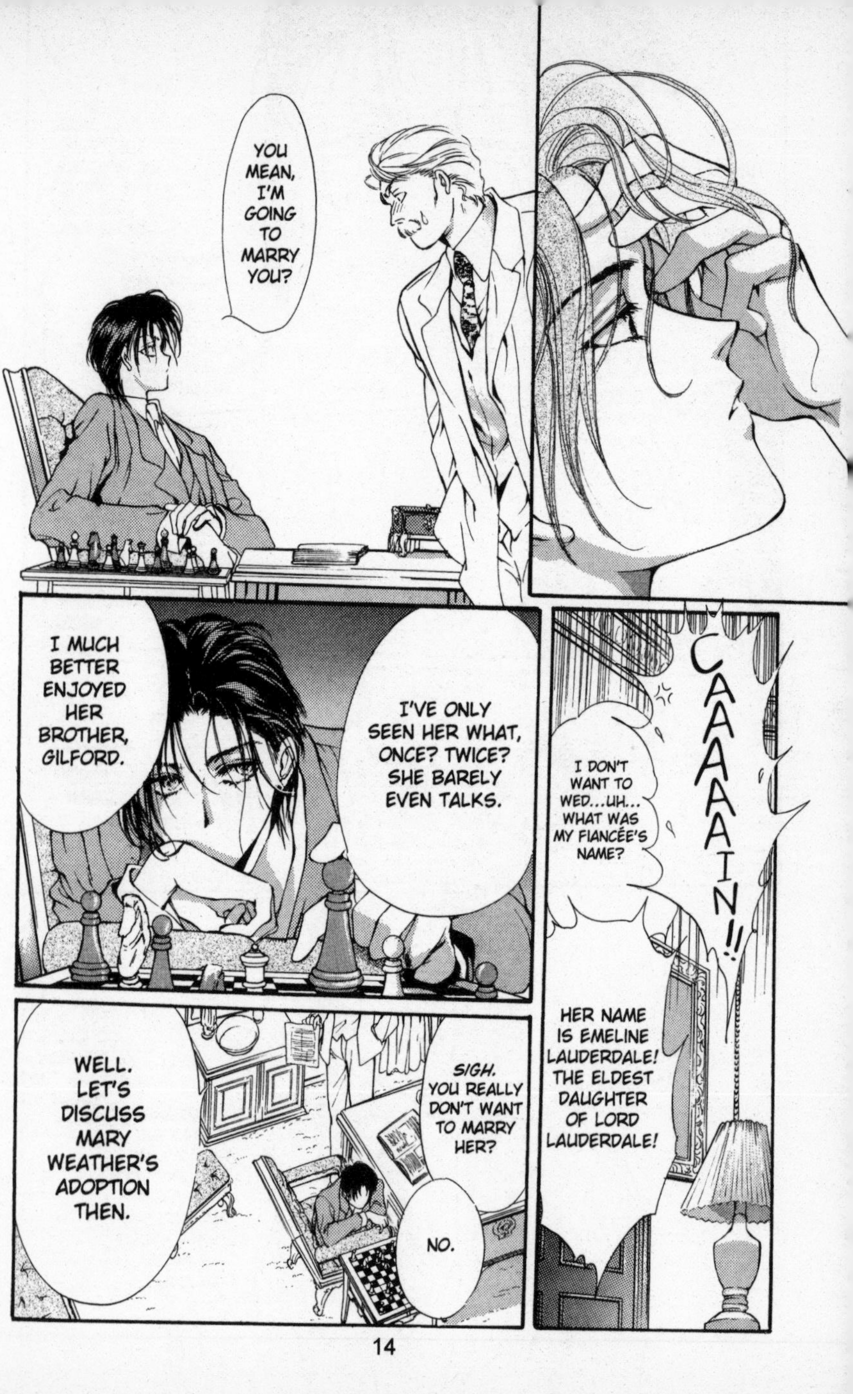
YOU MEAN, I'M GOING TO MARRY YOU?
I DON'T WANT TO WED...UH... WHAT WAS MY FIANCÉE'S NAME?
CAAAAAIN!!
HER NAME IS EMELINE LAUDERDALE! THE ELDEST DAUGHTER OF LORD LAUDERDALE!
I'VE ONLY SEEN HER WHAT, ONCE? TWICE? SHE BARELY EVEN TALKS.
I MUCH BETTER ENJOYED HER BROTHER, GILFORD.
SIGH. YOU REALLY DON'T WANT TO MARRY HER?
NO.
WELL. LET'S DISCUSS MARY WEATHER'S ADOPTION THEN.

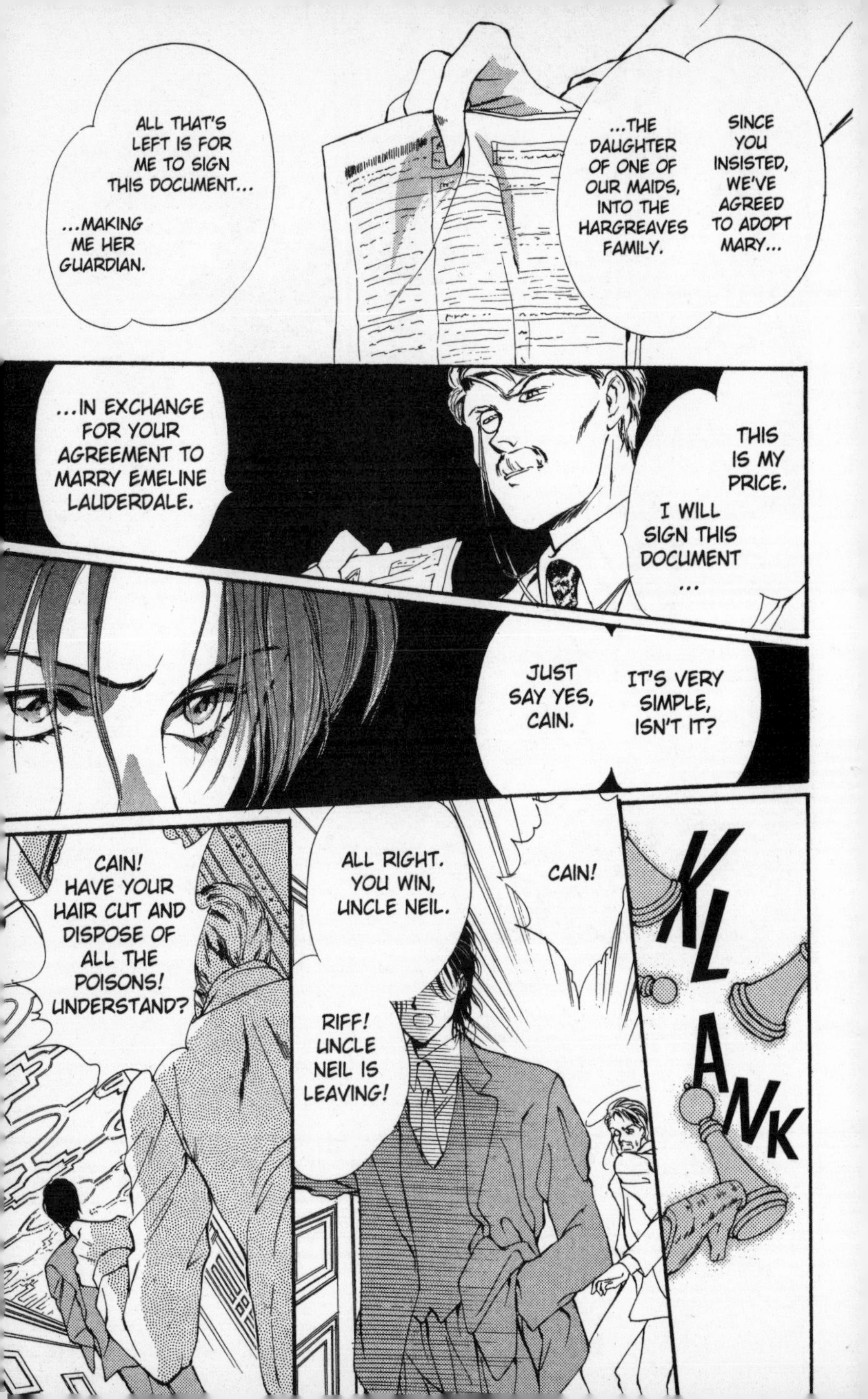
SINCE YOU INSISTED, WE'VE AGREED TO ADOPT MARY...
...THE DAUGHTER OF ONE OF OUR MAIDS, INTO THE HARGREAVES FAMILY.
ALL THAT'S LEFT IS FOR ME TO SIGN THIS DOCUMENT...
...MAKING ME HER GUARDIAN.
THIS IS MY PRICE.
I WILL SIGN THIS DOCUMENT ...
...IN EXCHANGE FOR YOUR AGREEMENT TO MARRY EMELINE LAUDERDALE.
IT'S VERY SIMPLE, ISN'T IT?
JUST SAY YES, CAIN.
KLANK
CAIN!
ALL RIGHT. YOU WIN, UNCLE NEIL.
RIFF! UNCLE NEIL IS LEAVING!
CAIN! HAVE YOUR HAIR CUT AND DISPOSE OF ALL THE POISONS! UNDERSTAND?

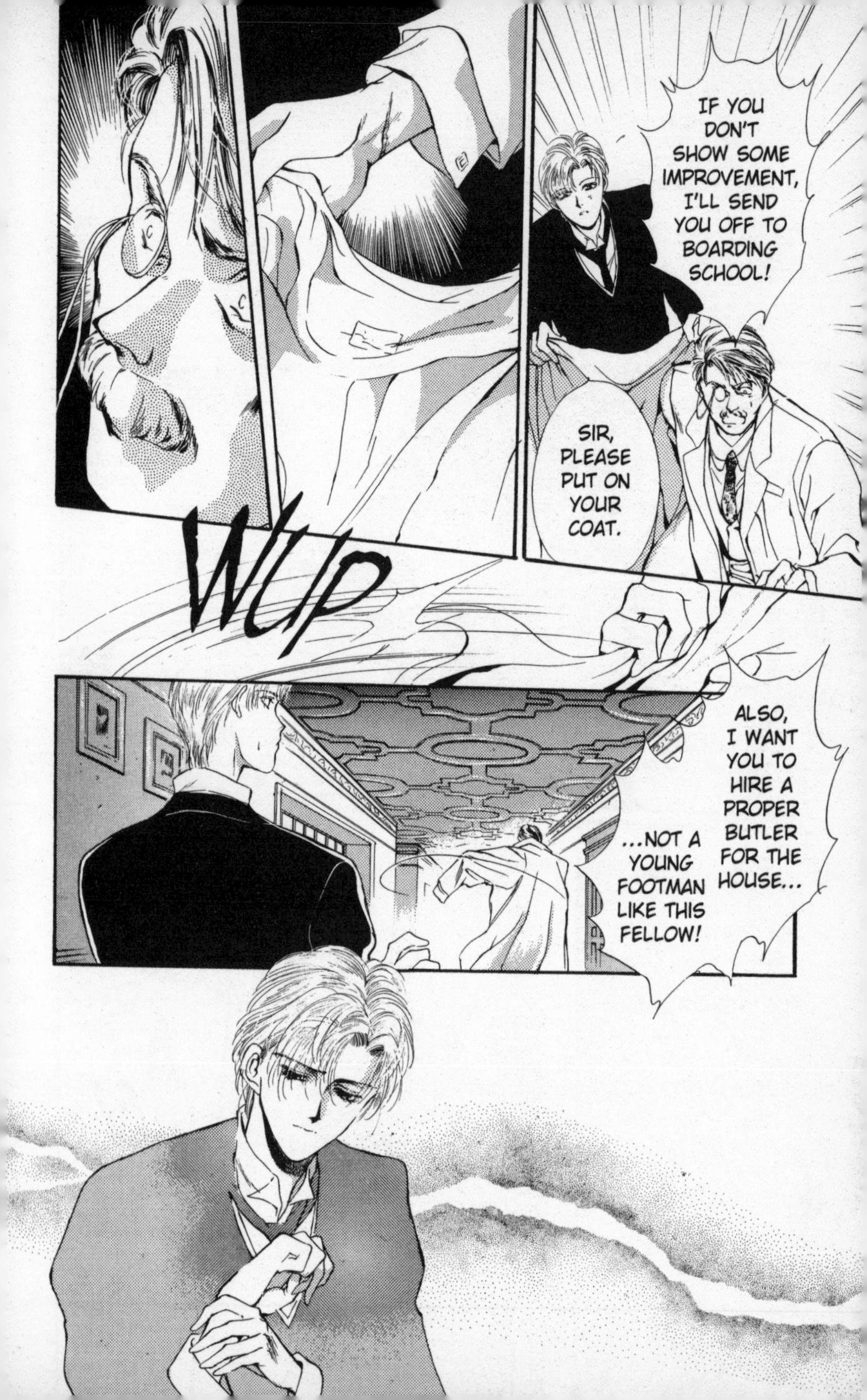
IF YOU DON'T SHOW SOME IMPROVEMENT, I'LL SEND YOU OFF TO BOARDING SCHOOL!
SIR, PLEASE PUT ON YOUR COAT.
WUP
ALSO, I WANT YOU TO HIRE A PROPER BUTLER FOR THE HOUSE...
...NOT A YOUNG FOOTMAN LIKE THIS FELLOW!

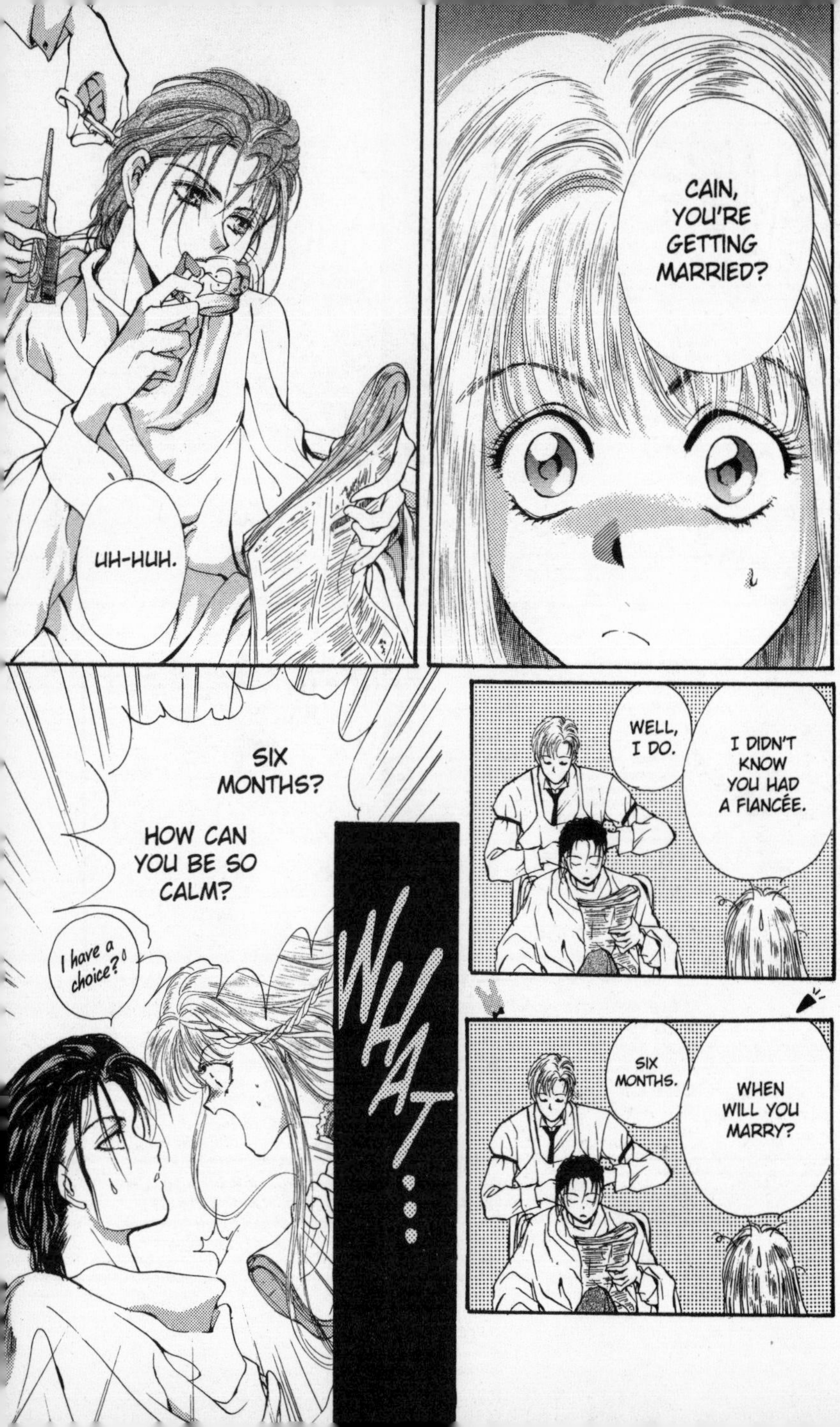
CAIN, YOU'RE GETTING MARRIED?
UH-HUH.
I DIDN'T KNOW YOU HAD A FIANCÉE.
WELL, I DO.
WHEN WILL YOU MARRY?
SIX MONTHS.
SIX MONTHS?
HOW CAN YOU BE SO CALM?
WHAT...
I have a choice?

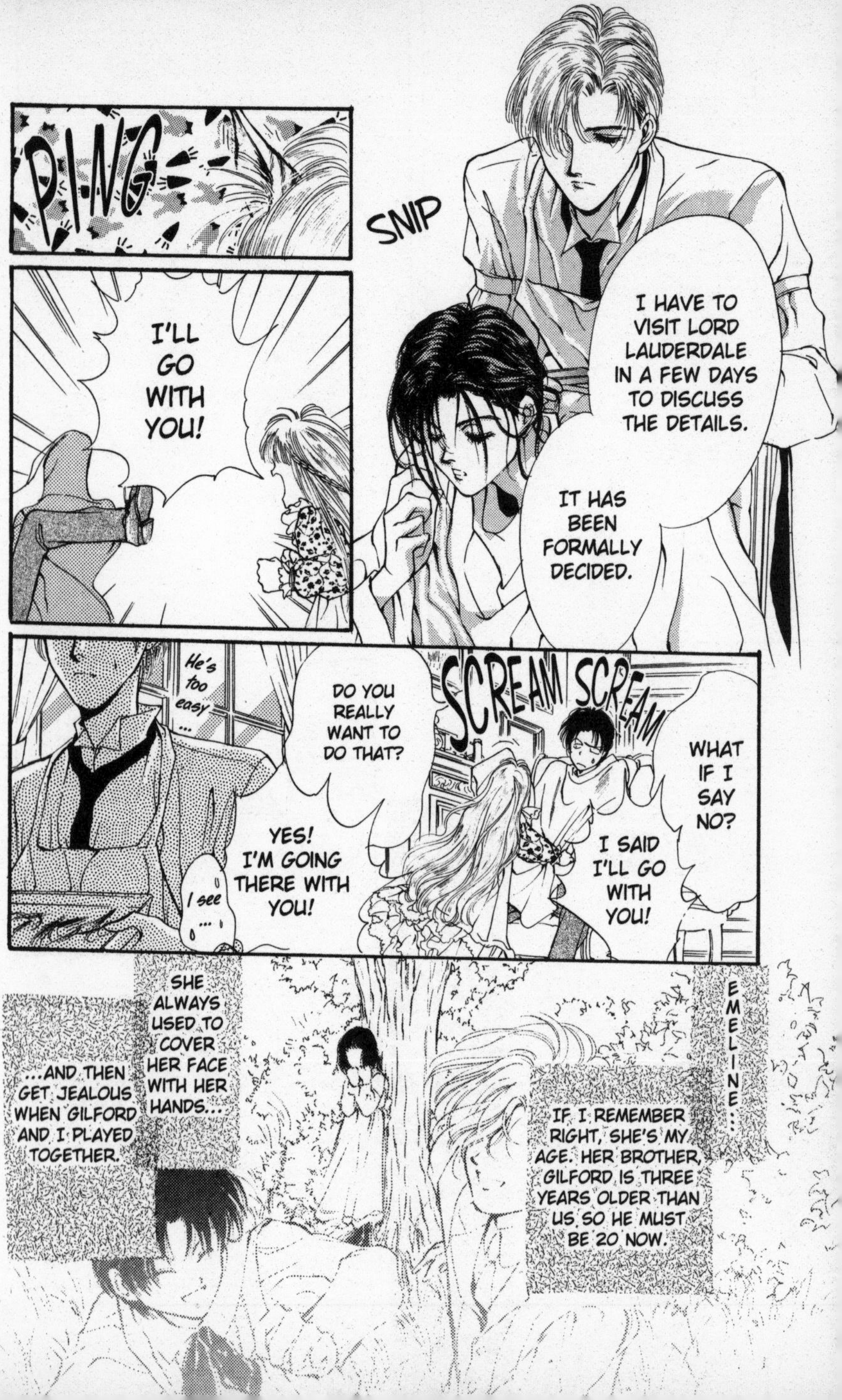
SNIP
I HAVE TO VISIT LORD LAUDERDALE IN A FEW DAYS TO DISCUSS THE DETAILS.
IT HAS BEEN FORMALLY DECIDED.
PING
I'LL GO WITH YOU!
SCREAM SCREAM
WHAT IF I SAY NO?
I SAID I'LL GO WITH YOU!
DO YOU REALLY WANT TO DO THAT?
YES! I'M GOING THERE WITH YOU!
I see...
He's too easy...
EMELINE...
IF I REMEMBER RIGHT, SHE'S MY AGE. HER BROTHER, GILFORD IS THREE YEARS OLDER THAN US SO HE MUST BE 20 NOW.
SHE ALWAYS USED TO COVER HER FACE WITH HER HANDS...
...AND THEN GET JEALOUS WHEN GILFORD AND I PLAYED TOGETHER.

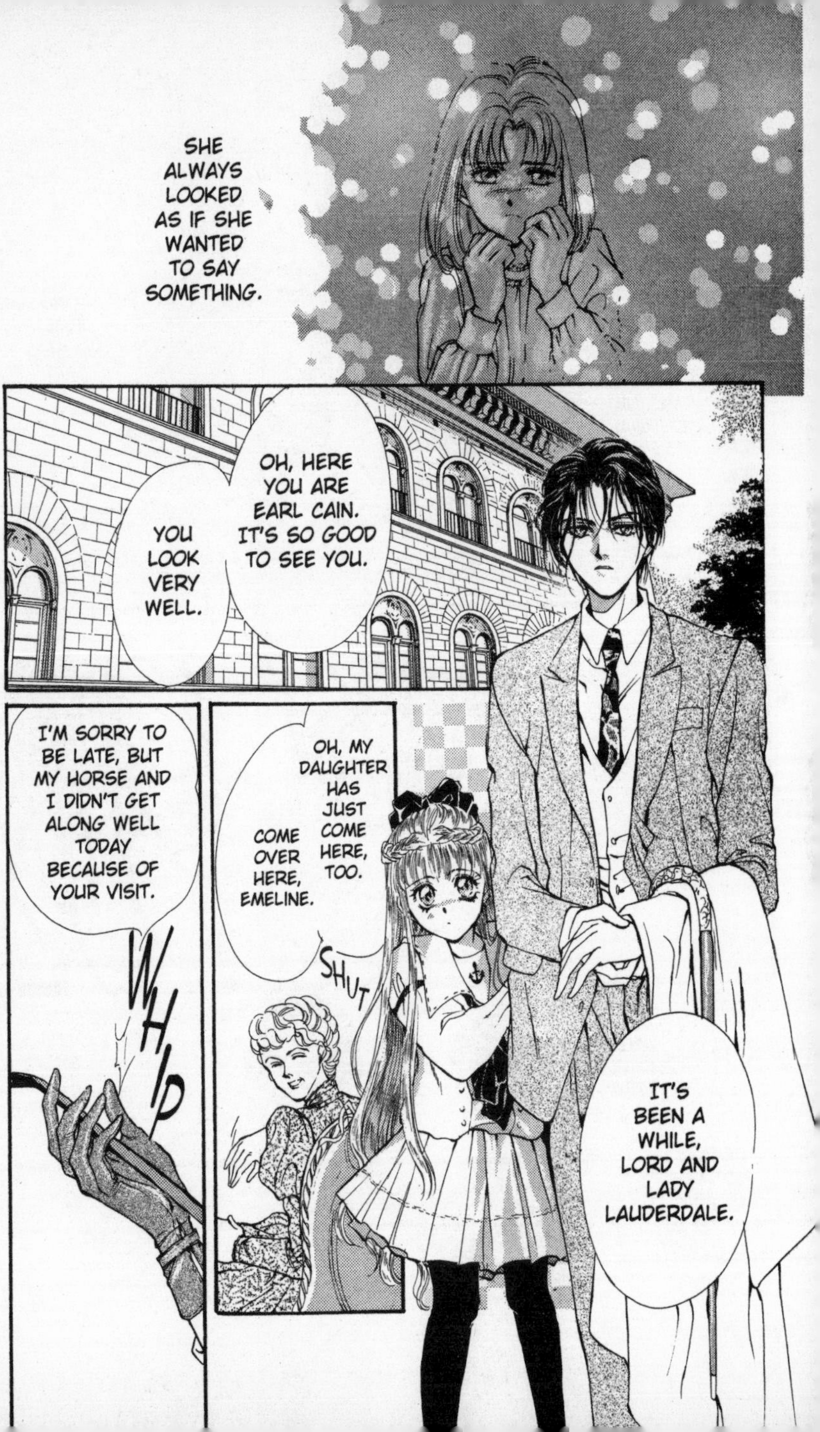
SHE ALWAYS LOOKED AS IF SHE WANTED TO SAY SOMETHING.
OH, HERE YOU ARE EARL CAIN. IT'S SO GOOD TO SEE YOU.
YOU LOOK VERY WELL.
IT'S BEEN A WHILE, LORD AND LADY LAUDERDALE.
OH, MY DAUGHTER HAS JUST COME HERE, TOO.
COME OVER HERE, EMELINE.
SHUT
I'M SORRY TO BE LATE, BUT MY HORSE AND I DIDN'T GET ALONG WELL TODAY BECAUSE OF YOUR VISIT.
WHIP

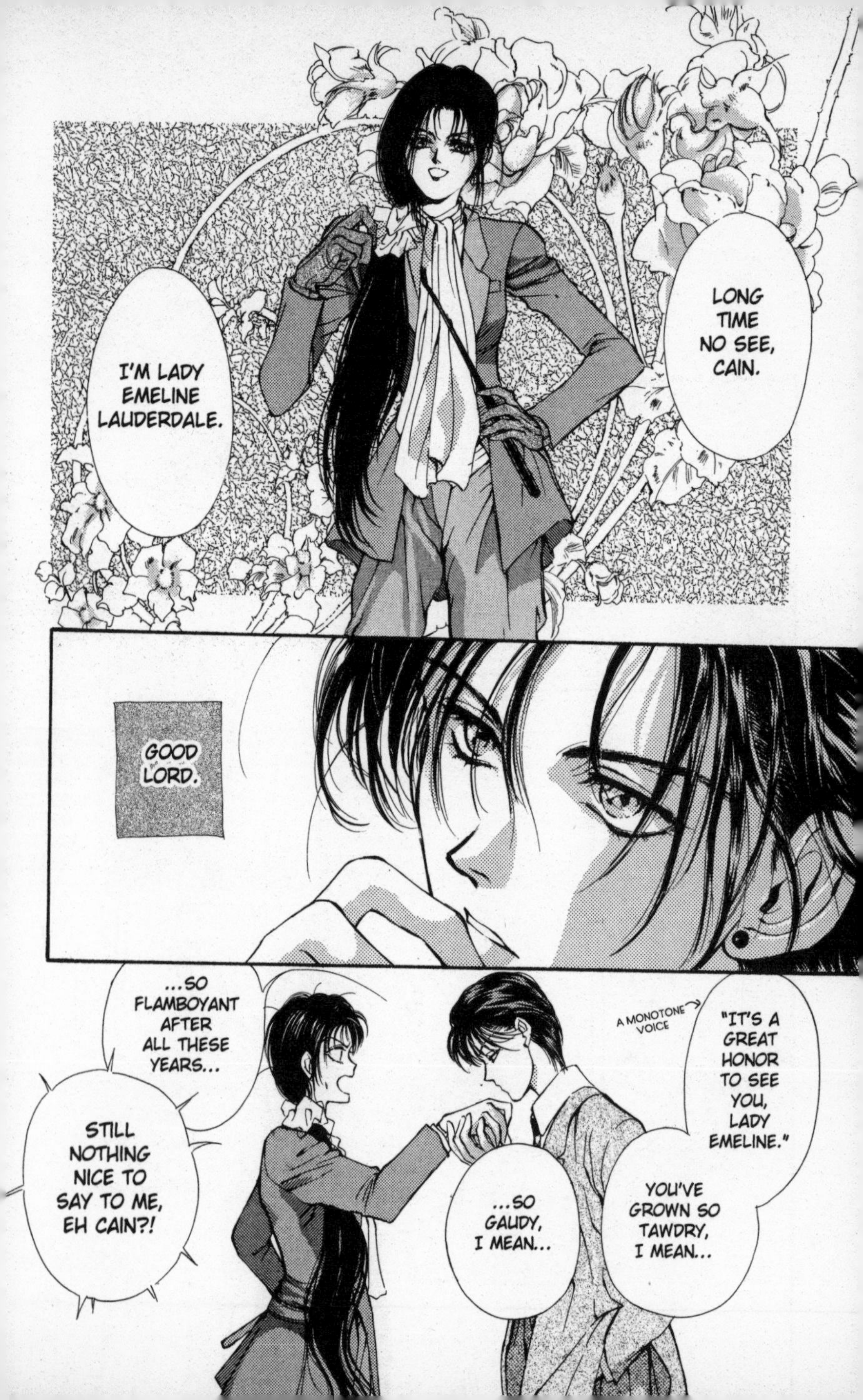
LONG TIME NO SEE, CAIN.
I'M LADY EMELINE LAUDERDALE.
GOOD LORD.
A MONOTONE VOICE
"IT'S A GREAT HONOR TO SEE YOU, LADY EMELINE."
YOU'VE GROWN SO TAWDRY, I MEAN...
...SO GAUDY, I MEAN...
...SO FLAMBOYANT AFTER ALL THESE YEARS...
STILL NOTHING NICE TO SAY TO ME, EH CAIN?!

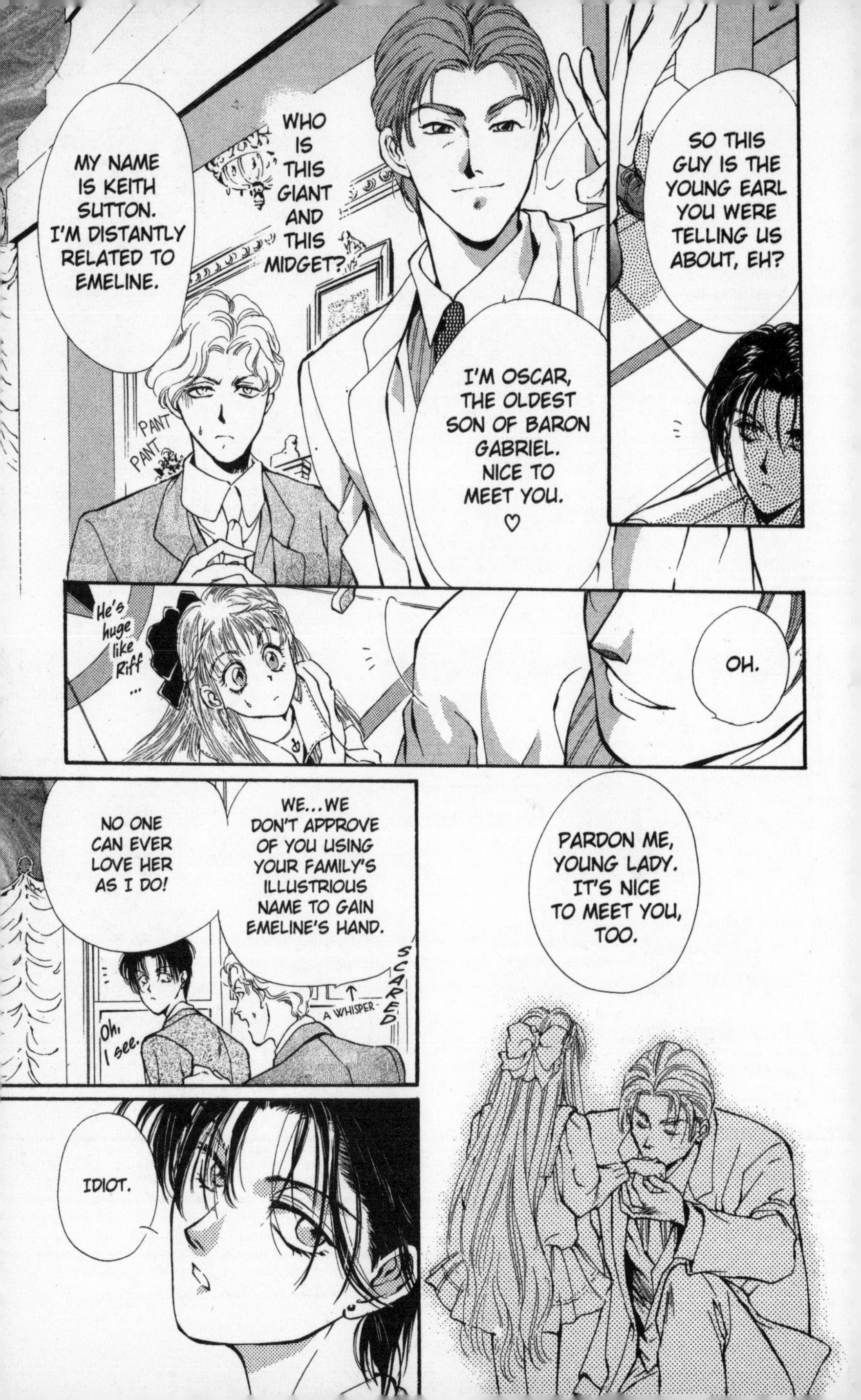

SO THIS GUY IS THE YOUNG EARL YOU WERE TELLING US ABOUT, EH?
I'M OSCAR, THE OLDEST SON OF BARON GABRIEL. NICE TO MEET YOU. ♡
WHO IS THIS GIANT AND THIS MIDGET?
MY NAME IS KEITH SUTTON. I'M DISTANTLY RELATED TO EMELINE.
PANT PANT
OH.
He's huge like Riff ...
PARDON ME, YOUNG LADY. IT'S NICE TO MEET YOU, TOO.
WE...WE DON'T APPROVE OF YOU USING YOUR FAMILY'S ILLUSTRIOUS NAME TO GAIN EMELINE'S HAND.
SCARED
A WHISPER
NO ONE CAN EVER LOVE HER AS I DO!
Oh, I see.
IDIOT.

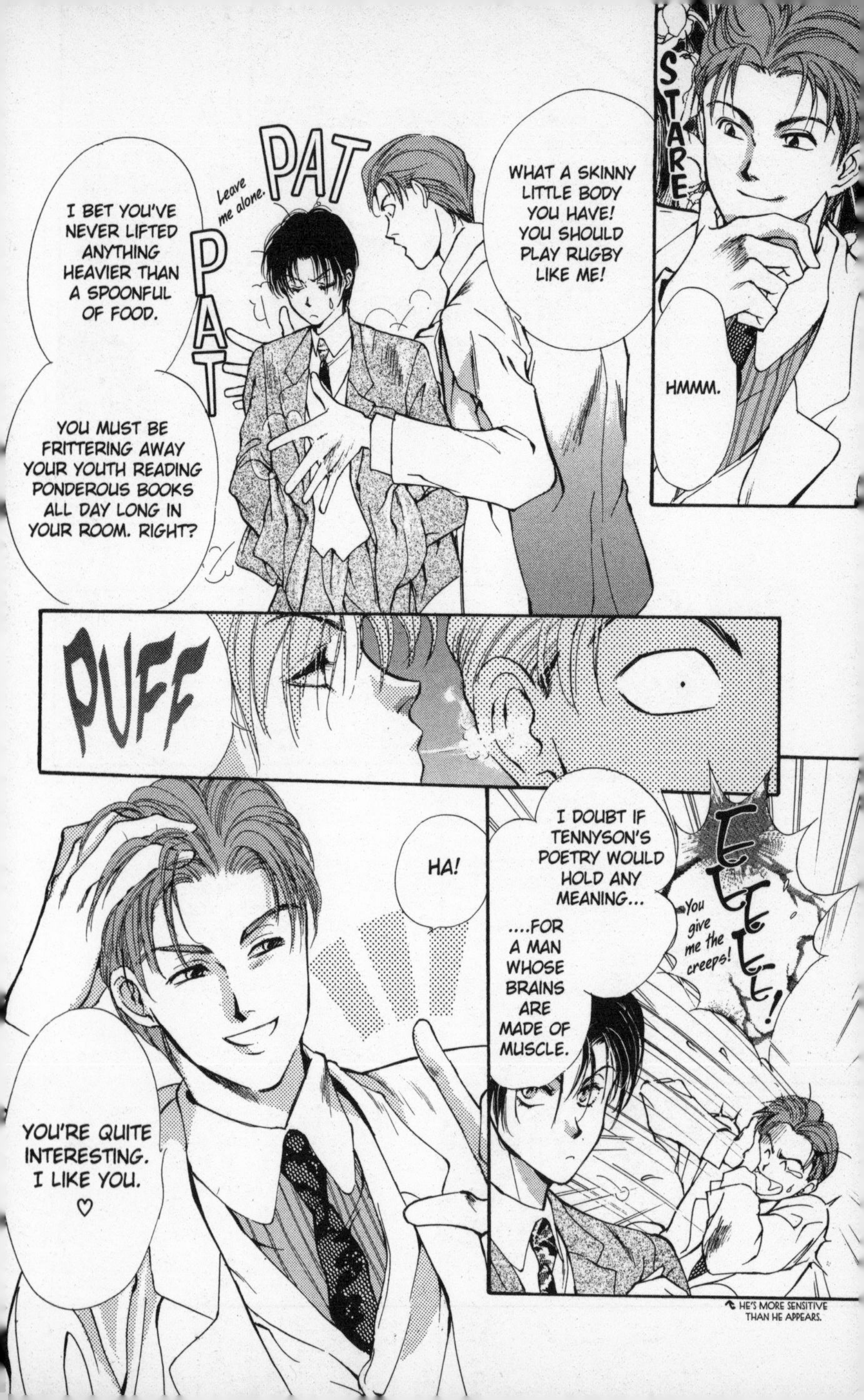
STARE
HMMM.
WHAT A SKINNY LITTLE BODY YOU HAVE! YOU SHOULD PLAY RUGBY LIKE ME!
PAT
Leave me alone.
PAT
I BET YOU'VE NEVER LIFTED ANYTHING HEAVIER THAN A SPOONFUL OF FOOD.
YOU MUST BE FRITTERING AWAY YOUR YOUTH READING PONDEROUS BOOKS ALL DAY LONG IN YOUR ROOM. RIGHT?
PUFF
EEEEE!
You give me the creeps!
I DOUBT IF TENNYSON'S POETRY WOULD HOLD ANY MEANING...
....FOR A MAN WHOSE BRAINS ARE MADE OF MUSCLE.
HA!
YOU'RE QUITE INTERESTING. I LIKE YOU. ♡
HE'S MORE SENSITIVE THAN HE APPEARS.

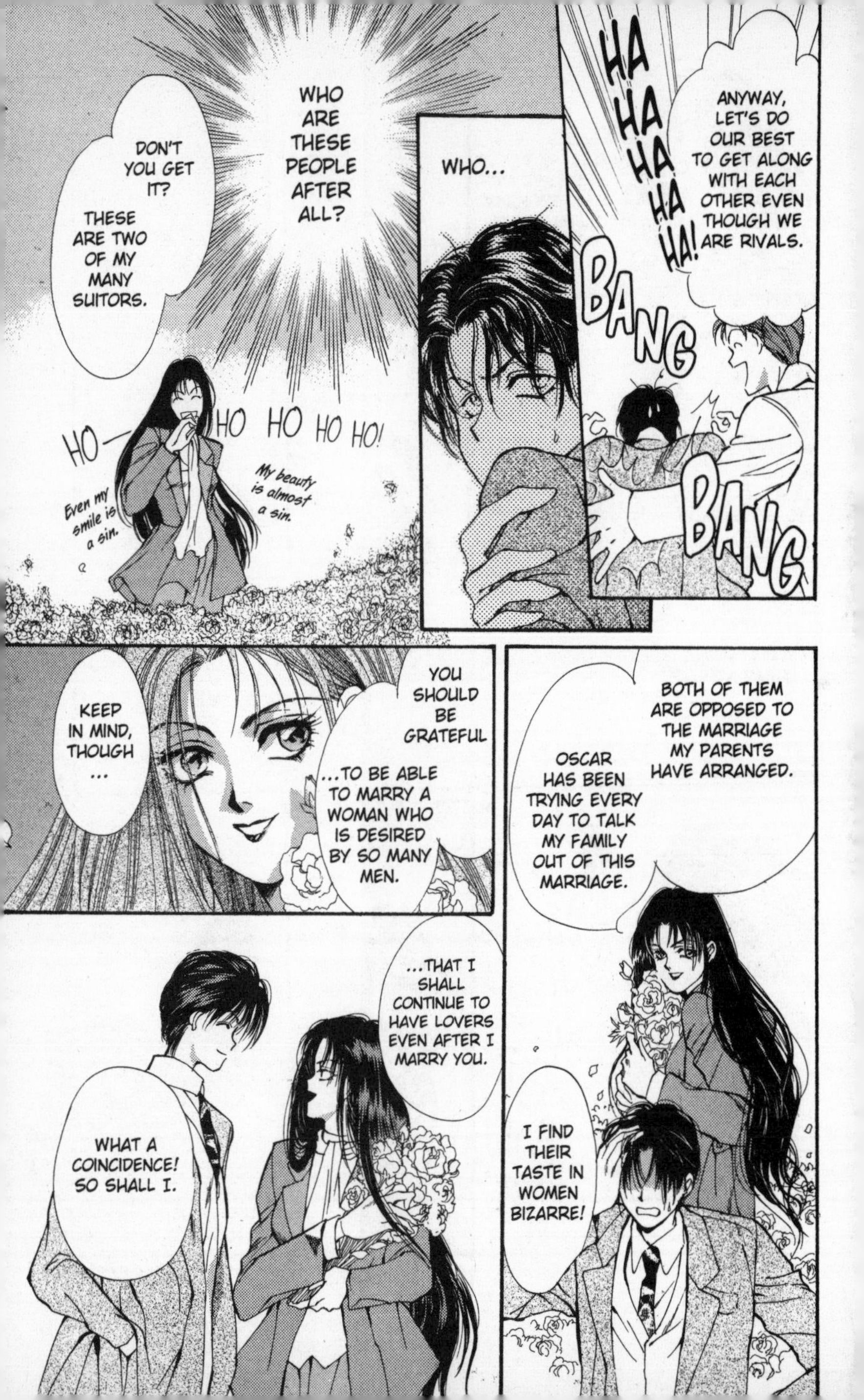
HA HA HA HA HA!
ANYWAY, LET'S DO OUR BEST TO GET ALONG WITH EACH OTHER EVEN THOUGH WE ARE RIVALS.
BANG
BANG
WHO...
WHO ARE THESE PEOPLE AFTER ALL?
DON'T YOU GET IT?
THESE ARE TWO OF MY MANY SUITORS.
HO— HO HO HO HO!
My beauty is almost a sin.
Even my smile is a sin.
BOTH OF THEM ARE OPPOSED TO THE MARRIAGE MY PARENTS HAVE ARRANGED.
OSCAR HAS BEEN TRYING EVERY DAY TO TALK MY FAMILY OUT OF THIS MARRIAGE.
I FIND THEIR TASTE IN WOMEN BIZARRE!
YOU SHOULD BE GRATEFUL
...TO BE ABLE TO MARRY A WOMAN WHO IS DESIRED BY SO MANY MEN.
KEEP IN MIND, THOUGH...
...THAT I SHALL CONTINUE TO HAVE LOVERS EVEN AFTER I MARRY YOU.
WHAT A COINCIDENCE! SO SHALL I.

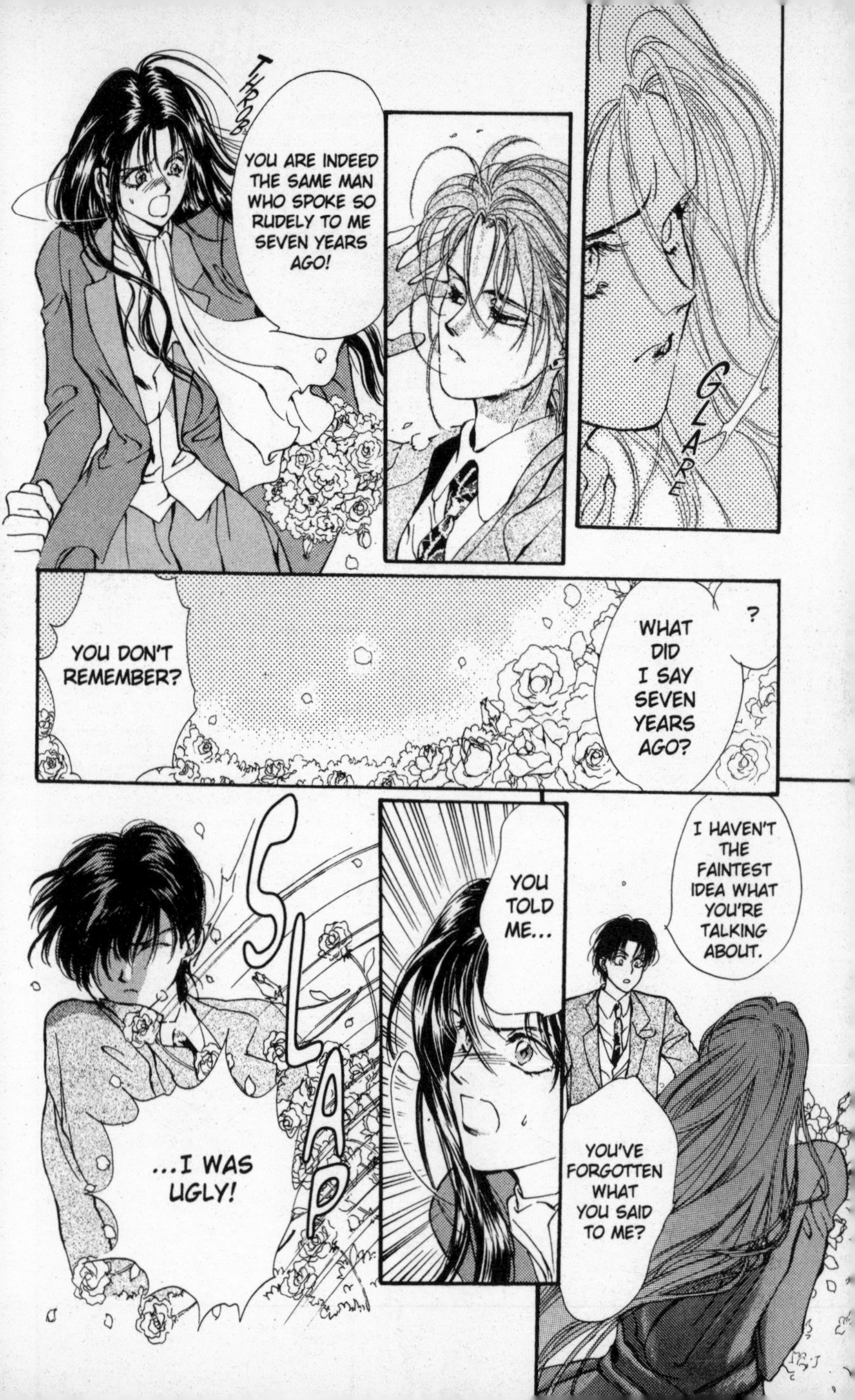
GLARE
THROB
YOU ARE INDEED THE SAME MAN WHO SPOKE SO RUDELY TO ME SEVEN YEARS AGO!
?
WHAT DID I SAY SEVEN YEARS AGO?
YOU DON'T REMEMBER?
I HAVEN'T THE FAINTEST IDEA WHAT YOU'RE TALKING ABOUT.
YOU'VE FORGOTTEN WHAT YOU SAID TO ME?
YOU TOLD ME...
SLAP
...I WAS UGLY!

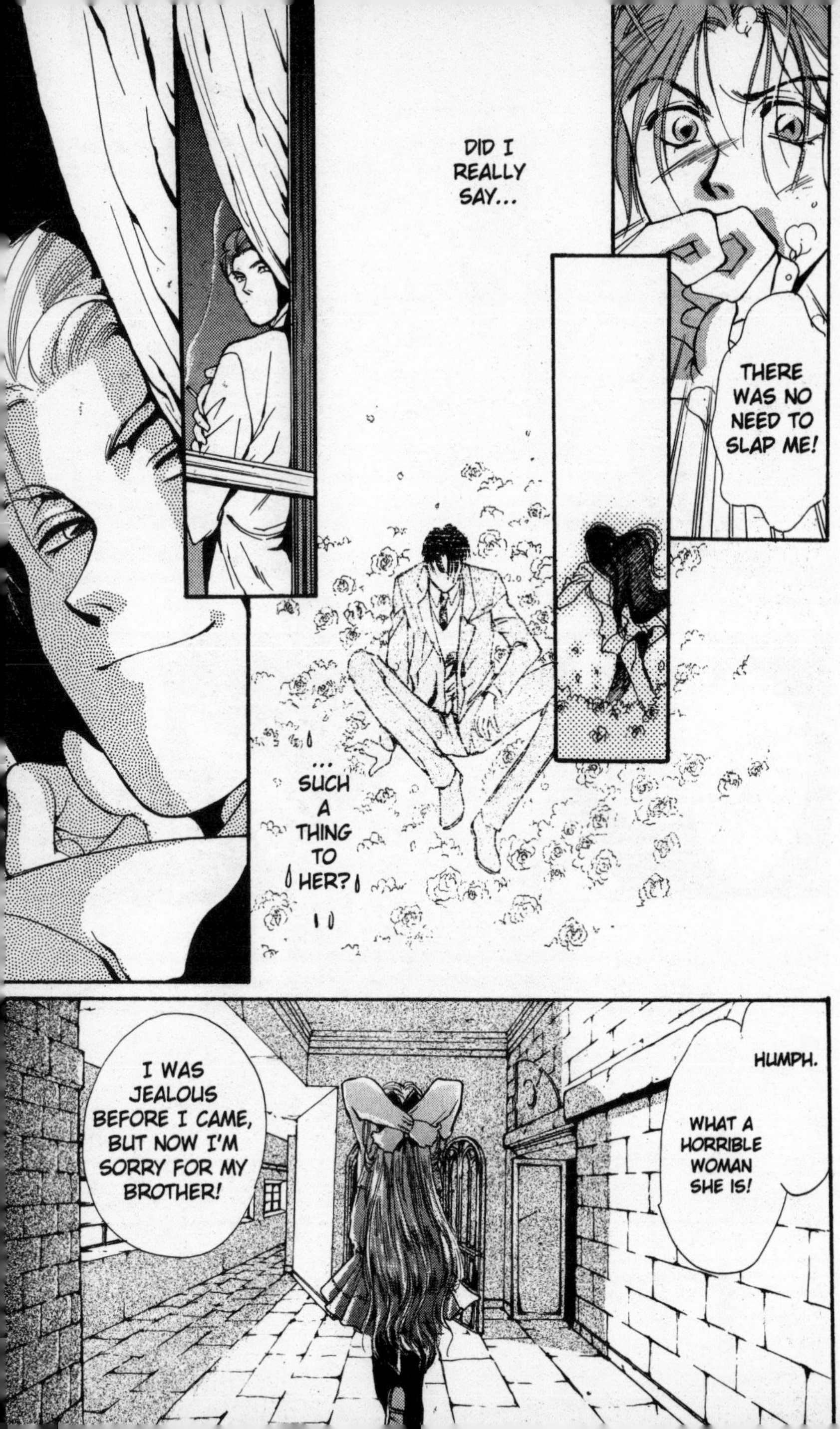
THERE WAS NO NEED TO SLAP ME!
DID I REALLY SAY...
...SUCH A THING TO HER?
HUMPH.
WHAT A HORRIBLE WOMAN SHE IS!
I WAS JEALOUS BEFORE I CAME, BUT NOW I'M SORRY FOR MY BROTHER!

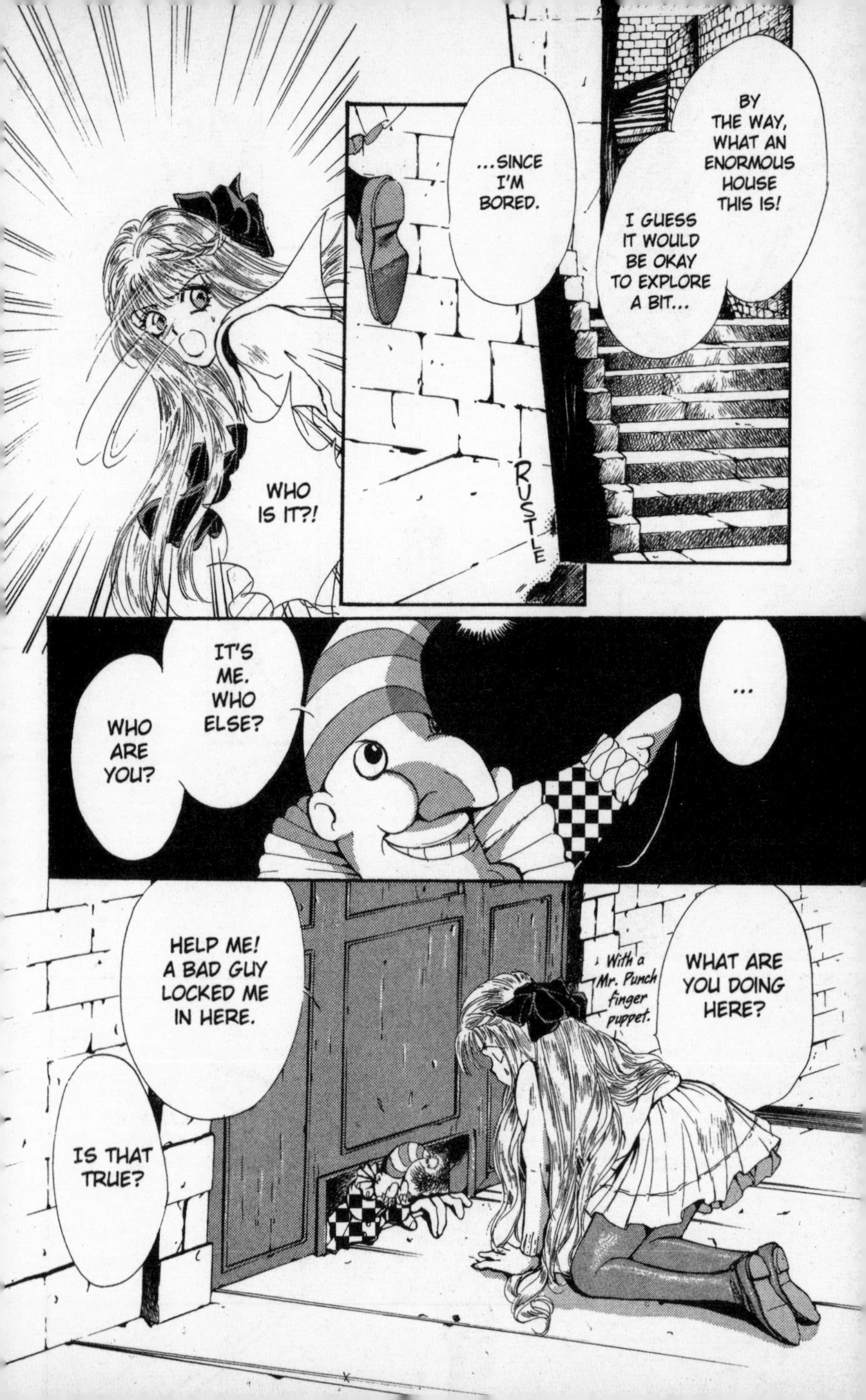
BY THE WAY, WHAT AN ENORMOUS HOUSE THIS IS!
I GUESS IT WOULD BE OKAY TO EXPLORE A BIT...
...SINCE I'M BORED.
RUSTLE
WHO IS IT?!
...
IT'S ME. WHO ELSE?
WHO ARE YOU?
WHAT ARE YOU DOING HERE?
With a Mr. Punch finger puppet.
HELP ME! A BAD GUY LOCKED ME IN HERE.
IS THAT TRUE?

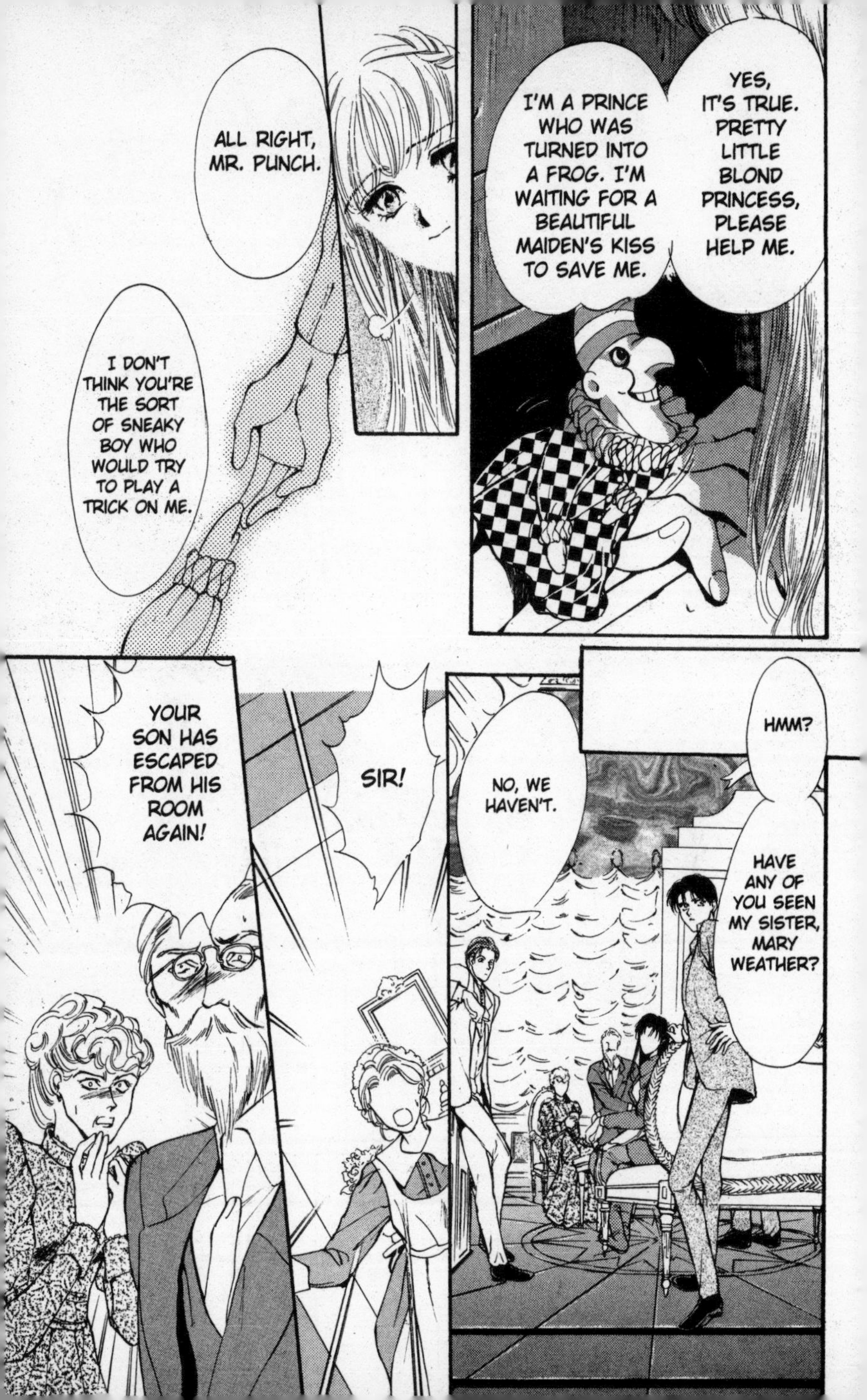

YES, IT'S TRUE. PRETTY LITTLE BLOND PRINCESS, PLEASE HELP ME.
I'M A PRINCE WHO WAS TURNED INTO A FROG. I'M WAITING FOR A BEAUTIFUL MAIDEN'S KISS TO SAVE ME.
ALL RIGHT, MR. PUNCH.
I DON'T THINK YOU'RE THE SORT OF SNEAKY BOY WHO WOULD TRY TO PLAY A TRICK ON ME.
HMM?
HAVE ANY OF YOU SEEN MY SISTER, MARY WEATHER?
NO, WE HAVEN'T.
SIR!
YOUR SON HAS ESCAPED FROM HIS ROOM AGAIN!

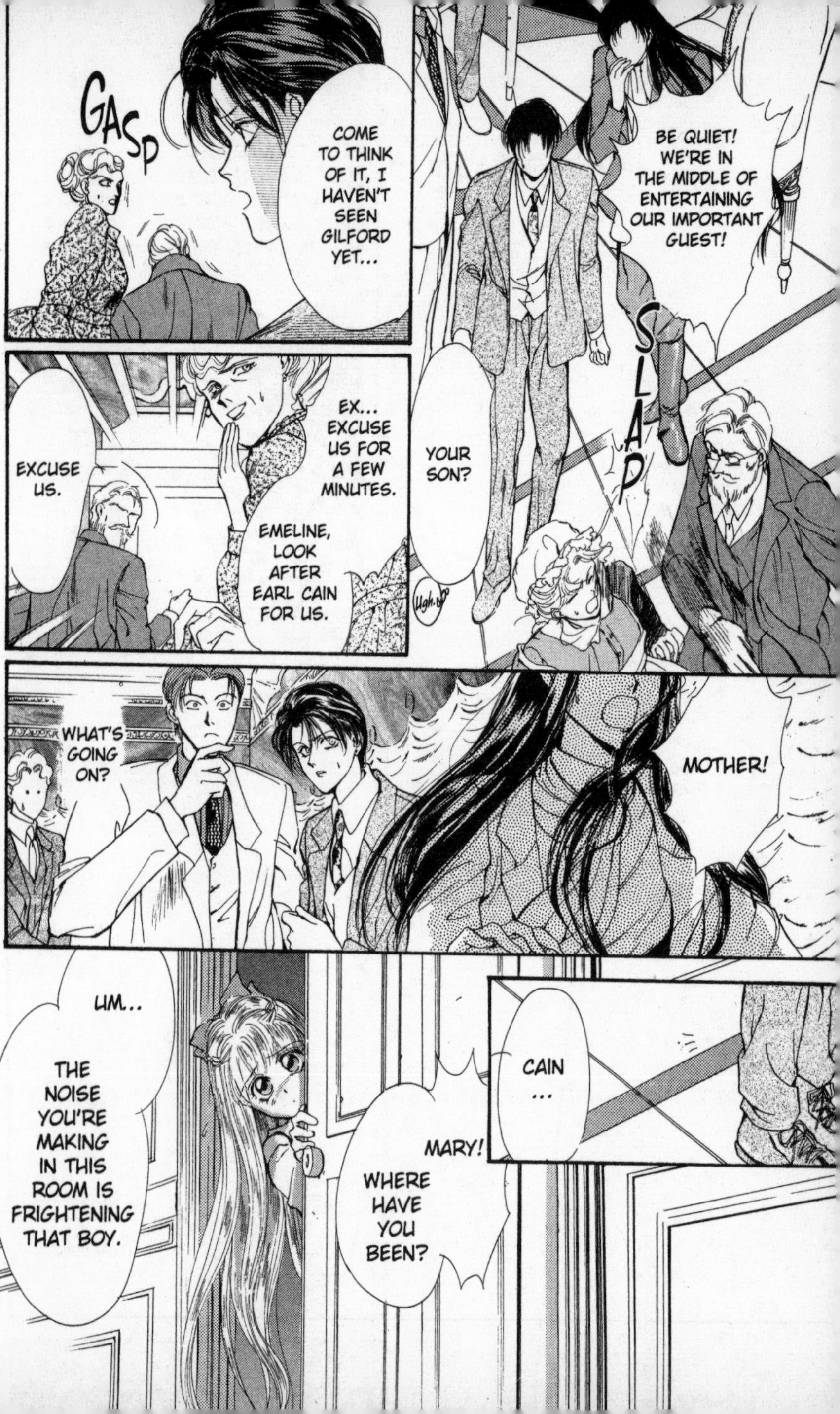
BE QUIET! WE'RE IN THE MIDDLE OF ENTERTAINING OUR IMPORTANT GUEST!
SLAP
YOUR SON?
Ugh.
COME TO THINK OF IT, I HAVEN'T SEEN GILFORD YET...
GASP
EX... EXCUSE US FOR A FEW MINUTES.
EMELINE, LOOK AFTER EARL CAIN FOR US.
EXCUSE US.
MOTHER!
WHAT'S GOING ON?
CAIN ...
MARY!
WHERE HAVE YOU BEEN?
UM...
THE NOISE YOU'RE MAKING IN THIS ROOM IS FRIGHTENING THAT BOY.

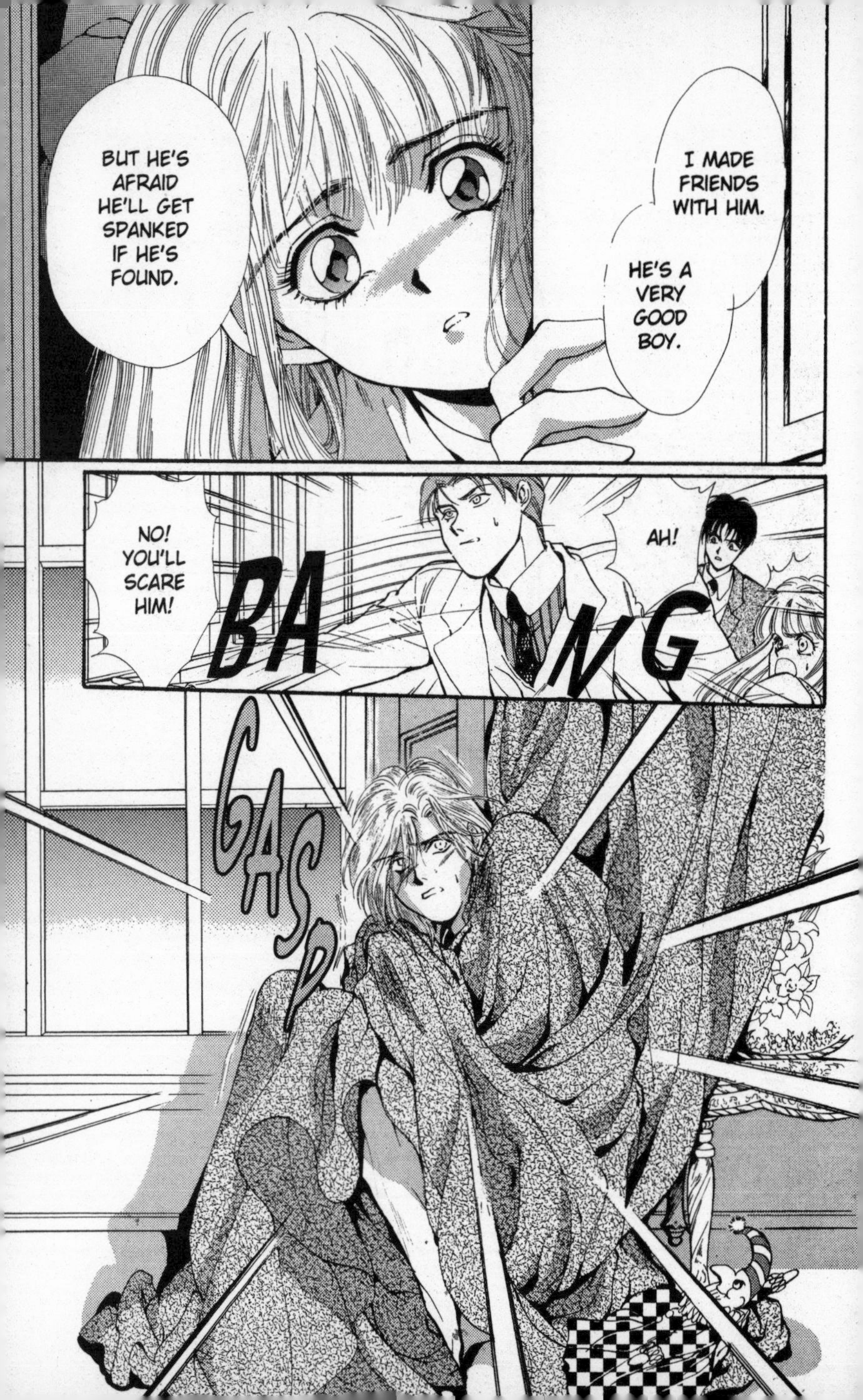
I MADE FRIENDS WITH HIM.
HE'S A VERY GOOD BOY.
BUT HE'S AFRAID HE'LL GET SPANKED IF HE'S FOUND.
AH!
NO! YOU'LL SCARE HIM!
BANG
GASP

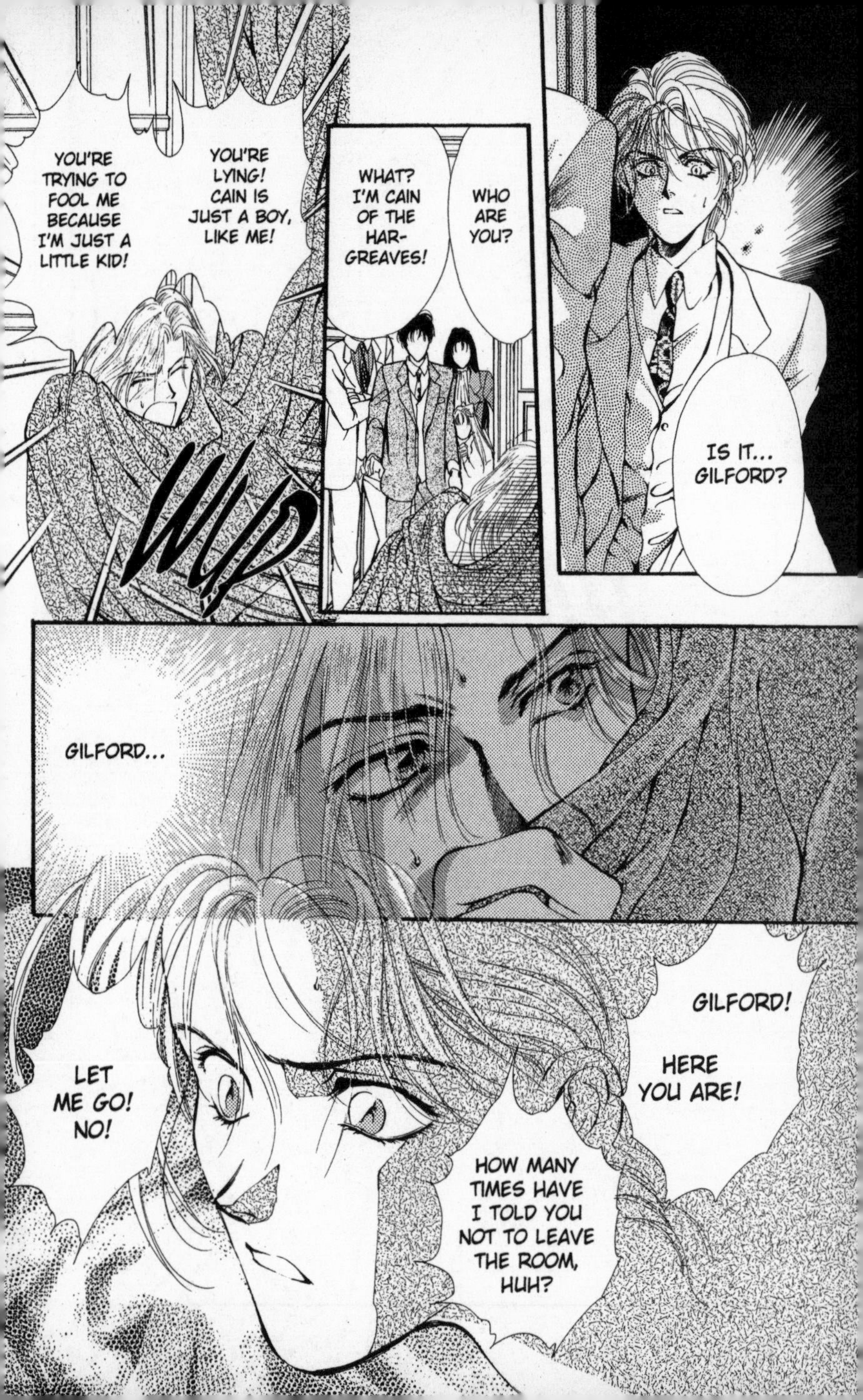
IS IT... GILFORD?
WHO ARE YOU?
WHAT? I'M CAIN OF THE HAR-GREAVES!
YOU'RE LYING! CAIN IS JUST A BOY, LIKE ME!
YOU'RE TRYING TO FOOL ME BECAUSE I'M JUST A LITTLE KID!
WUP
GILFORD...
GILFORD!
HERE YOU ARE!
HOW MANY TIMES HAVE I TOLD YOU NOT TO LEAVE THE ROOM, HUH?
LET ME GO! NO!

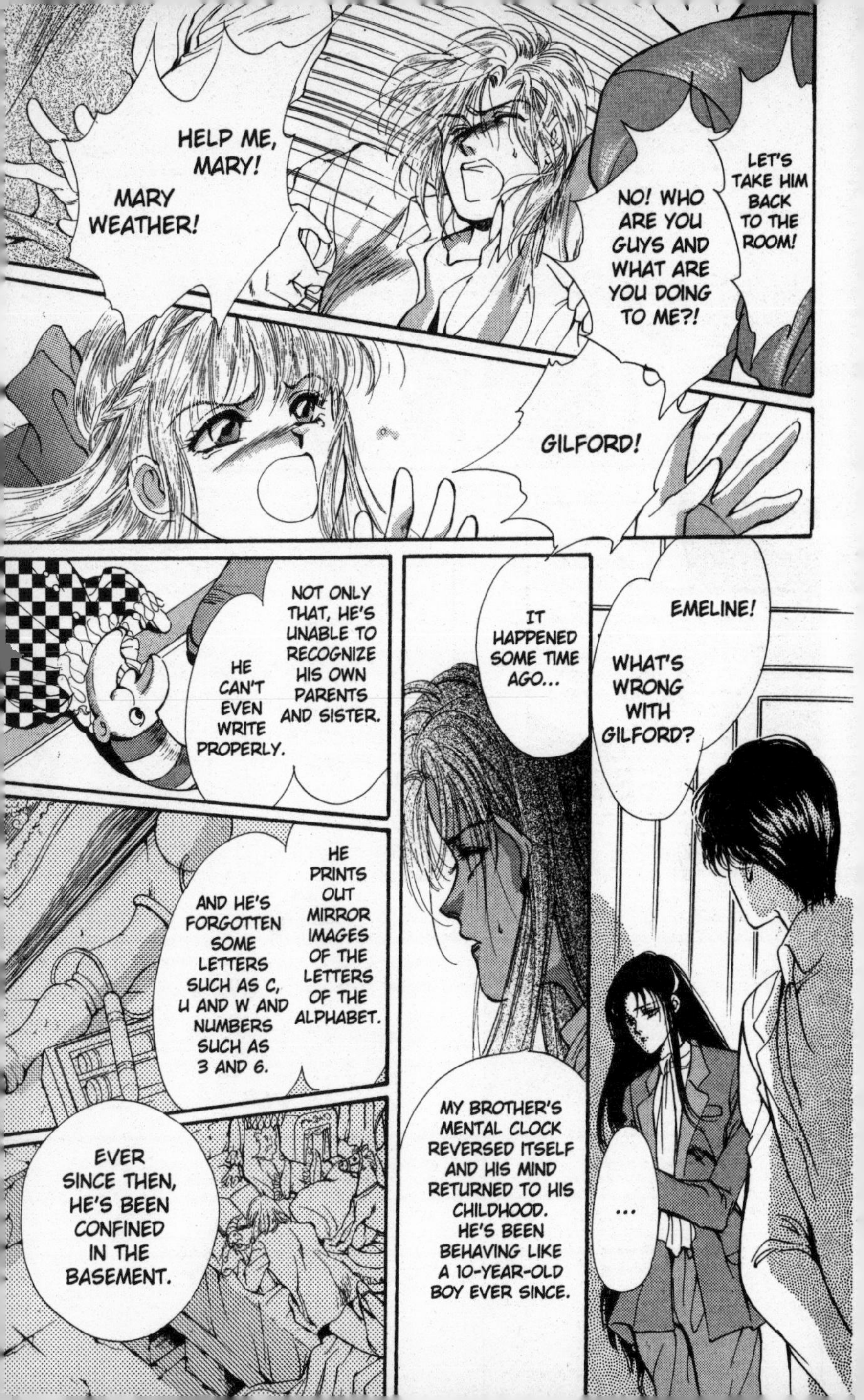
LET'S TAKE HIM BACK TO THE ROOM!
NO! WHO ARE YOU GUYS AND WHAT ARE YOU DOING TO ME?!
HELP ME, MARY!
MARY WEATHER!
GILFORD!
EMELINE!
WHAT'S WRONG WITH GILFORD?
IT HAPPENED SOME TIME AGO...
MY BROTHER'S MENTAL CLOCK REVERSED ITSELF AND HIS MIND RETURNED TO HIS CHILDHOOD. HE'S BEEN BEHAVING LIKE A 10-YEAR-OLD BOY EVER SINCE.
...
NOT ONLY THAT, HE'S UNABLE TO RECOGNIZE HIS OWN PARENTS AND SISTER.
HE CAN'T EVEN WRITE PROPERLY.
HE PRINTS OUT MIRROR IMAGES OF THE LETTERS OF THE ALPHABET.
AND HE'S FORGOTTEN SOME LETTERS SUCH AS C, U AND W AND NUMBERS SUCH AS 3 AND 6.
EVER SINCE THEN, HE'S BEEN CONFINED IN THE BASEMENT.

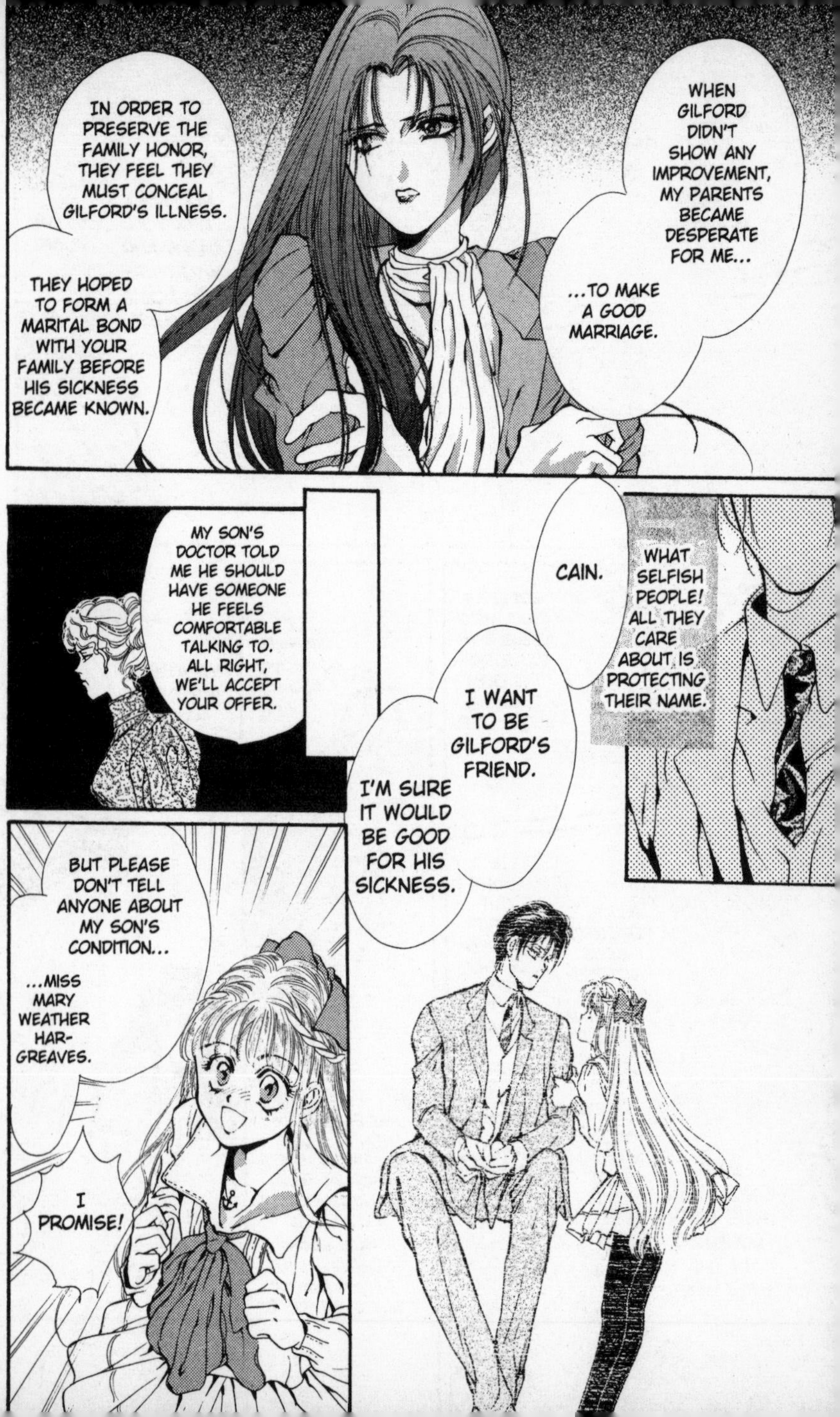
WHEN GILFORD DIDN'T SHOW ANY IMPROVEMENT, MY PARENTS BECAME DESPERATE FOR ME...
...TO MAKE A GOOD MARRIAGE.
IN ORDER TO PRESERVE THE FAMILY HONOR, THEY FEEL THEY MUST CONCEAL GILFORD'S ILLNESS.
THEY HOPED TO FORM A MARITAL BOND WITH YOUR FAMILY BEFORE HIS SICKNESS BECAME KNOWN.
WHAT SELFISH PEOPLE! ALL THEY CARE ABOUT IS PROTECTING THEIR NAME.
CAIN.
I WANT TO BE GILFORD'S FRIEND.
I'M SURE IT WOULD BE GOOD FOR HIS SICKNESS.
MY SON'S DOCTOR TOLD ME HE SHOULD HAVE SOMEONE HE FEELS COMFORTABLE TALKING TO. ALL RIGHT, WE'LL ACCEPT YOUR OFFER.
BUT PLEASE DON'T TELL ANYONE ABOUT MY SON'S CONDITION...
...MISS MARY WEATHER HAR-GREAVES.
I PROMISE!

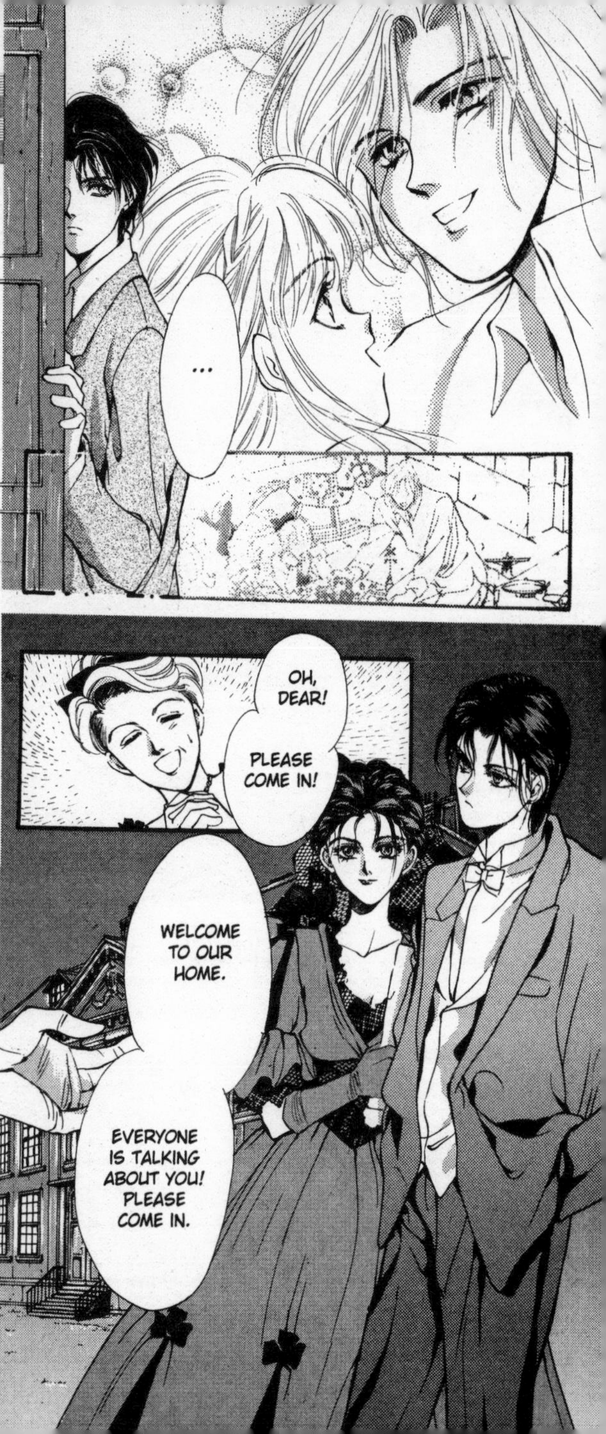
...
OH, DEAR!
PLEASE COME IN!
WELCOME TO OUR HOME.
EVERYONE IS TALKING ABOUT YOU! PLEASE COME IN.

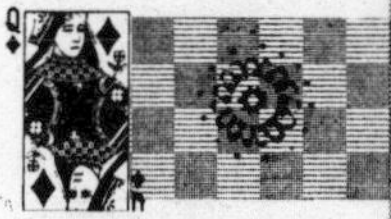

The *Cain* series is already in its fourth episode, ha ha ha. I am thrilled that this episode is going to be serialized in more than five installments. Furthermore, the publisher has fulfilled a dream of mine by using my work on the cover of a "Hana to Yume Comics" magazine, and printing the first page of this episode in color. I almost fainted with happiness when I learned of his decision. This decision has made me extremely busy because I was determined to do a good job. (Consequently, I have been unable to reply to fan mail...) In this new episode, I revealed Cain's age for the first time. Everyone said he looked much older than 17. (Does he?) I guess the clothes he wears make him look older than he is. In any case, I've been wanting to adapt the story of Jack the Ripper in my comic work, so I am very happy to be working on this particular episode. Let's see what happens.

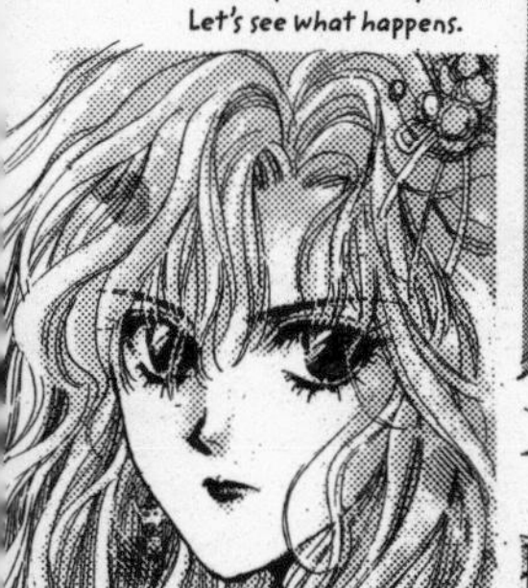

X· WHEEL OF FORTUNE

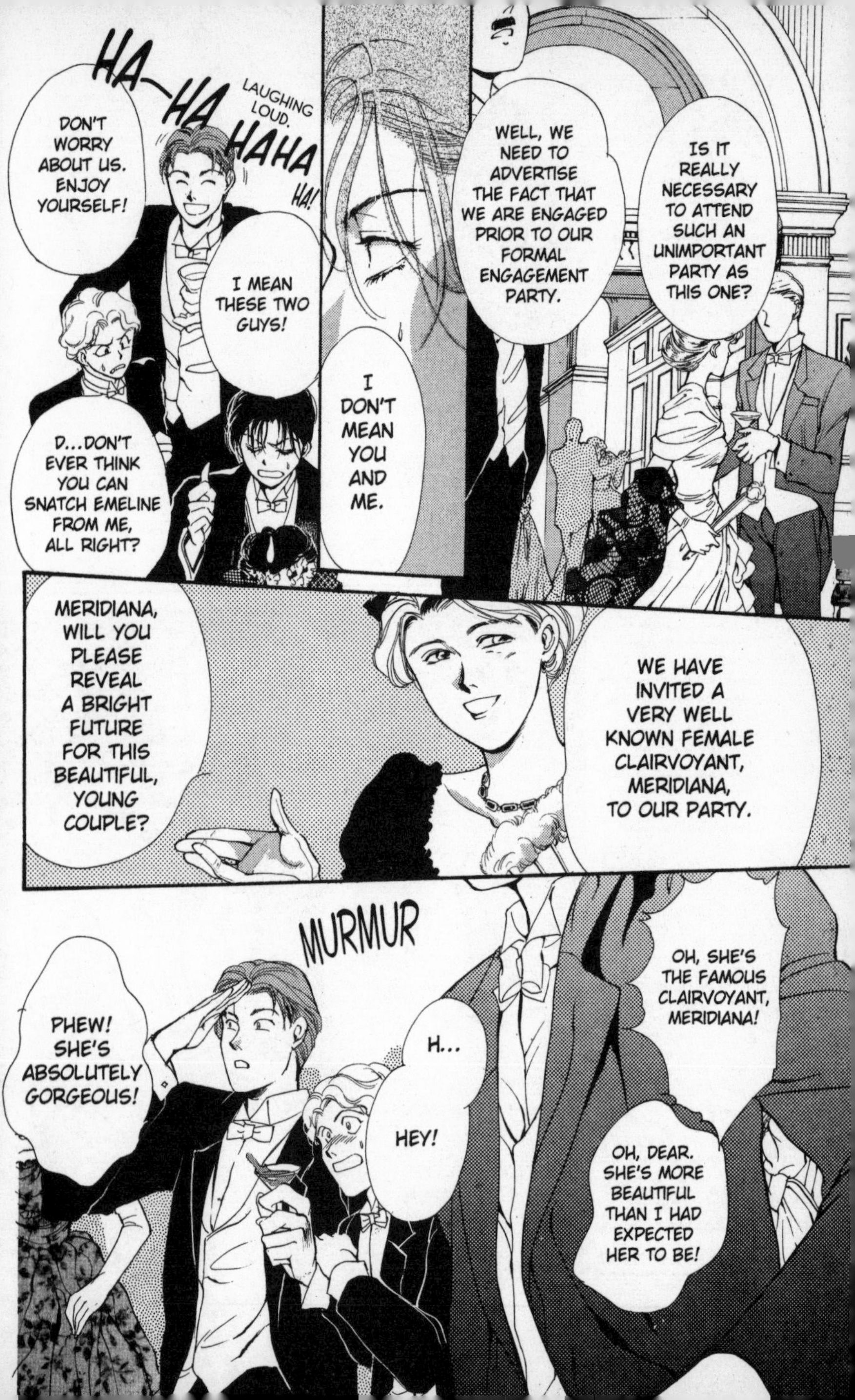
IS IT REALLY NECESSARY TO ATTEND SUCH AN UNIMPORTANT PARTY AS THIS ONE?
WELL, WE NEED TO ADVERTISE THE FACT THAT WE ARE ENGAGED PRIOR TO OUR FORMAL ENGAGEMENT PARTY.
I DON'T MEAN YOU AND ME.
HA-HA HAHA HA!
LAUGHING LOUD.
I MEAN THESE TWO GUYS!
DON'T WORRY ABOUT US. ENJOY YOURSELF!
D...DON'T EVER THINK YOU CAN SNATCH EMELINE FROM ME, ALL RIGHT?
WE HAVE INVITED A VERY WELL KNOWN FEMALE CLAIRVOYANT, MERIDIANA, TO OUR PARTY.
MERIDIANA, WILL YOU PLEASE REVEAL A BRIGHT FUTURE FOR THIS BEAUTIFUL, YOUNG COUPLE?
MURMUR
OH, SHE'S THE FAMOUS CLAIRVOYANT, MERIDIANA!
OH, DEAR. SHE'S MORE BEAUTIFUL THAN I HAD EXPECTED HER TO BE!
H...
HEY!
PHEW! SHE'S ABSOLUTELY GORGEOUS!

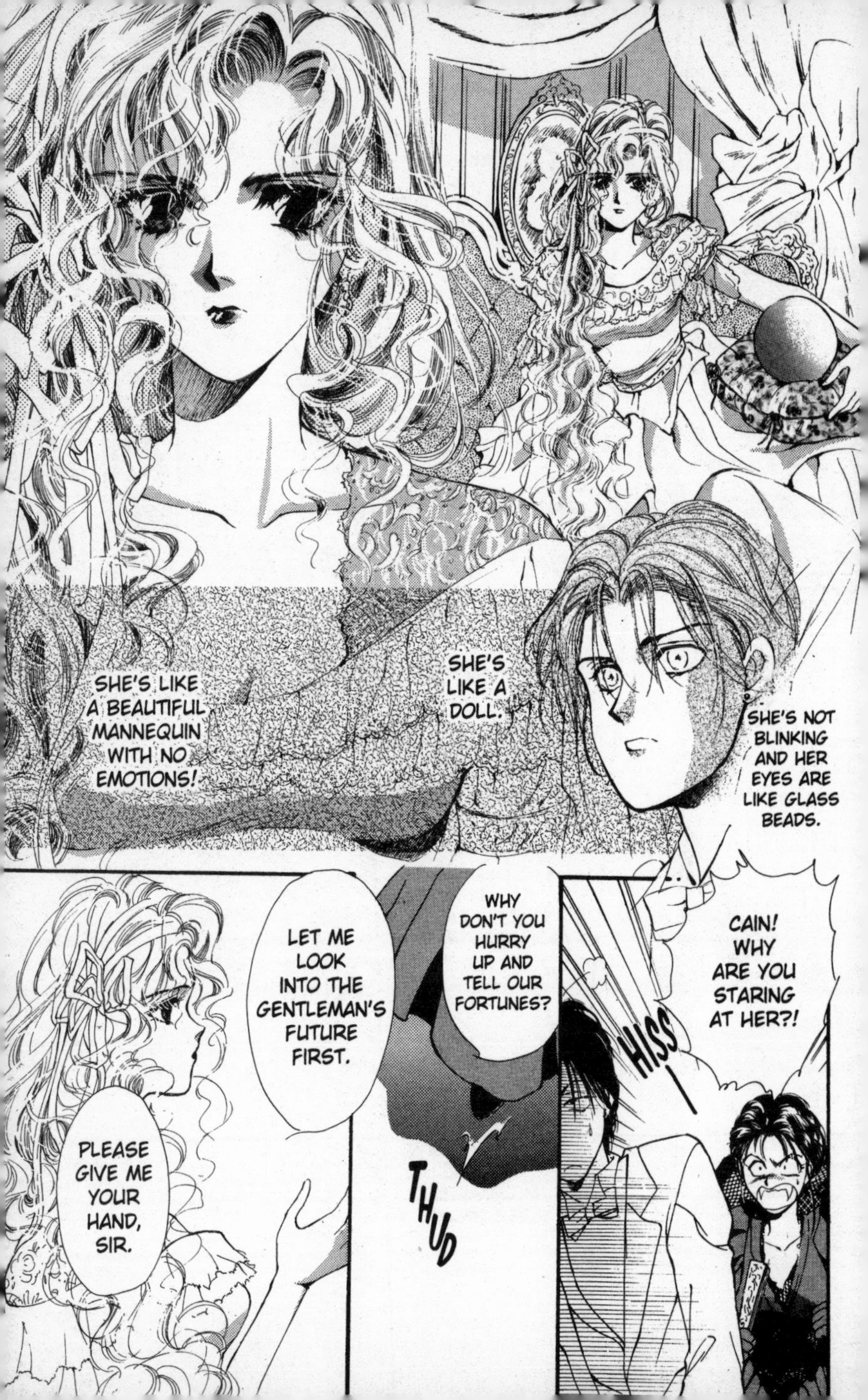

SHE'S NOT BLINKING AND HER EYES ARE LIKE GLASS BEADS.
SHE'S LIKE A DOLL.
SHE'S LIKE A BEAUTIFUL MANNEQUIN WITH NO EMOTIONS!
CAIN! WHY ARE YOU STARING AT HER?!
HISS
WHY DON'T YOU HURRY UP AND TELL OUR FORTUNES?
THUD
LET ME LOOK INTO THE GENTLEMAN'S FUTURE FIRST.
PLEASE GIVE ME YOUR HAND, SIR.

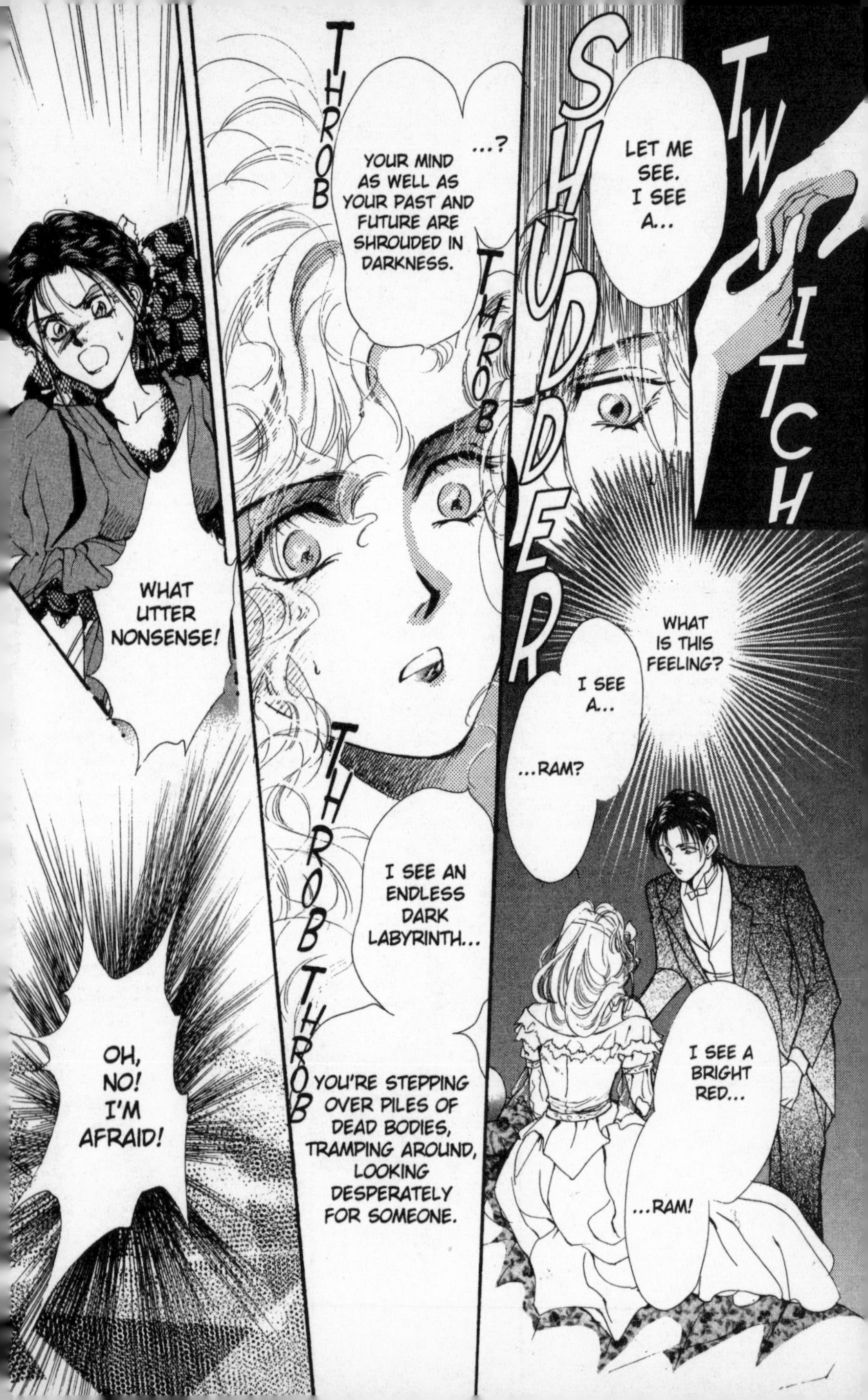
TWITCH
LET ME SEE. I SEE A...
SHUDDER
WHAT IS THIS FEELING?
I SEE A...
...RAM?
I SEE A BRIGHT RED...
...RAM!
...?
THROB
YOUR MIND AS WELL AS YOUR PAST AND FUTURE ARE SHROUDED IN DARKNESS.
THROB
THROB
I SEE AN ENDLESS DARK LABYRINTH...
THROB
YOU'RE STEPPING OVER PILES OF DEAD BODIES, TRAMPING AROUND, LOOKING DESPERATELY FOR SOMEONE.
WHAT UTTER NONSENSE!
OH, NO! I'M AFRAID!

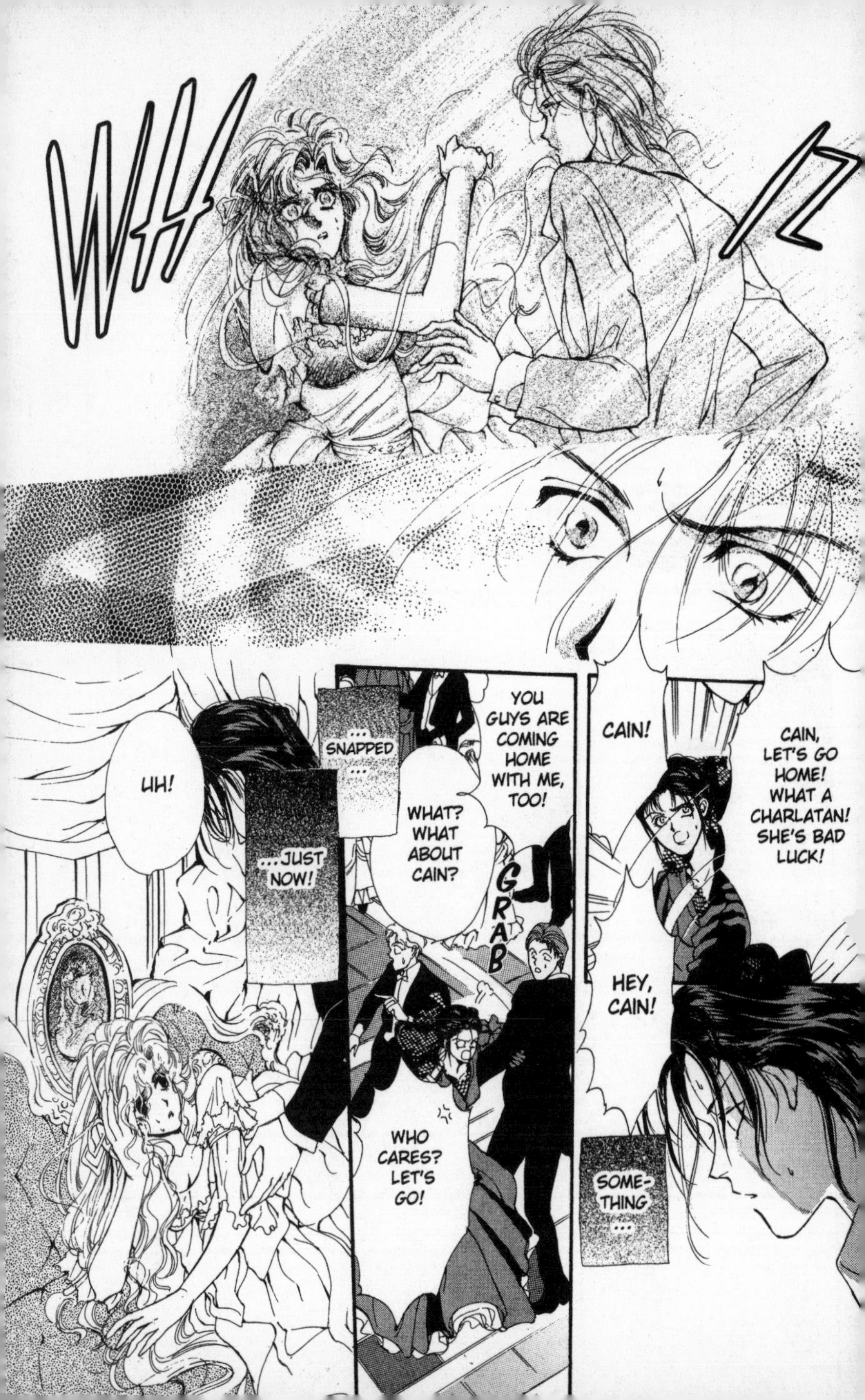
WHIZ
CAIN, LET'S GO HOME! WHAT A CHARLATAN! SHE'S BAD LUCK!
CAIN!
HEY, CAIN!
SOME-THING ...
YOU GUYS ARE COMING HOME WITH ME, TOO!
... SNAPPED ...
WHAT? WHAT ABOUT CAIN?
GRAB
WHO CARES? LET'S GO!
...JUST NOW!
UH!

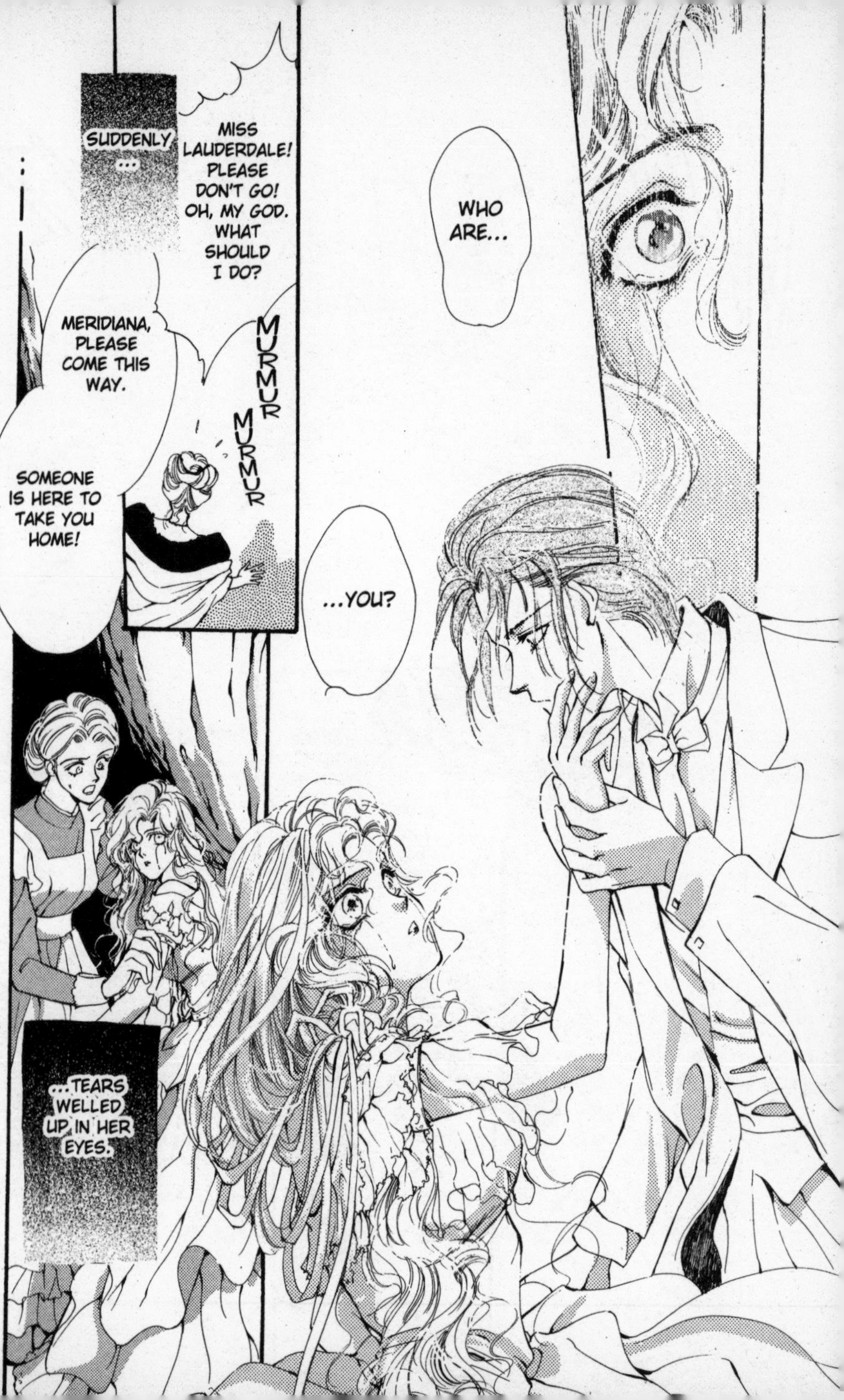
WHO ARE...
...YOU?
SUDDENLY, ...
MISS LAUDERDALE! PLEASE DON'T GO! OH, MY GOD. WHAT SHOULD I DO?
MURMUR MURMUR
MERIDIANA, PLEASE COME THIS WAY.
SOMEONE IS HERE TO TAKE YOU HOME!
...TEARS WELLED UP IN HER EYES.

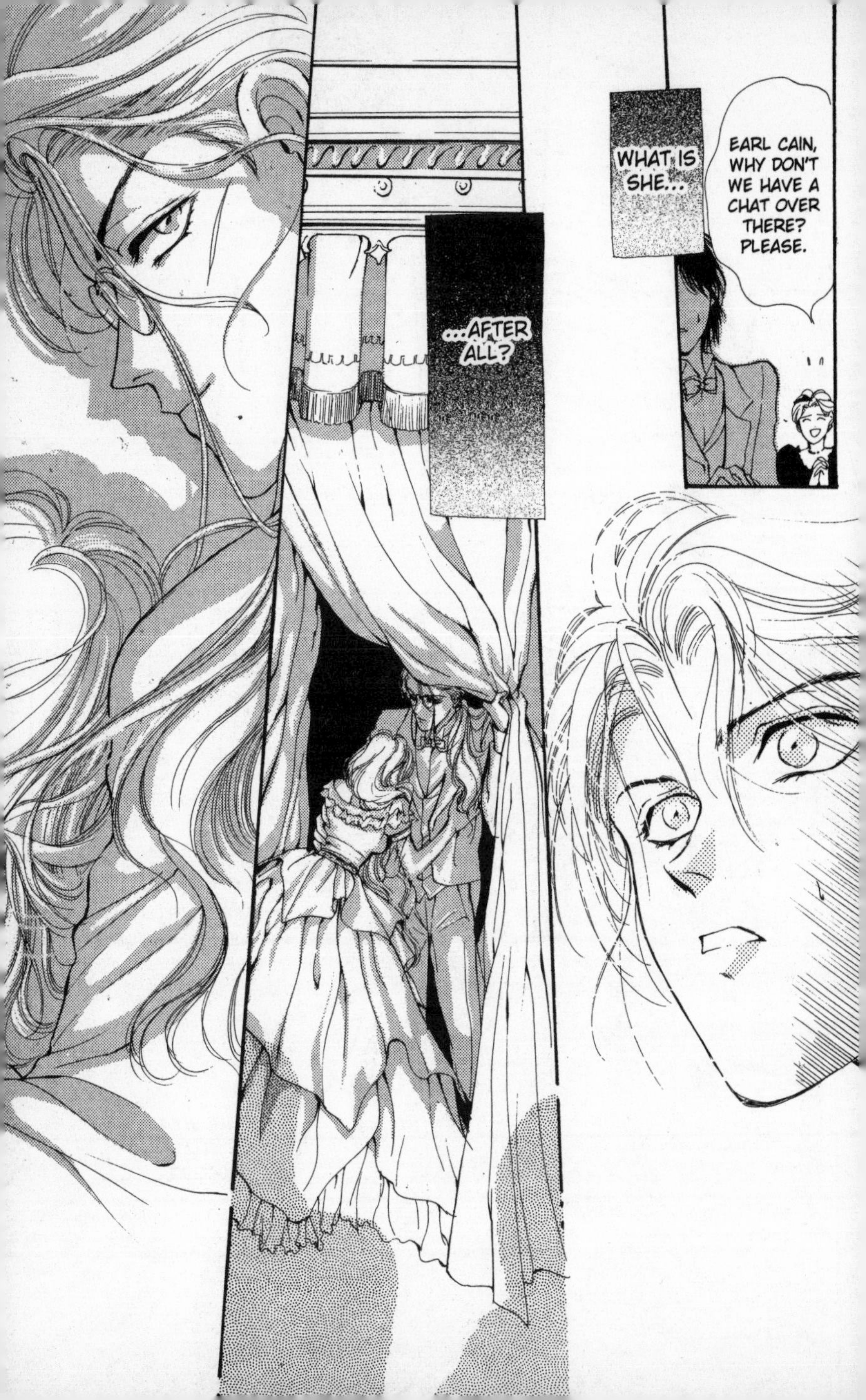
EARL CAIN, WHY DON'T WE HAVE A CHAT OVER THERE? PLEASE.
WHAT IS SHE...
...AFTER ALL?

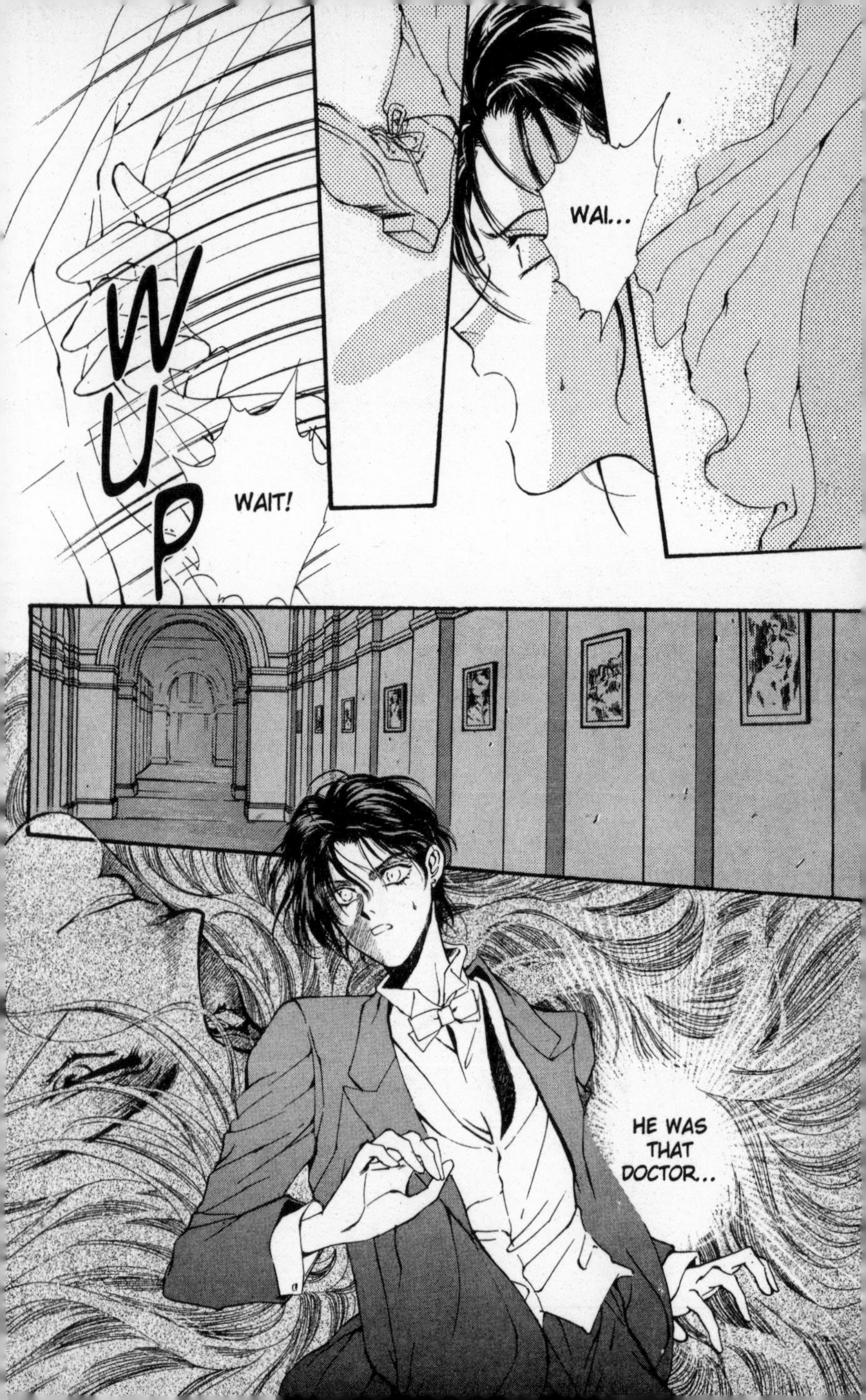
WAI...
WUP
WAIT!
HE WAS THAT DOCTOR...

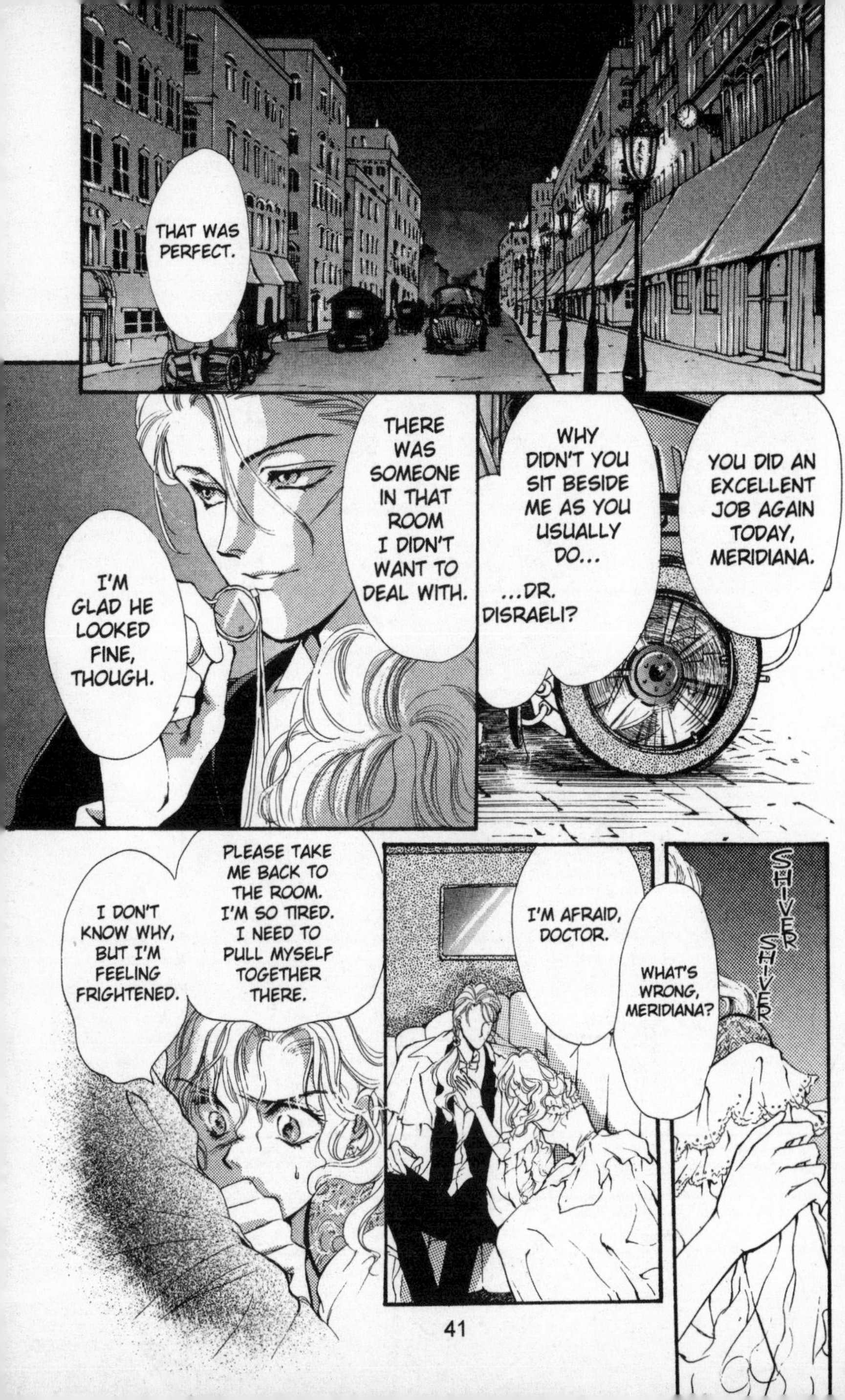
THAT WAS PERFECT.
YOU DID AN EXCELLENT JOB AGAIN TODAY, MERIDIANA.
WHY DIDN'T YOU SIT BESIDE ME AS YOU USUALLY DO...
...DR. DISRAELI?
THERE WAS SOMEONE IN THAT ROOM I DIDN'T WANT TO DEAL WITH.
I'M GLAD HE LOOKED FINE, THOUGH.
SHIVER SHIVER
WHAT'S WRONG, MERIDIANA?
I'M AFRAID, DOCTOR.
PLEASE TAKE ME BACK TO THE ROOM. I'M SO TIRED. I NEED TO PULL MYSELF TOGETHER THERE.
I DON'T KNOW WHY, BUT I'M FEELING FRIGHTENED.

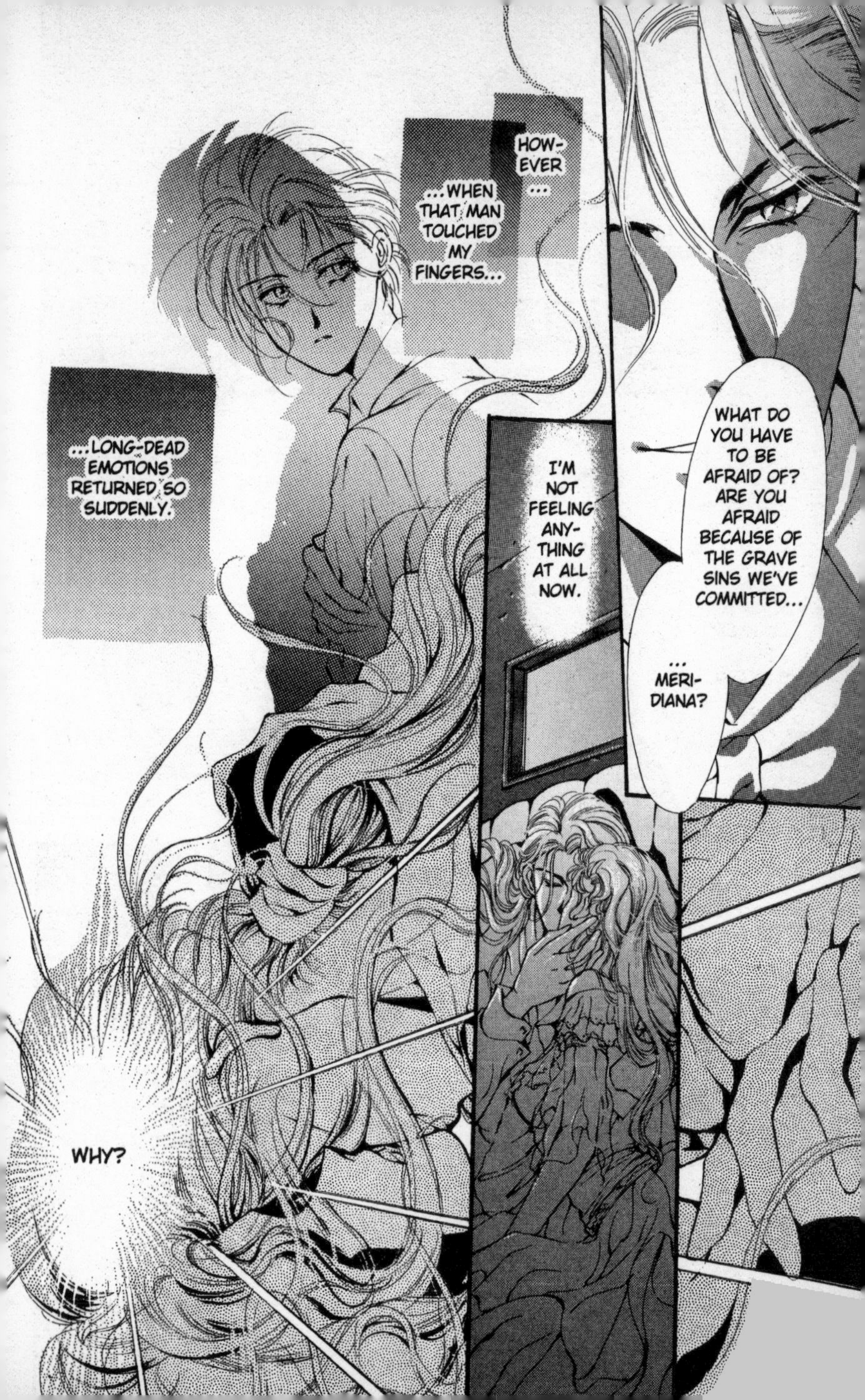
WHAT DO YOU HAVE TO BE AFRAID OF? ARE YOU AFRAID BECAUSE OF THE GRAVE SINS WE'VE COMMITTED...
...MERIDIANA?
HOW-EVER...
...WHEN THAT MAN TOUCHED MY FINGERS...
...LONG-DEAD EMOTIONS RETURNED SO SUDDENLY.
I'M NOT FEELING ANYTHING AT ALL NOW.
WHY?

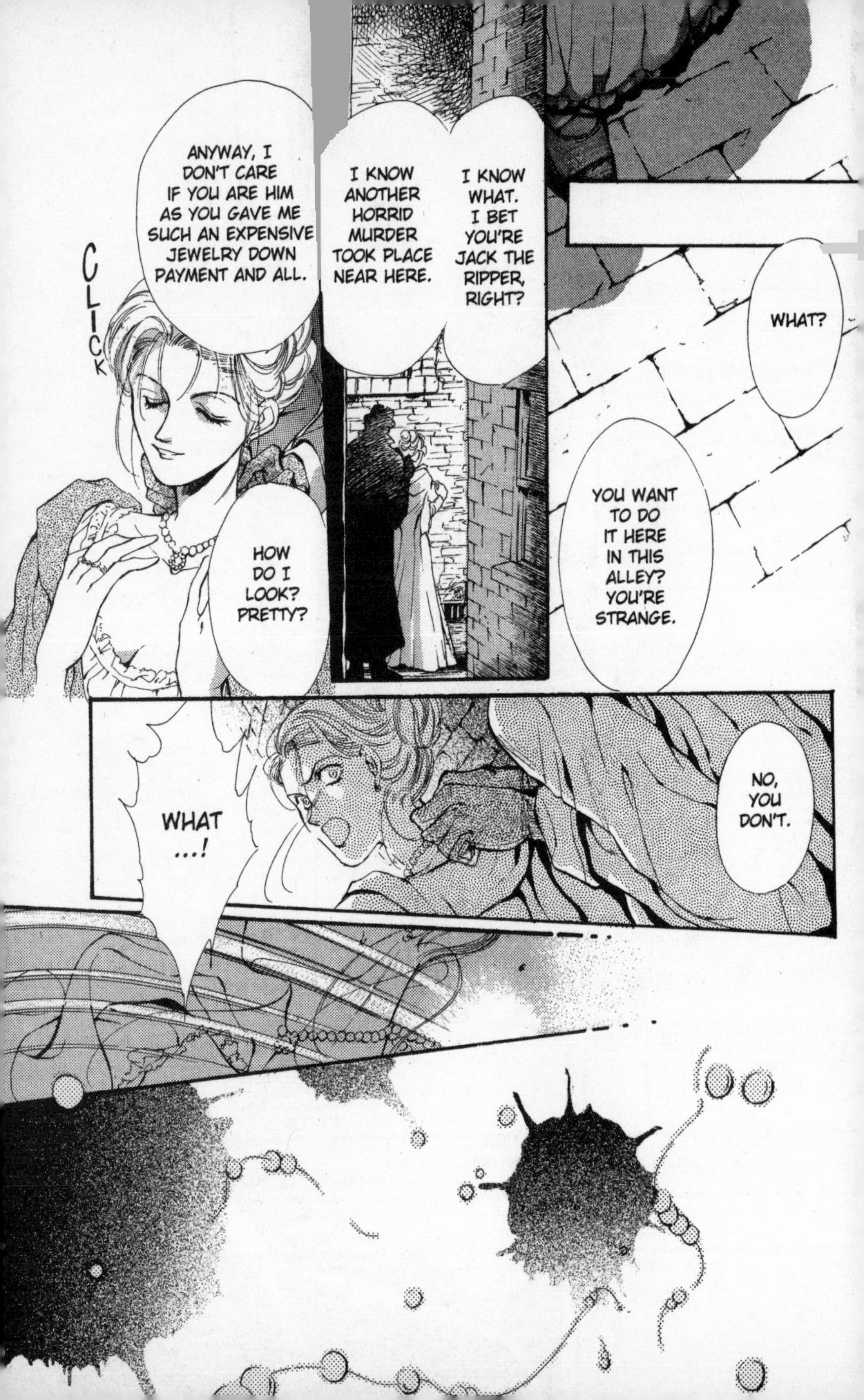
WHAT?
YOU WANT TO DO IT HERE IN THIS ALLEY? YOU'RE STRANGE.
I KNOW WHAT. I BET YOU'RE JACK THE RIPPER, RIGHT?
I KNOW ANOTHER HORRID MURDER TOOK PLACE NEAR HERE.
ANYWAY, I DON'T CARE IF YOU ARE HIM AS YOU GAVE ME SUCH AN EXPENSIVE JEWELRY DOWN PAYMENT AND ALL.
CLICK
HOW DO I LOOK? PRETTY?
NO, YOU DON'T.
WHAT ...!

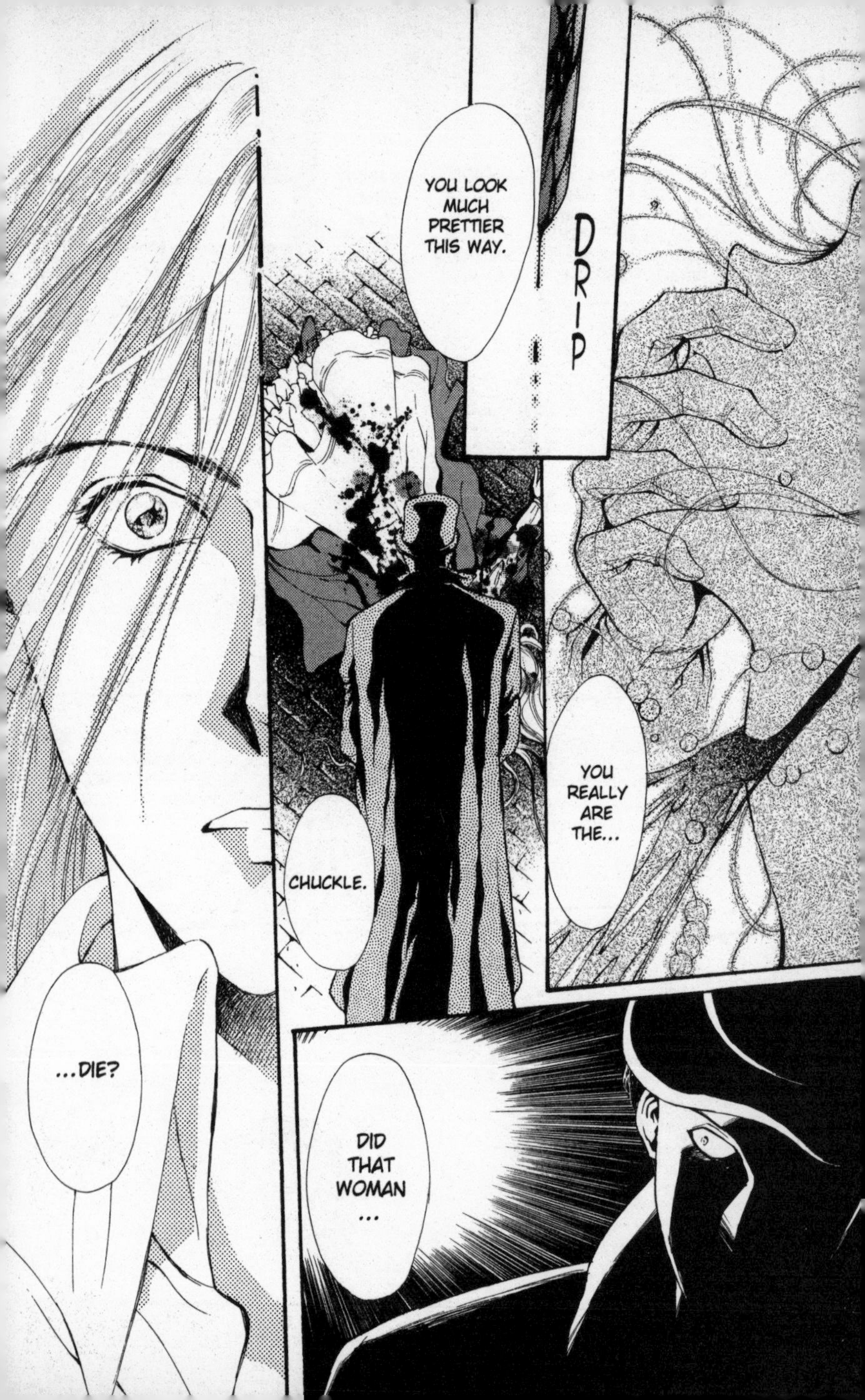
YOU REALLY ARE THE...
DRIP
YOU LOOK MUCH PRETTIER THIS WAY.
CHUCKLE.
DID THAT WOMAN ...
...DIE?

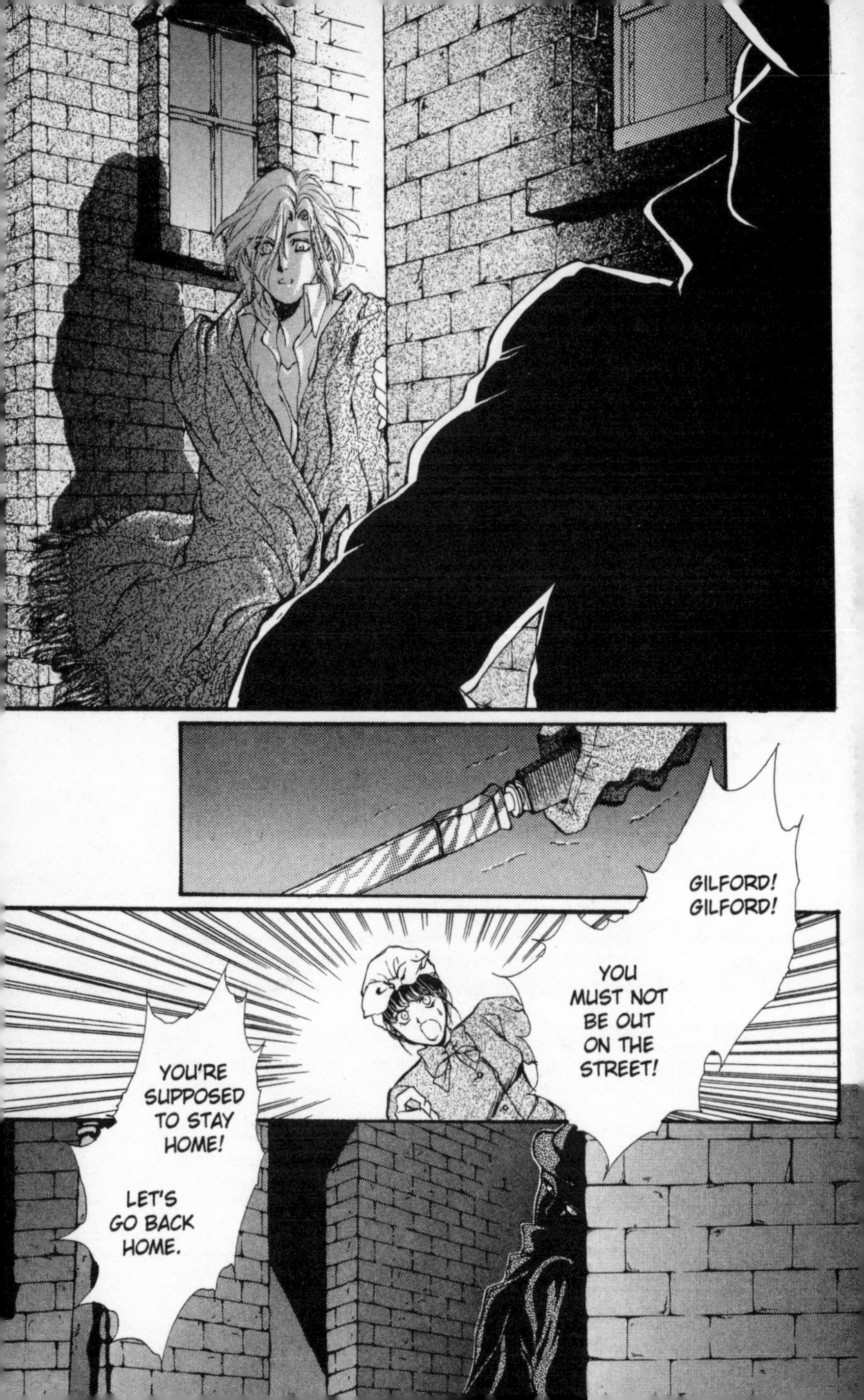
GILFORD! GILFORD!
YOU MUST NOT BE OUT ON THE STREET!
YOU'RE SUPPOSED TO STAY HOME!
LET'S GO BACK HOME.

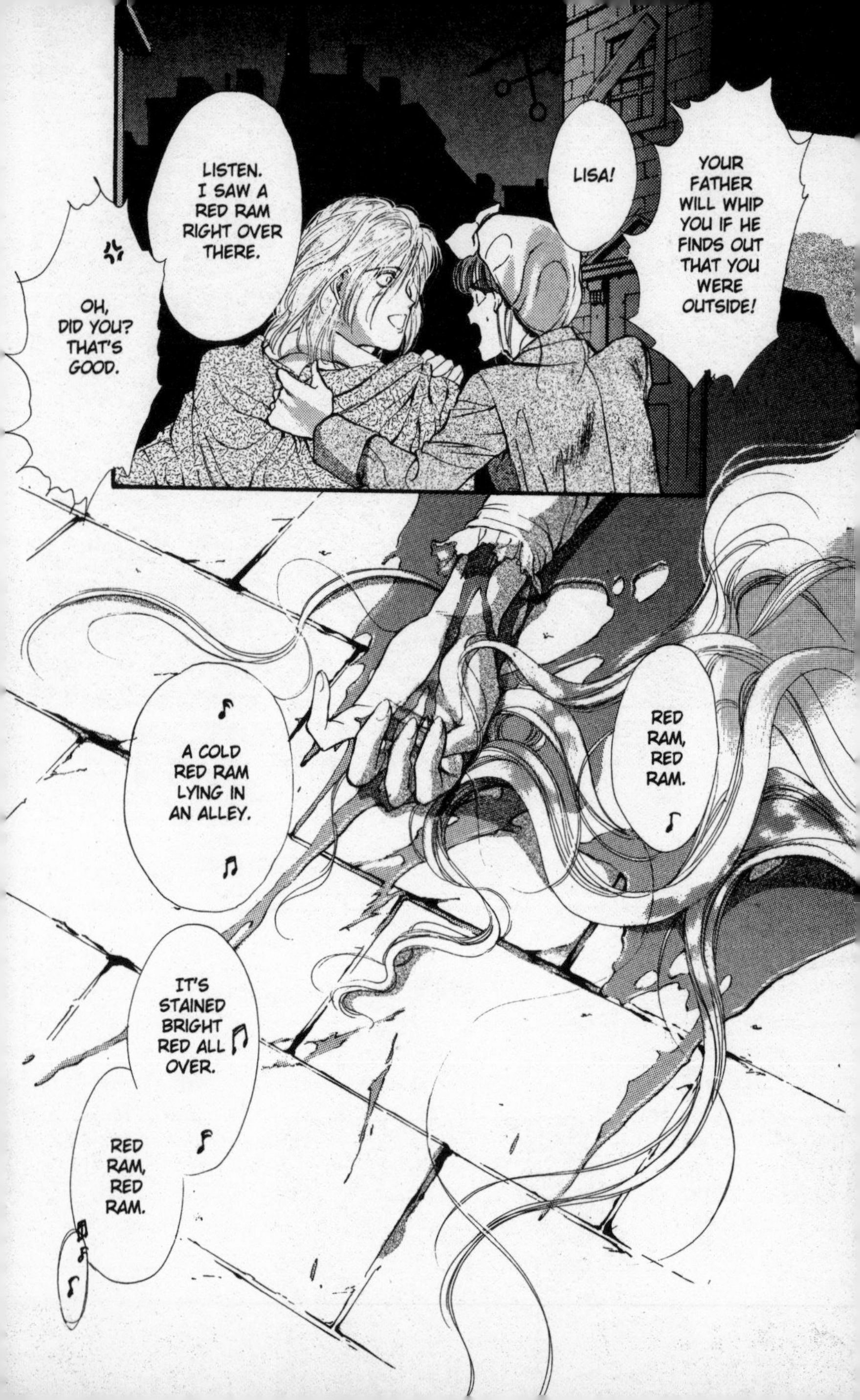
LISA!
YOUR FATHER WILL WHIP YOU IF HE FINDS OUT THAT YOU WERE OUTSIDE!
LISTEN. I SAW A RED RAM RIGHT OVER THERE.
OH, DID YOU? THAT'S GOOD.
RED RAM, RED RAM.
A COLD RED RAM LYING IN AN ALLEY.
IT'S STAINED BRIGHT RED ALL OVER.
RED RAM, RED RAM.

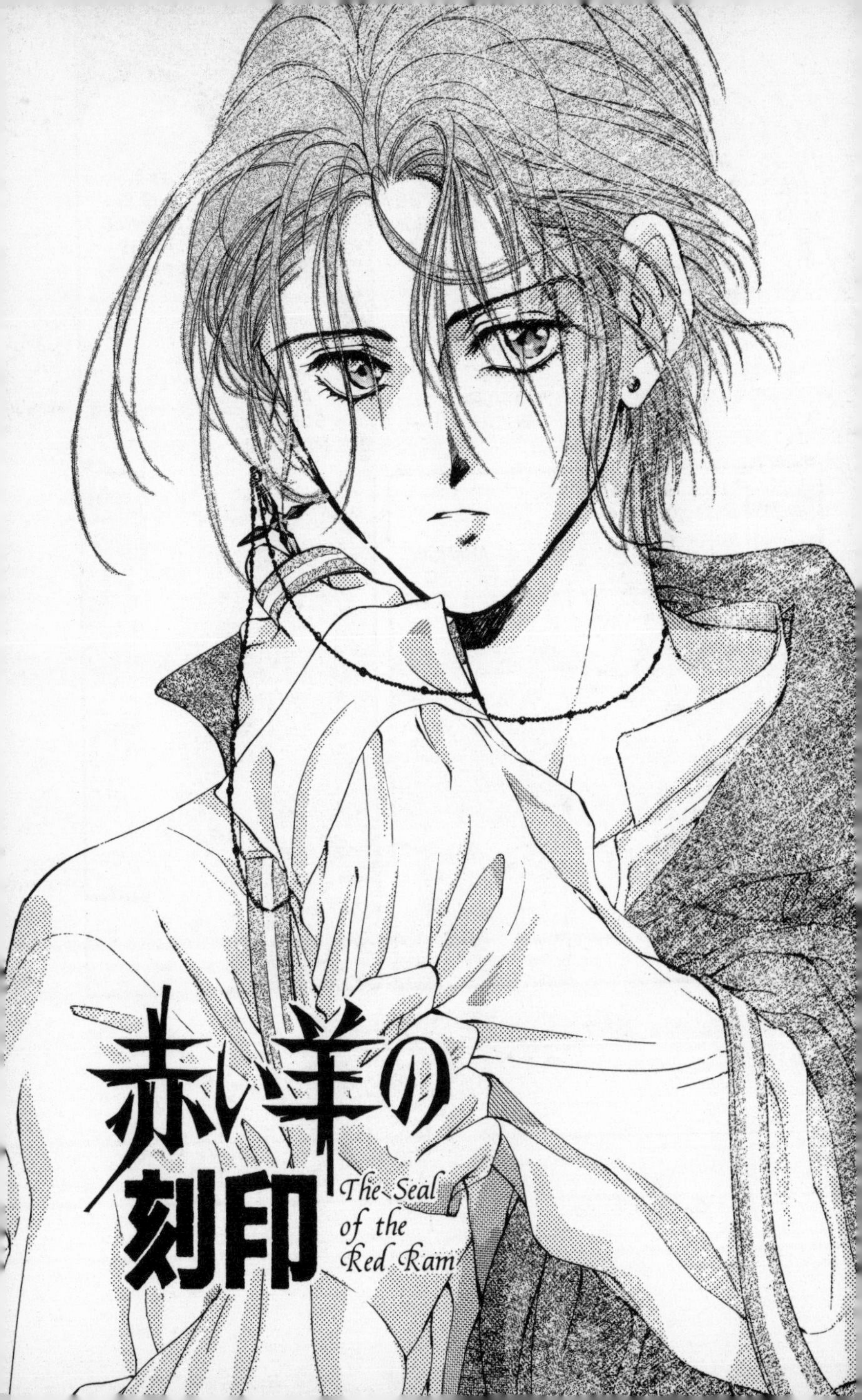
赤い羊の刻印
The Seal of the Red Ram

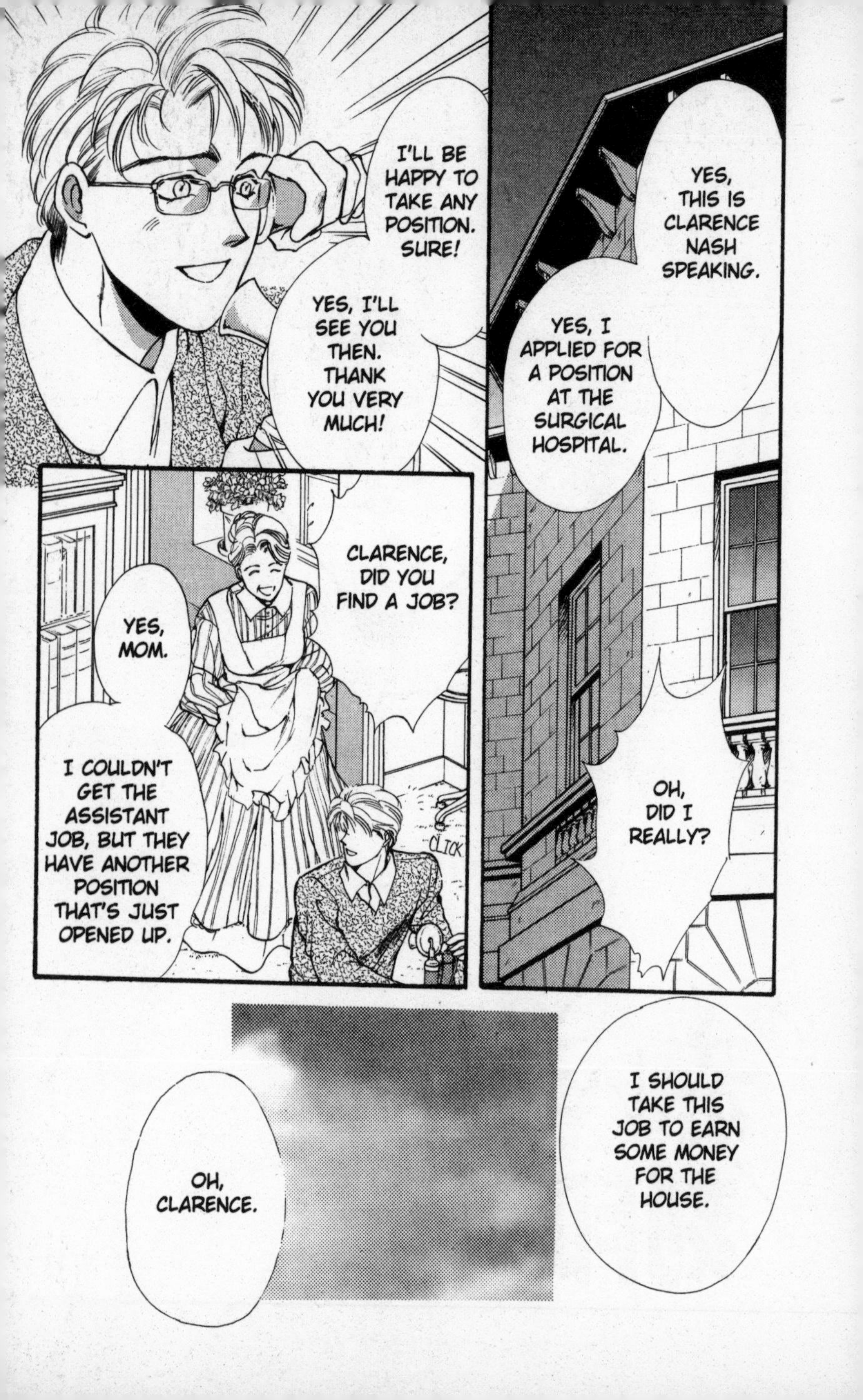
YES, THIS IS CLARENCE NASH SPEAKING.
YES, I APPLIED FOR A POSITION AT THE SURGICAL HOSPITAL.
OH, DID I REALLY?
I'LL BE HAPPY TO TAKE ANY POSITION. SURE!
YES, I'LL SEE YOU THEN. THANK YOU VERY MUCH!
CLARENCE, DID YOU FIND A JOB?
YES, MOM.
I COULDN'T GET THE ASSISTANT JOB, BUT THEY HAVE ANOTHER POSITION THAT'S JUST OPENED UP.
CLICK
I SHOULD TAKE THIS JOB TO EARN SOME MONEY FOR THE HOUSE.
OH, CLARENCE.

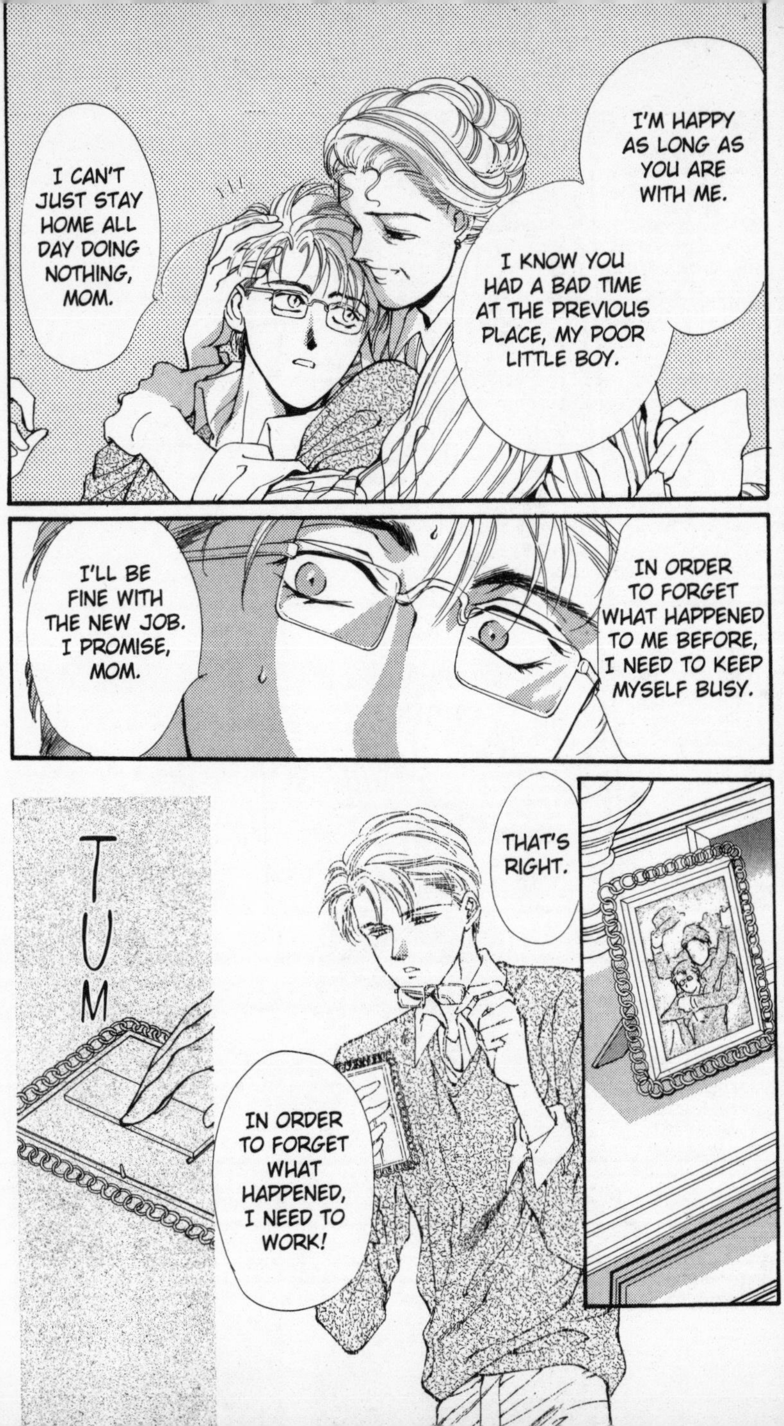
I'M HAPPY AS LONG AS YOU ARE WITH ME.
I KNOW YOU HAD A BAD TIME AT THE PREVIOUS PLACE, MY POOR LITTLE BOY.
I CAN'T JUST STAY HOME ALL DAY DOING NOTHING, MOM.
IN ORDER TO FORGET WHAT HAPPENED TO ME BEFORE, I NEED TO KEEP MYSELF BUSY.
I'LL BE FINE WITH THE NEW JOB. I PROMISE, MOM.
THAT'S RIGHT.
IN ORDER TO FORGET WHAT HAPPENED, I NEED TO WORK!
TUM

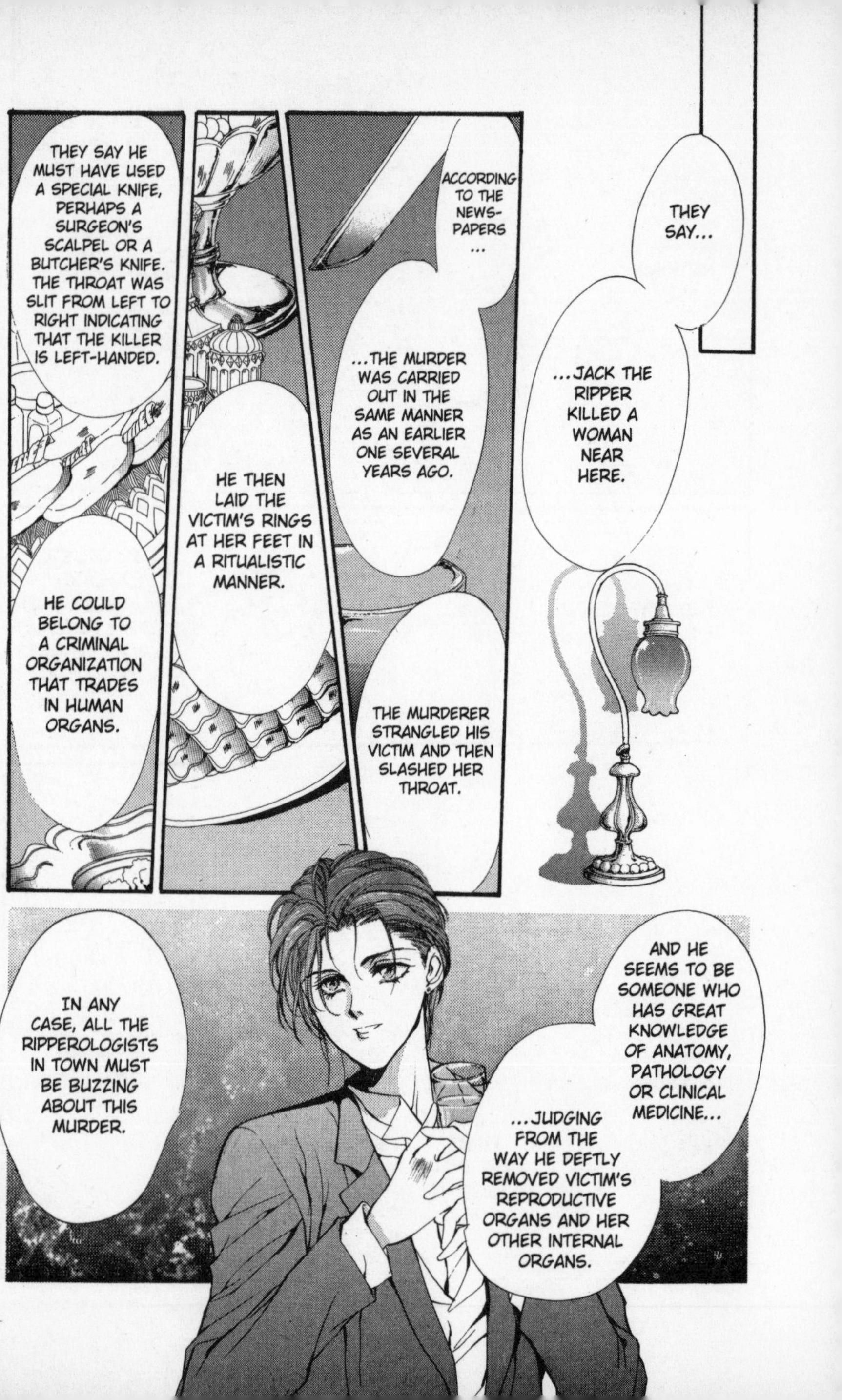
THEY SAY...
...JACK THE RIPPER KILLED A WOMAN NEAR HERE.
ACCORDING TO THE NEWS-PAPERS ...
...THE MURDER WAS CARRIED OUT IN THE SAME MANNER AS AN EARLIER ONE SEVERAL YEARS AGO.
THE MURDERER STRANGLED HIS VICTIM AND THEN SLASHED HER THROAT.
HE THEN LAID THE VICTIM'S RINGS AT HER FEET IN A RITUALISTIC MANNER.
THEY SAY HE MUST HAVE USED A SPECIAL KNIFE, PERHAPS A SURGEON'S SCALPEL OR A BUTCHER'S KNIFE. THE THROAT WAS SLIT FROM LEFT TO RIGHT INDICATING THAT THE KILLER IS LEFT-HANDED.
HE COULD BELONG TO A CRIMINAL ORGANIZATION THAT TRADES IN HUMAN ORGANS.
AND HE SEEMS TO BE SOMEONE WHO HAS GREAT KNOWLEDGE OF ANATOMY, PATHOLOGY OR CLINICAL MEDICINE...
...JUDGING FROM THE WAY HE DEFTLY REMOVED VICTIM'S REPRODUCTIVE ORGANS AND HER OTHER INTERNAL ORGANS.
IN ANY CASE, ALL THE RIPPEROLOGISTS IN TOWN MUST BE BUZZING ABOUT THIS MURDER.

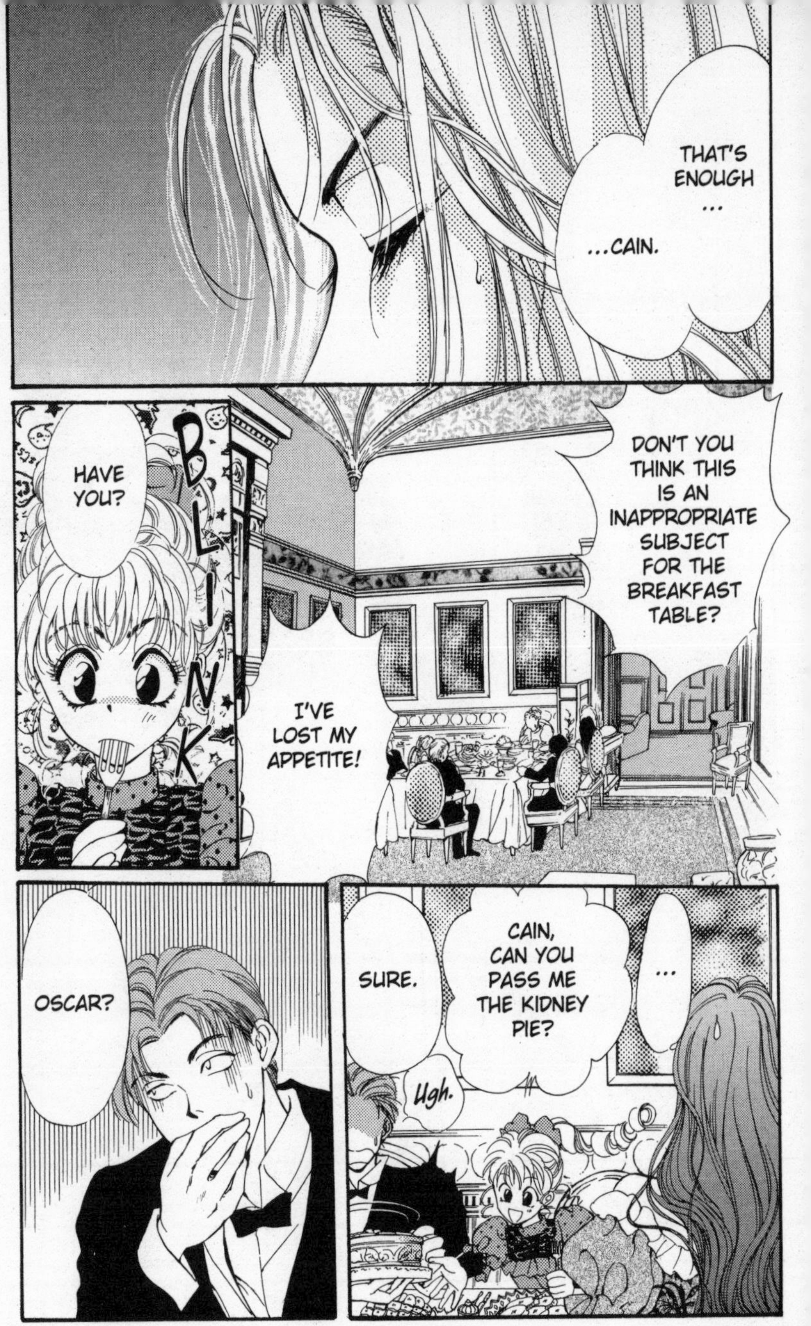
THAT'S ENOUGH ...
...CAIN.
DON'T YOU THINK THIS IS AN INAPPROPRIATE SUBJECT FOR THE BREAKFAST TABLE?
I'VE LOST MY APPETITE!
BLINK
HAVE YOU?
...
CAIN, CAN YOU PASS ME THE KIDNEY PIE?
SURE.
Ugh.
OSCAR?

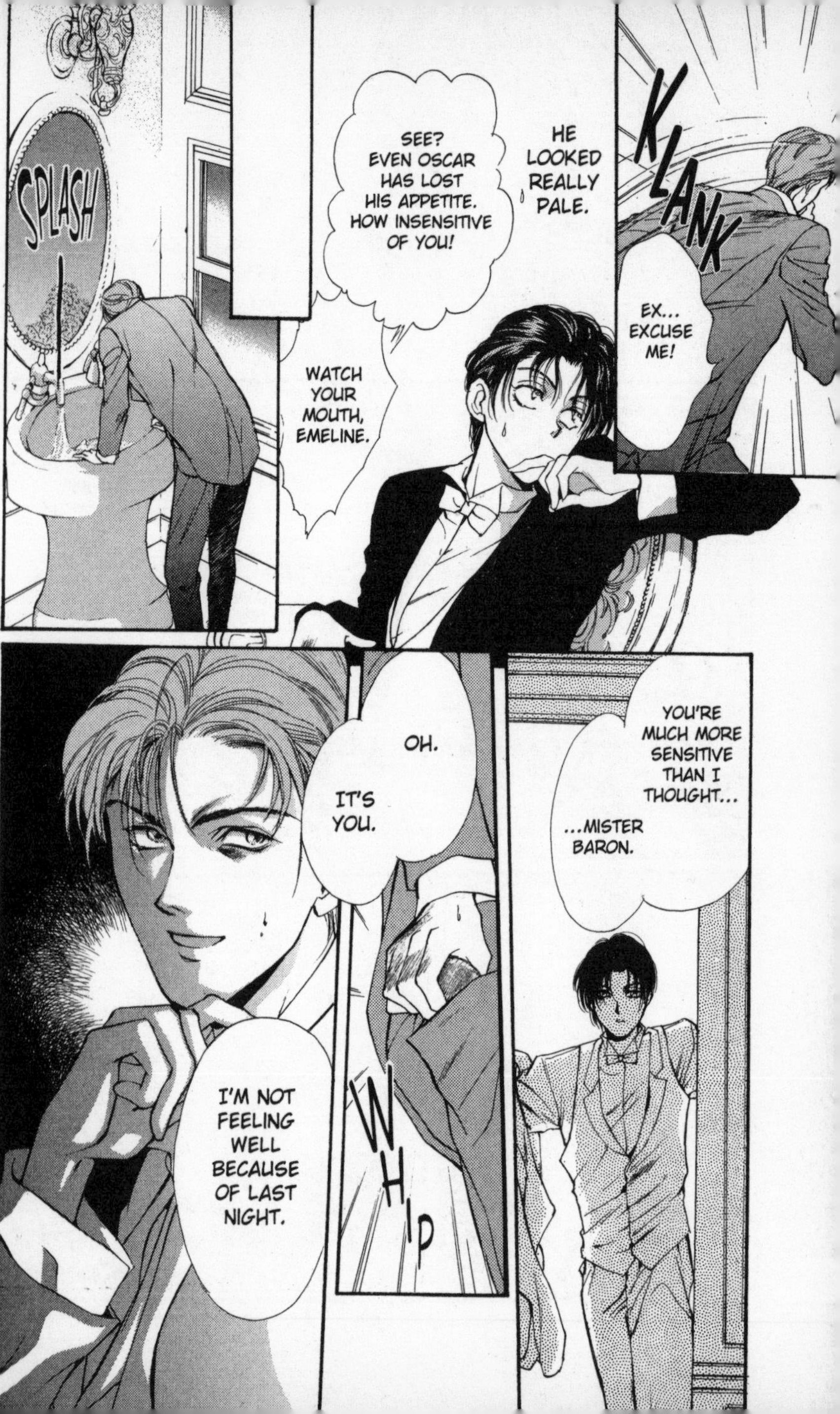
KLANK
EX... EXCUSE ME!
HE LOOKED REALLY PALE.
SEE? EVEN OSCAR HAS LOST HIS APPETITE. HOW INSENSITIVE OF YOU!
WATCH YOUR MOUTH, EMELINE.
SPLASH
YOU'RE MUCH MORE SENSITIVE THAN I THOUGHT...
...MISTER BARON.
OH.
IT'S YOU.
WHIP
I'M NOT FEELING WELL BECAUSE OF LAST NIGHT.

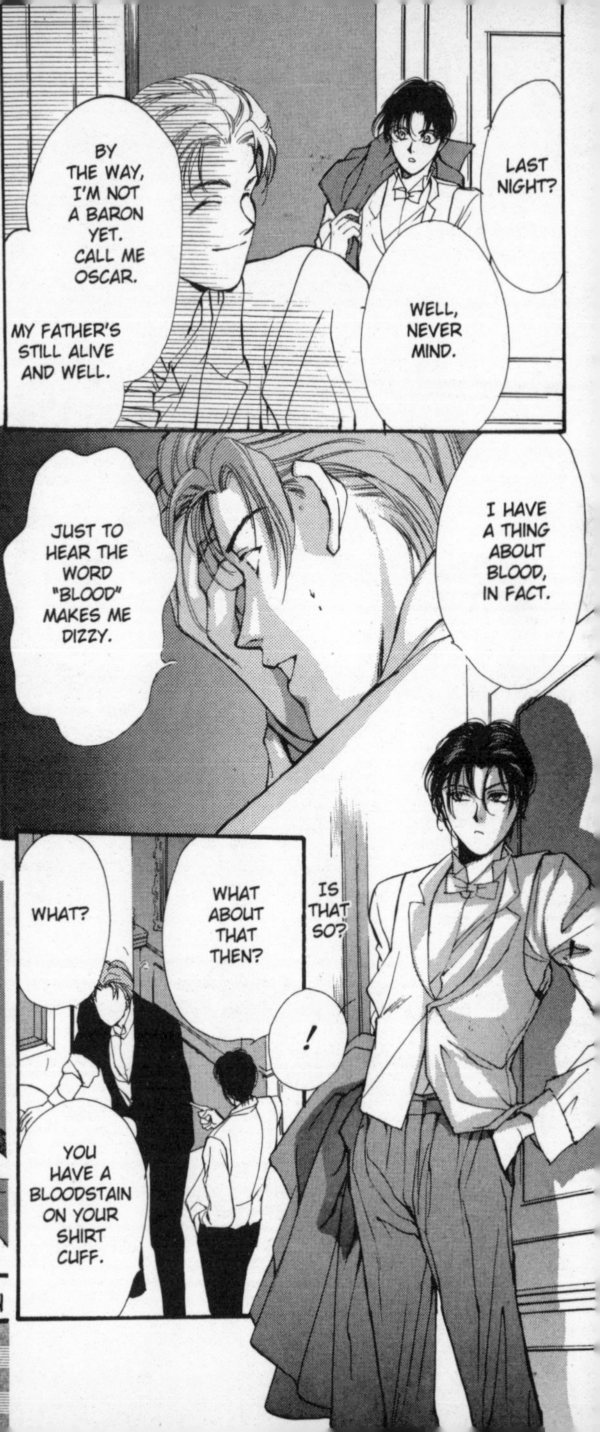
LAST NIGHT?
WELL, NEVER MIND.
BY THE WAY, I'M NOT A BARON YET. CALL ME OSCAR.
MY FATHER'S STILL ALIVE AND WELL.
I HAVE A THING ABOUT BLOOD, IN FACT.
JUST TO HEAR THE WORD "BLOOD" MAKES ME DIZZY.
IS THAT SO?
WHAT ABOUT THAT THEN?
WHAT?
!
YOU HAVE A BLOODSTAIN ON YOUR SHIRT CUFF.

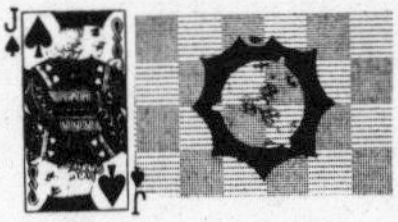

Many readers hate Cain's uncle, Neil, because of Riff's suicide attempt. (Well, that's entirely reasonable.) By the way, Riff's real name is Riffael Raffit...a strange name, eh? It's Riff Raff in abbreviation. There is a butler in the movie, *The Rocky Horror Show*, whose name is Riff Raff. The movie has inspired a cult: viewers dress up like the characters and act out the story as they watch the movie. I only borrowed this character's name for Cain's butler, not his personality. I'm often asked what the "C" for Cain's middle name stands for, but it's a secret. (Only people who read the second episode of *The Earl Cain Series* in the supplementary volume of "Hana to Yume" in Japan will know the answer... it's such a twisted world we live in, isn't it?!)

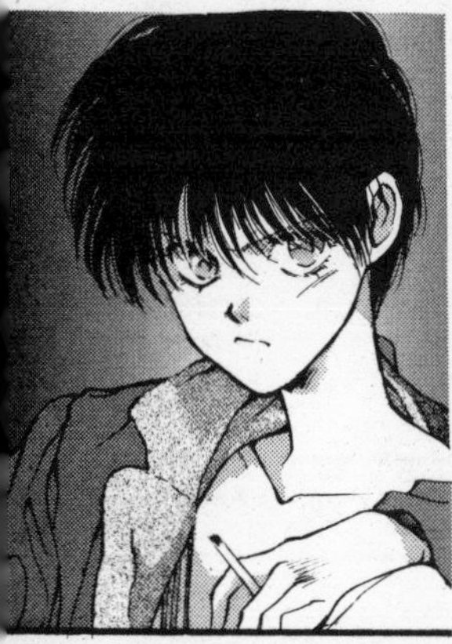

XVIII · THE MOON

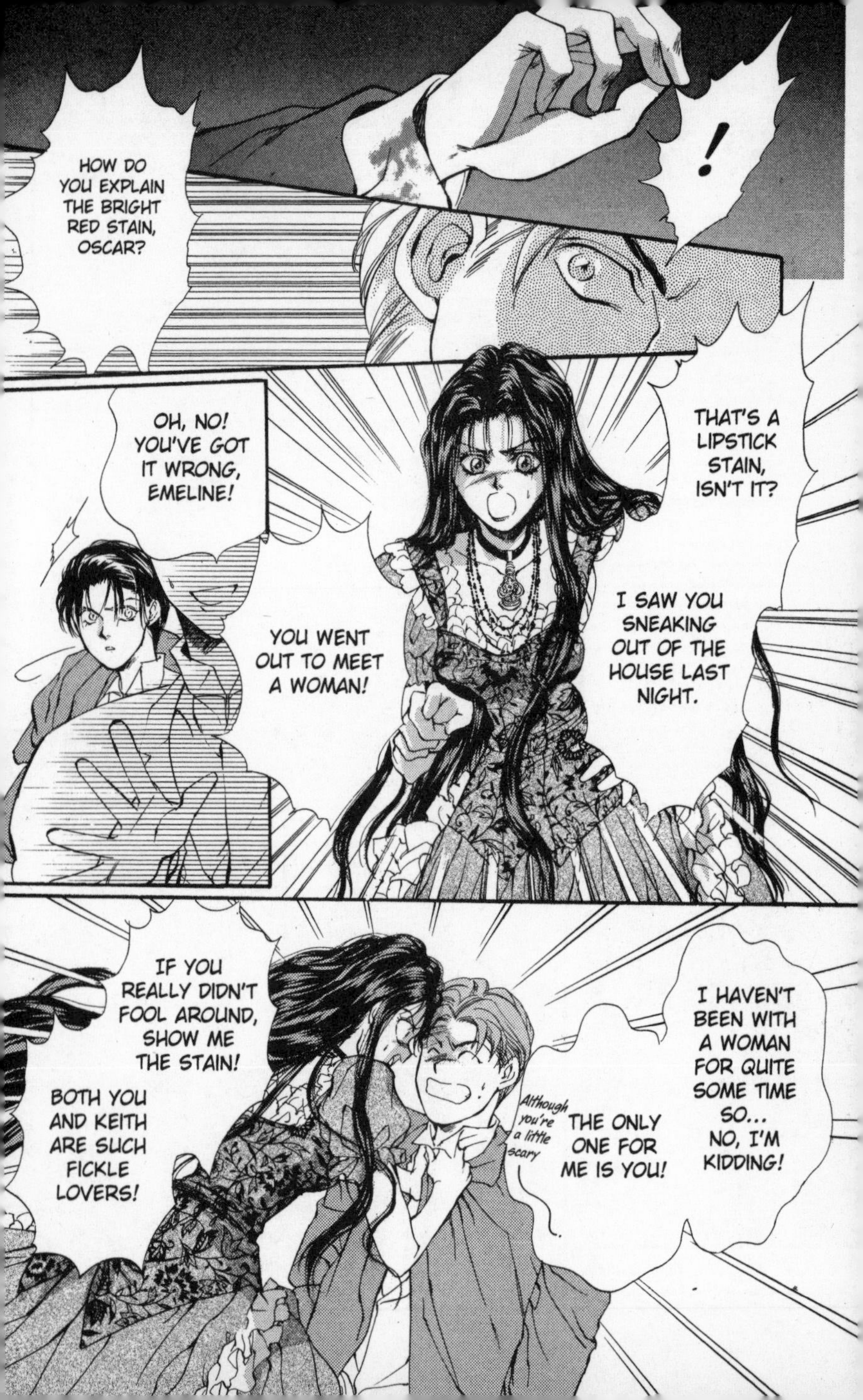
!
HOW DO YOU EXPLAIN THE BRIGHT RED STAIN, OSCAR?
THAT'S A LIPSTICK STAIN, ISN'T IT?
I SAW YOU SNEAKING OUT OF THE HOUSE LAST NIGHT.
YOU WENT OUT TO MEET A WOMAN!
OH, NO! YOU'VE GOT IT WRONG, EMELINE!
I HAVEN'T BEEN WITH A WOMAN FOR QUITE SOME TIME SO... NO, I'M KIDDING!
THE ONLY ONE FOR ME IS YOU!
Although you're a little scary
IF YOU REALLY DIDN'T FOOL AROUND, SHOW ME THE STAIN!
BOTH YOU AND KEITH ARE SUCH FICKLE LOVERS!

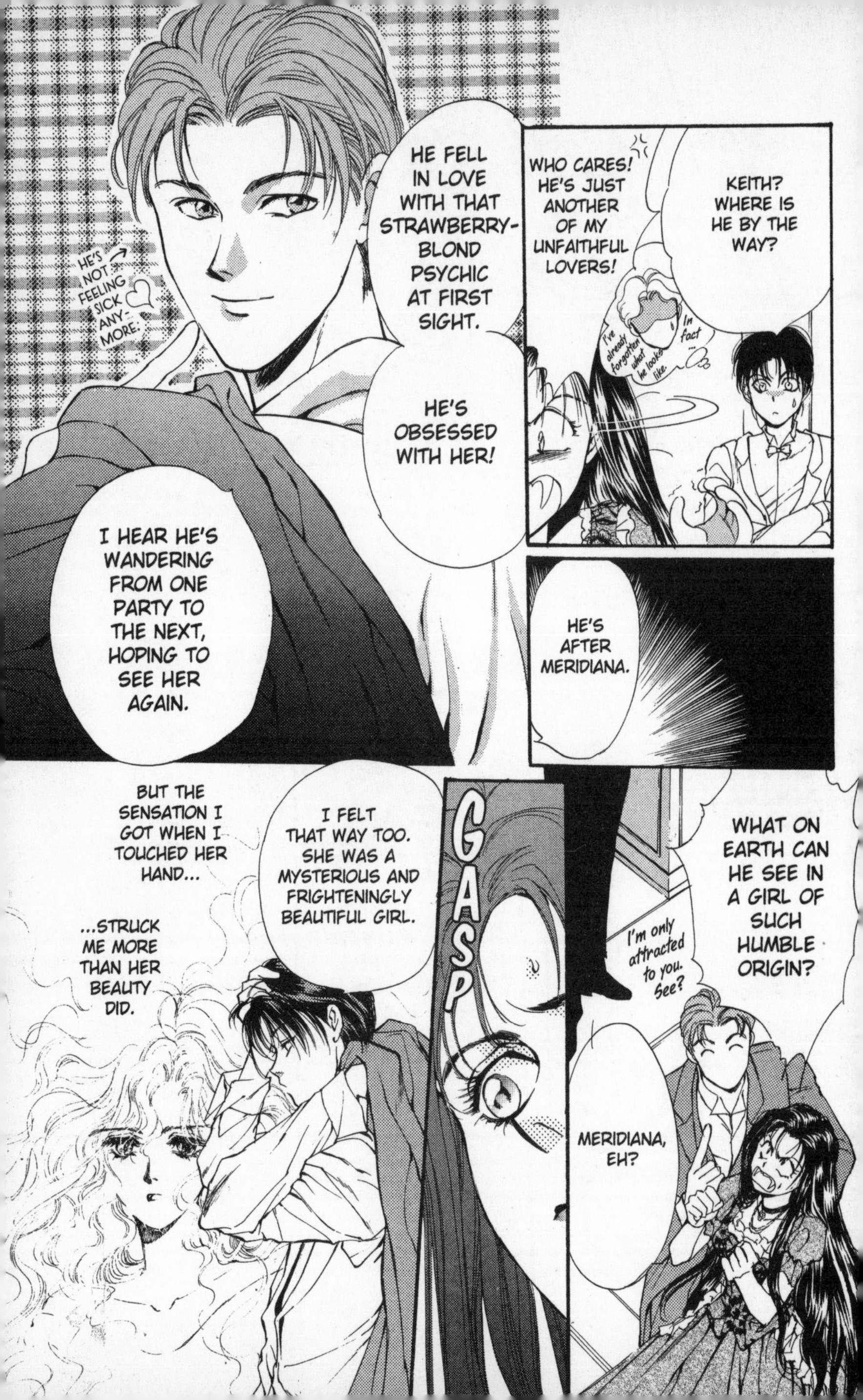
KEITH? WHERE IS HE BY THE WAY?
WHO CARES! HE'S JUST ANOTHER OF MY UNFAITHFUL LOVERS!
In fact...
I've already forgotten what he looks like.
HE'S AFTER MERIDIANA.
HE FELL IN LOVE WITH THAT STRAWBERRY-BLOND PSYCHIC AT FIRST SIGHT.
HE'S OBSESSED WITH HER!
I HEAR HE'S WANDERING FROM ONE PARTY TO THE NEXT, HOPING TO SEE HER AGAIN.
HE'S NOT FEELING SICK ANY-MORE.
WHAT ON EARTH CAN HE SEE IN A GIRL OF SUCH HUMBLE ORIGIN?
I'm only attracted to you. See?
MERIDIANA, EH?
GASP
I FELT THAT WAY TOO. SHE WAS A MYSTERIOUS AND FRIGHTENINGLY BEAUTIFUL GIRL.
BUT THE SENSATION I GOT WHEN I TOUCHED HER HAND...
...STRUCK ME MORE THAN HER BEAUTY DID.

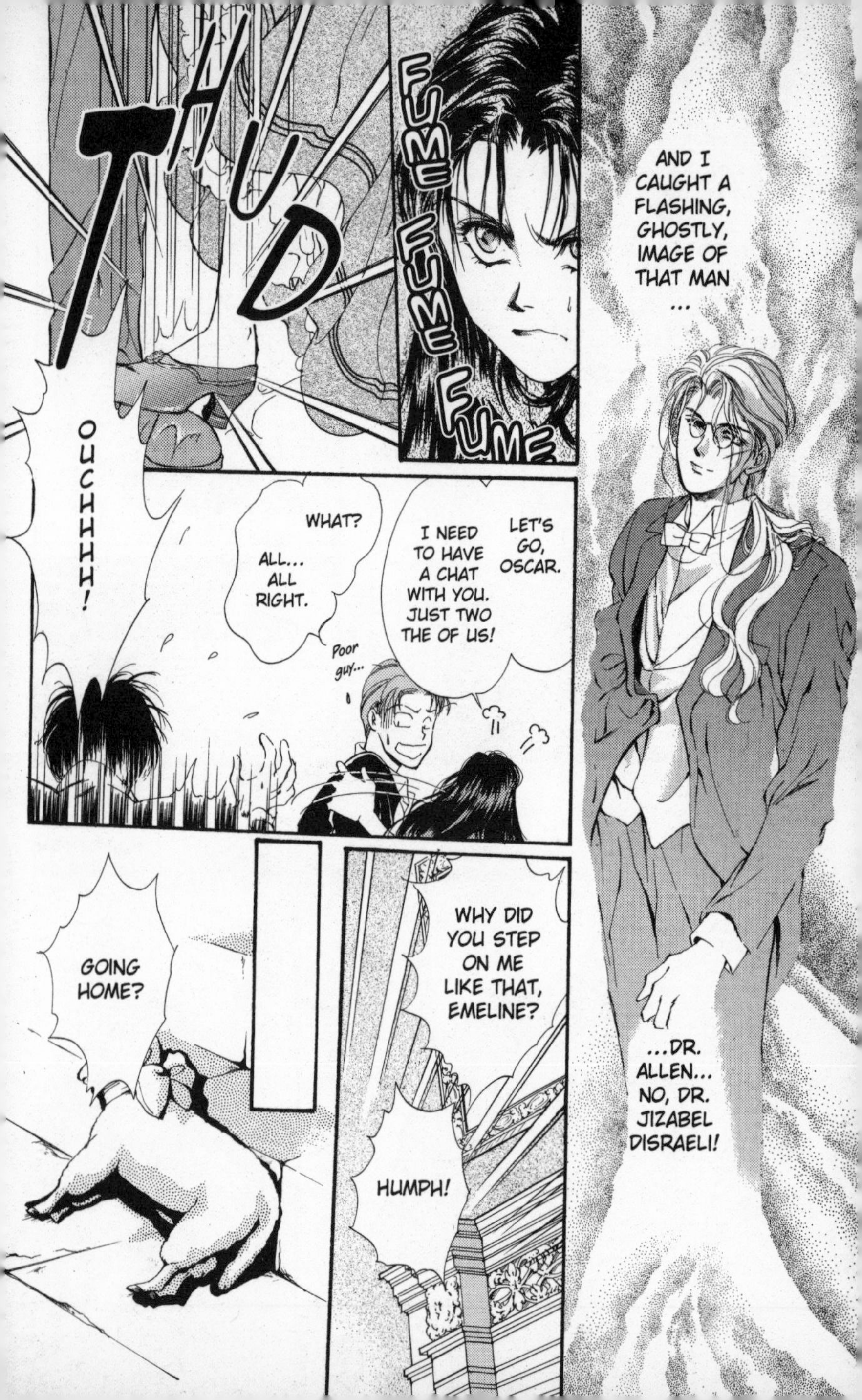
AND I CAUGHT A FLASHING, GHOSTLY, IMAGE OF THAT MAN ...
...DR. ALLEN... NO, DR. JIZABEL DISRAELI!
FUME FUME FUME
THUD
OUCHHHH!
LET'S GO, OSCAR.
I NEED TO HAVE A CHAT WITH YOU. JUST TWO THE OF US!
Poor guy...
WHAT?
ALL... ALL RIGHT.
WHY DID YOU STEP ON ME LIKE THAT, EMELINE?
HUMPH!
GOING HOME?

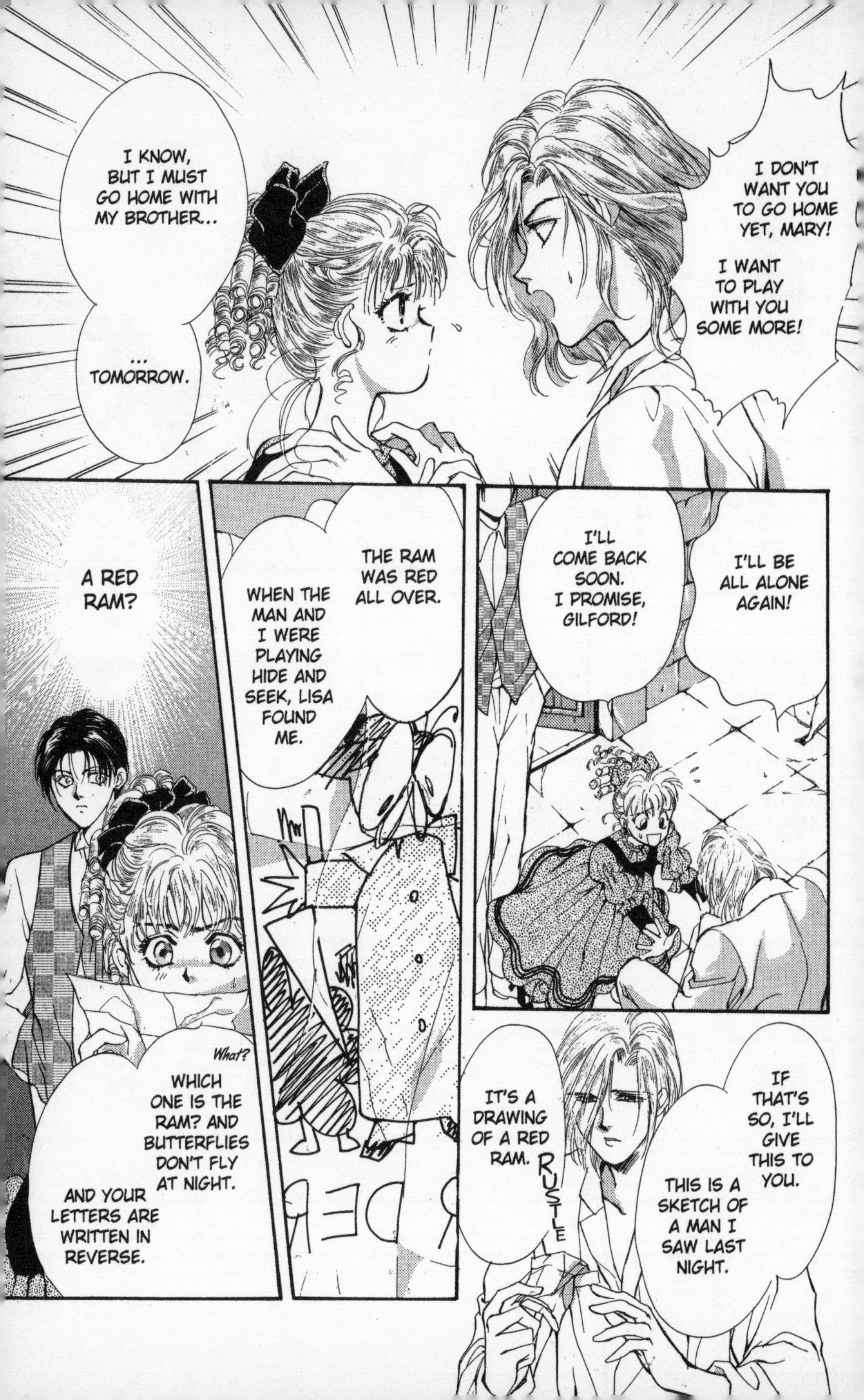
I DON'T WANT YOU TO GO HOME YET, MARY!
I WANT TO PLAY WITH YOU SOME MORE!
I KNOW, BUT I MUST GO HOME WITH MY BROTHER...
... TOMORROW.
I'LL BE ALL ALONE AGAIN!
I'LL COME BACK SOON. I PROMISE, GILFORD!
IF THAT'S SO, I'LL GIVE THIS TO YOU.
THIS IS A SKETCH OF A MAN I SAW LAST NIGHT.
IT'S A DRAWING OF A RED RAM.
RUSTLE
THE RAM WAS RED ALL OVER.
WHEN THE MAN AND I WERE PLAYING HIDE AND SEEK, LISA FOUND ME.
A RED RAM?
What?
WHICH ONE IS THE RAM? AND BUTTERFLIES DON'T FLY AT NIGHT.
AND YOUR LETTERS ARE WRITTEN IN REVERSE.

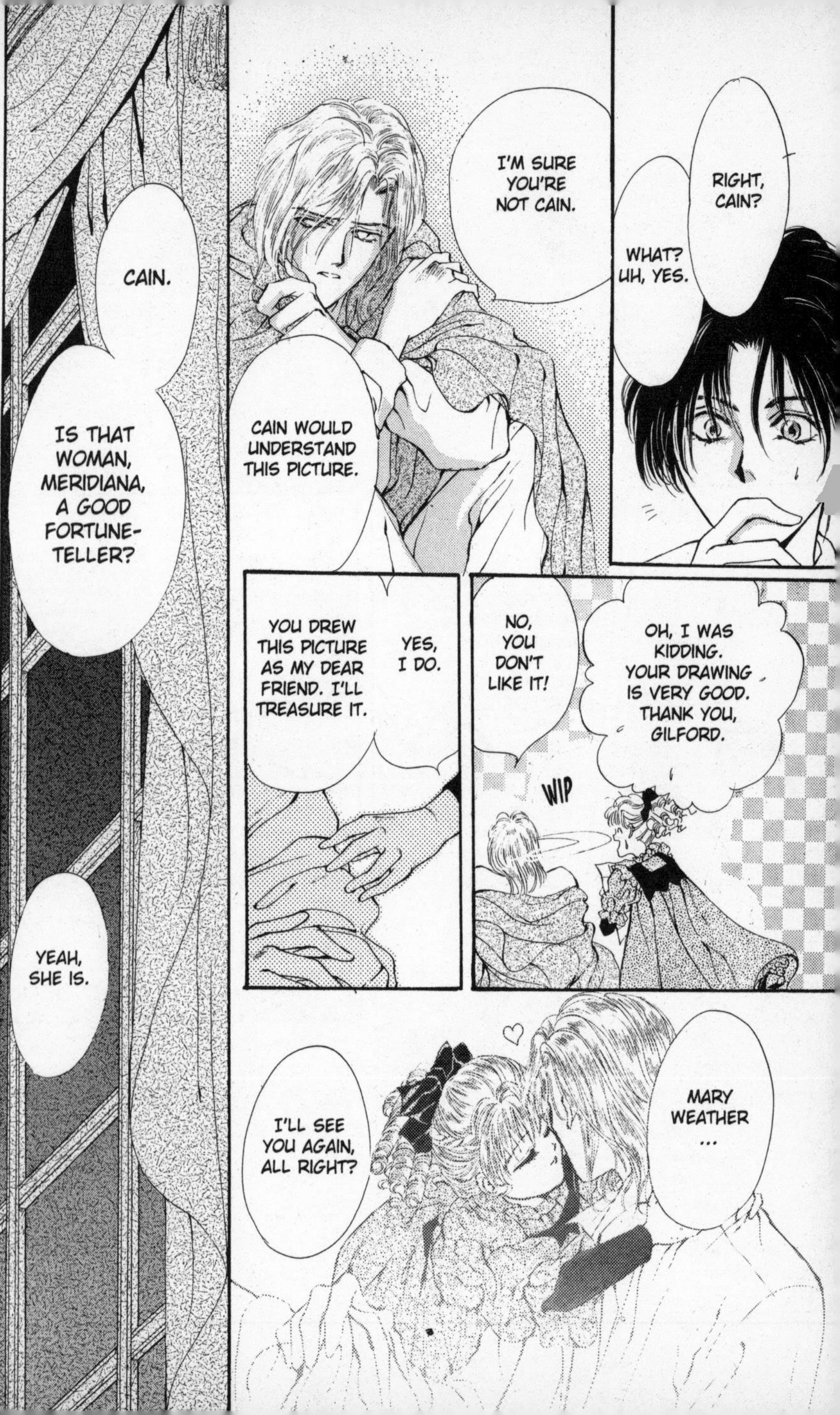
RIGHT, CAIN?
WHAT? UH, YES.
I'M SURE YOU'RE NOT CAIN.
CAIN WOULD UNDERSTAND THIS PICTURE.
OH, I WAS KIDDING. YOUR DRAWING IS VERY GOOD. THANK YOU, GILFORD.
NO, YOU DON'T LIKE IT!
WIP
YES, I DO.
YOU DREW THIS PICTURE AS MY DEAR FRIEND. I'LL TREASURE IT.
MARY WEATHER ...
I'LL SEE YOU AGAIN, ALL RIGHT?
CAIN.
IS THAT WOMAN, MERIDIANA, A GOOD FORTUNE-TELLER?
YEAH, SHE IS.

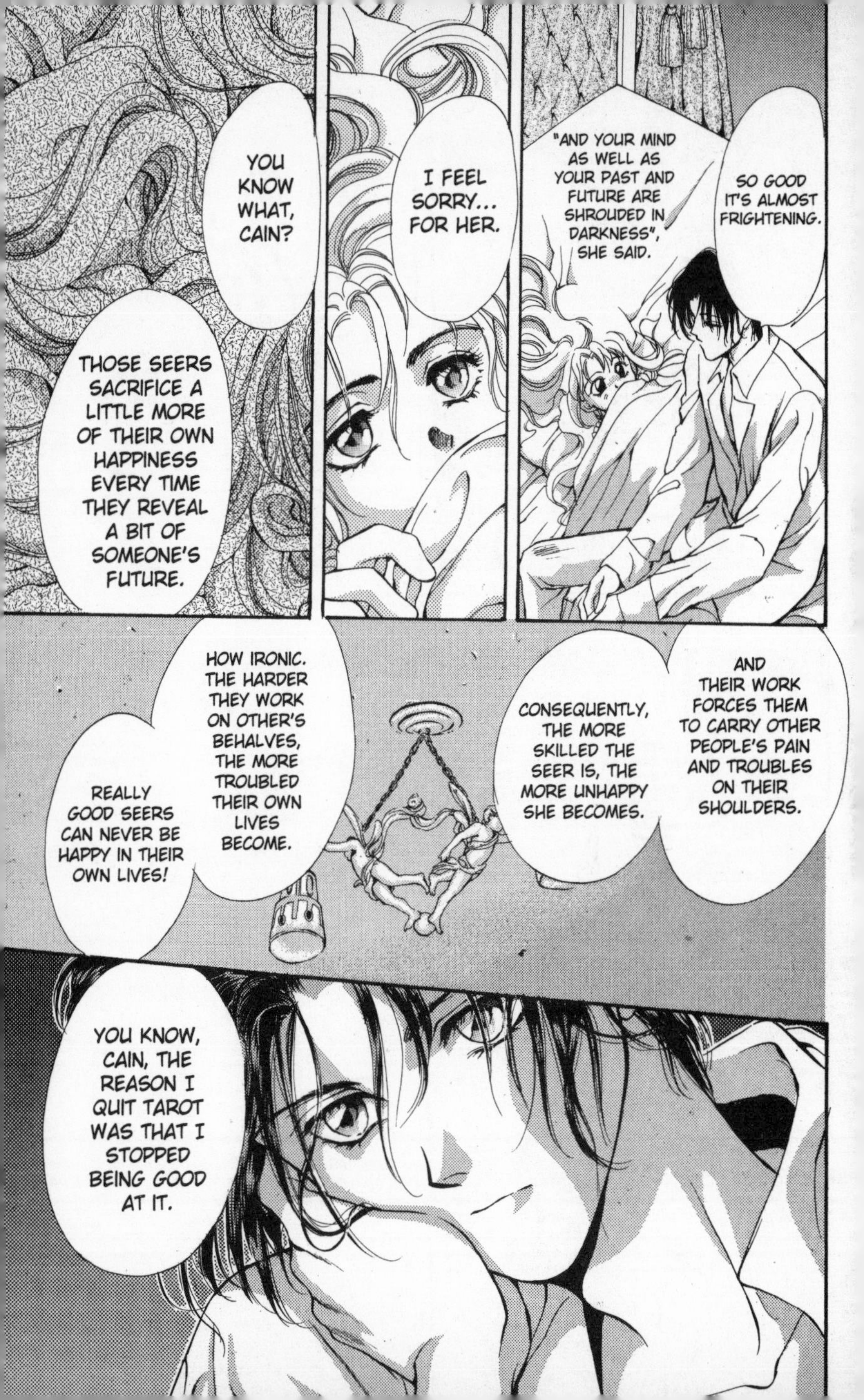
SO GOOD IT'S ALMOST FRIGHTENING.
"AND YOUR MIND AS WELL AS YOUR PAST AND FUTURE ARE SHROUDED IN DARKNESS", SHE SAID.
I FEEL SORRY... FOR HER.
YOU KNOW WHAT, CAIN?
THOSE SEERS SACRIFICE A LITTLE MORE OF THEIR OWN HAPPINESS EVERY TIME THEY REVEAL A BIT OF SOMEONE'S FUTURE.
AND THEIR WORK FORCES THEM TO CARRY OTHER PEOPLE'S PAIN AND TROUBLES ON THEIR SHOULDERS.
CONSEQUENTLY, THE MORE SKILLED THE SEER IS, THE MORE UNHAPPY SHE BECOMES.
HOW IRONIC. THE HARDER THEY WORK ON OTHER'S BEHALVES, THE MORE TROUBLED THEIR OWN LIVES BECOME.
REALLY GOOD SEERS CAN NEVER BE HAPPY IN THEIR OWN LIVES!
YOU KNOW, CAIN, THE REASON I QUIT TAROT WAS THAT I STOPPED BEING GOOD AT IT.

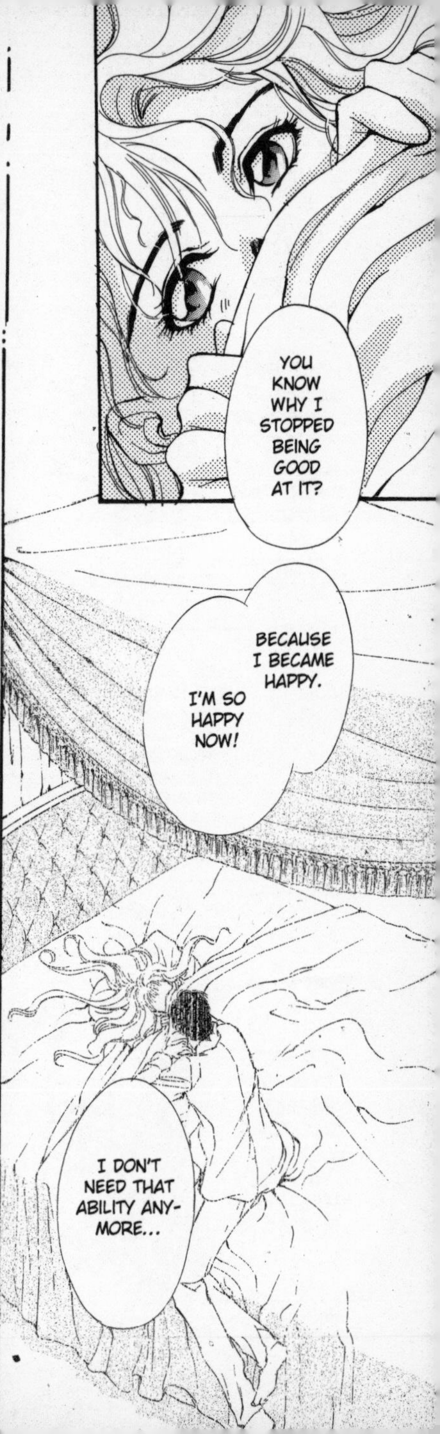
YOU KNOW WHY I STOPPED BEING GOOD AT IT?
BECAUSE I BECAME HAPPY.
I'M SO HAPPY NOW!
I DON'T NEED THAT ABILITY ANY-MORE...
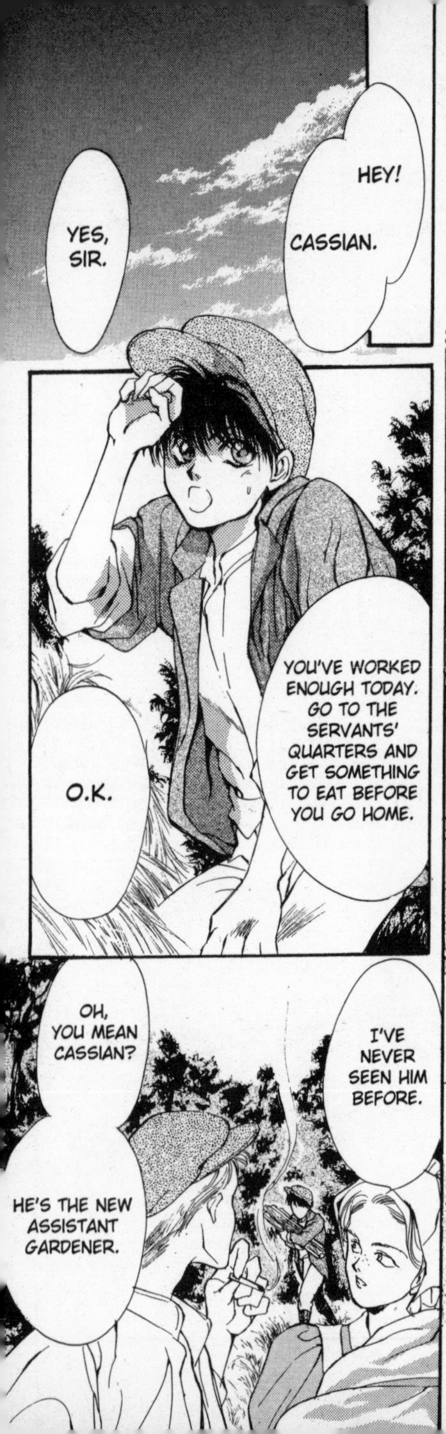
HEY!
CASSIAN.
YES, SIR.
YOU'VE WORKED ENOUGH TODAY. GO TO THE SERVANTS' QUARTERS AND GET SOMETHING TO EAT BEFORE YOU GO HOME.
O.K.
I'VE NEVER SEEN HIM BEFORE.
OH, YOU MEAN CASSIAN?
HE'S THE NEW ASSISTANT GARDENER.

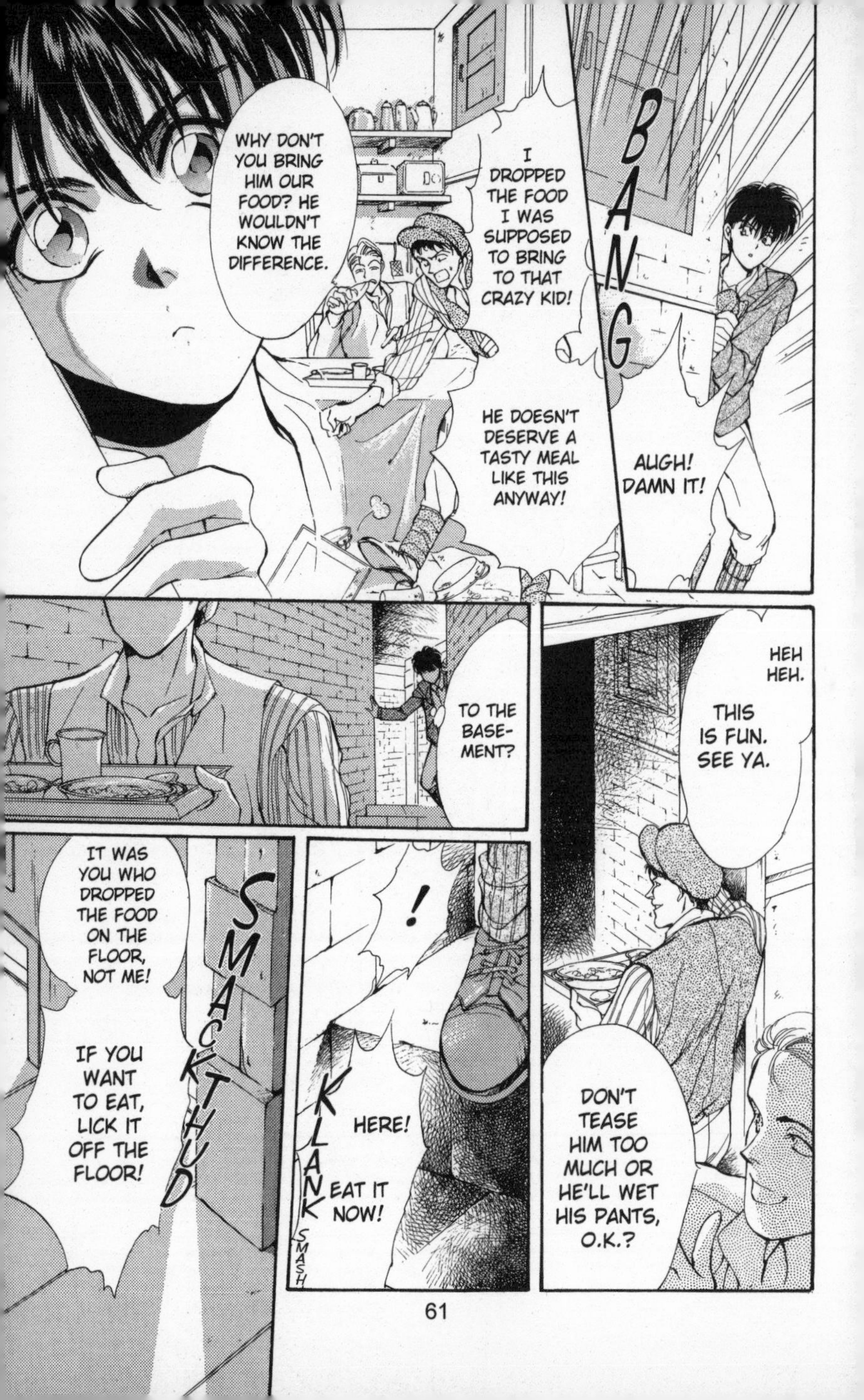
BANG
AUGH! DAMN IT!
I DROPPED THE FOOD I WAS SUPPOSED TO BRING TO THAT CRAZY KID!
WHY DON'T YOU BRING HIM OUR FOOD? HE WOULDN'T KNOW THE DIFFERENCE.
HE DOESN'T DESERVE A TASTY MEAL LIKE THIS ANYWAY!
HEH HEH.
THIS IS FUN. SEE YA.
DON'T TEASE HIM TOO MUCH OR HE'LL WET HIS PANTS, O.K.?
TO THE BASE-MENT?
!
HERE!
EAT IT NOW!
KLANK
SMASH
IT WAS YOU WHO DROPPED THE FOOD ON THE FLOOR, NOT ME!
SMACK
THUD
IF YOU WANT TO EAT, LICK IT OFF THE FLOOR!

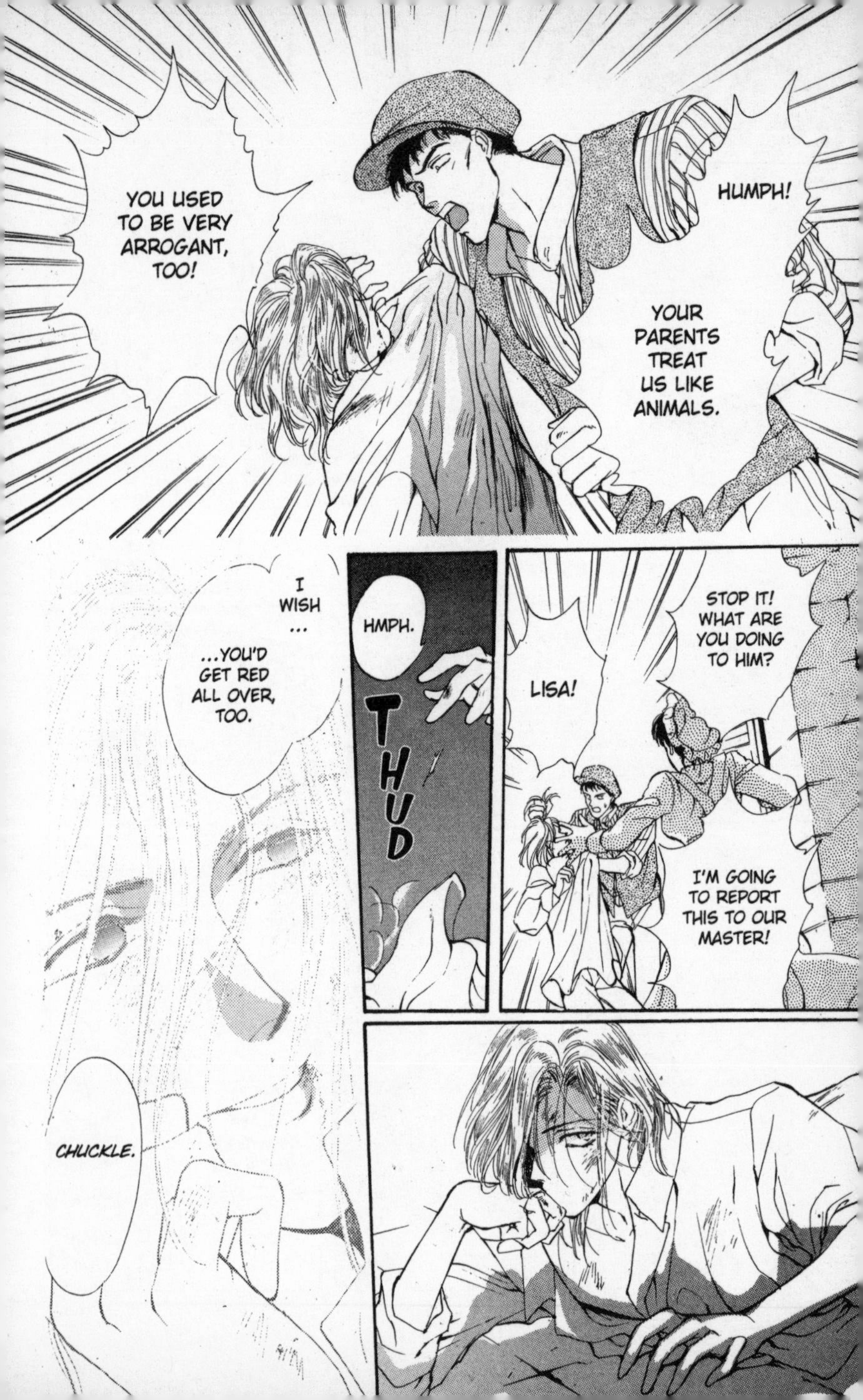
HUMPH!
YOUR PARENTS TREAT US LIKE ANIMALS.
YOU USED TO BE VERY ARROGANT, TOO!
STOP IT! WHAT ARE YOU DOING TO HIM?
LISA!
I'M GOING TO REPORT THIS TO OUR MASTER!
HMPH.
THUD
I WISH ...
...YOU'D GET RED ALL OVER, TOO.
CHUCKLE.

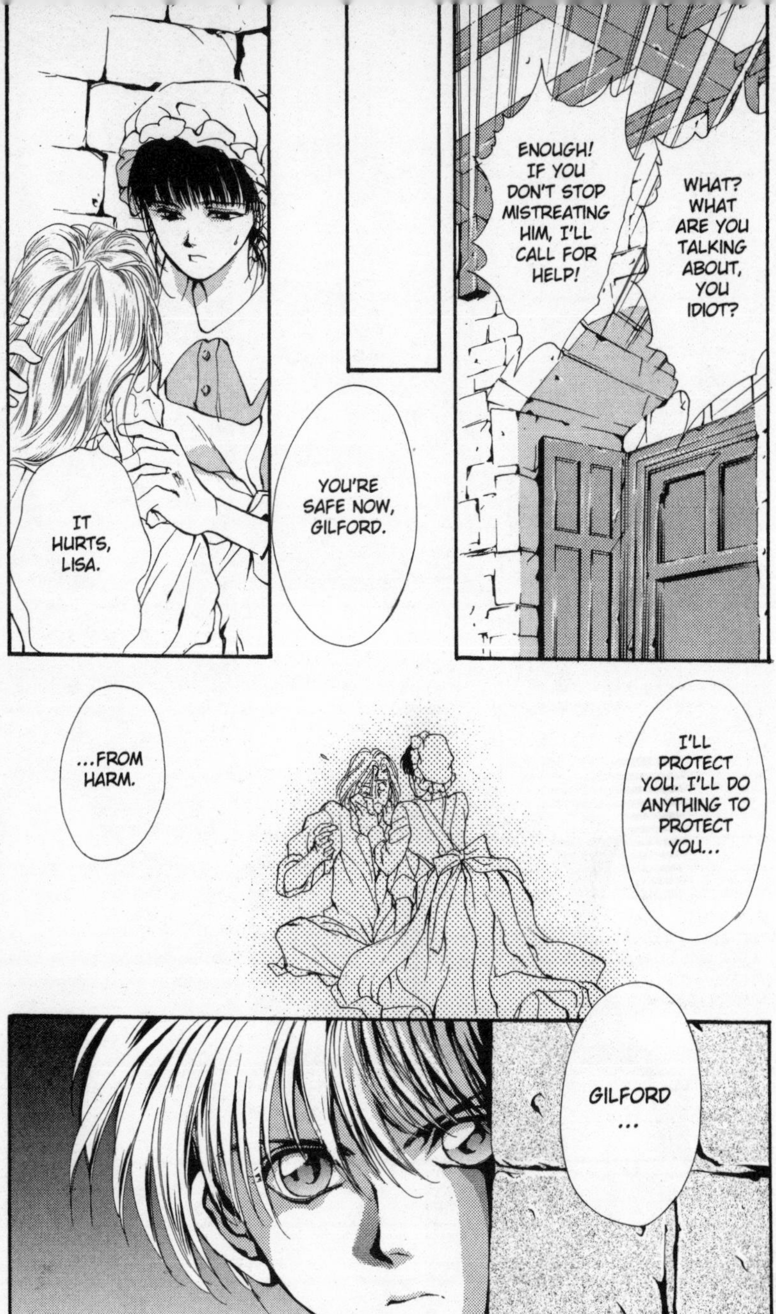
ENOUGH! IF YOU DON'T STOP MISTREATING HIM, I'LL CALL FOR HELP!
WHAT? WHAT ARE YOU TALKING ABOUT, YOU IDIOT?
YOU'RE SAFE NOW, GILFORD.
IT HURTS, LISA.
I'LL PROTECT YOU. I'LL DO ANYTHING TO PROTECT YOU...
...FROM HARM.
GILFORD ...

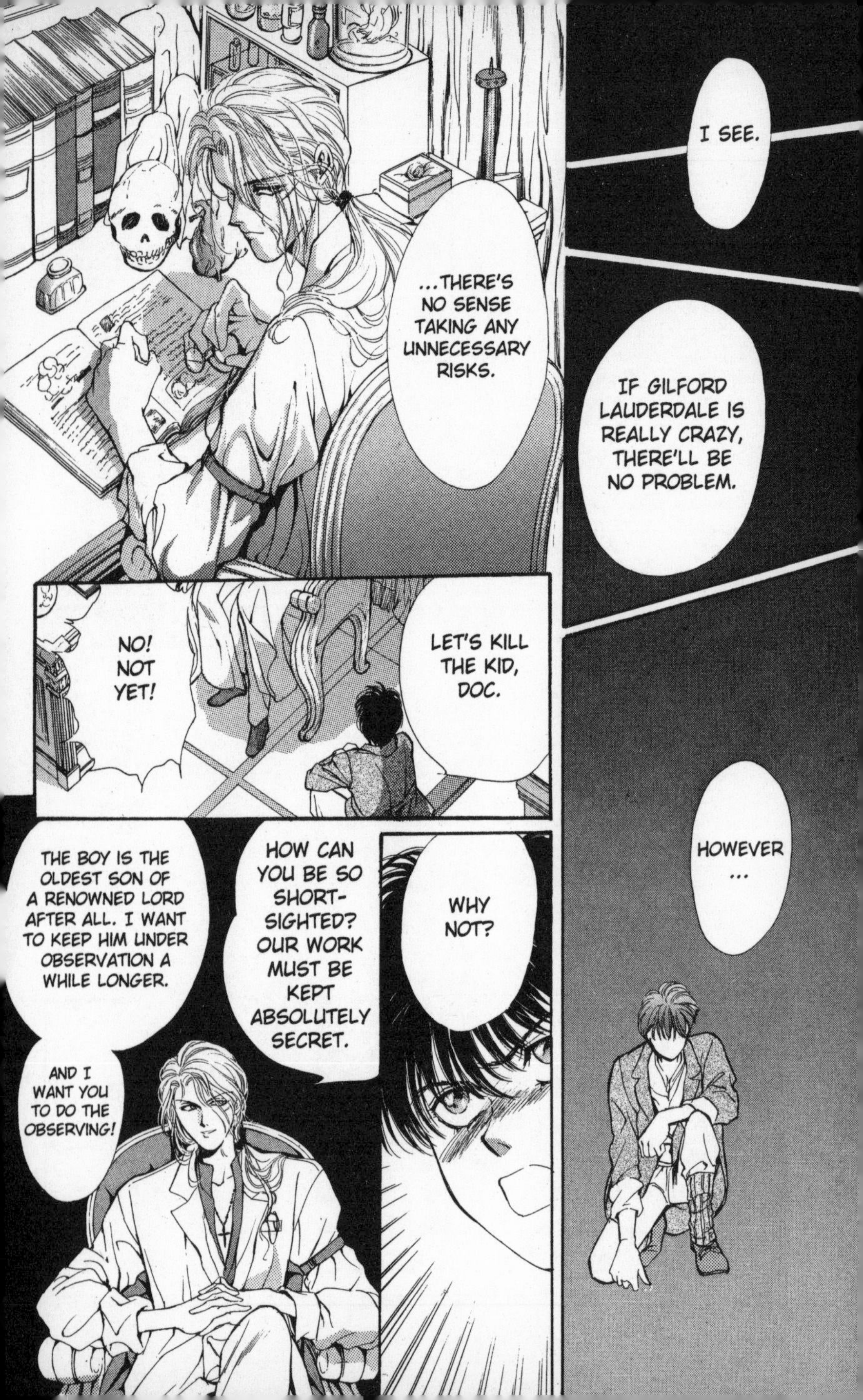
I SEE.
IF GILFORD LAUDERDALE IS REALLY CRAZY, THERE'LL BE NO PROBLEM.
HOWEVER ...
...THERE'S NO SENSE TAKING ANY UNNECESSARY RISKS.
LET'S KILL THE KID, DOC.
NO! NOT YET!
WHY NOT?
HOW CAN YOU BE SO SHORT-SIGHTED? OUR WORK MUST BE KEPT ABSOLUTELY SECRET.
THE BOY IS THE OLDEST SON OF A RENOWNED LORD AFTER ALL. I WANT TO KEEP HIM UNDER OBSERVATION A WHILE LONGER.
AND I WANT YOU TO DO THE OBSERVING!

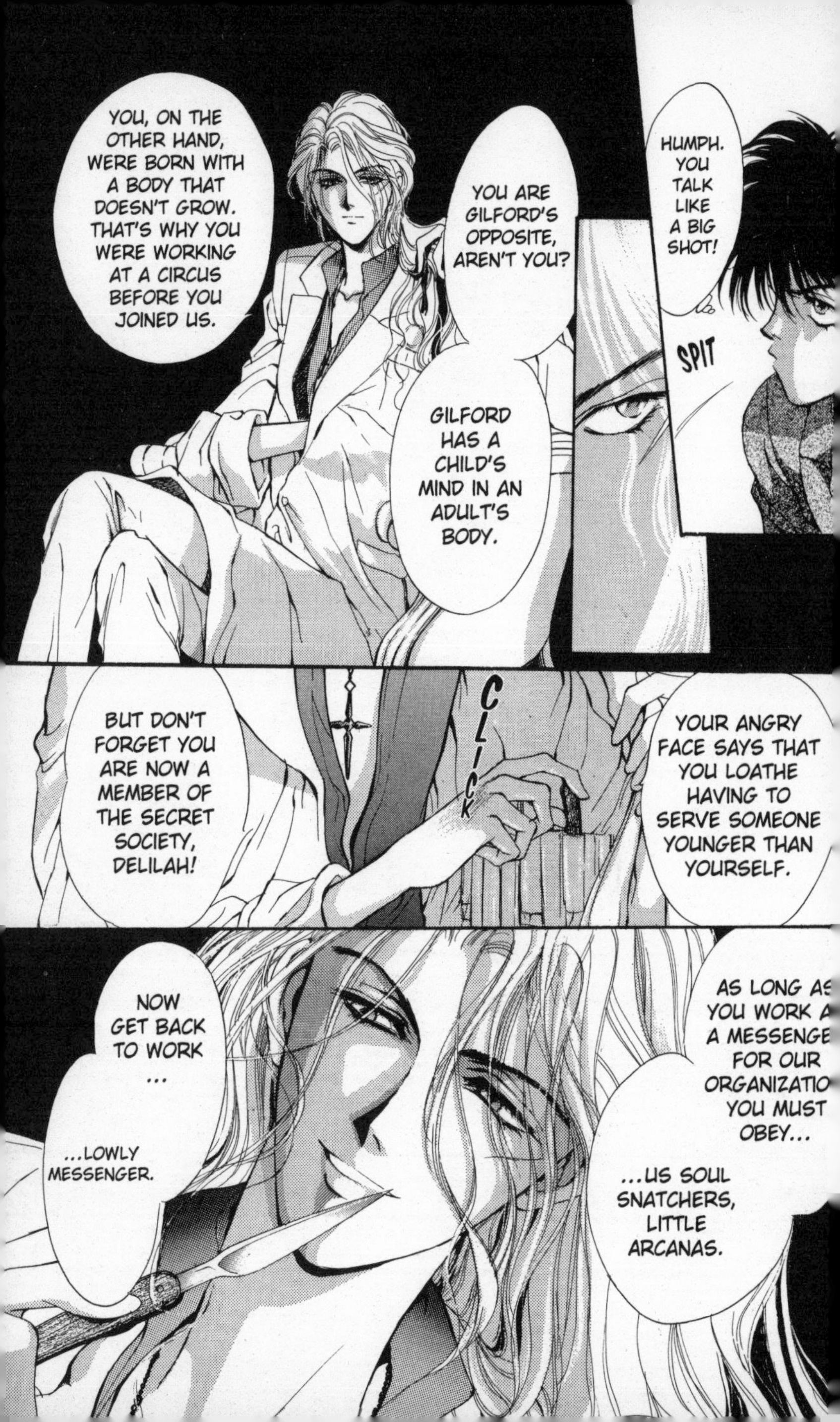
HUMPH. YOU TALK LIKE A BIG SHOT!
SPIT
YOU ARE GILFORD'S OPPOSITE, AREN'T YOU?
GILFORD HAS A CHILD'S MIND IN AN ADULT'S BODY.
YOU, ON THE OTHER HAND, WERE BORN WITH A BODY THAT DOESN'T GROW. THAT'S WHY YOU WERE WORKING AT A CIRCUS BEFORE YOU JOINED US.
YOUR ANGRY FACE SAYS THAT YOU LOATHE HAVING TO SERVE SOMEONE YOUNGER THAN YOURSELF.
CLICK
BUT DON'T FORGET YOU ARE NOW A MEMBER OF THE SECRET SOCIETY, DELILAH!
AS LONG AS YOU WORK A A MESSENGE FOR OUR ORGANIZATIO YOU MUST OBEY...
...US SOUL SNATCHERS, LITTLE ARCANAS.
NOW GET BACK TO WORK ...
...LOWLY MESSENGER.

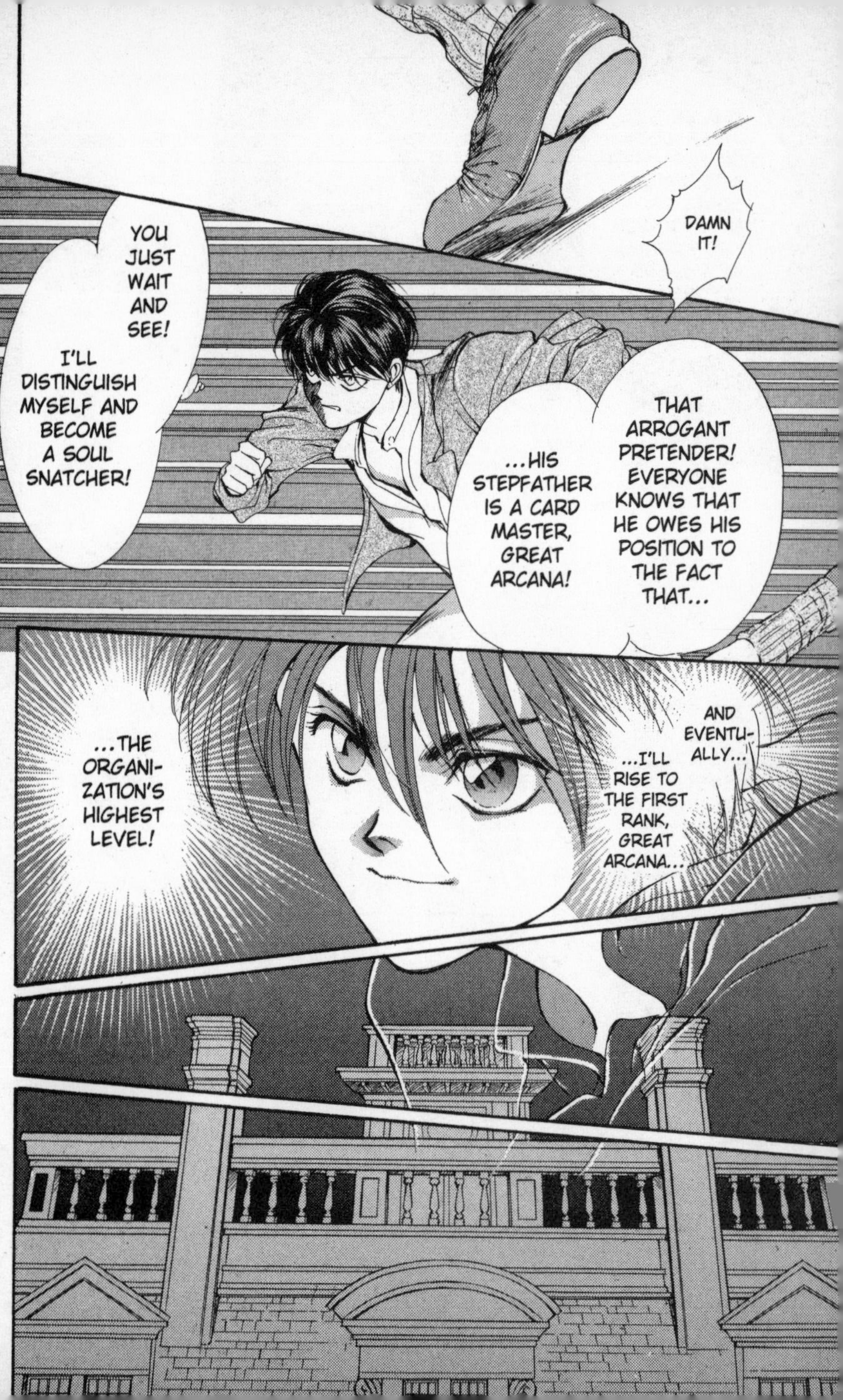
DAMN IT!
THAT ARROGANT PRETENDER! EVERYONE KNOWS THAT HE OWES HIS POSITION TO THE FACT THAT...
...HIS STEPFATHER IS A CARD MASTER, GREAT ARCANA!
YOU JUST WAIT AND SEE!
I'LL DISTINGUISH MYSELF AND BECOME A SOUL SNATCHER!
AND EVENTUALLY...
...I'LL RISE TO THE FIRST RANK, GREAT ARCANA...
...THE ORGANIZATION'S HIGHEST LEVEL!

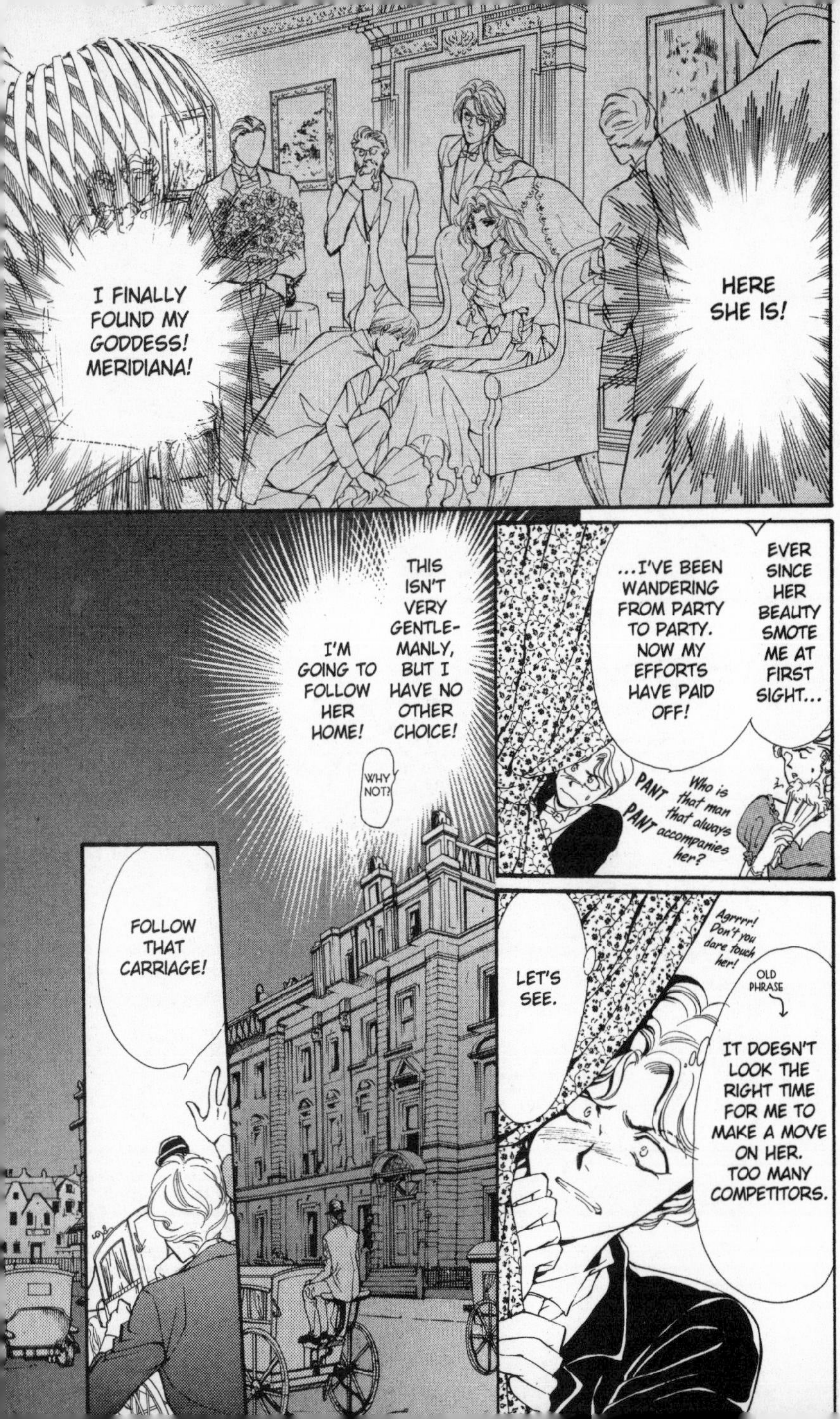
HERE SHE IS!
I FINALLY FOUND MY GODDESS! MERIDIANA!
EVER SINCE HER BEAUTY SMOTE ME AT FIRST SIGHT...
...I'VE BEEN WANDERING FROM PARTY TO PARTY. NOW MY EFFORTS HAVE PAID OFF!
PANT PANT
Who is that man that always accompanies her?
Agrrrr! Don't you dare touch her!
LET'S SEE.
OLD PHRASE
IT DOESN'T LOOK THE RIGHT TIME FOR ME TO MAKE A MOVE ON HER. TOO MANY COMPETITORS.
THIS ISN'T VERY GENTLE-MANLY, BUT I HAVE NO OTHER CHOICE!
I'M GOING TO FOLLOW HER HOME!
WHY NOT?
FOLLOW THAT CARRIAGE!

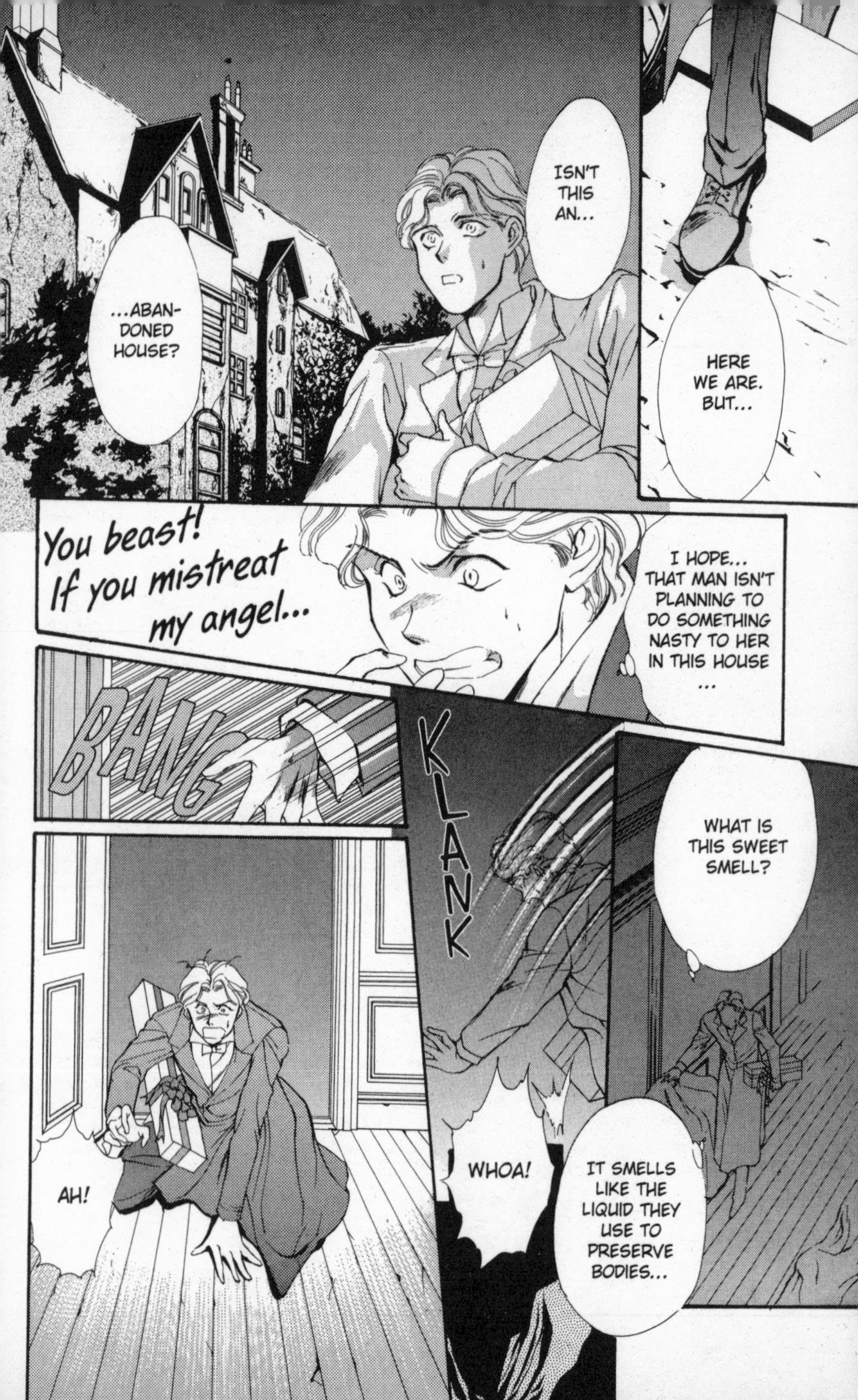
HERE WE ARE. BUT...
ISN'T THIS AN...
...ABAN-DONED HOUSE?
I HOPE... THAT MAN ISN'T PLANNING TO DO SOMETHING NASTY TO HER IN THIS HOUSE ...
You beast! If you mistreat my angel...
WHAT IS THIS SWEET SMELL?
IT SMELLS LIKE THE LIQUID THEY USE TO PRESERVE BODIES...
KLANK
WHOA!
BANG
AH!

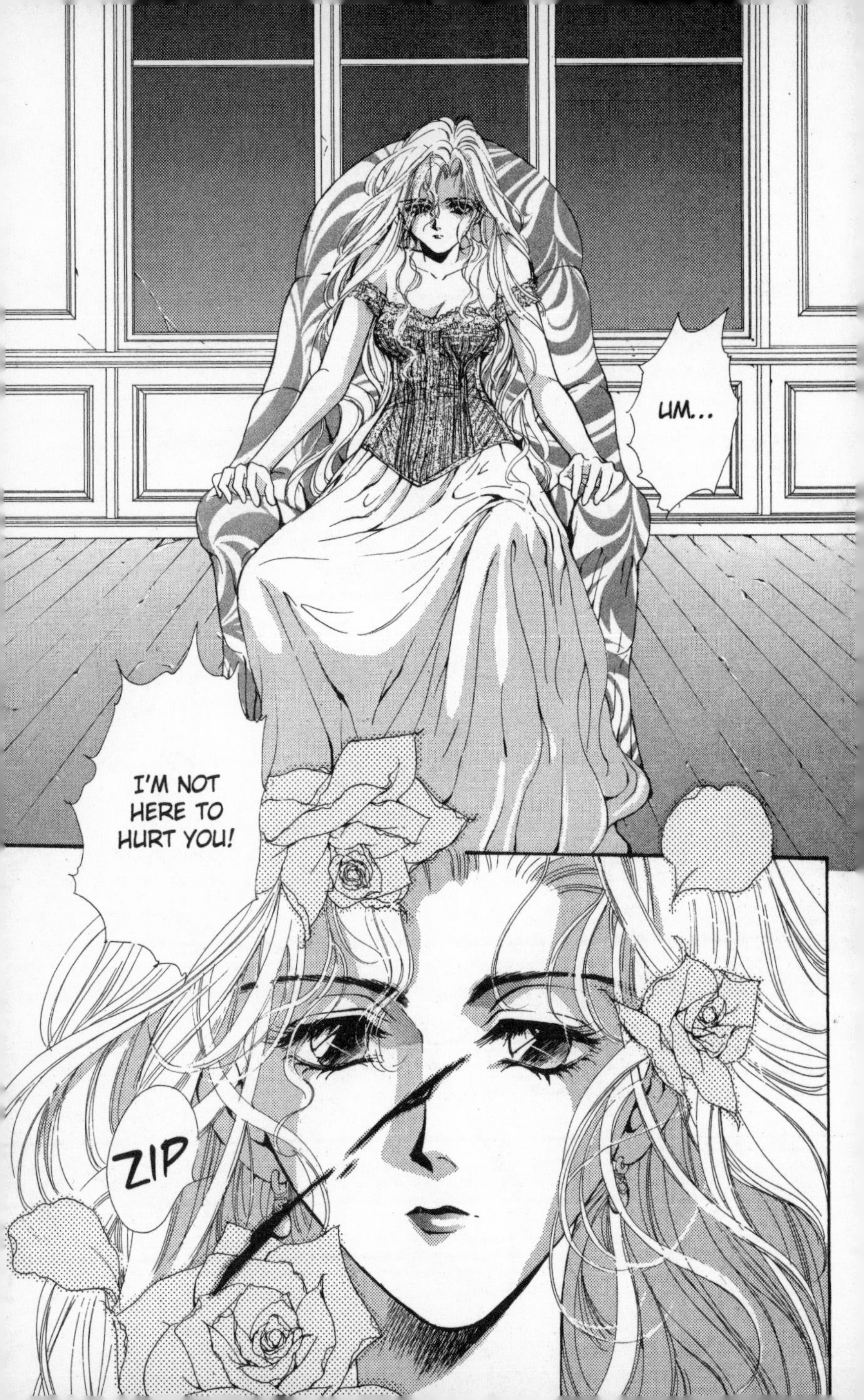
UM...
I'M NOT HERE TO HURT YOU!
ZIP

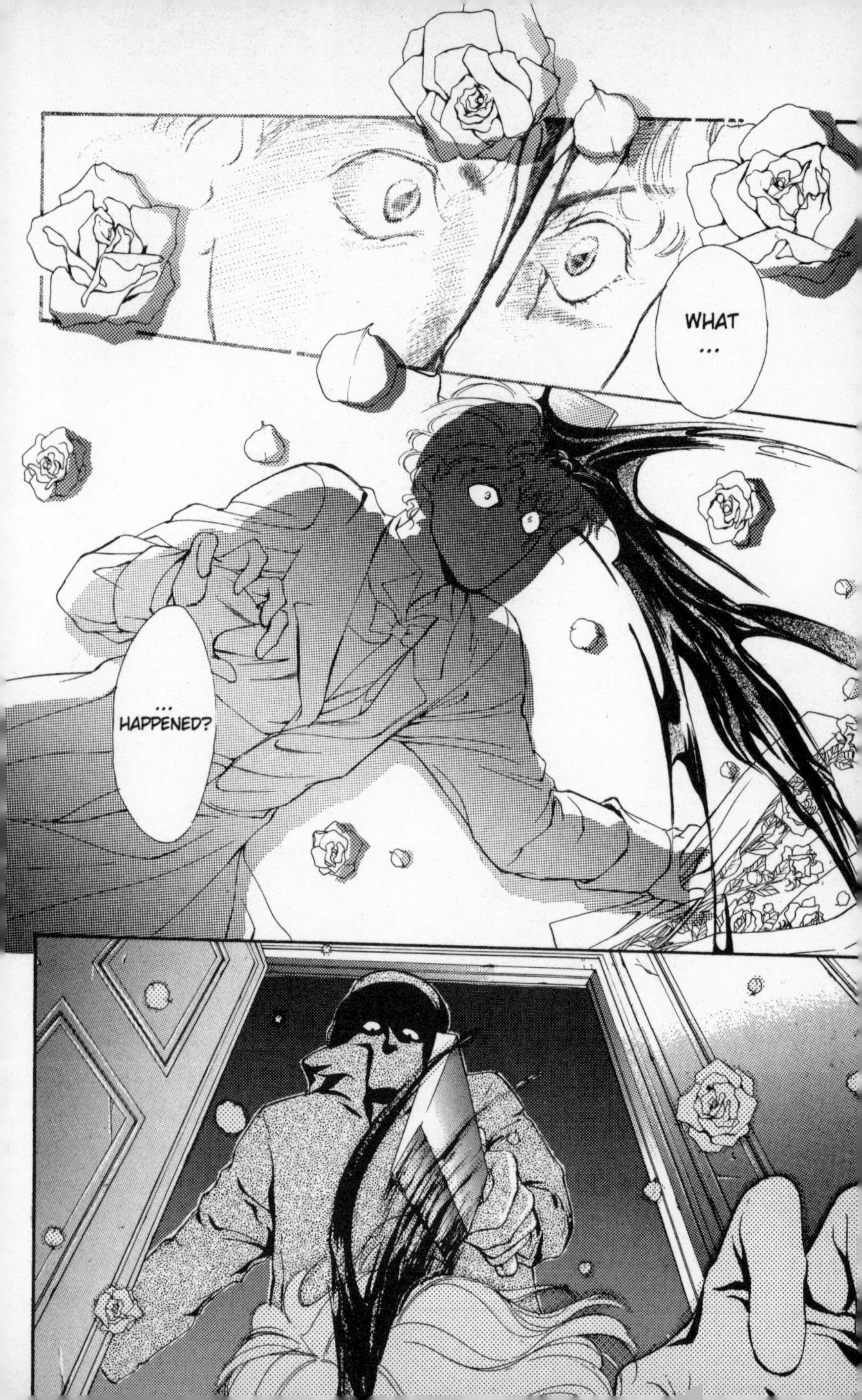
WHAT ...
... HAPPENED?

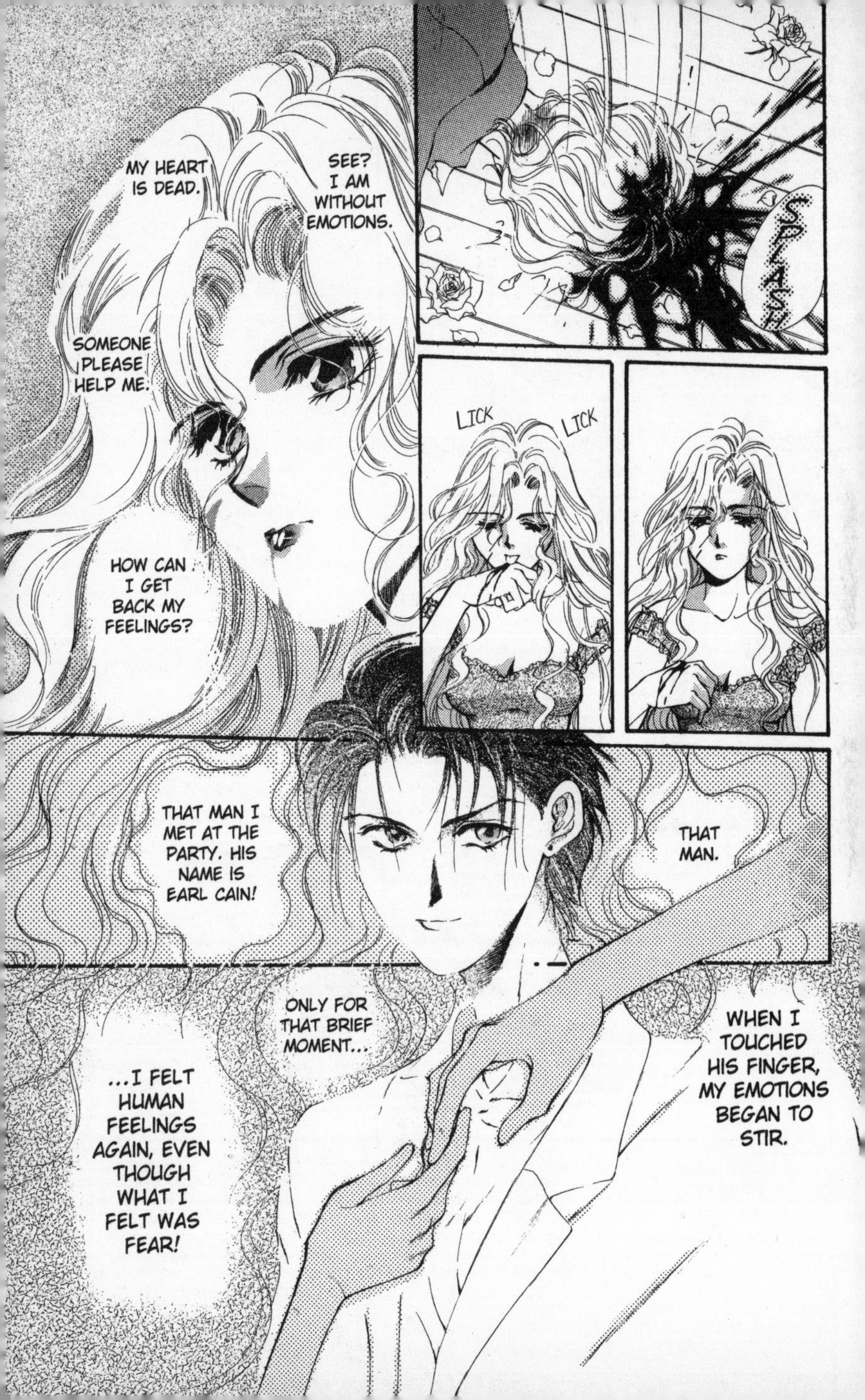
SPLASH
LICK
LICK
SEE? I AM WITHOUT EMOTIONS.
MY HEART IS DEAD.
SOMEONE PLEASE HELP ME.
HOW CAN I GET BACK MY FEELINGS?
THAT MAN.
THAT MAN I MET AT THE PARTY. HIS NAME IS EARL CAIN!
WHEN I TOUCHED HIS FINGER, MY EMOTIONS BEGAN TO STIR.
ONLY FOR THAT BRIEF MOMENT...
...I FELT HUMAN FEELINGS AGAIN, EVEN THOUGH WHAT I FELT WAS FEAR!

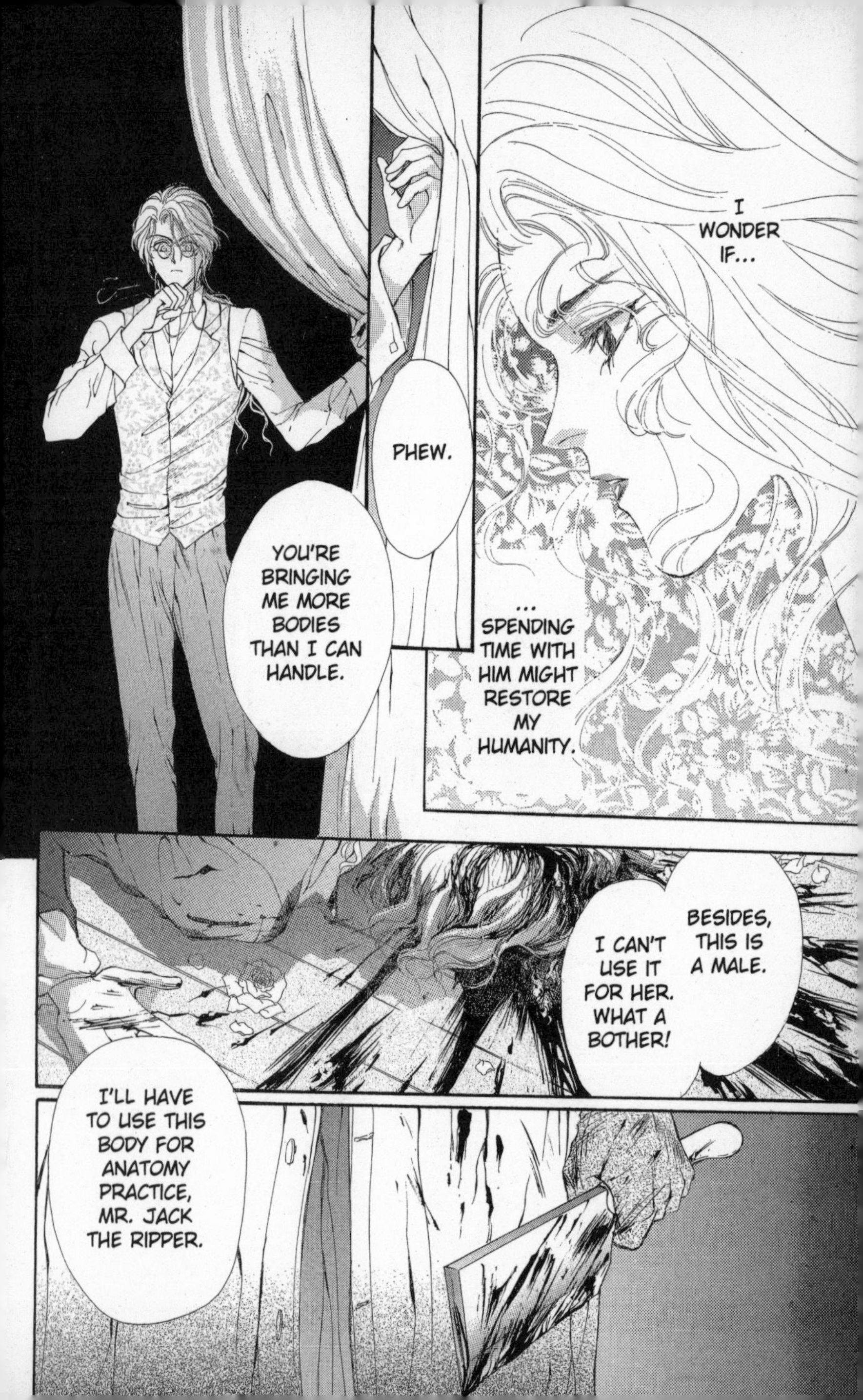
I WONDER IF...
...SPENDING TIME WITH HIM MIGHT RESTORE MY HUMANITY.
PHEW.
YOU'RE BRINGING ME MORE BODIES THAN I CAN HANDLE.
BESIDES, THIS IS A MALE.
I CAN'T USE IT FOR HER. WHAT A BOTHER!
I'LL HAVE TO USE THIS BODY FOR ANATOMY PRACTICE, MR. JACK THE RIPPER.

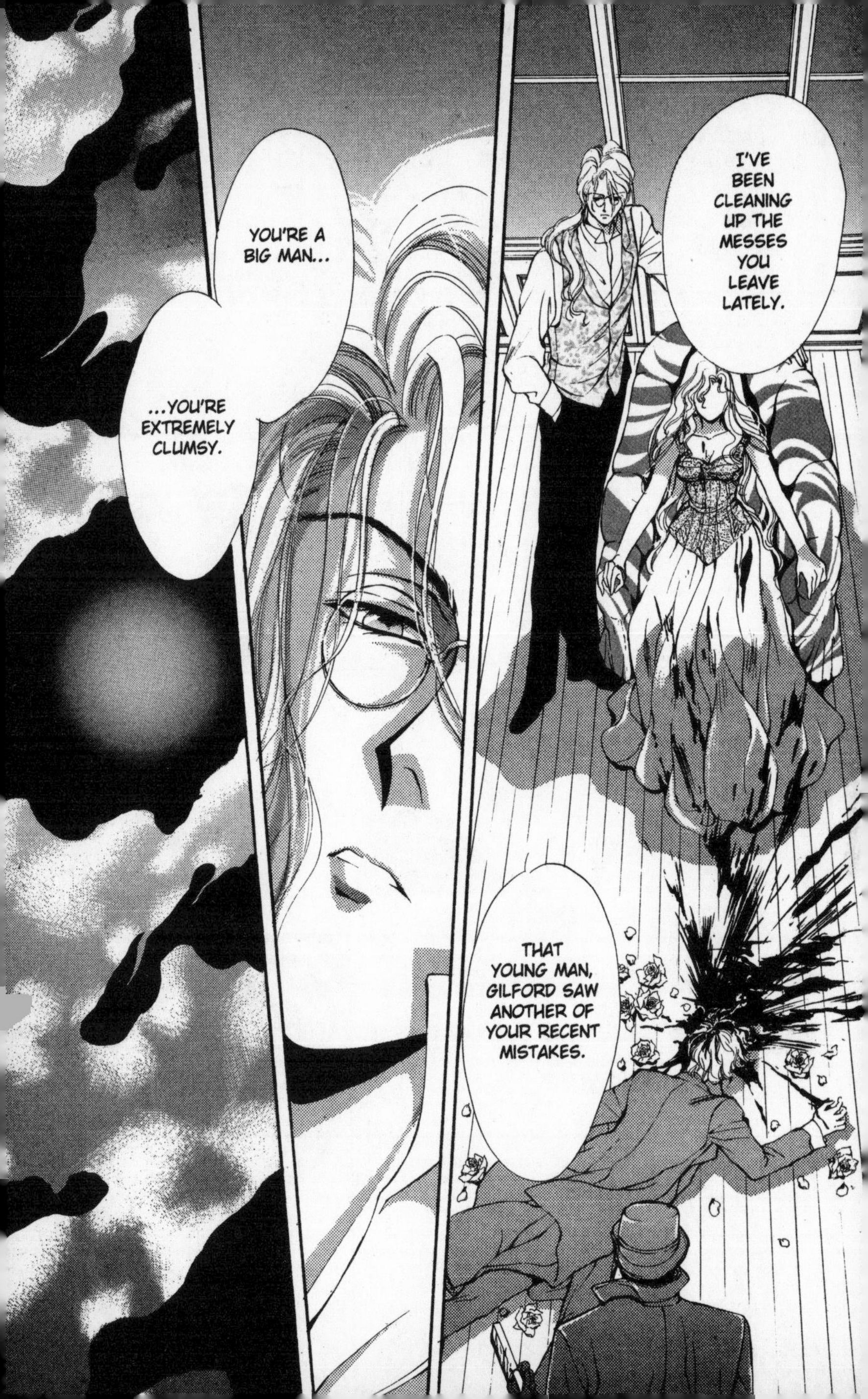
I'VE BEEN CLEANING UP THE MESSES YOU LEAVE LATELY.
THAT YOUNG MAN, GILFORD SAW ANOTHER OF YOUR RECENT MISTAKES.
YOU'RE A BIG MAN...
...YOU'RE EXTREMELY CLUMSY.

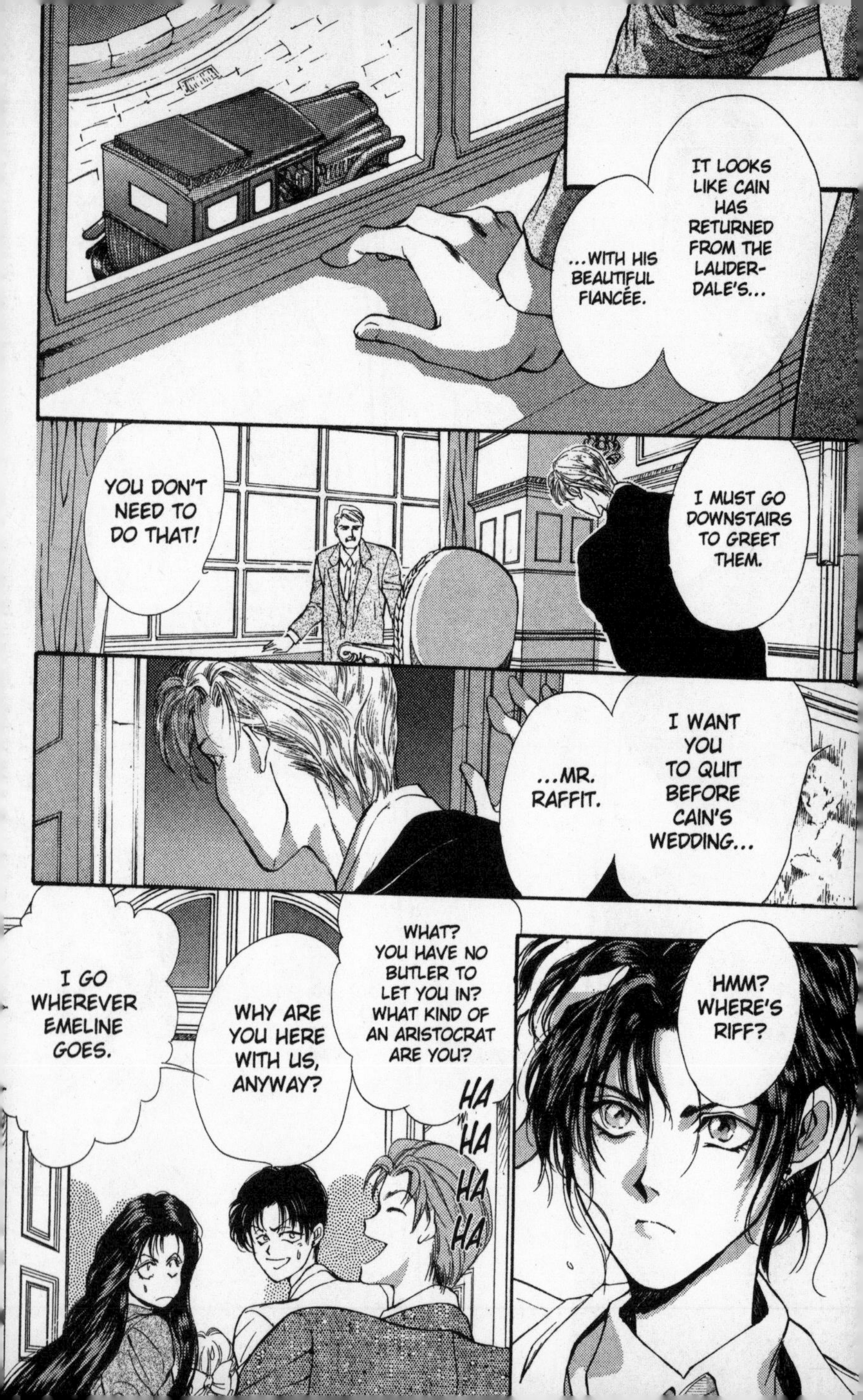
IT LOOKS LIKE CAIN HAS RETURNED FROM THE LAUDER-DALE'S...
...WITH HIS BEAUTIFUL FIANCÉE.
I MUST GO DOWNSTAIRS TO GREET THEM.
YOU DON'T NEED TO DO THAT!
I WANT YOU TO QUIT BEFORE CAIN'S WEDDING...
...MR. RAFFIT.
HMM? WHERE'S RIFF?
WHAT? YOU HAVE NO BUTLER TO LET YOU IN? WHAT KIND OF AN ARISTOCRAT ARE YOU?
HA HA HA HA HA
WHY ARE YOU HERE WITH US, ANYWAY?
I GO WHEREVER EMELINE GOES.

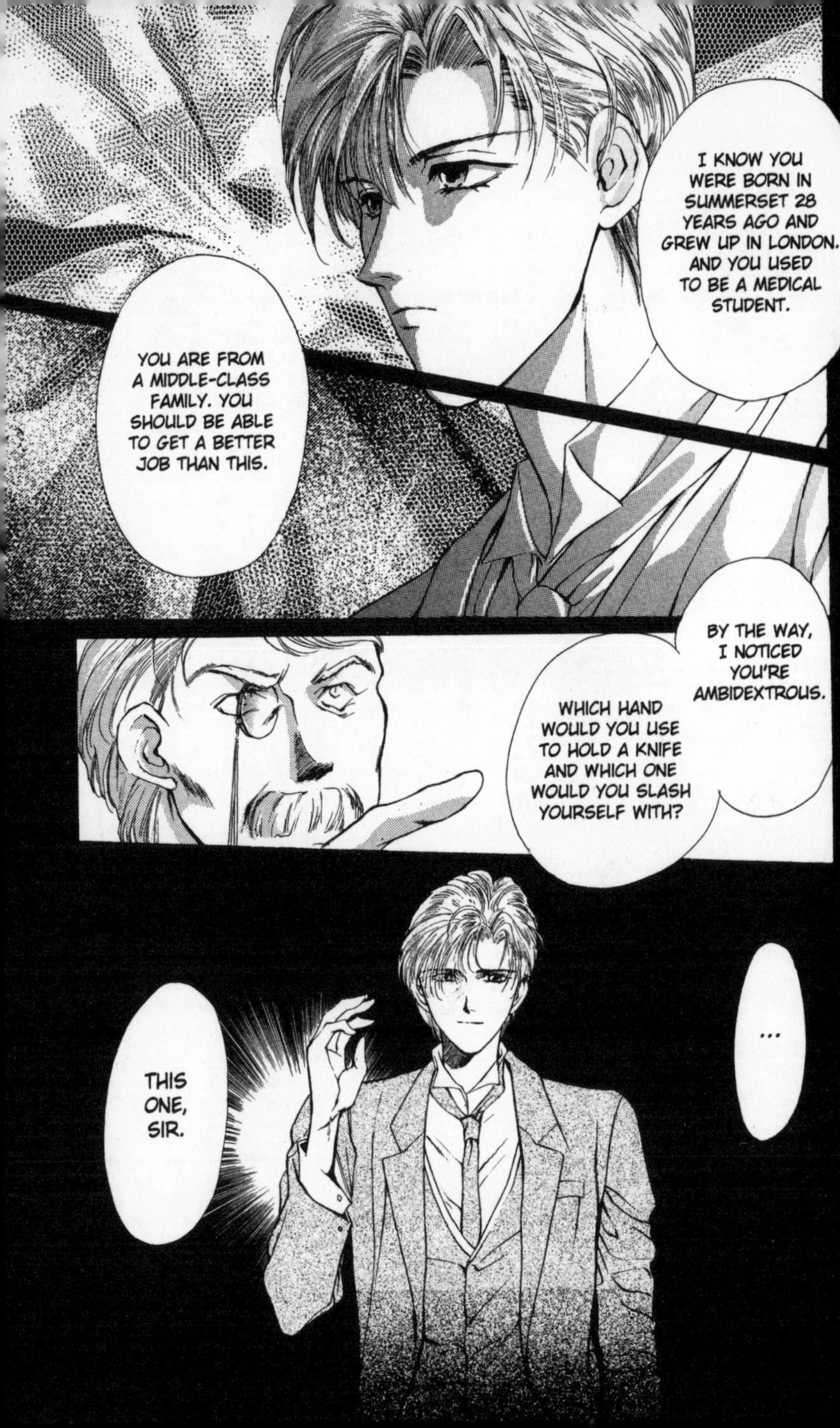
I KNOW YOU WERE BORN IN SUMMERSET 28 YEARS AGO AND GREW UP IN LONDON. AND YOU USED TO BE A MEDICAL STUDENT.
YOU ARE FROM A MIDDLE-CLASS FAMILY. YOU SHOULD BE ABLE TO GET A BETTER JOB THAN THIS.
BY THE WAY, I NOTICED YOU'RE AMBIDEXTROUS.
WHICH HAND WOULD YOU USE TO HOLD A KNIFE AND WHICH ONE WOULD YOU SLASH YOURSELF WITH?
...
THIS ONE, SIR.

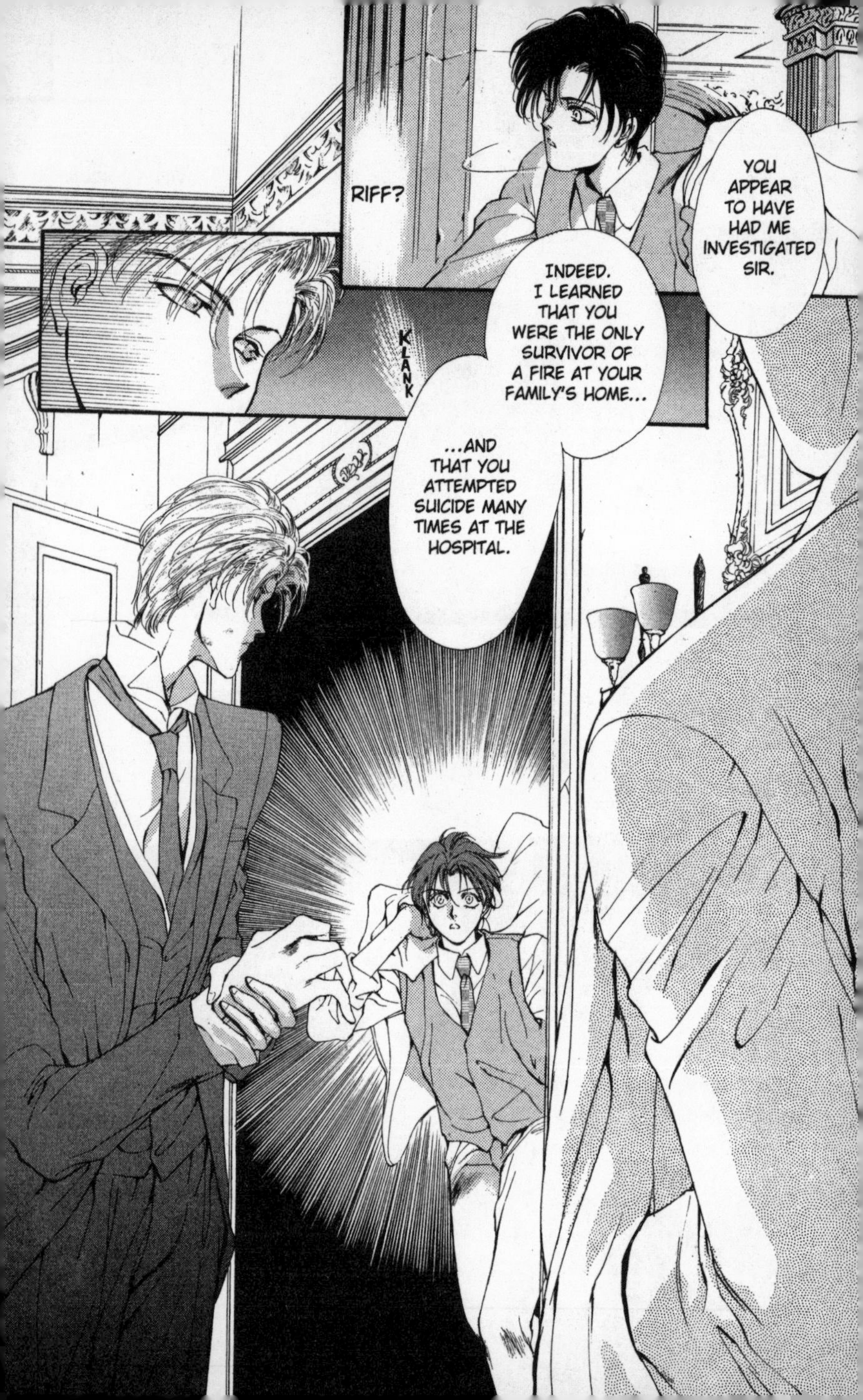
YOU APPEAR TO HAVE HAD ME INVESTIGATED SIR.
RIFF?
INDEED. I LEARNED THAT YOU WERE THE ONLY SURVIVOR OF A FIRE AT YOUR FAMILY'S HOME...
KLANK
...AND THAT YOU ATTEMPTED SUICIDE MANY TIMES AT THE HOSPITAL.

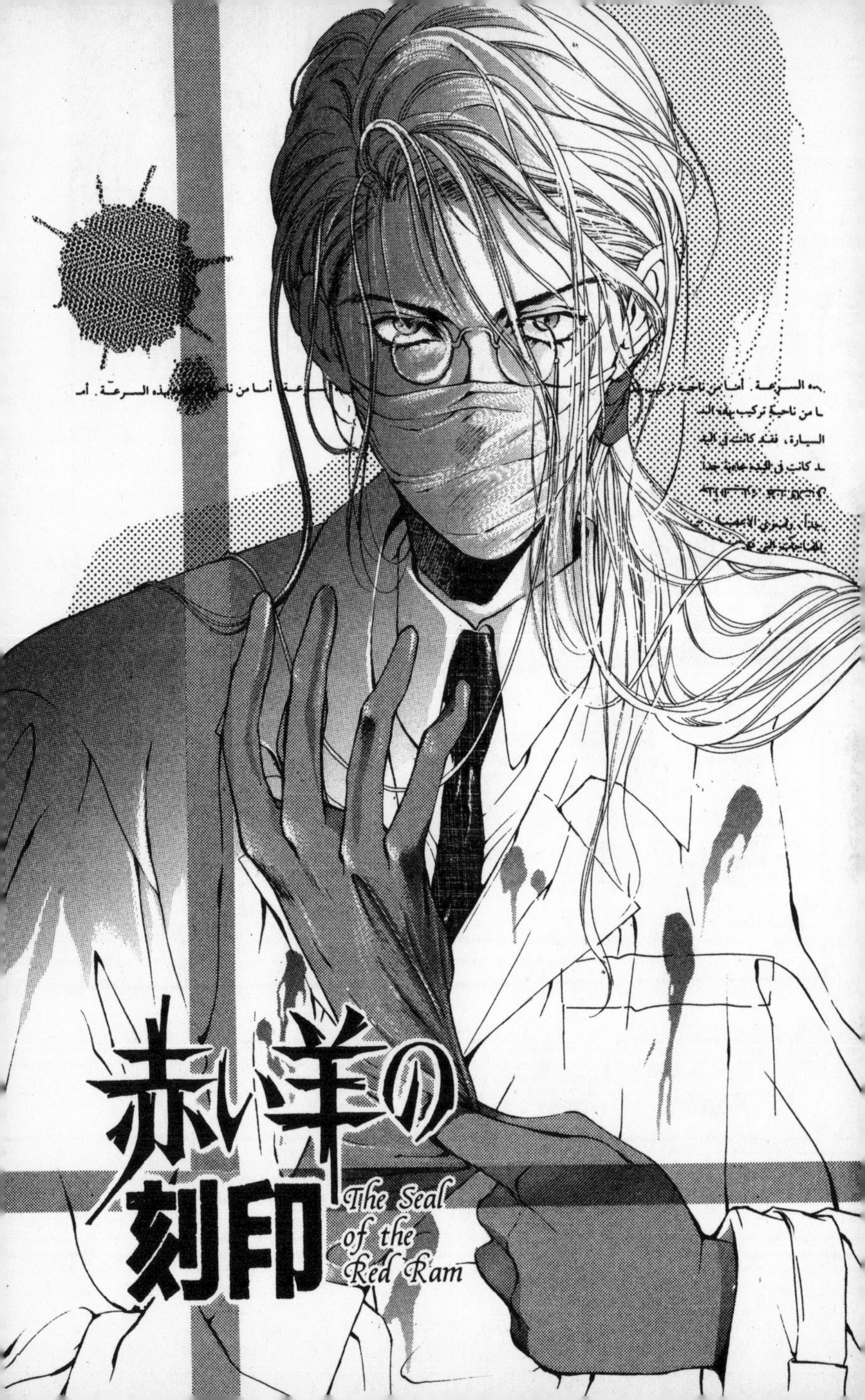
赤い羊の刻印
The Seal of the Red Ram

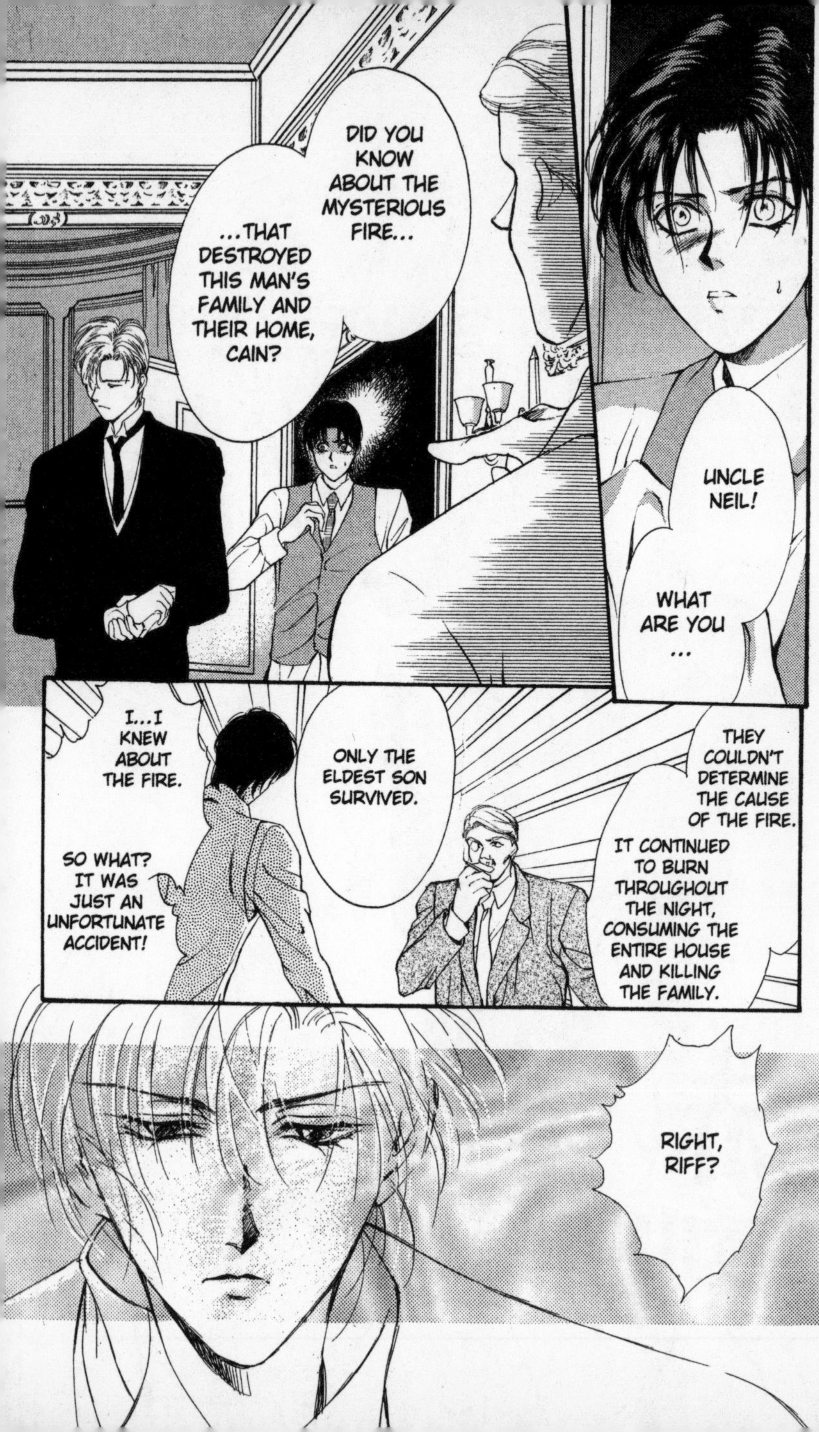
UNCLE NEIL!
WHAT ARE YOU ...
DID YOU KNOW ABOUT THE MYSTERIOUS FIRE...
...THAT DESTROYED THIS MAN'S FAMILY AND THEIR HOME, CAIN?
THEY COULDN'T DETERMINE THE CAUSE OF THE FIRE.
IT CONTINUED TO BURN THROUGHOUT THE NIGHT, CONSUMING THE ENTIRE HOUSE AND KILLING THE FAMILY.
ONLY THE ELDEST SON SURVIVED.
I...I KNEW ABOUT THE FIRE.
SO WHAT? IT WAS JUST AN UNFORTUNATE ACCIDENT!
RIGHT, RIFF?

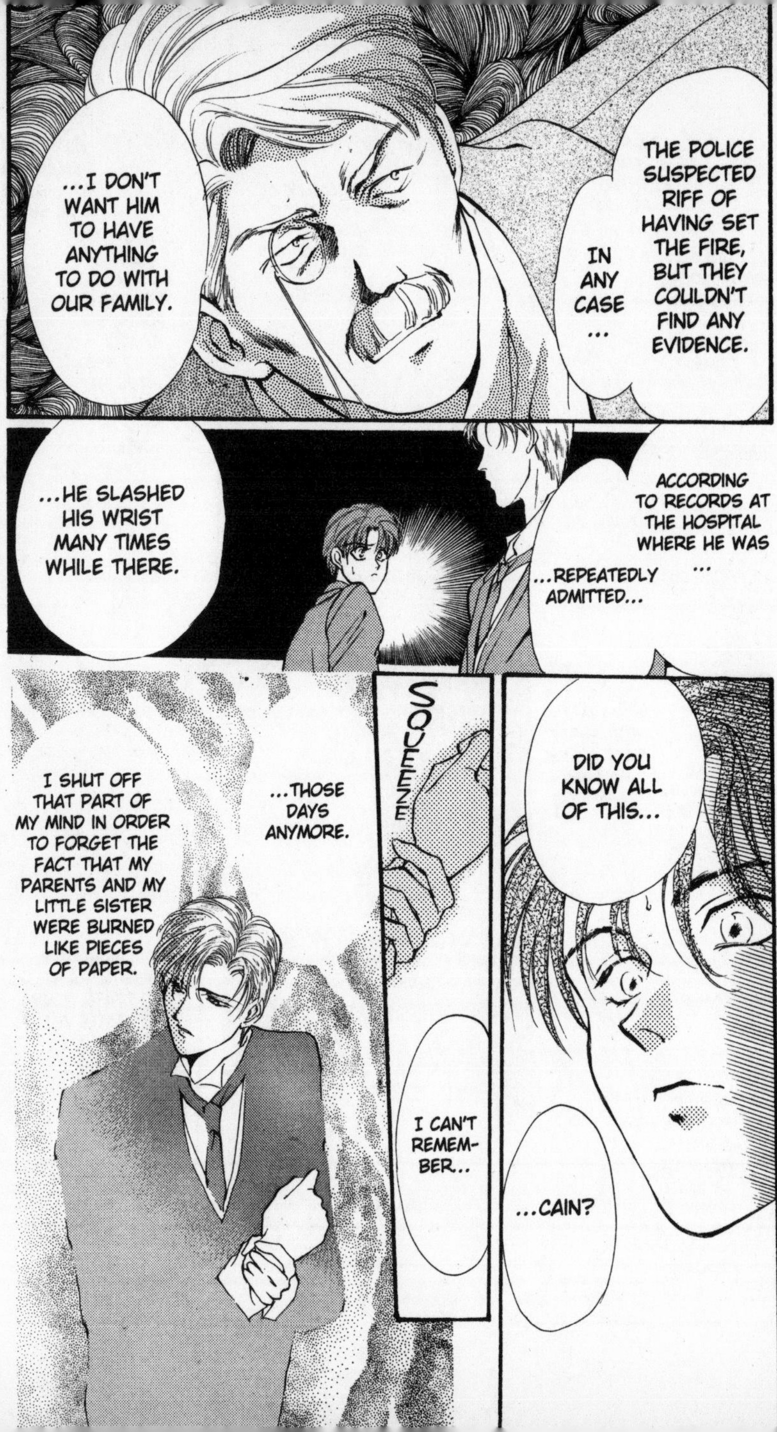
THE POLICE SUSPECTED RIFF OF HAVING SET THE FIRE, BUT THEY COULDN'T FIND ANY EVIDENCE.
IN ANY CASE...
...I DON'T WANT HIM TO HAVE ANYTHING TO DO WITH OUR FAMILY.
ACCORDING TO RECORDS AT THE HOSPITAL WHERE HE WAS...
...REPEATEDLY ADMITTED...
...HE SLASHED HIS WRIST MANY TIMES WHILE THERE.
DID YOU KNOW ALL OF THIS...
...CAIN?
SQUEEZE
I CAN'T REMEMBER...
...THOSE DAYS ANYMORE.
I SHUT OFF THAT PART OF MY MIND IN ORDER TO FORGET THE FACT THAT MY PARENTS AND MY LITTLE SISTER WERE BURNED LIKE PIECES OF PAPER.

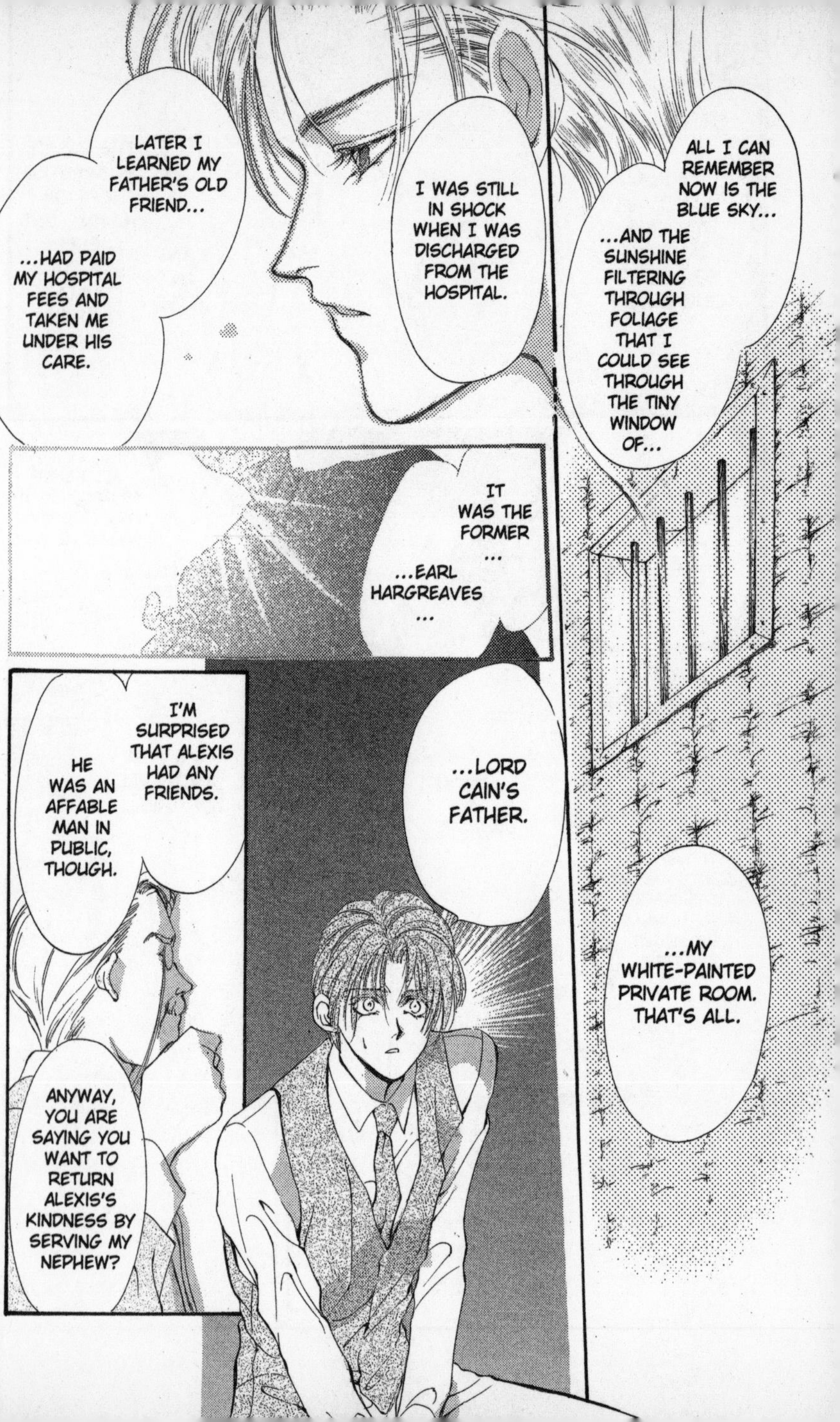
ALL I CAN REMEMBER NOW IS THE BLUE SKY...
...AND THE SUNSHINE FILTERING THROUGH FOLIAGE THAT I COULD SEE THROUGH THE TINY WINDOW OF...
...MY WHITE-PAINTED PRIVATE ROOM. THAT'S ALL.
I WAS STILL IN SHOCK WHEN I WAS DISCHARGED FROM THE HOSPITAL.
LATER I LEARNED MY FATHER'S OLD FRIEND...
...HAD PAID MY HOSPITAL FEES AND TAKEN ME UNDER HIS CARE.
IT WAS THE FORMER ...
...EARL HARGREAVES ...
...LORD CAIN'S FATHER.
I'M SURPRISED THAT ALEXIS HAD ANY FRIENDS.
HE WAS AN AFFABLE MAN IN PUBLIC, THOUGH.
ANYWAY, YOU ARE SAYING YOU WANT TO RETURN ALEXIS'S KINDNESS BY SERVING MY NEPHEW?

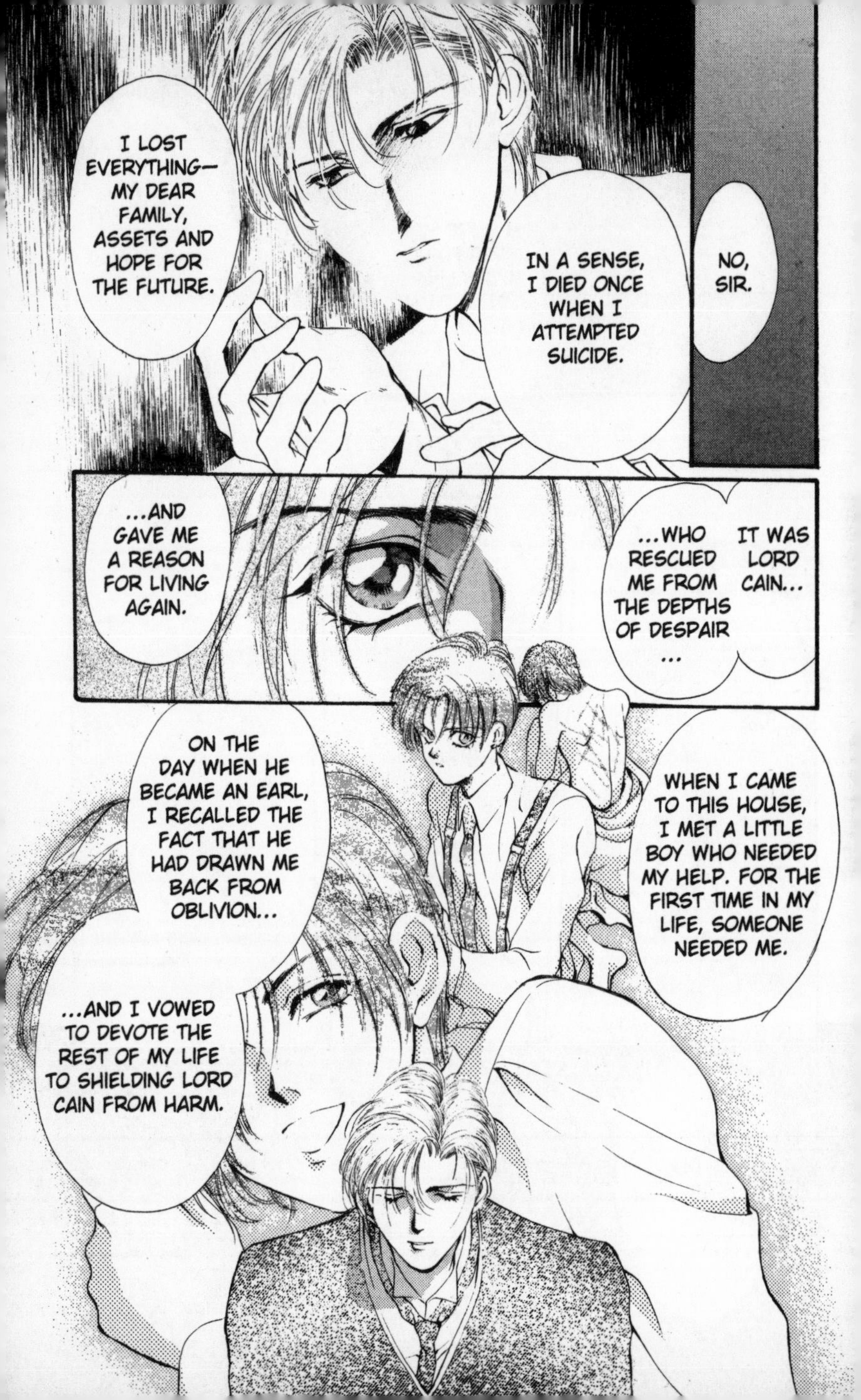
NO, SIR.
IN A SENSE, I DIED ONCE WHEN I ATTEMPTED SUICIDE.
I LOST EVERYTHING— MY DEAR FAMILY, ASSETS AND HOPE FOR THE FUTURE.
IT WAS LORD CAIN...
...WHO RESCUED ME FROM THE DEPTHS OF DESPAIR ...
...AND GAVE ME A REASON FOR LIVING AGAIN.
WHEN I CAME TO THIS HOUSE, I MET A LITTLE BOY WHO NEEDED MY HELP. FOR THE FIRST TIME IN MY LIFE, SOMEONE NEEDED ME.
ON THE DAY WHEN HE BECAME AN EARL, I RECALLED THE FACT THAT HE HAD DRAWN ME BACK FROM OBLIVION...
...AND I VOWED TO DEVOTE THE REST OF MY LIFE TO SHIELDING LORD CAIN FROM HARM.

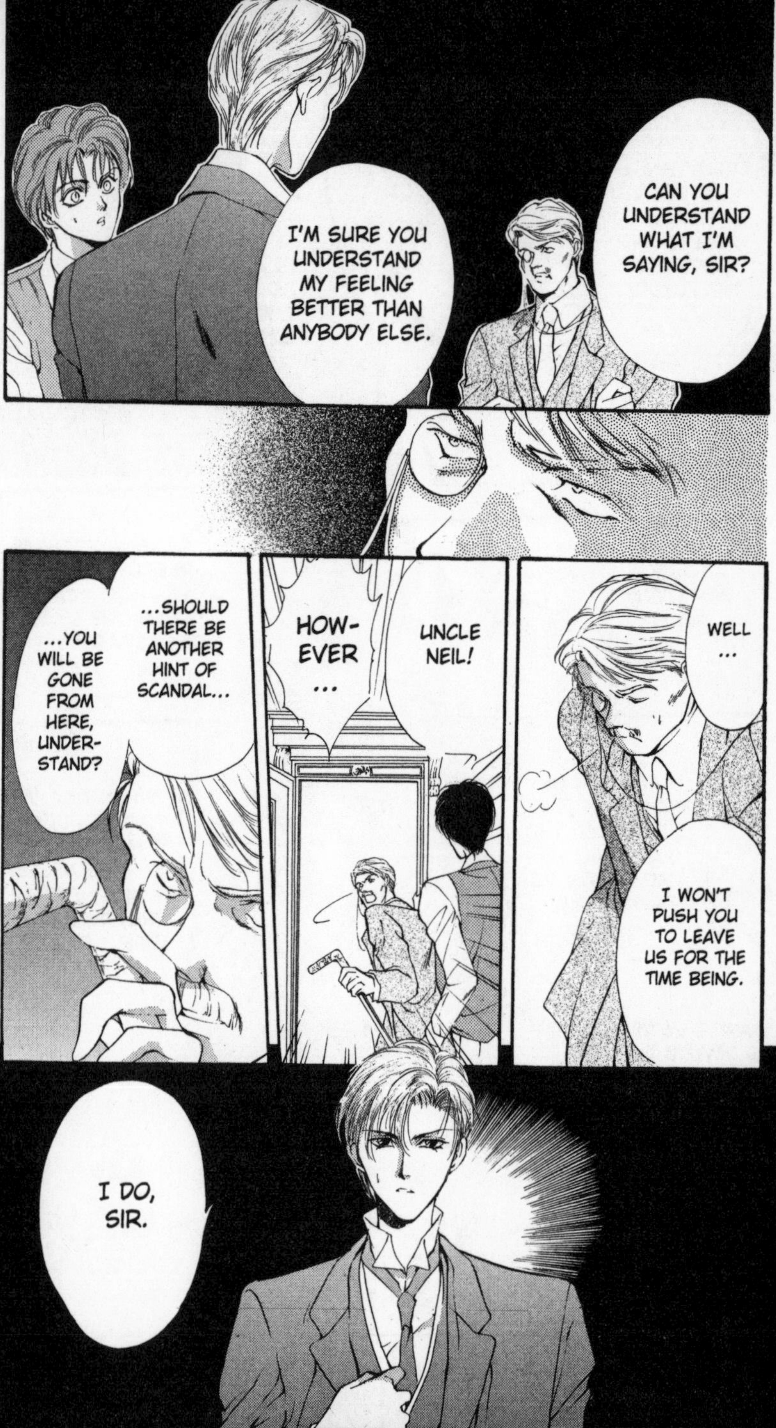
CAN YOU UNDERSTAND WHAT I'M SAYING, SIR?
I'M SURE YOU UNDERSTAND MY FEELING BETTER THAN ANYBODY ELSE.
WELL ...
I WON'T PUSH YOU TO LEAVE US FOR THE TIME BEING.
UNCLE NEIL!
HOW-EVER ...
...SHOULD THERE BE ANOTHER HINT OF SCANDAL...
...YOU WILL BE GONE FROM HERE, UNDER-STAND?
I DO, SIR.

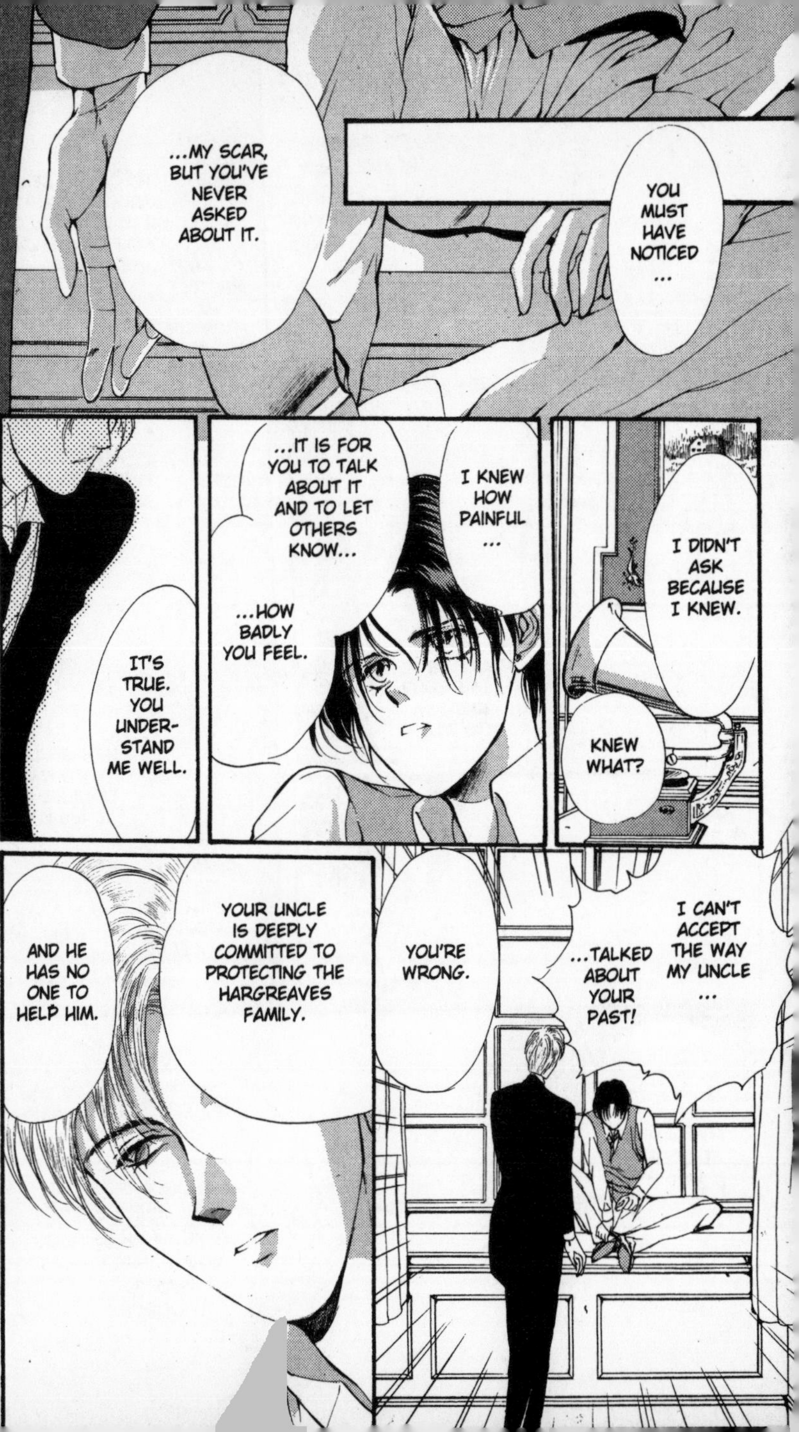
YOU MUST HAVE NOTICED ...
...MY SCAR, BUT YOU'VE NEVER ASKED ABOUT IT.
I DIDN'T ASK BECAUSE I KNEW.
KNEW WHAT?
I KNEW HOW PAINFUL ...
...IT IS FOR YOU TO TALK ABOUT IT AND TO LET OTHERS KNOW...
...HOW BADLY YOU FEEL.
IT'S TRUE. YOU UNDER-STAND ME WELL.
I CAN'T ACCEPT THE WAY MY UNCLE ...
...TALKED ABOUT YOUR PAST!
YOU'RE WRONG.
YOUR UNCLE IS DEEPLY COMMITTED TO PROTECTING THE HARGREAVES FAMILY.
AND HE HAS NO ONE TO HELP HIM.

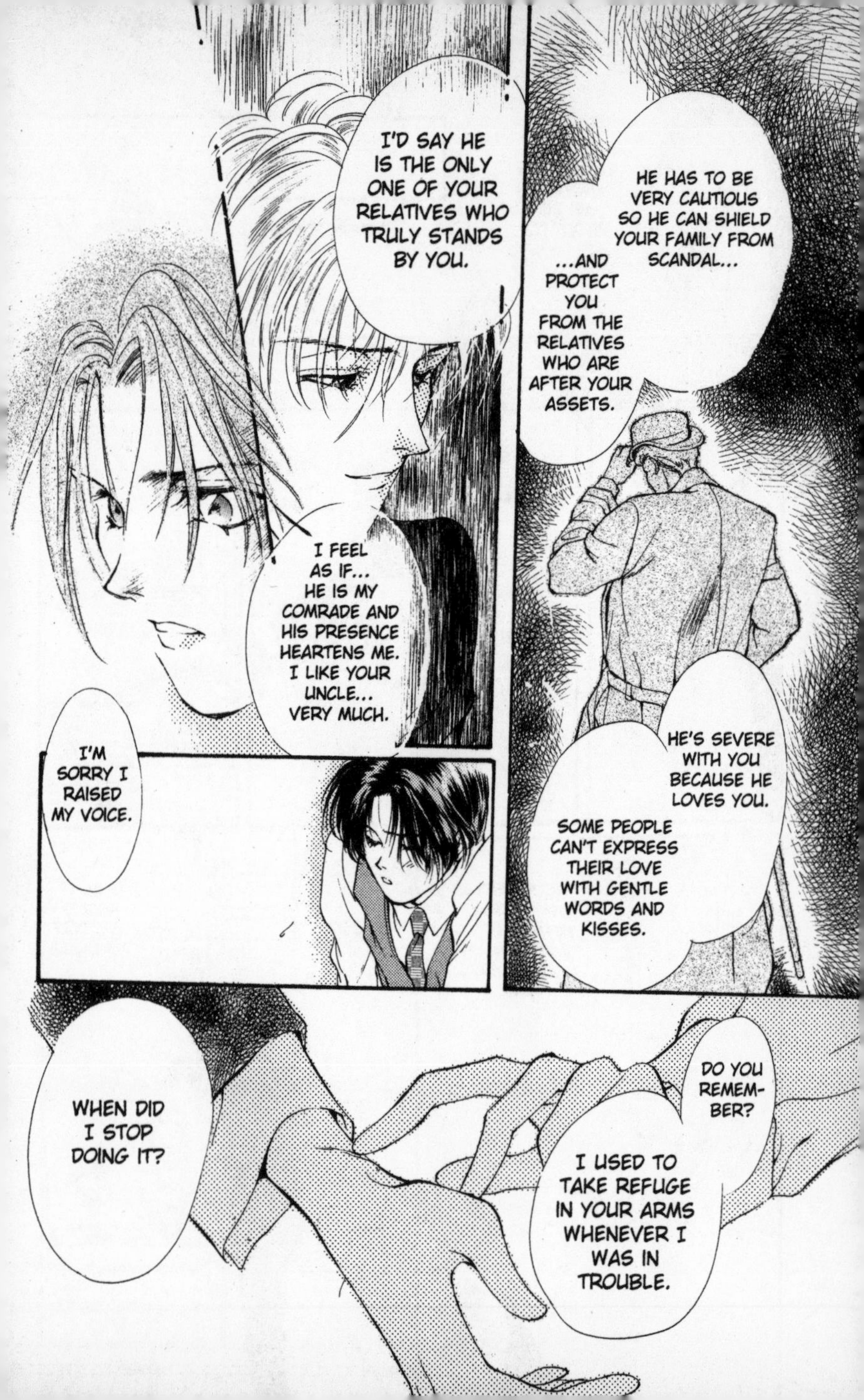
HE HAS TO BE VERY CAUTIOUS SO HE CAN SHIELD YOUR FAMILY FROM SCANDAL...
...AND PROTECT YOU FROM THE RELATIVES WHO ARE AFTER YOUR ASSETS.
HE'S SEVERE WITH YOU BECAUSE HE LOVES YOU.
SOME PEOPLE CAN'T EXPRESS THEIR LOVE WITH GENTLE WORDS AND KISSES.
I'D SAY HE IS THE ONLY ONE OF YOUR RELATIVES WHO TRULY STANDS BY YOU.
I FEEL AS IF... HE IS MY COMRADE AND HIS PRESENCE HEARTENS ME. I LIKE YOUR UNCLE... VERY MUCH.
I'M SORRY I RAISED MY VOICE.
DO YOU REMEMBER?
I USED TO TAKE REFUGE IN YOUR ARMS WHENEVER I WAS IN TROUBLE.
WHEN DID I STOP DOING IT?

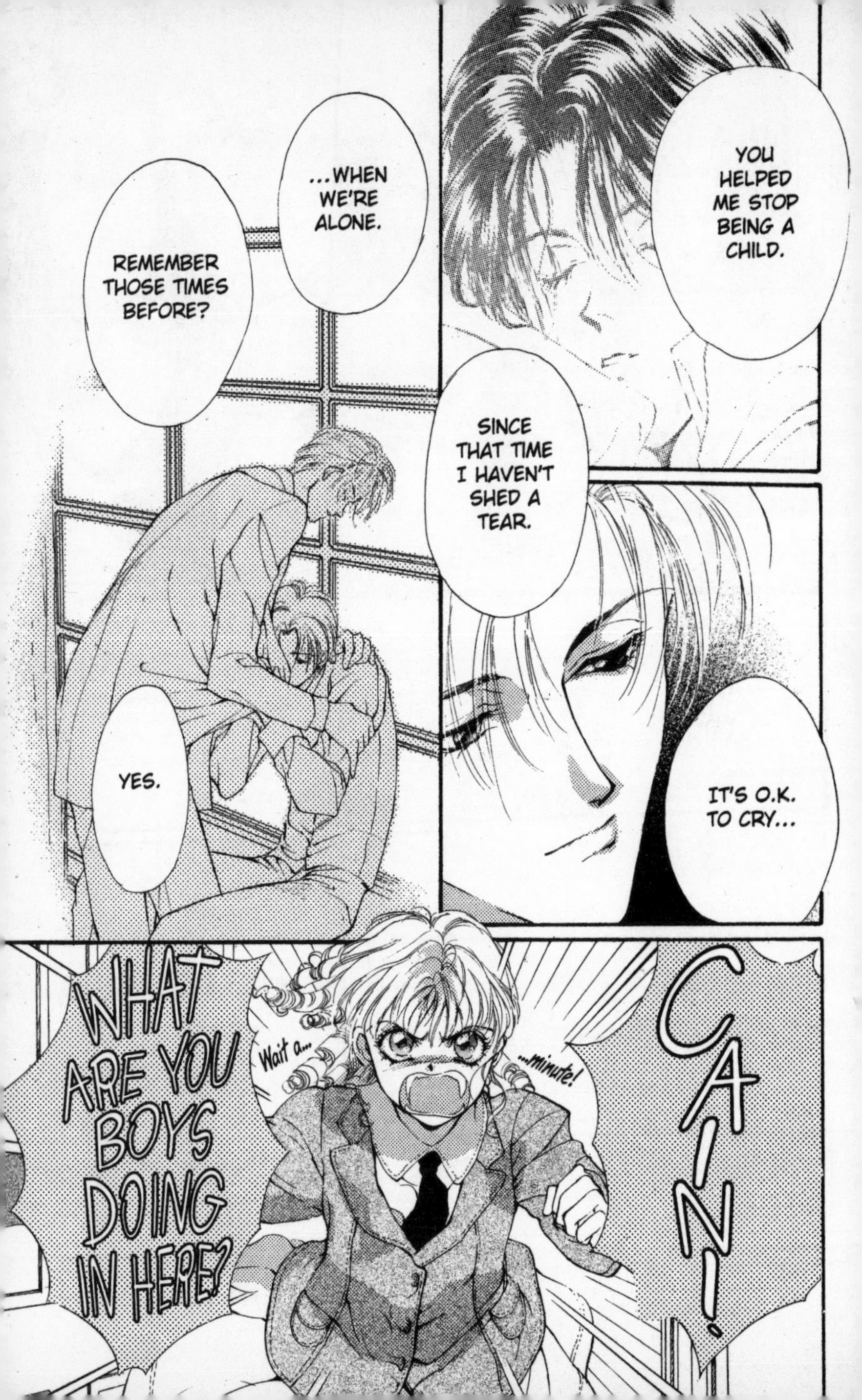
YOU HELPED ME STOP BEING A CHILD.
SINCE THAT TIME I HAVEN'T SHED A TEAR.
IT'S O.K. TO CRY...
...WHEN WE'RE ALONE.
REMEMBER THOSE TIMES BEFORE?
YES.
CAIN!
Wait a...
...minute!
WHAT ARE YOU BOYS DOING IN HERE?

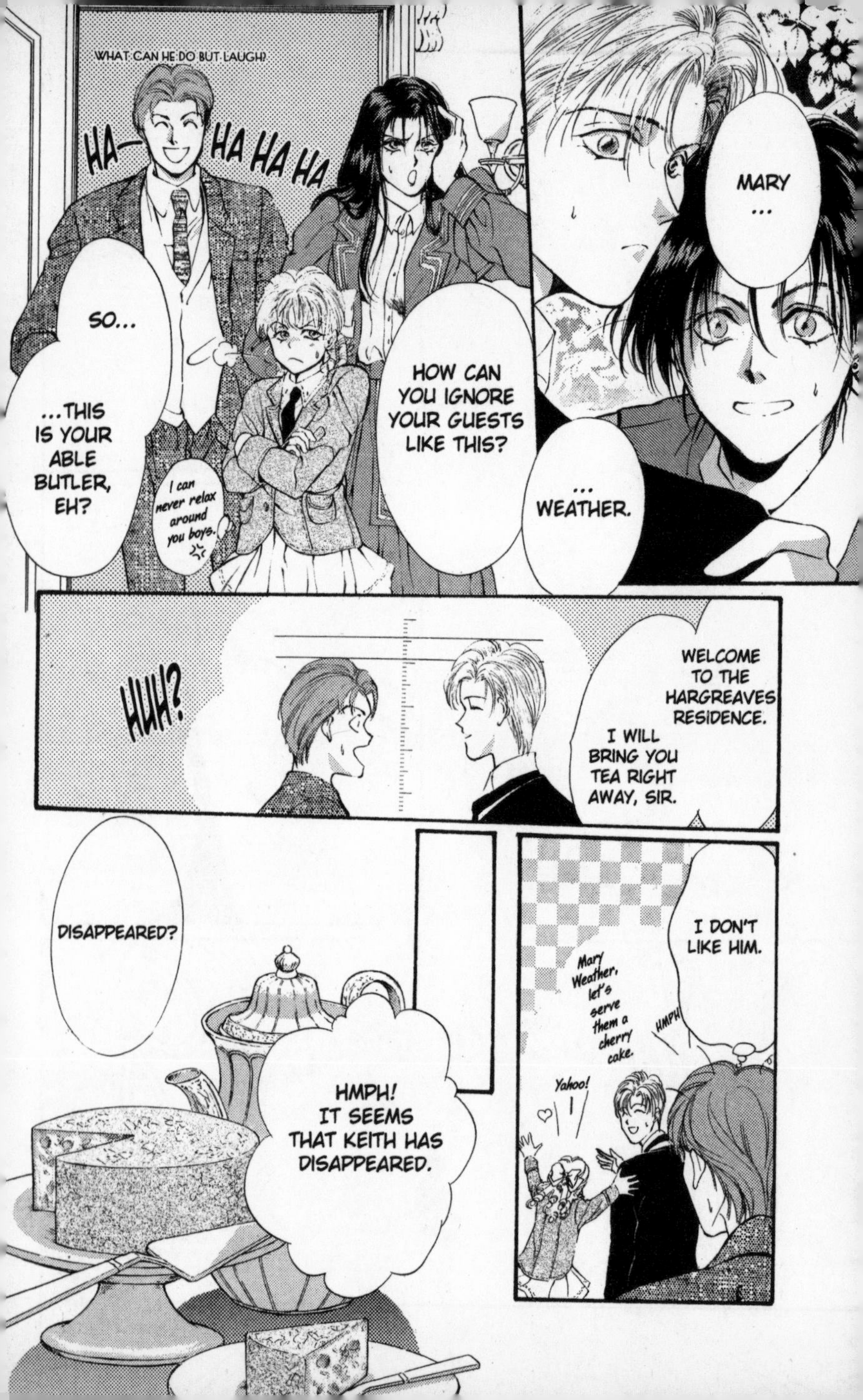
MARY ...
... WEATHER.
WHAT CAN HE DO BUT LAUGH?
HA— HA HA HA
HOW CAN YOU IGNORE YOUR GUESTS LIKE THIS?
SO...
...THIS IS YOUR ABLE BUTLER, EH?
I can never relax around you boys.
WELCOME TO THE HARGREAVES RESIDENCE.
I WILL BRING YOU TEA RIGHT AWAY, SIR.
HUH?
I DON'T LIKE HIM.
HMPH
Mary Weather, let's serve them a cherry cake.
Yahoo!
HMPH! IT SEEMS THAT KEITH HAS DISAPPEARED.
DISAPPEARED?

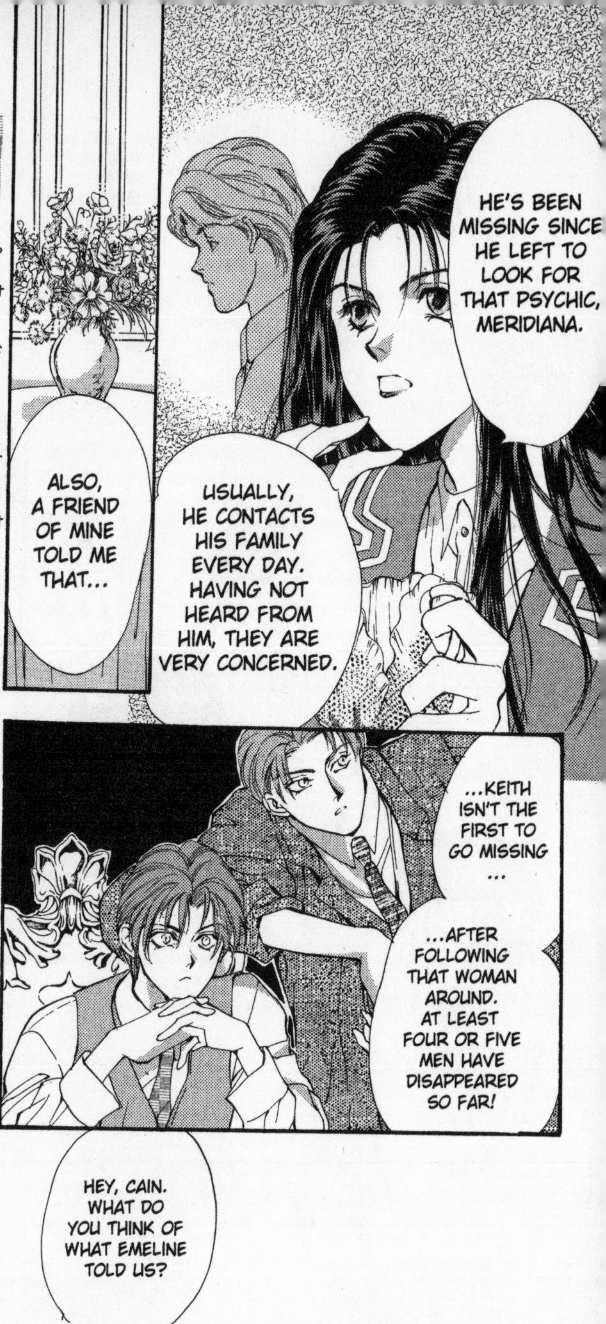
HE'S BEEN MISSING SINCE HE LEFT TO LOOK FOR THAT PSYCHIC, MERIDIANA.
USUALLY, HE CONTACTS HIS FAMILY EVERY DAY. HAVING NOT HEARD FROM HIM, THEY ARE VERY CONCERNED.
ALSO, A FRIEND OF MINE TOLD ME THAT...
...KEITH ISN'T THE FIRST TO GO MISSING ...
...AFTER FOLLOWING THAT WOMAN AROUND. AT LEAST FOUR OR FIVE MEN HAVE DISAPPEARED SO FAR!
HEY, CAIN. WHAT DO YOU THINK OF WHAT EMELINE TOLD US?

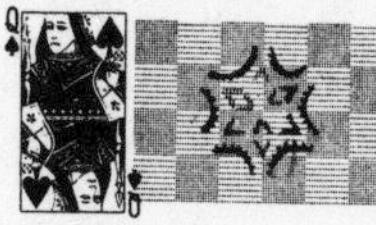

The scene you witnessed two pages earlier is not another instance of my bad old habit with Cain and Riff. Please take a close look at the panel. The panel where Riff appears to be holding Cain. (Someone told me it looked as if they were flirting with each other.) The two men aren't holding each other at all. Cain is simply sniffing Riff's jacket. Cain used to bury his face in Riff's jacket and cry when he was little. (It reminds me of the way an animal sniffs at places it has been before!) But it's true that Riff looks happy. I appreciate the honesty of the reader who wrote: "Mary Weather shouldn't interrupt Cain and Riff!" I can understand her feeling. Dr. Disraeli will start talking really weird in a few pages. I truly enjoyed composing his bizarre monologue. (Don't ask me why.)

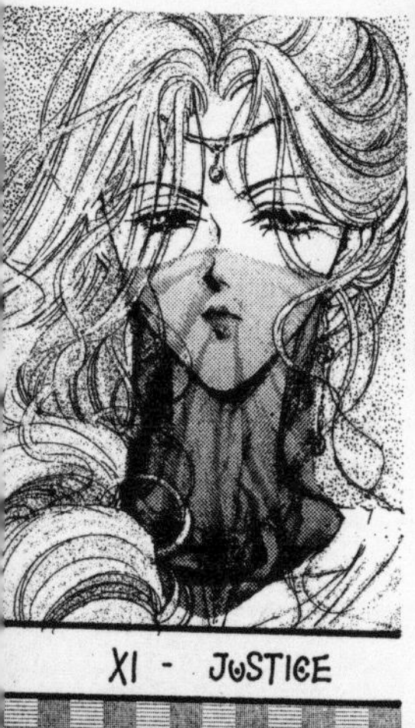

XI - JUSTICE

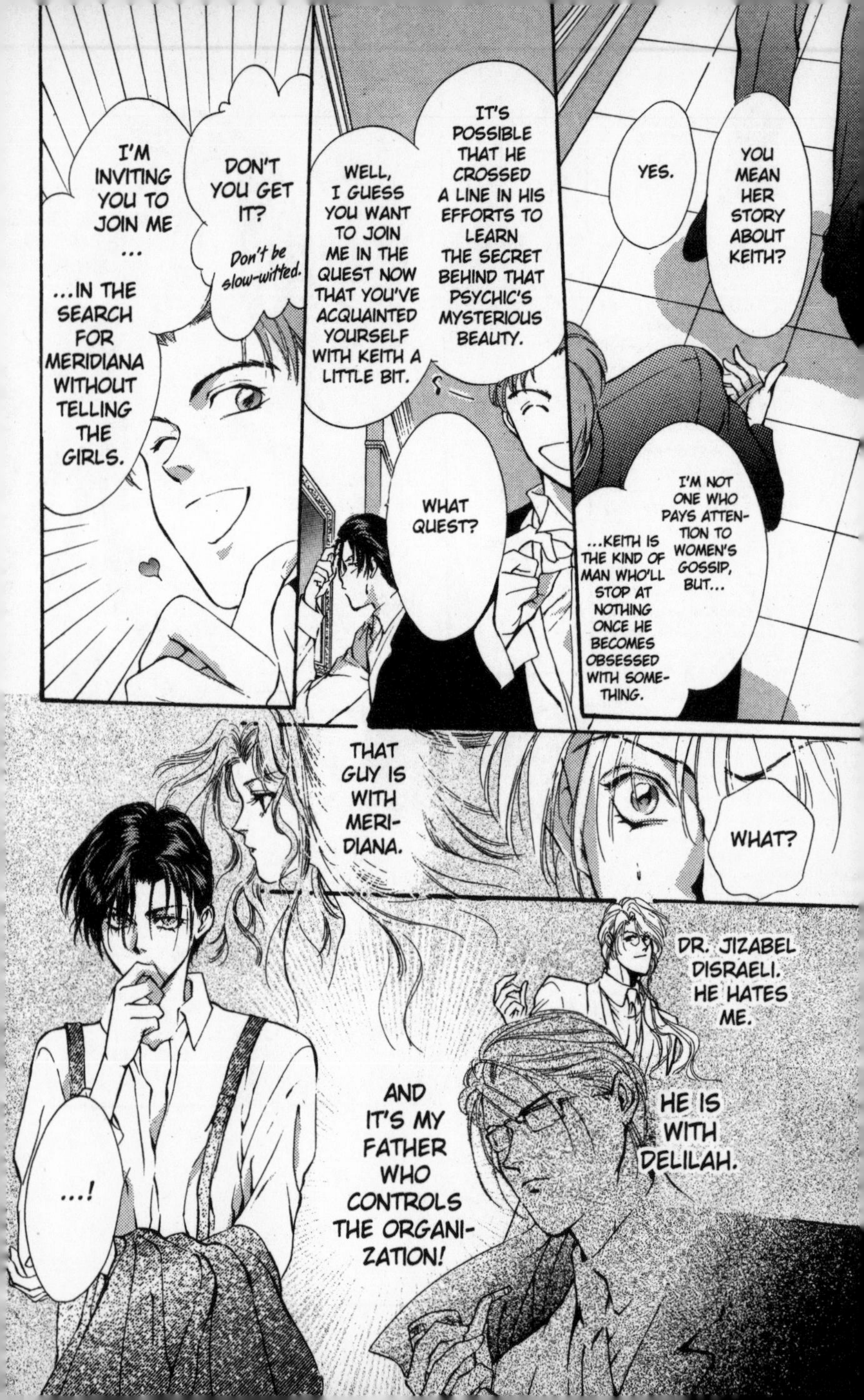
YOU MEAN HER STORY ABOUT KEITH?
YES.
I'M NOT ONE WHO PAYS ATTENTION TO WOMEN'S GOSSIP, BUT...
...KEITH IS THE KIND OF MAN WHO'LL STOP AT NOTHING ONCE HE BECOMES OBSESSED WITH SOMETHING.
IT'S POSSIBLE THAT HE CROSSED A LINE IN HIS EFFORTS TO LEARN THE SECRET BEHIND THAT PSYCHIC'S MYSTERIOUS BEAUTY.
WELL, I GUESS YOU WANT TO JOIN ME IN THE QUEST NOW THAT YOU'VE ACQUAINTED YOURSELF WITH KEITH A LITTLE BIT.
WHAT QUEST?
DON'T YOU GET IT?
Don't be slow-witted.
I'M INVITING YOU TO JOIN ME ...
...IN THE SEARCH FOR MERIDIANA WITHOUT TELLING THE GIRLS.
WHAT?
THAT GUY IS WITH MERIDIANA.
DR. JIZABEL DISRAELI. HE HATES ME.
HE IS WITH DELILAH.
AND IT'S MY FATHER WHO CONTROLS THE ORGANIZATION!
...!

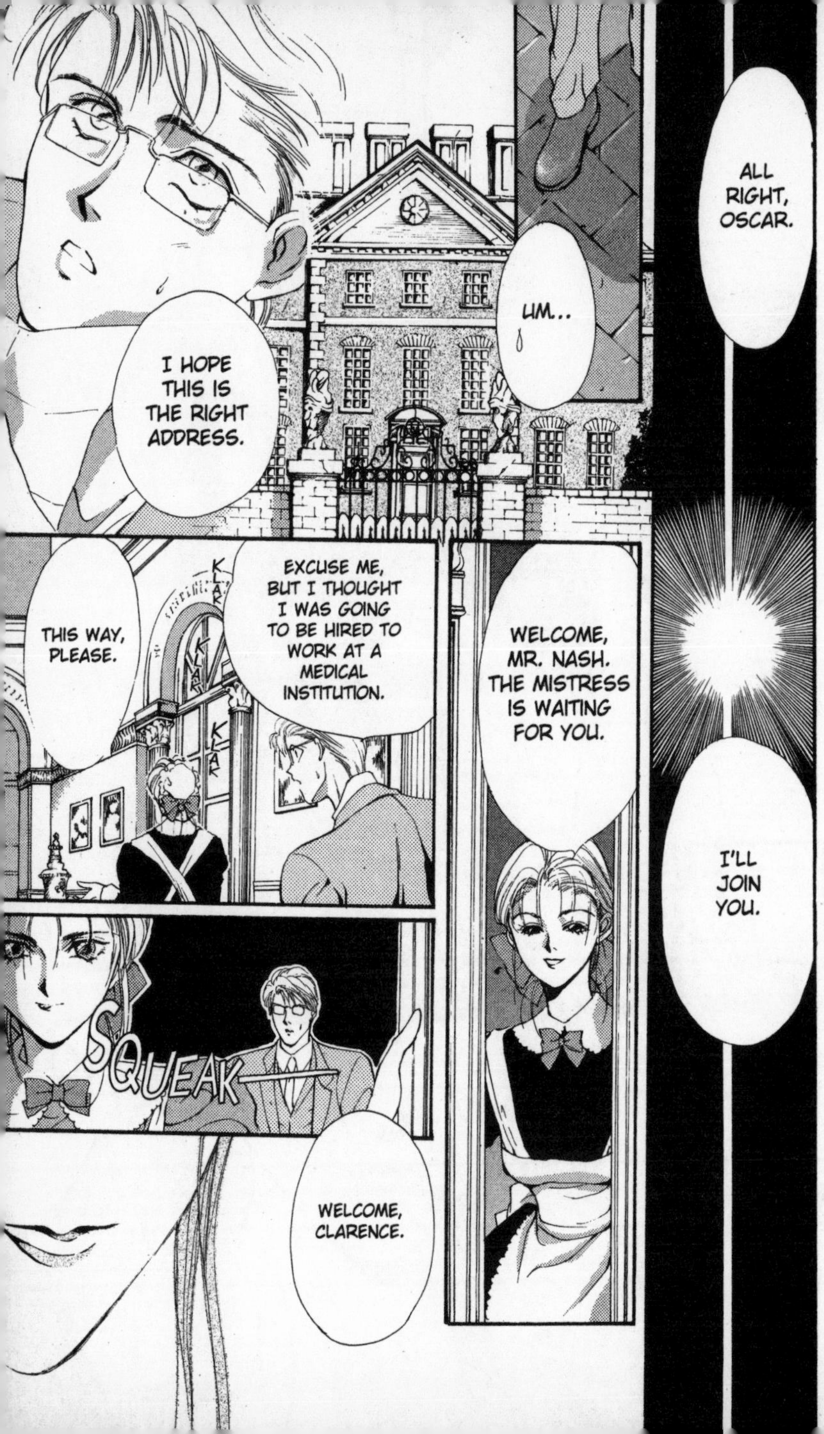

ALL RIGHT, OSCAR.
I'LL JOIN YOU.
UM...
I HOPE THIS IS THE RIGHT ADDRESS.
WELCOME, MR. NASH. THE MISTRESS IS WAITING FOR YOU.
KLAK KLAK KLAK
EXCUSE ME, BUT I THOUGHT I WAS GOING TO BE HIRED TO WORK AT A MEDICAL INSTITUTION.
THIS WAY, PLEASE.
SQUEAK
WELCOME, CLARENCE.

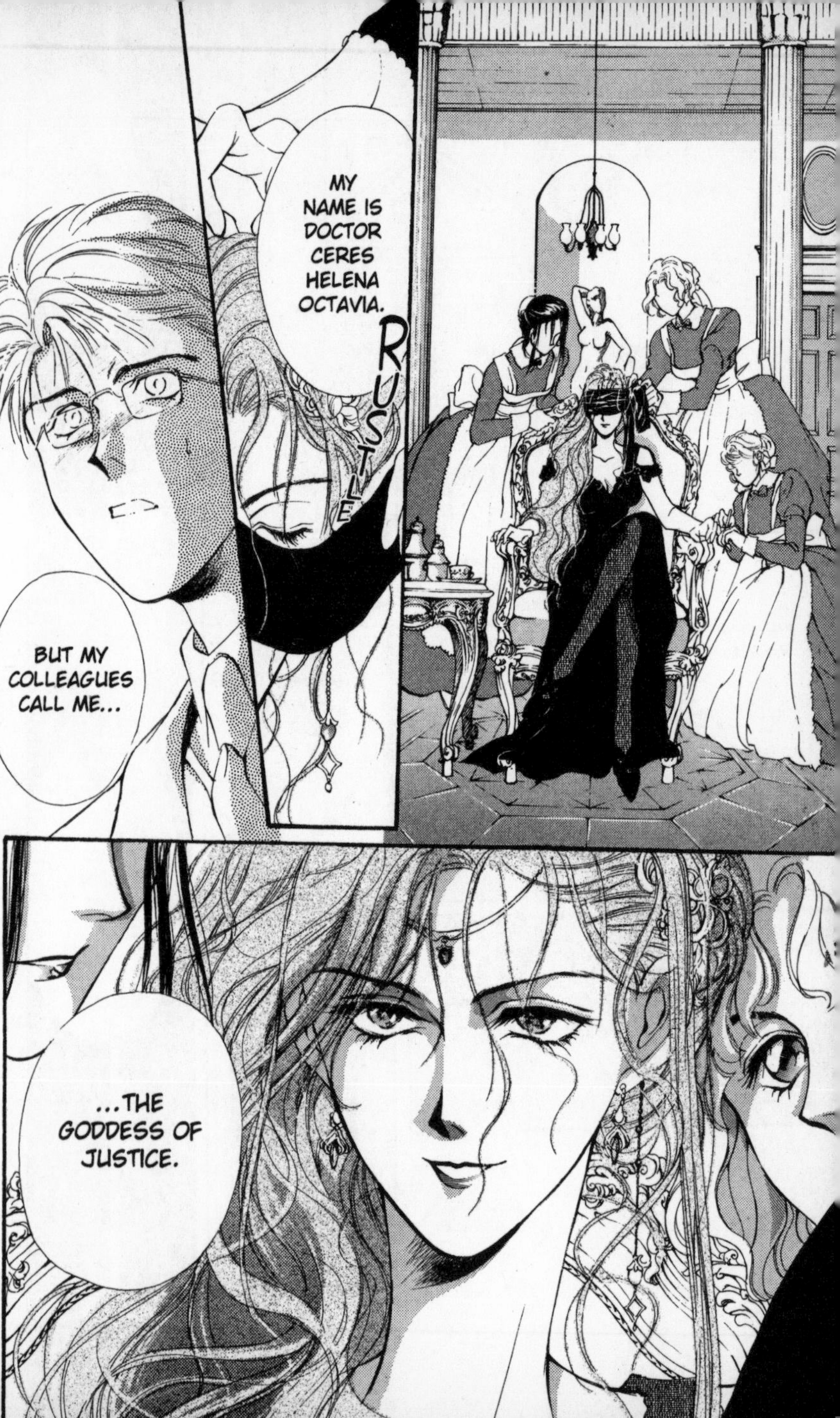
MY NAME IS DOCTOR CERES HELENA OCTAVIA.
RUSTLE
BUT MY COLLEAGUES CALL ME...
...THE GODDESS OF JUSTICE.

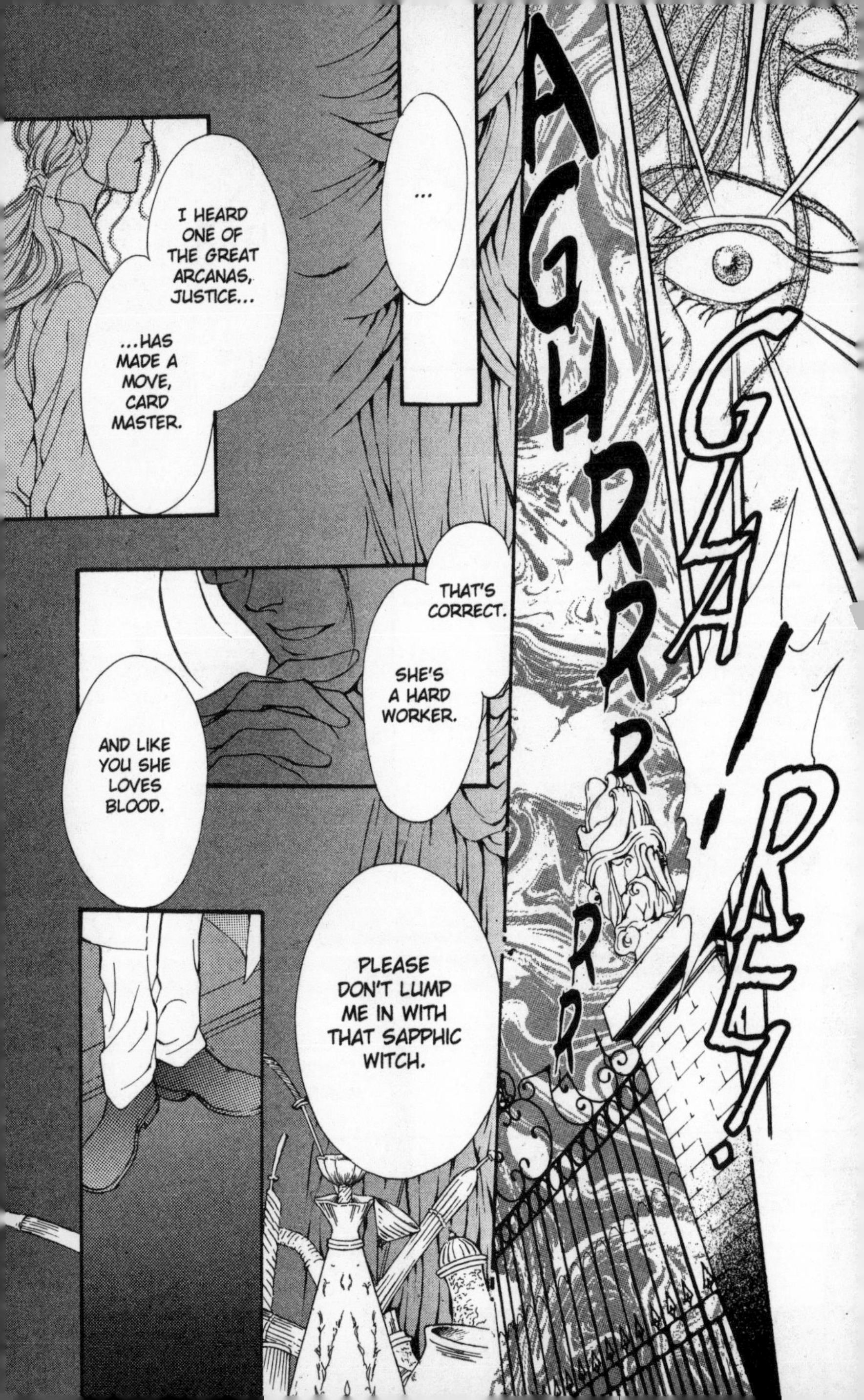
GLA! RAE!
AGHRRRRRR
...
I HEARD ONE OF THE GREAT ARCANAS, JUSTICE...
...HAS MADE A MOVE, CARD MASTER.
THAT'S CORRECT.
SHE'S A HARD WORKER.
AND LIKE YOU SHE LOVES BLOOD.
PLEASE DON'T LUMP ME IN WITH THAT SAPPHIC WITCH.

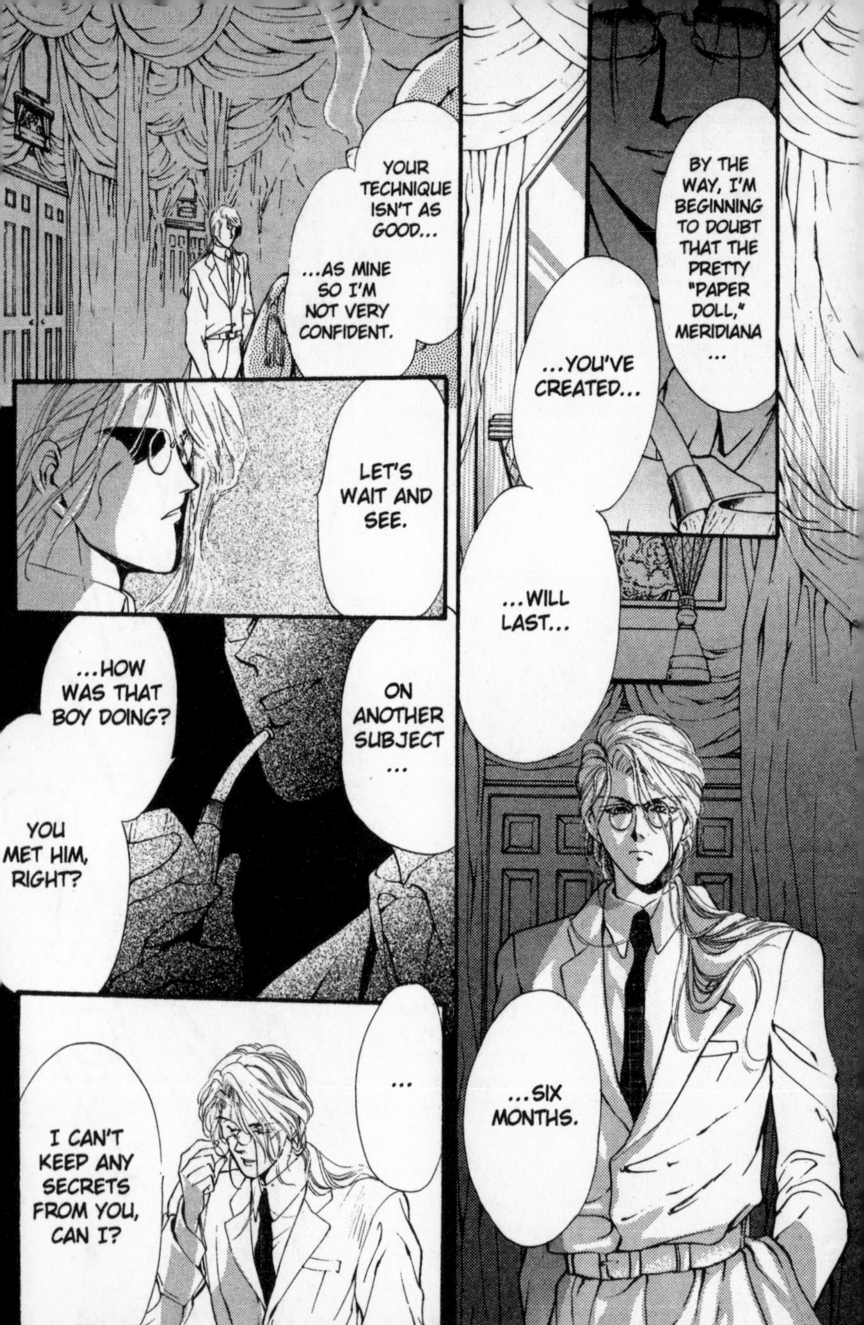

BY THE WAY, I'M BEGINNING TO DOUBT THAT THE PRETTY "PAPER DOLL," MERIDIANA ...
...YOU'VE CREATED...
...WILL LAST...
YOUR TECHNIQUE ISN'T AS GOOD...
...AS MINE SO I'M NOT VERY CONFIDENT.
LET'S WAIT AND SEE.
...SIX MONTHS.
ON ANOTHER SUBJECT ...
...HOW WAS THAT BOY DOING?
YOU MET HIM, RIGHT?
...
I CAN'T KEEP ANY SECRETS FROM YOU, CAN I?

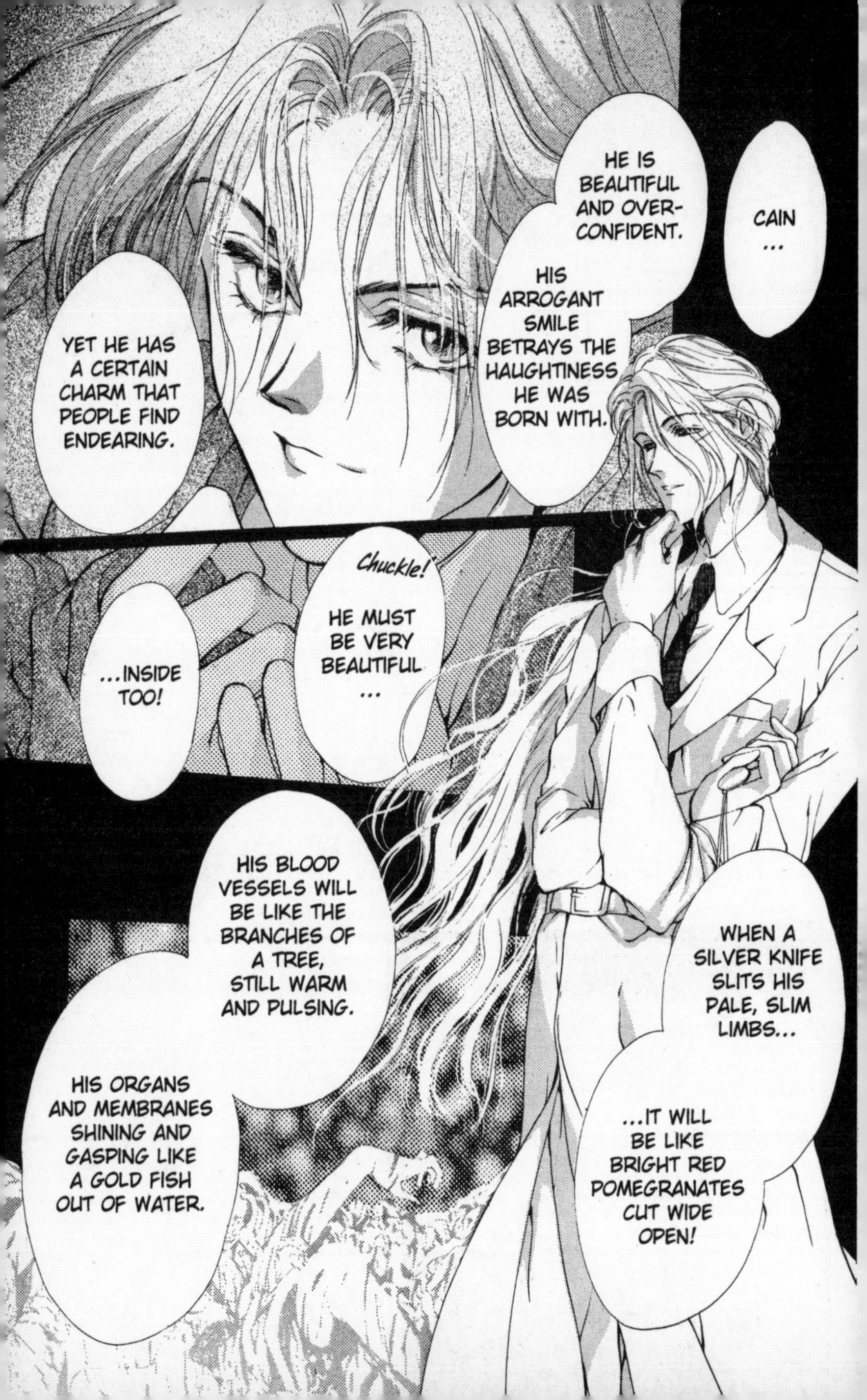
CAIN ...
HE IS BEAUTIFUL AND OVER-CONFIDENT.
HIS ARROGANT SMILE BETRAYS THE HAUGHTINESS HE WAS BORN WITH.
YET HE HAS A CERTAIN CHARM THAT PEOPLE FIND ENDEARING.
Chuckle!
HE MUST BE VERY BEAUTIFUL ...
...INSIDE TOO!
WHEN A SILVER KNIFE SLITS HIS PALE, SLIM LIMBS...
...IT WILL BE LIKE BRIGHT RED POMEGRANATES CUT WIDE OPEN!
HIS BLOOD VESSELS WILL BE LIKE THE BRANCHES OF A TREE, STILL WARM AND PULSING.
HIS ORGANS AND MEMBRANES SHINING AND GASPING LIKE A GOLD FISH OUT OF WATER.

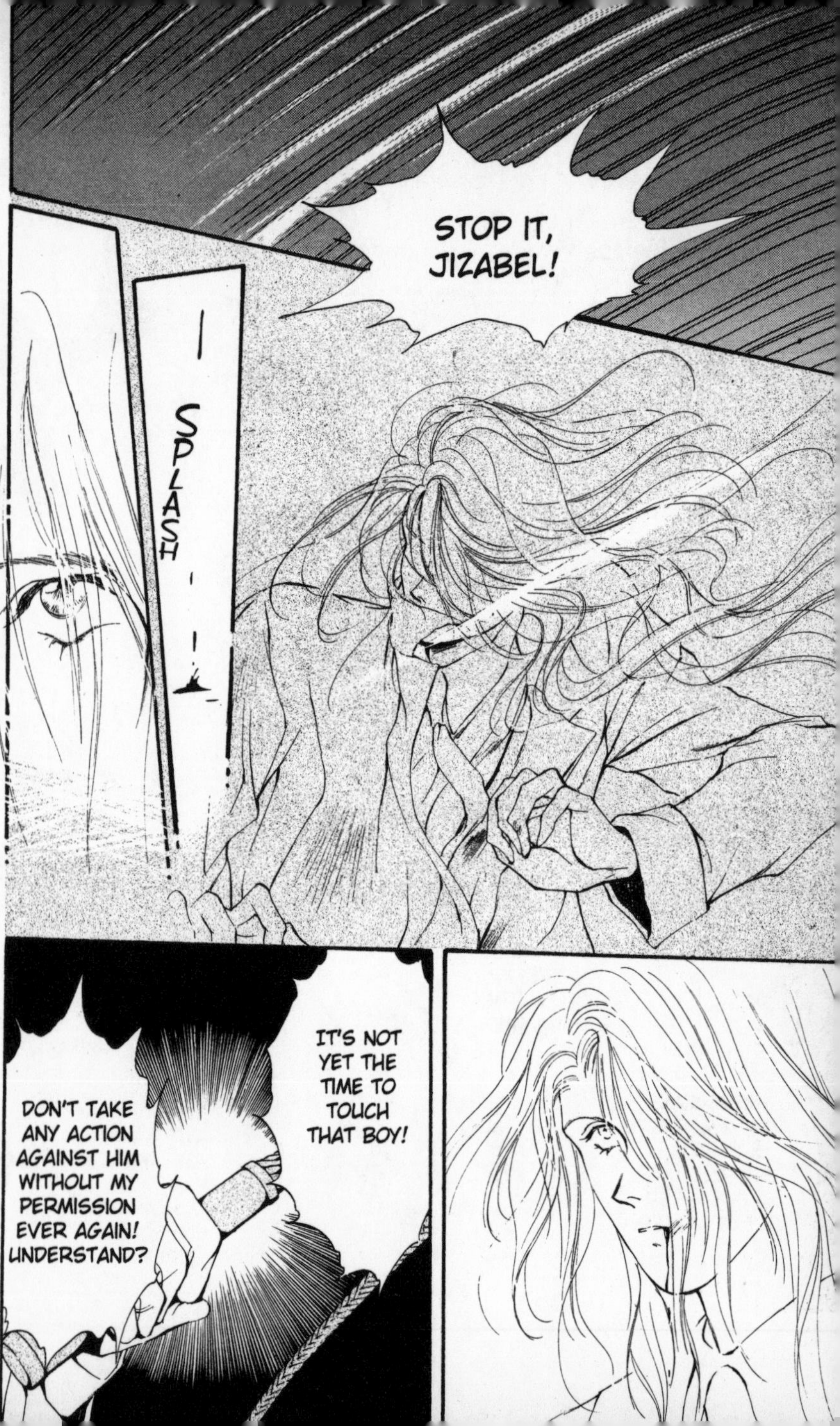
STOP IT, JIZABEL!
SPLASH
IT'S NOT YET THE TIME TO TOUCH THAT BOY!
DON'T TAKE ANY ACTION AGAINST HIM WITHOUT MY PERMISSION EVER AGAIN! UNDERSTAND?

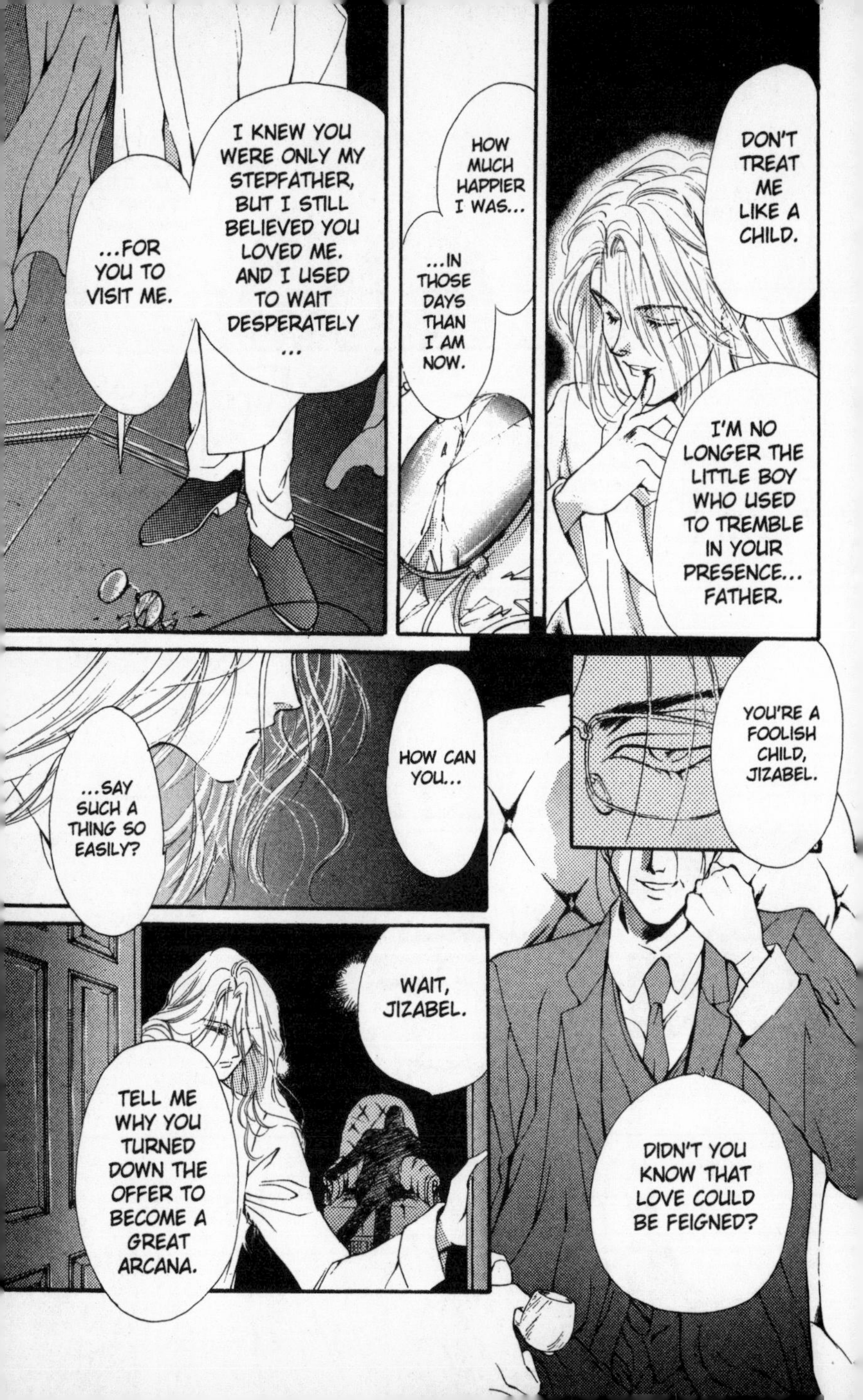
DON'T TREAT ME LIKE A CHILD.
I'M NO LONGER THE LITTLE BOY WHO USED TO TREMBLE IN YOUR PRESENCE... FATHER.
HOW MUCH HAPPIER I WAS...
...IN THOSE DAYS THAN I AM NOW.
I KNEW YOU WERE ONLY MY STEPFATHER, BUT I STILL BELIEVED YOU LOVED ME. AND I USED TO WAIT DESPERATELY ...
...FOR YOU TO VISIT ME.
YOU'RE A FOOLISH CHILD, JIZABEL.
HOW CAN YOU...
...SAY SUCH A THING SO EASILY?
DIDN'T YOU KNOW THAT LOVE COULD BE FEIGNED?
WAIT, JIZABEL.
TELL ME WHY YOU TURNED DOWN THE OFFER TO BECOME A GREAT ARCANA.

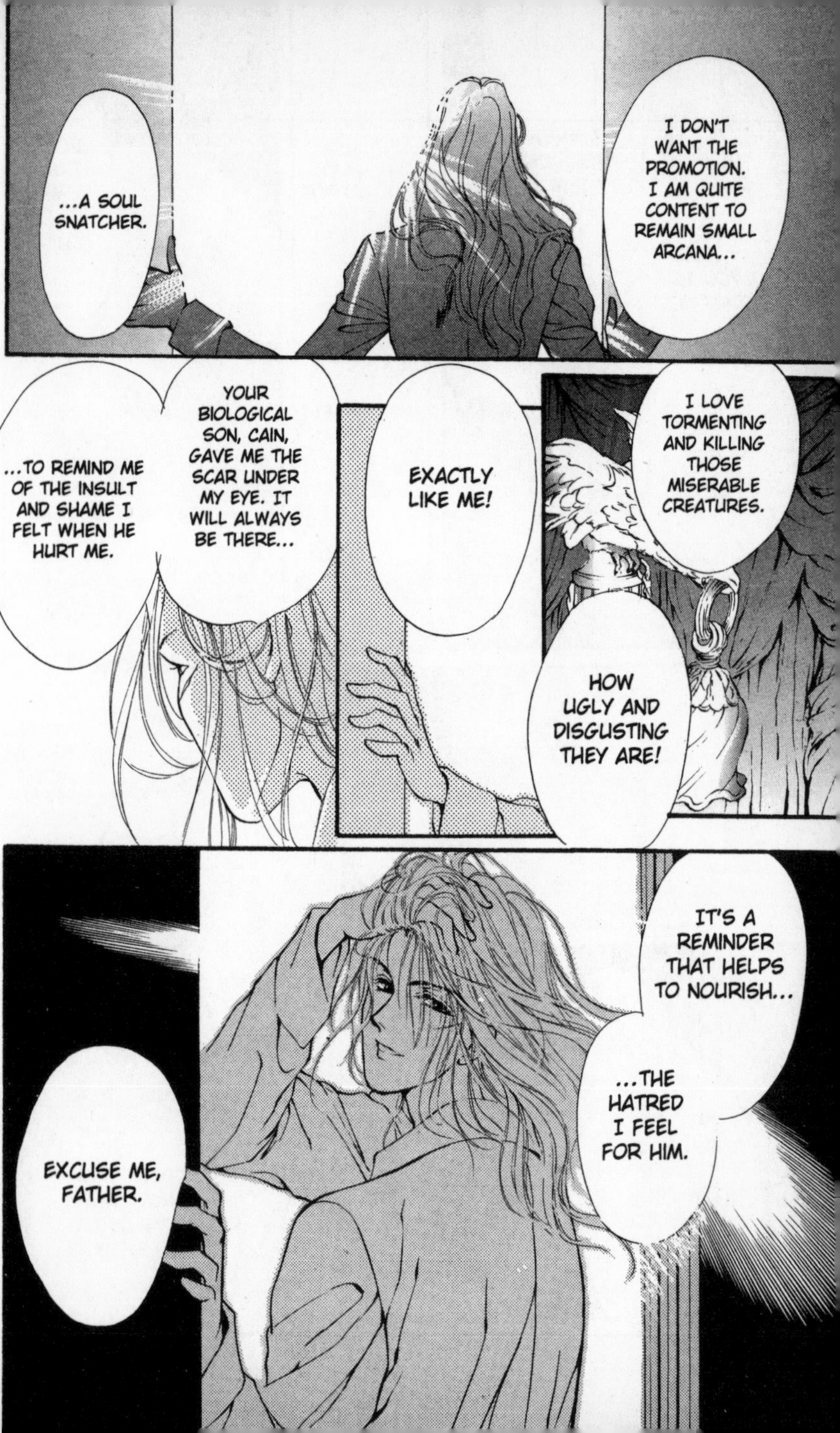
I DON'T WANT THE PROMOTION. I AM QUITE CONTENT TO REMAIN SMALL ARCANA...
...A SOUL SNATCHER.
I LOVE TORMENTING AND KILLING THOSE MISERABLE CREATURES.
HOW UGLY AND DISGUSTING THEY ARE!
EXACTLY LIKE ME!
YOUR BIOLOGICAL SON, CAIN, GAVE ME THE SCAR UNDER MY EYE. IT WILL ALWAYS BE THERE...
...TO REMIND ME OF THE INSULT AND SHAME I FELT WHEN HE HURT ME.
IT'S A REMINDER THAT HELPS TO NOURISH...
...THE HATRED I FEEL FOR HIM.
EXCUSE ME, FATHER.

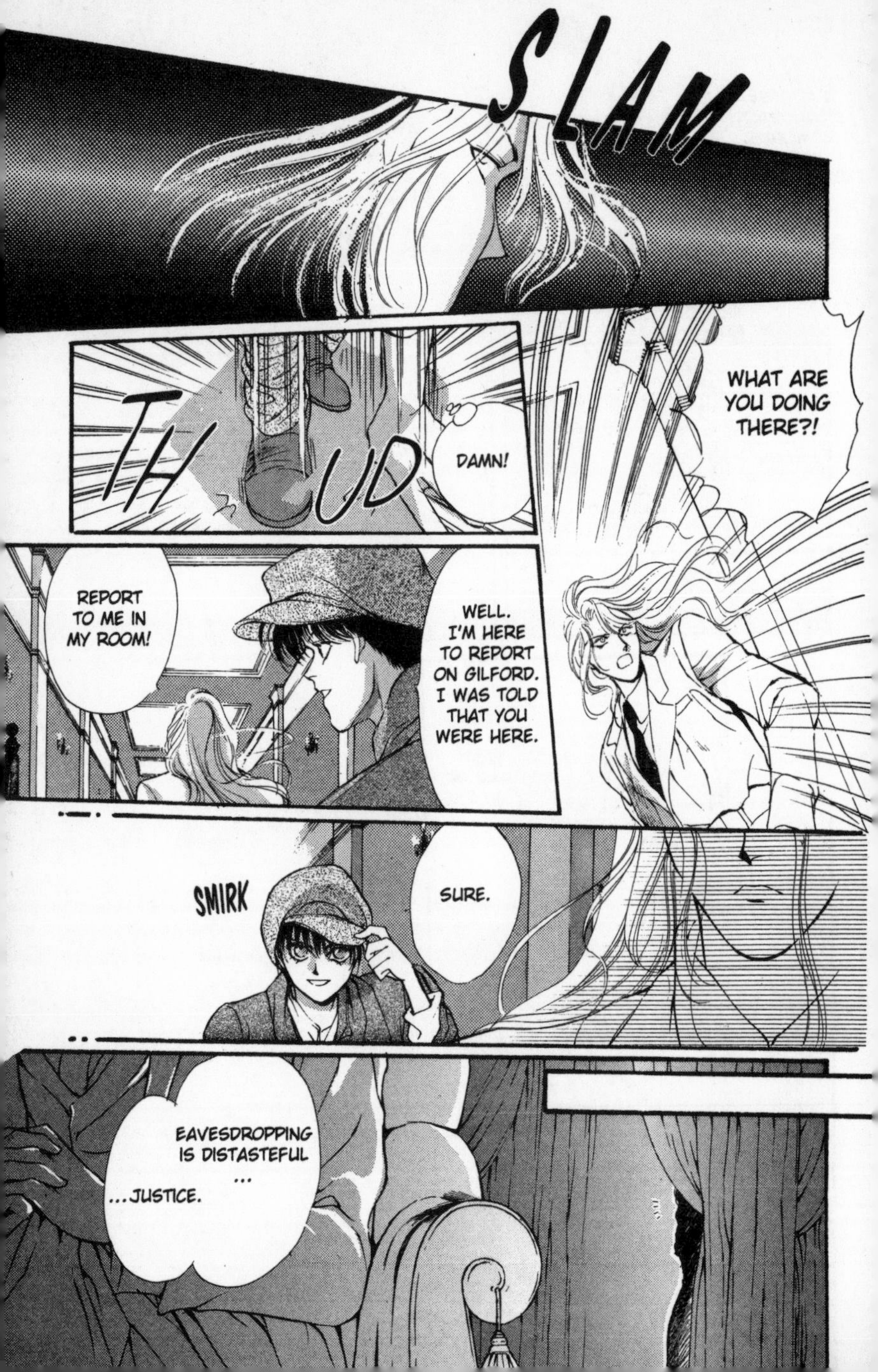
SLAM
WHAT ARE YOU DOING THERE?!
THUD
DAMN!
WELL. I'M HERE TO REPORT ON GILFORD. I WAS TOLD THAT YOU WERE HERE.
REPORT TO ME IN MY ROOM!
SURE.
SMIRK
EAVESDROPPING IS DISTASTEFUL ... ...JUSTICE.

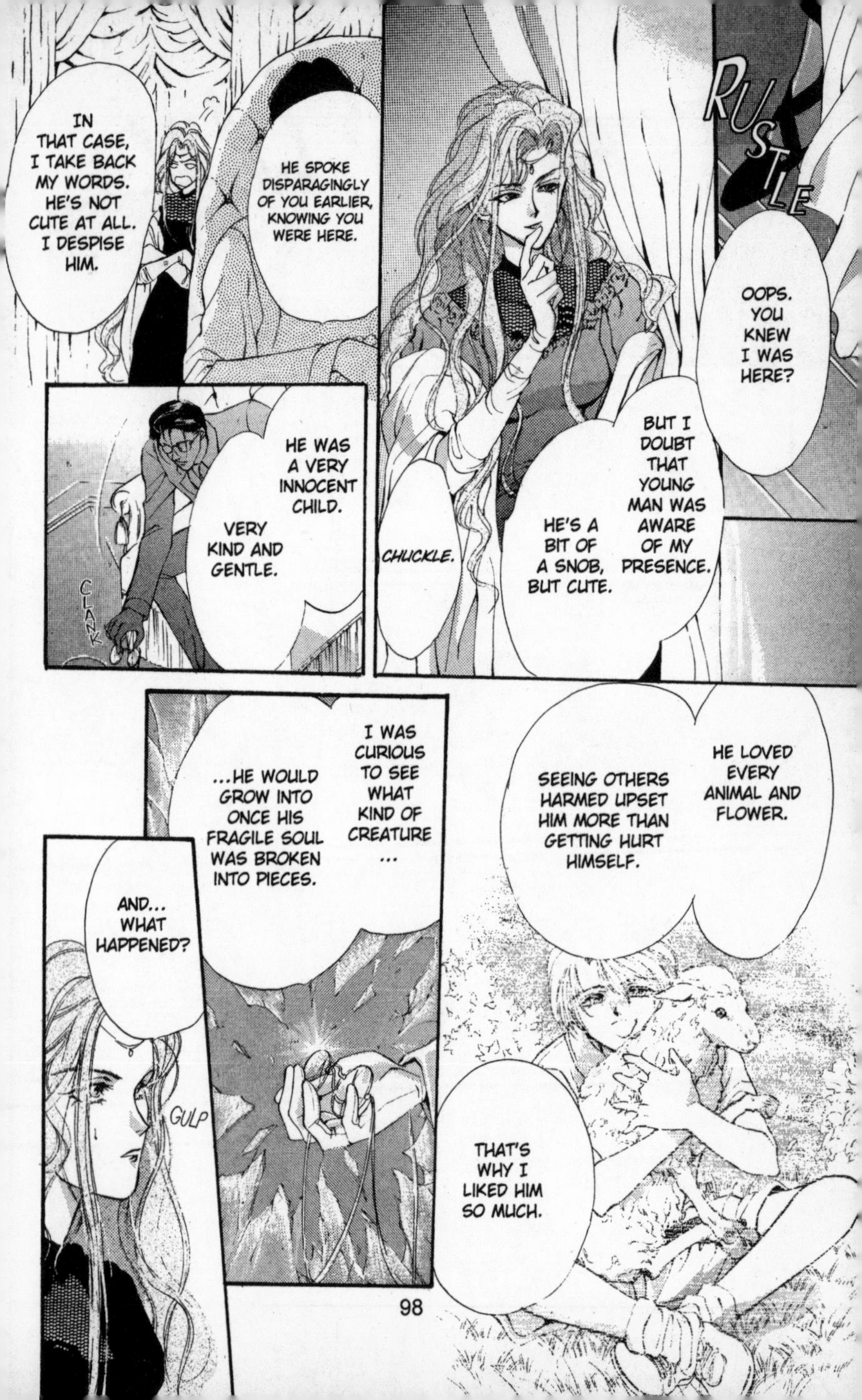
RUSTLE
OOPS. YOU KNEW I WAS HERE?
BUT I DOUBT THAT YOUNG MAN WAS AWARE OF MY PRESENCE.
HE'S A BIT OF A SNOB, BUT CUTE.
CHUCKLE.
HE SPOKE DISPARAGINGLY OF YOU EARLIER, KNOWING YOU WERE HERE.
IN THAT CASE, I TAKE BACK MY WORDS. HE'S NOT CUTE AT ALL. I DESPISE HIM.
HE WAS A VERY INNOCENT CHILD.
VERY KIND AND GENTLE.
CLANK
HE LOVED EVERY ANIMAL AND FLOWER.
SEEING OTHERS HARMED UPSET HIM MORE THAN GETTING HURT HIMSELF.
THAT'S WHY I LIKED HIM SO MUCH.
I WAS CURIOUS TO SEE WHAT KIND OF CREATURE ...
...HE WOULD GROW INTO ONCE HIS FRAGILE SOUL WAS BROKEN INTO PIECES.
AND... WHAT HAPPENED?
GULP

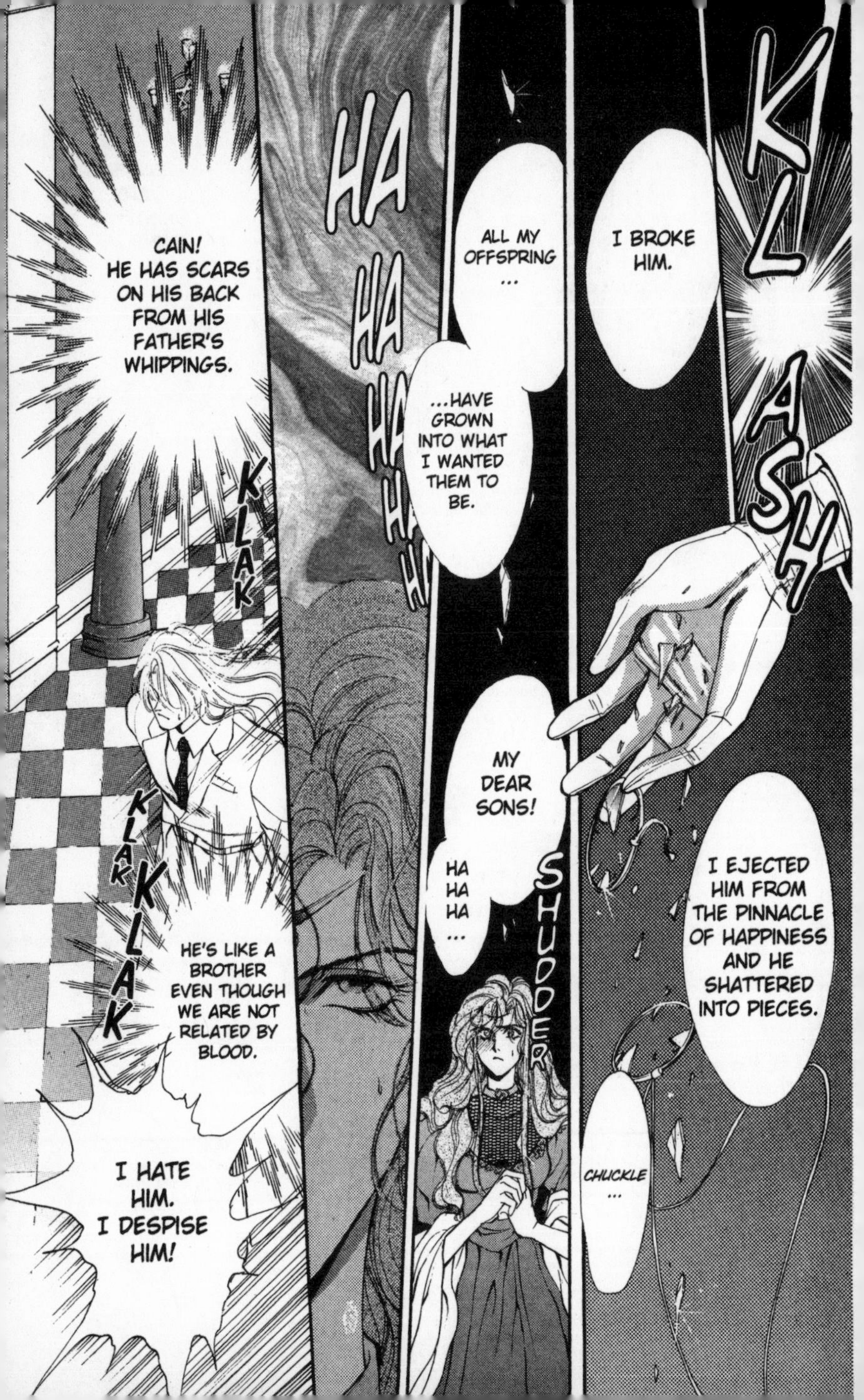
KLLASH
I BROKE HIM.
I EJECTED HIM FROM THE PINNACLE OF HAPPINESS AND HE SHATTERED INTO PIECES.
CHUCKLE...
ALL MY OFFSPRING...
...HAVE GROWN INTO WHAT I WANTED THEM TO BE.
MY DEAR SONS!
SHUDDER
HA HA HA...
HA HA HA HA HA
CAIN! HE HAS SCARS ON HIS BACK FROM HIS FATHER'S WHIPPINGS.
KLAK
KLAK KLAK
HE'S LIKE A BROTHER EVEN THOUGH WE ARE NOT RELATED BY BLOOD.
I HATE HIM. I DESPISE HIM!

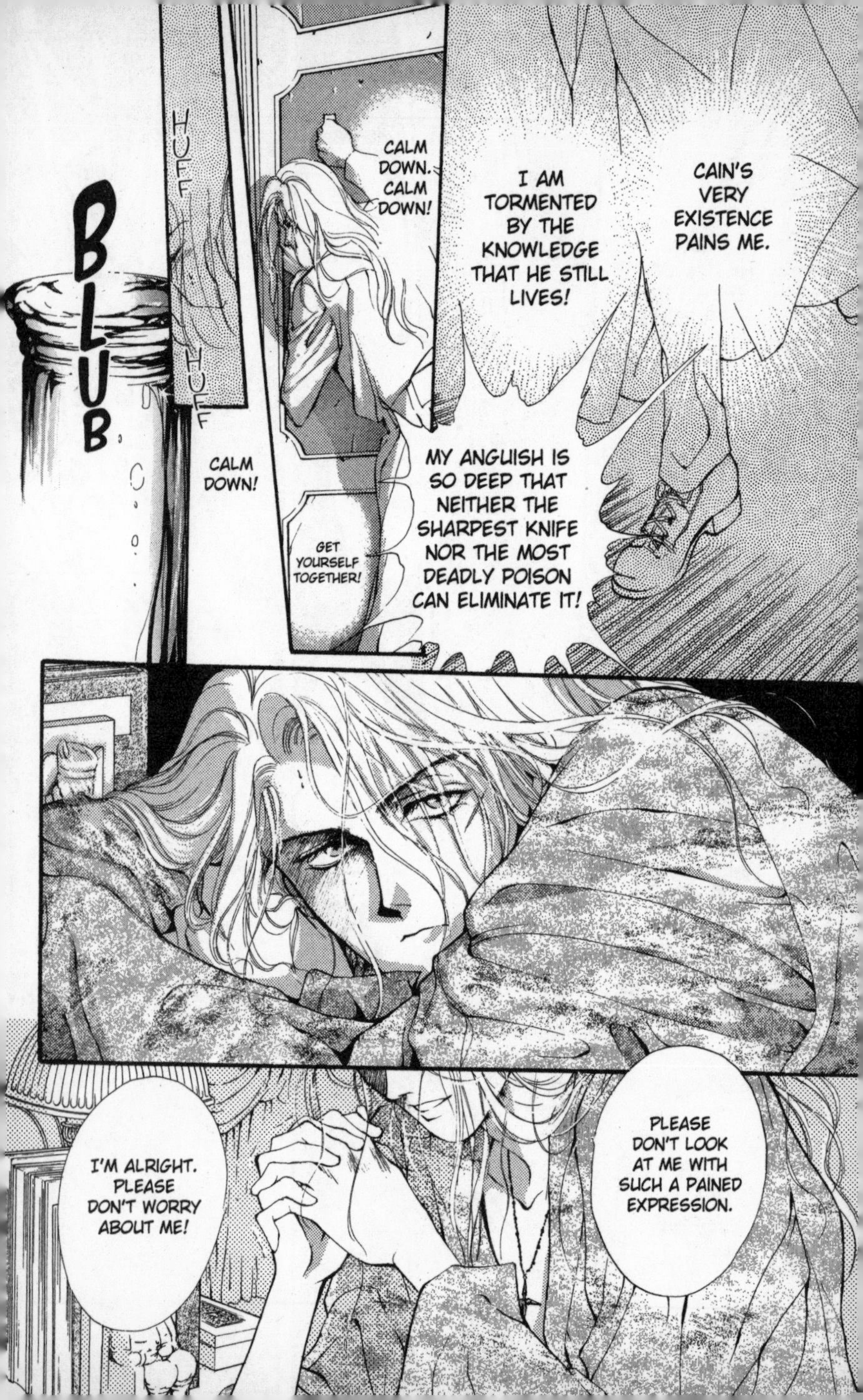
CAIN'S VERY EXISTENCE PAINS ME.
I AM TORMENTED BY THE KNOWLEDGE THAT HE STILL LIVES!
MY ANGUISH IS SO DEEP THAT NEITHER THE SHARPEST KNIFE NOR THE MOST DEADLY POISON CAN ELIMINATE IT!
HUFF
CALM DOWN. CALM DOWN!
HUFF
BLUB
CALM DOWN!
GET YOURSELF TOGETHER!
PLEASE DON'T LOOK AT ME WITH SUCH A PAINED EXPRESSION.
I'M ALRIGHT. PLEASE DON'T WORRY ABOUT ME!

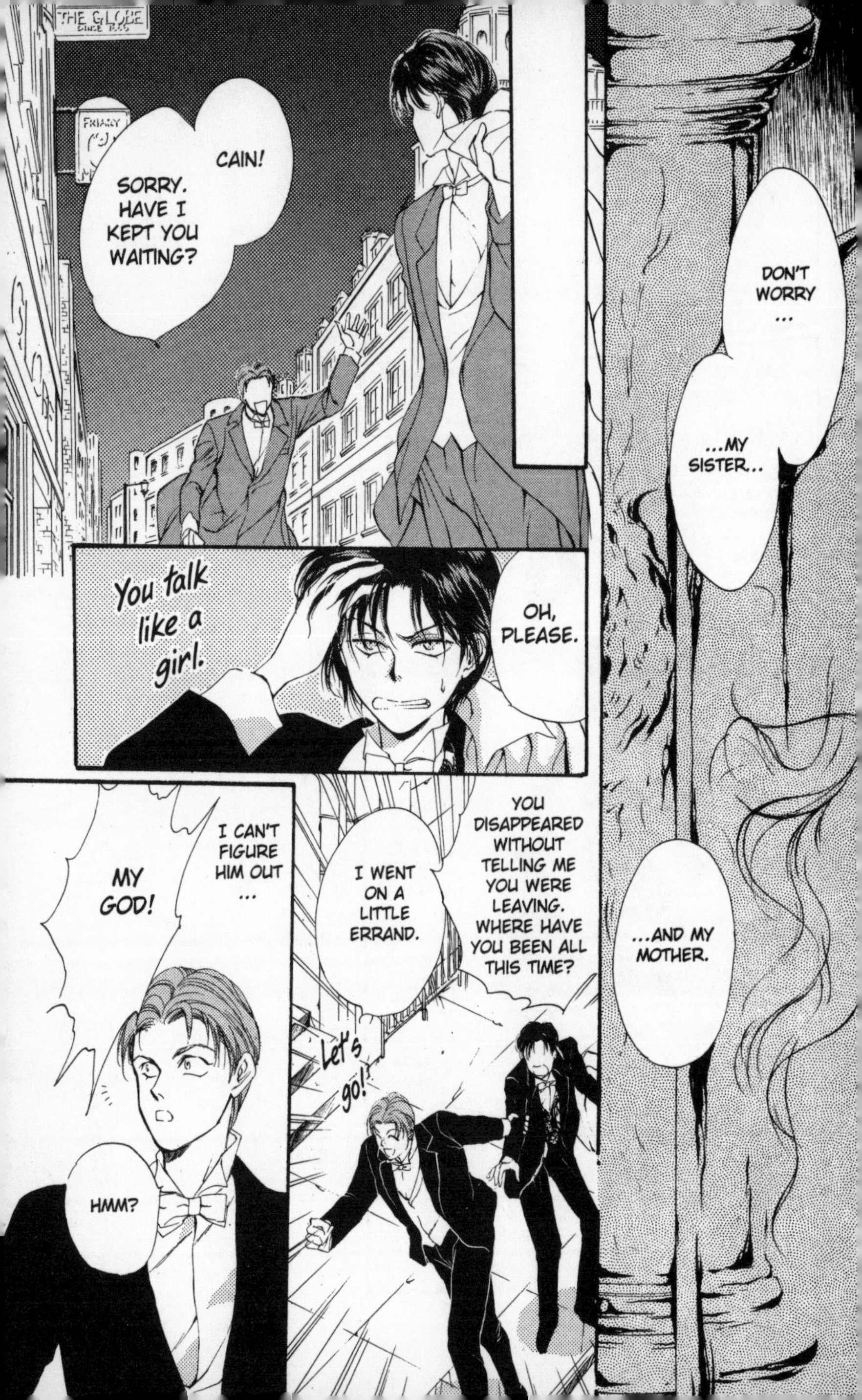
DON'T WORRY ...
...MY SISTER...
...AND MY MOTHER.
THE GLOBE
CAIN!
SORRY. HAVE I KEPT YOU WAITING?
OH, PLEASE.
You talk like a girl.
YOU DISAPPEARED WITHOUT TELLING ME YOU WERE LEAVING. WHERE HAVE YOU BEEN ALL THIS TIME?
I WENT ON A LITTLE ERRAND.
Let's go!
I CAN'T FIGURE HIM OUT ...
MY GOD!
HMM?

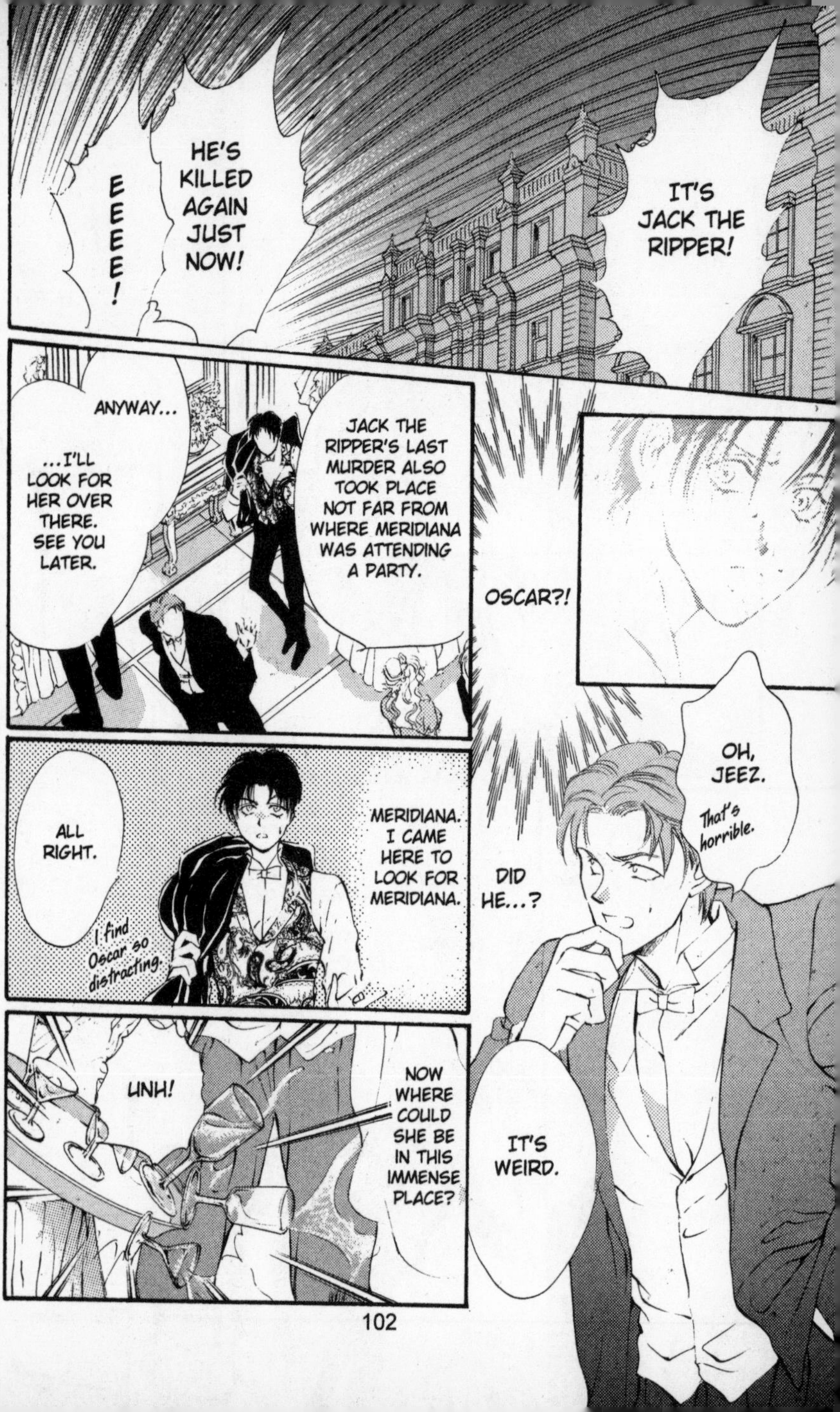
IT'S JACK THE RIPPER!
HE'S KILLED AGAIN JUST NOW!
EEEEE!
OSCAR?!
OH, JEEZ.
That's horrible.
DID HE...?
IT'S WEIRD.
JACK THE RIPPER'S LAST MURDER ALSO TOOK PLACE NOT FAR FROM WHERE MERIDIANA WAS ATTENDING A PARTY.
ANYWAY...
...I'LL LOOK FOR HER OVER THERE. SEE YOU LATER.
MERIDIANA. I CAME HERE TO LOOK FOR MERIDIANA.
ALL RIGHT.
I find Oscar so distracting.
NOW WHERE COULD SHE BE IN THIS IMMENSE PLACE?
UNH!

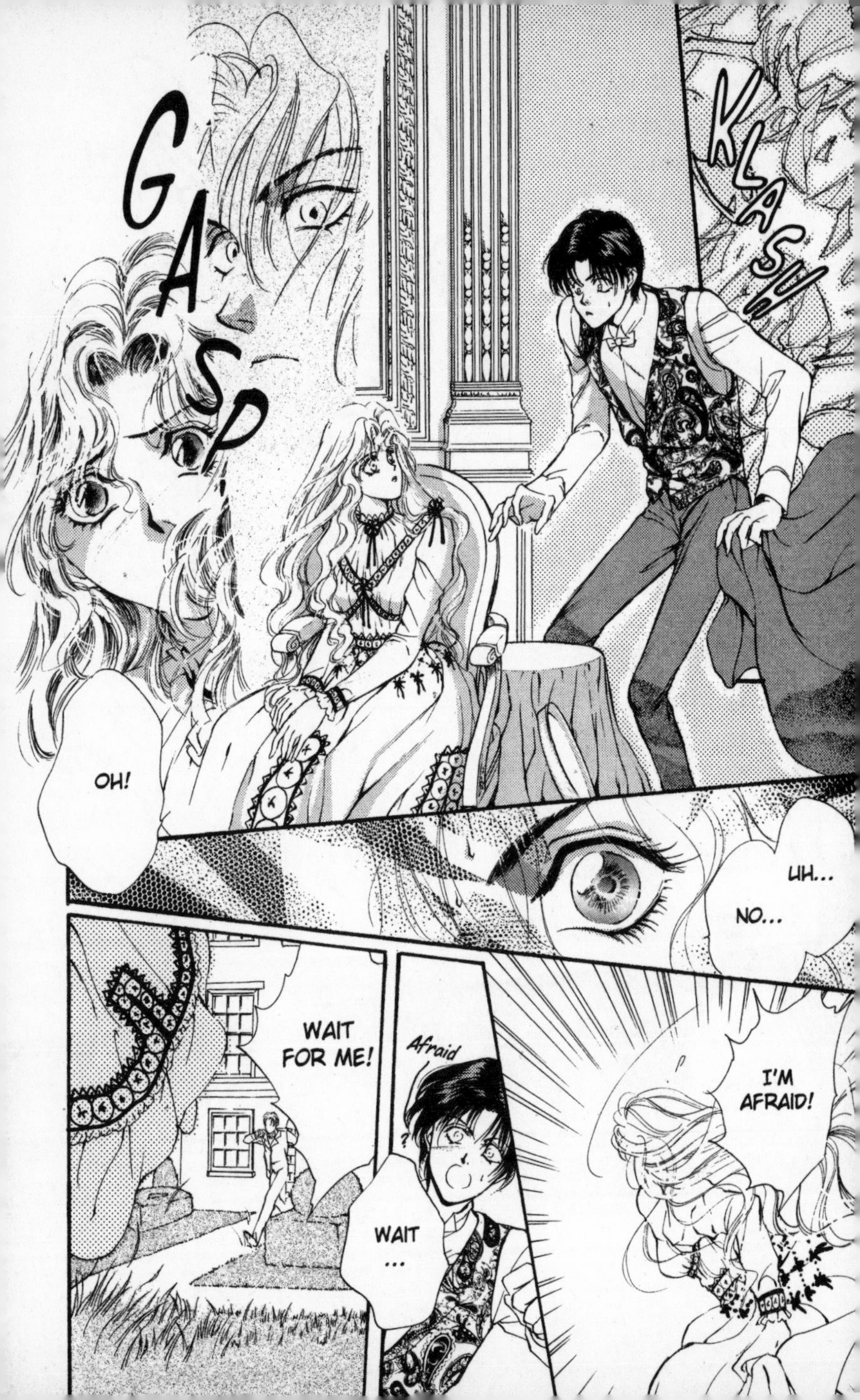
KLASH
GASP
OH!
UH...
NO...
I'M AFRAID!
Afraid
WAIT ...
WAIT FOR ME!

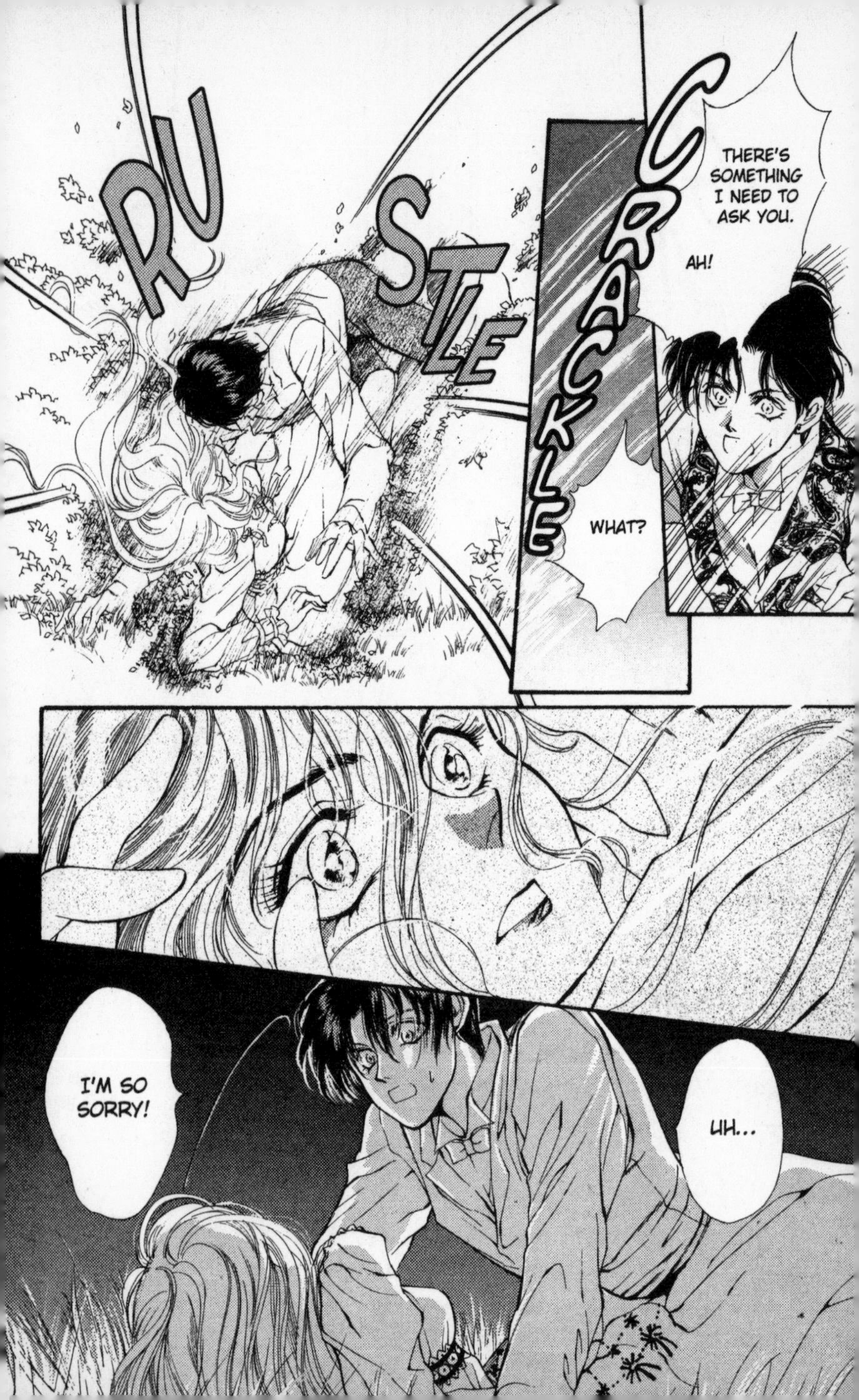
THERE'S SOMETHING I NEED TO ASK YOU.
AH!
CRACKLE
WHAT?
RUSTLE
UH...
I'M SO SORRY!

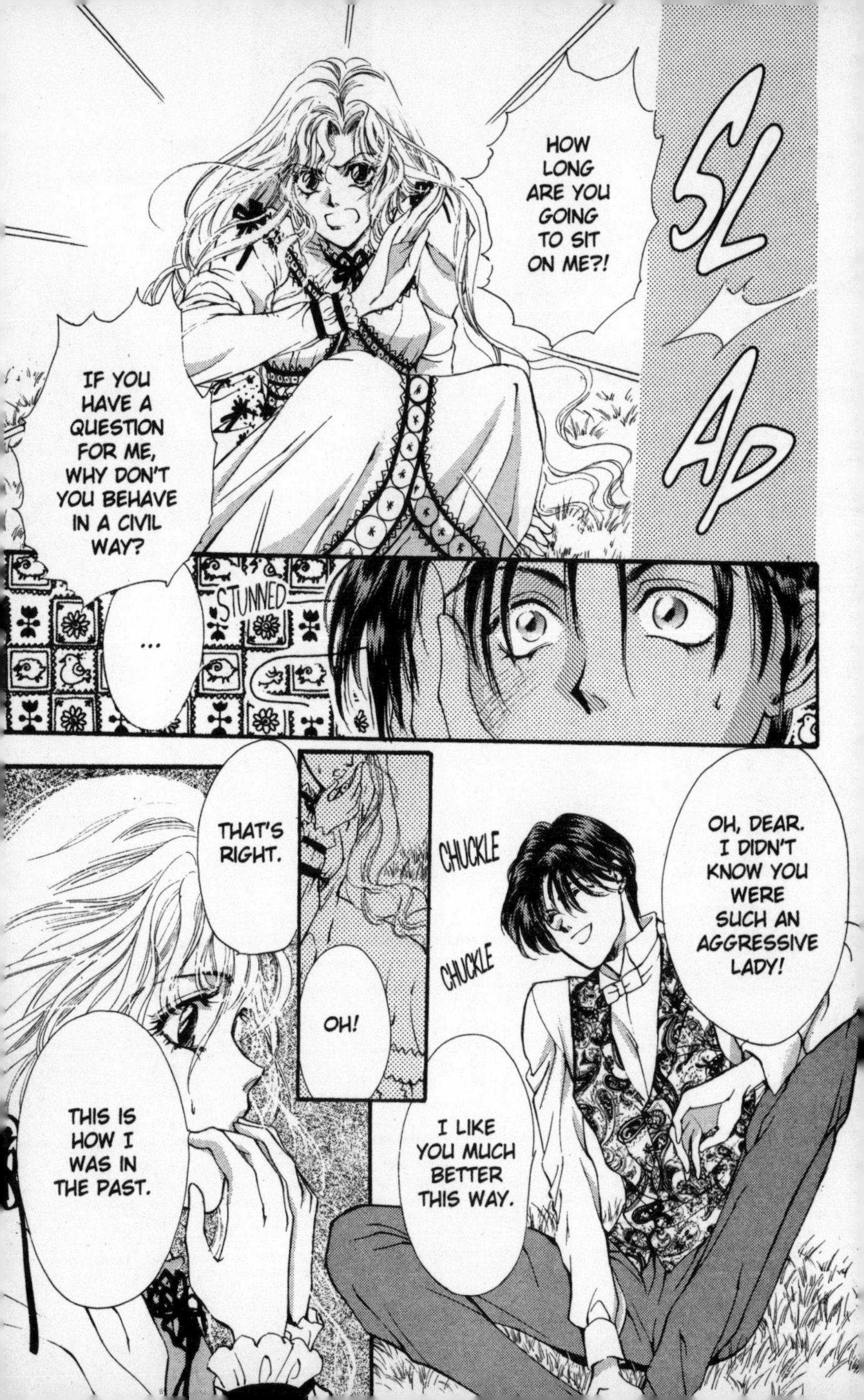
SLAP
HOW LONG ARE YOU GOING TO SIT ON ME?!
IF YOU HAVE A QUESTION FOR ME, WHY DON'T YOU BEHAVE IN A CIVIL WAY?
STUNNED
...
OH, DEAR. I DIDN'T KNOW YOU WERE SUCH AN AGGRESSIVE LADY!
CHUCKLE
CHUCKLE
I LIKE YOU MUCH BETTER THIS WAY.
OH!
THAT'S RIGHT.
THIS IS HOW I WAS IN THE PAST.

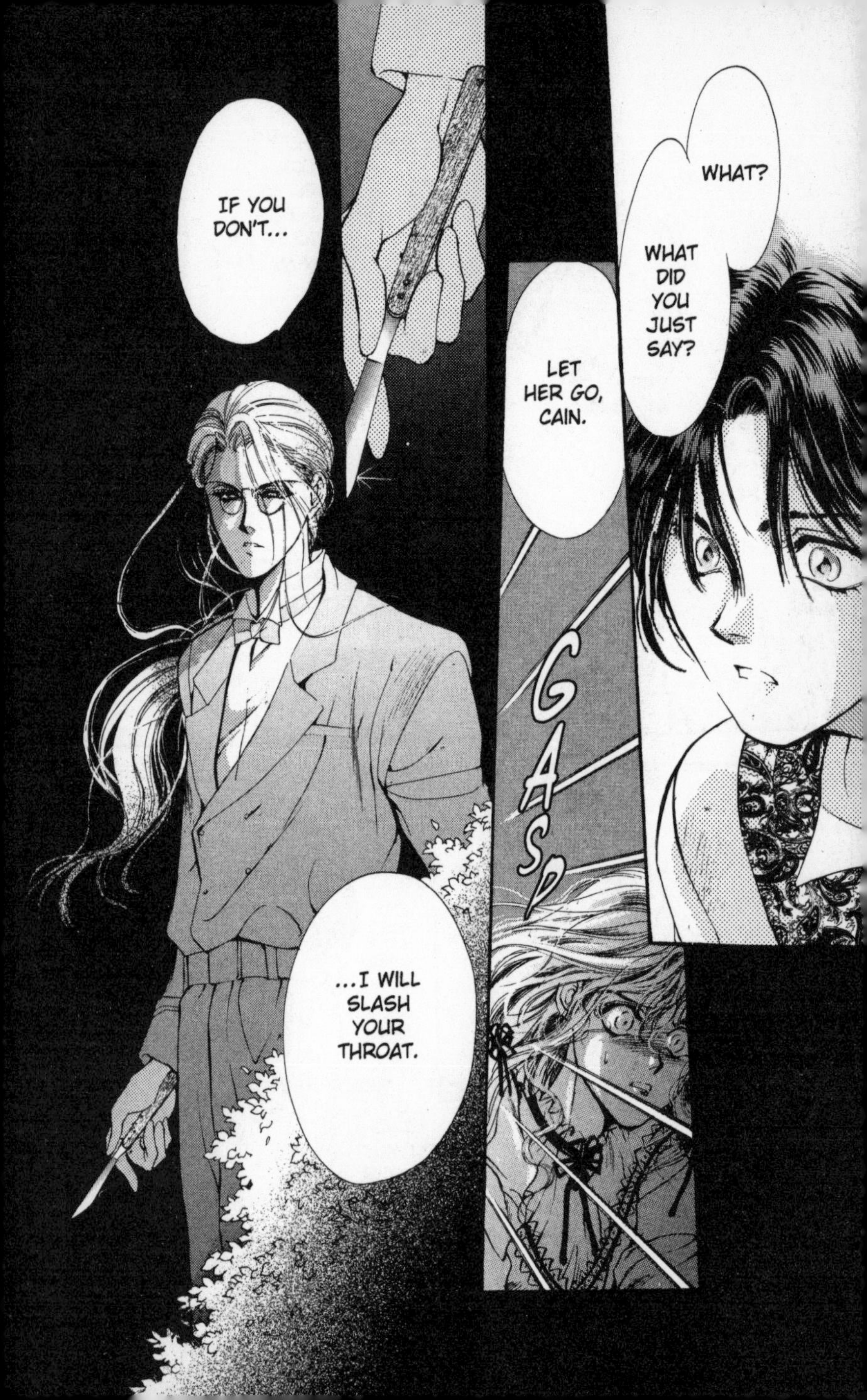
WHAT?
WHAT DID YOU JUST SAY?
LET HER GO, CAIN.
GASP
IF YOU DON'T...
...I WILL SLASH YOUR THROAT.

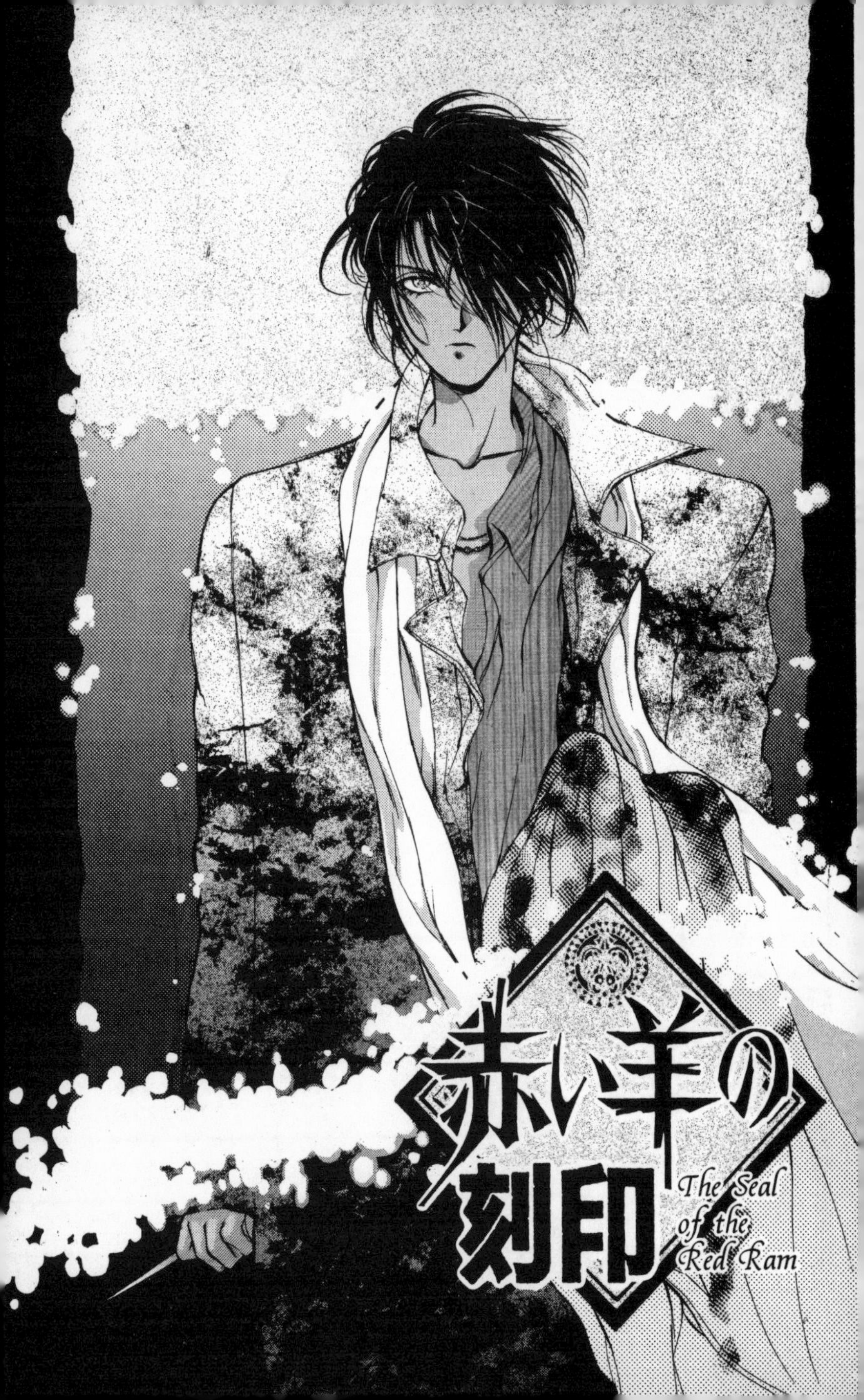
赤い羊の刻印
The Seal of the Red Ram

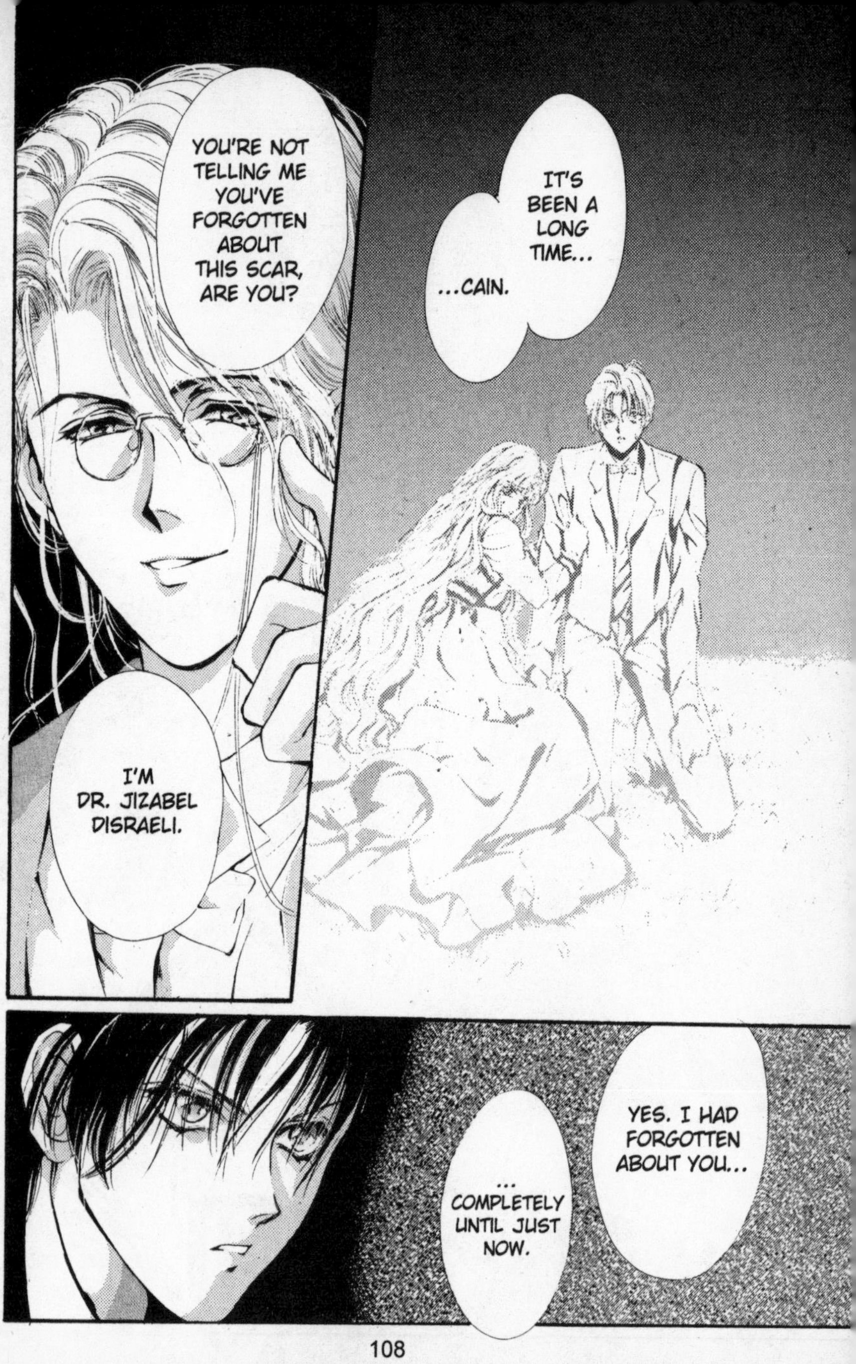
IT'S BEEN A LONG TIME...
...CAIN.
YOU'RE NOT TELLING ME YOU'VE FORGOTTEN ABOUT THIS SCAR, ARE YOU?
I'M DR. JIZABEL DISRAELI.
YES. I HAD FORGOTTEN ABOUT YOU...
...COMPLETELY UNTIL JUST NOW.

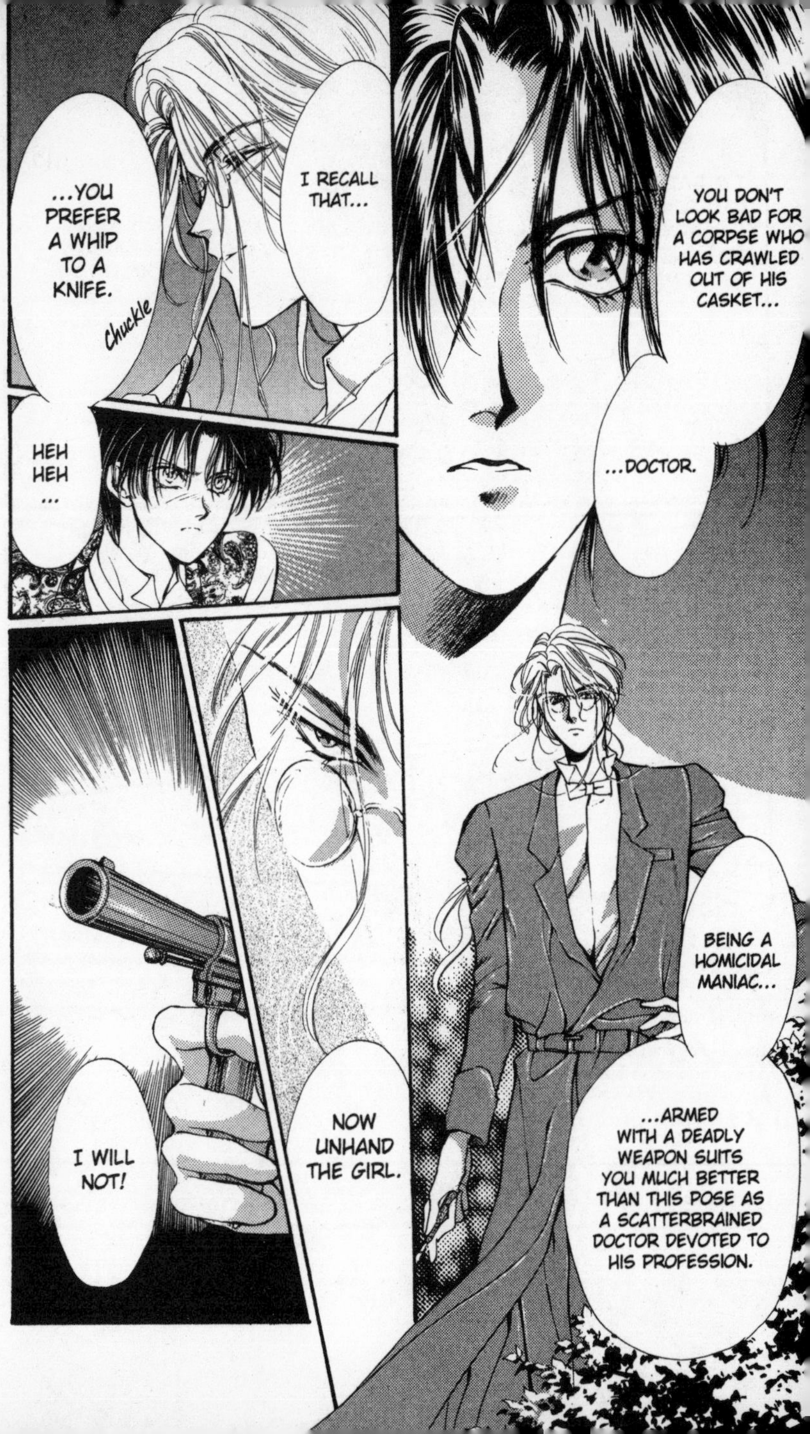
YOU DON'T LOOK BAD FOR A CORPSE WHO HAS CRAWLED OUT OF HIS CASKET...
...DOCTOR.
BEING A HOMICIDAL MANIAC...
...ARMED WITH A DEADLY WEAPON SUITS YOU MUCH BETTER THAN THIS POSE AS A SCATTERBRAINED DOCTOR DEVOTED TO HIS PROFESSION.
I RECALL THAT...
...YOU PREFER A WHIP TO A KNIFE.
Chuckle
HEH HEH ...
NOW UNHAND THE GIRL.
I WILL NOT!

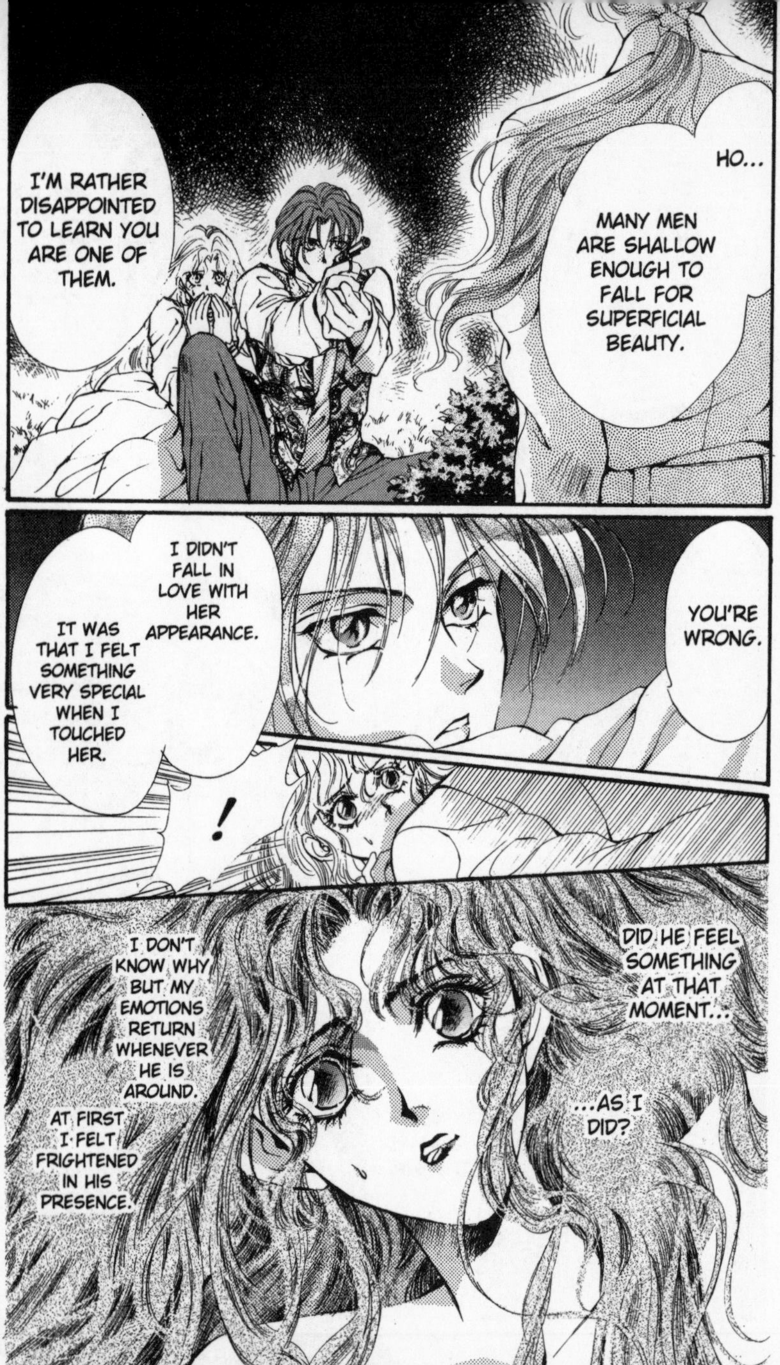
HO...
MANY MEN ARE SHALLOW ENOUGH TO FALL FOR SUPERFICIAL BEAUTY.
I'M RATHER DISAPPOINTED TO LEARN YOU ARE ONE OF THEM.
YOU'RE WRONG.
I DIDN'T FALL IN LOVE WITH HER APPEARANCE.
IT WAS THAT I FELT SOMETHING VERY SPECIAL WHEN I TOUCHED HER.
!
DID HE FEEL SOMETHING AT THAT MOMENT...
...AS I DID?
I DON'T KNOW WHY BUT MY EMOTIONS RETURN WHENEVER HE IS AROUND.
AT FIRST I FELT FRIGHTENED IN HIS PRESENCE.

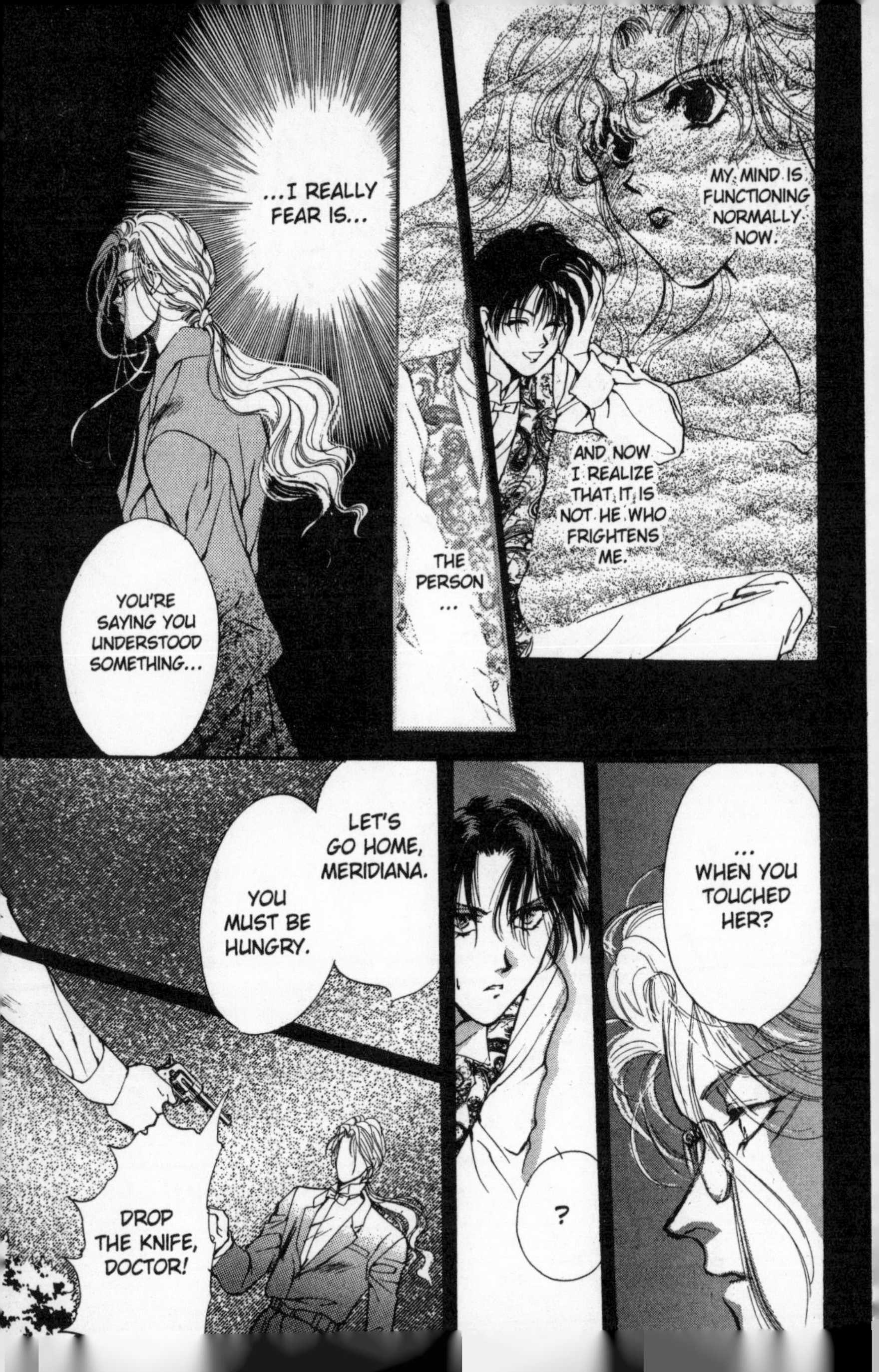
MY MIND IS FUNCTIONING NORMALLY NOW.
AND NOW I REALIZE THAT IT IS NOT HE WHO FRIGHTENS ME.
THE PERSON ...
...I REALLY FEAR IS...
YOU'RE SAYING YOU UNDERSTOOD SOMETHING...
... WHEN YOU TOUCHED HER?
?
LET'S GO HOME, MERIDIANA.
YOU MUST BE HUNGRY.
DROP THE KNIFE, DOCTOR!

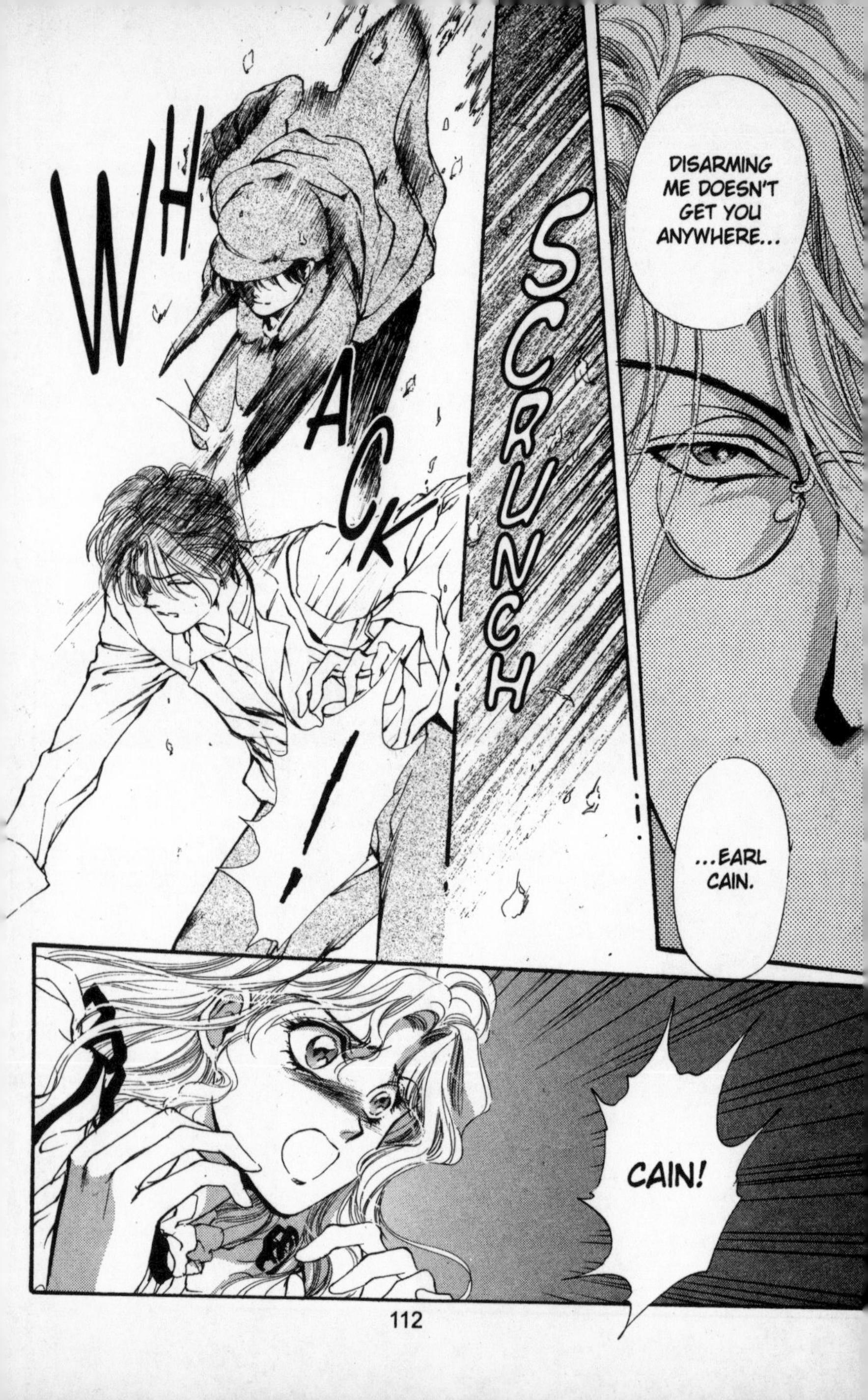
DISARMING ME DOESN'T GET YOU ANYWHERE...
...EARL CAIN.
SCRUNCH
WHACK
CAIN!

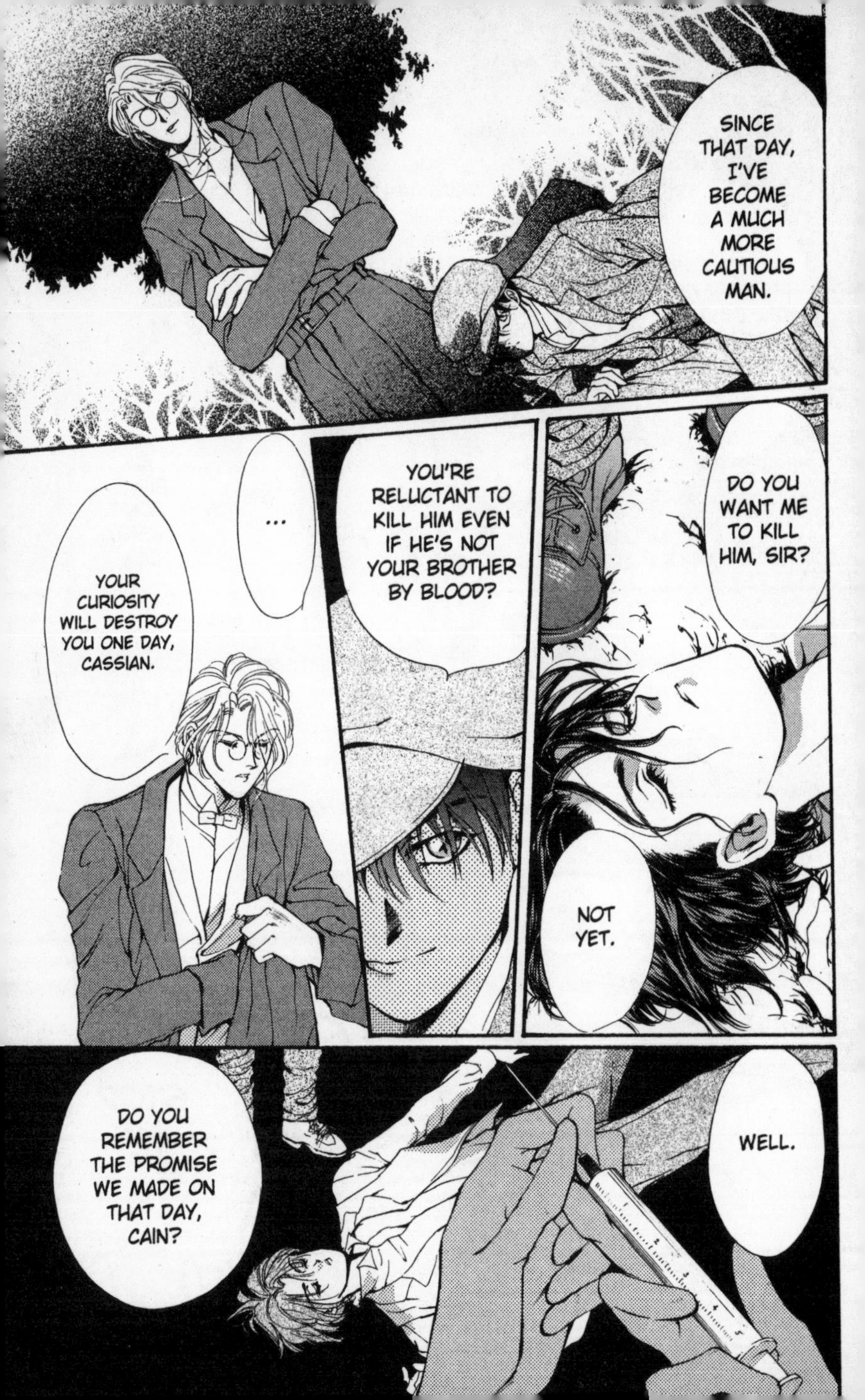
SINCE THAT DAY, I'VE BECOME A MUCH MORE CAUTIOUS MAN.
DO YOU WANT ME TO KILL HIM, SIR?
NOT YET.
YOU'RE RELUCTANT TO KILL HIM EVEN IF HE'S NOT YOUR BROTHER BY BLOOD?
...
YOUR CURIOSITY WILL DESTROY YOU ONE DAY, CASSIAN.
WELL.
DO YOU REMEMBER THE PROMISE WE MADE ON THAT DAY, CAIN?

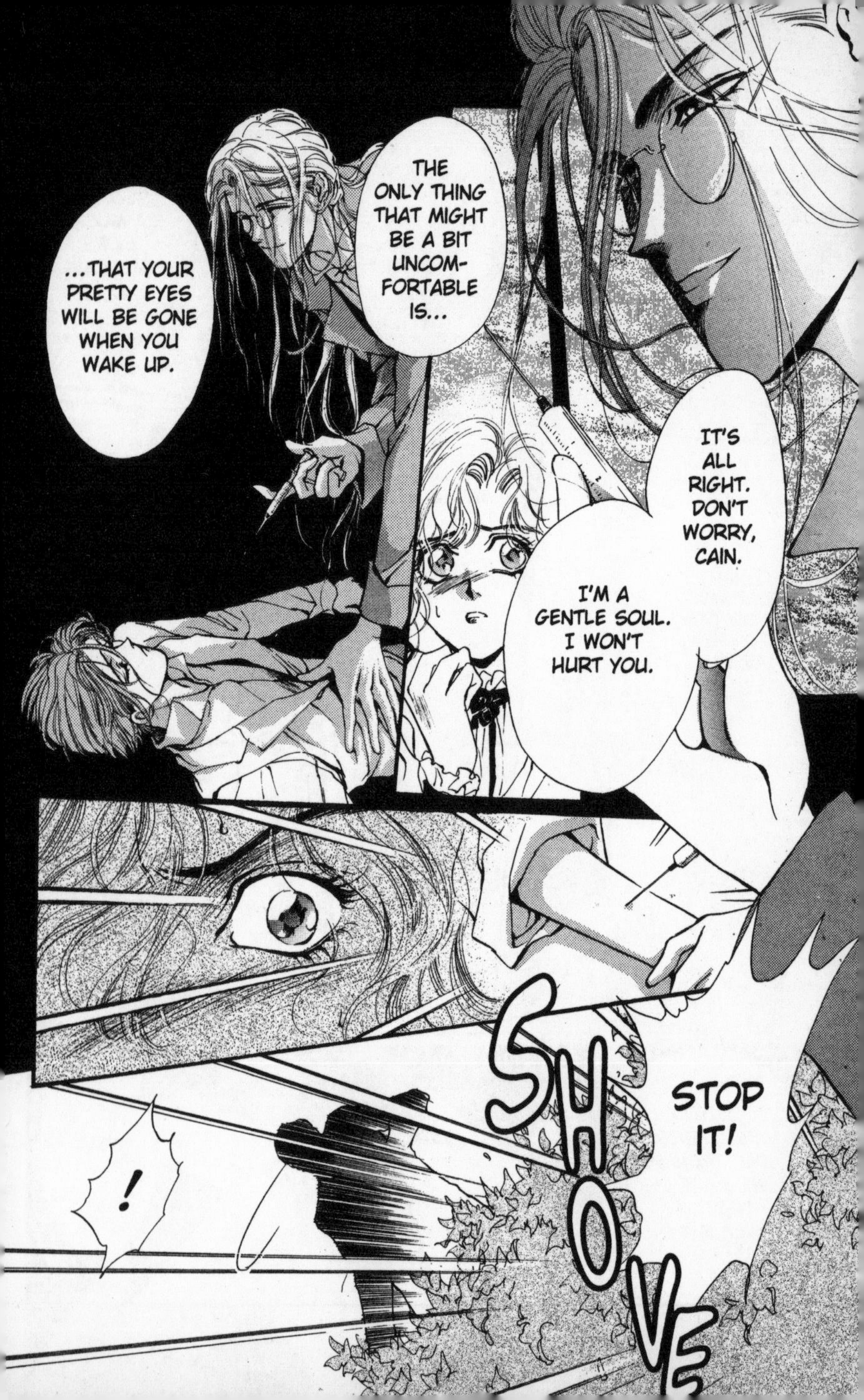
IT'S ALL RIGHT. DON'T WORRY, CAIN.
I'M A GENTLE SOUL. I WON'T HURT YOU.
THE ONLY THING THAT MIGHT BE A BIT UNCOM-FORTABLE IS...
...THAT YOUR PRETTY EYES WILL BE GONE WHEN YOU WAKE UP.
SHOVE
STOP IT!
!

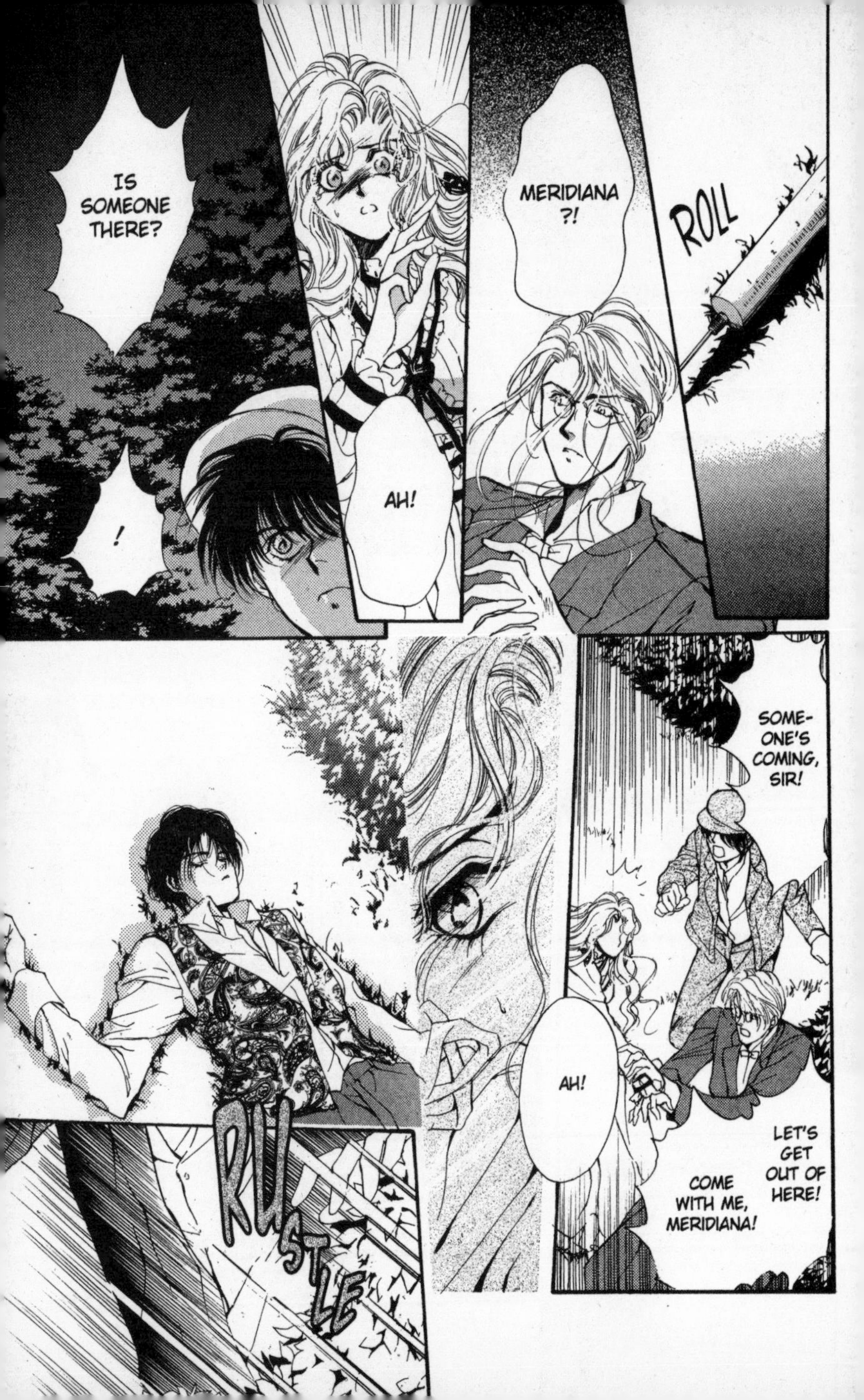
ROLL
MERIDIANA ?!
AH!
IS SOMEONE THERE?
!
SOME-ONE'S COMING, SIR!
LET'S GET OUT OF HERE!
COME WITH ME, MERIDIANA!
AH!
RUSTLE

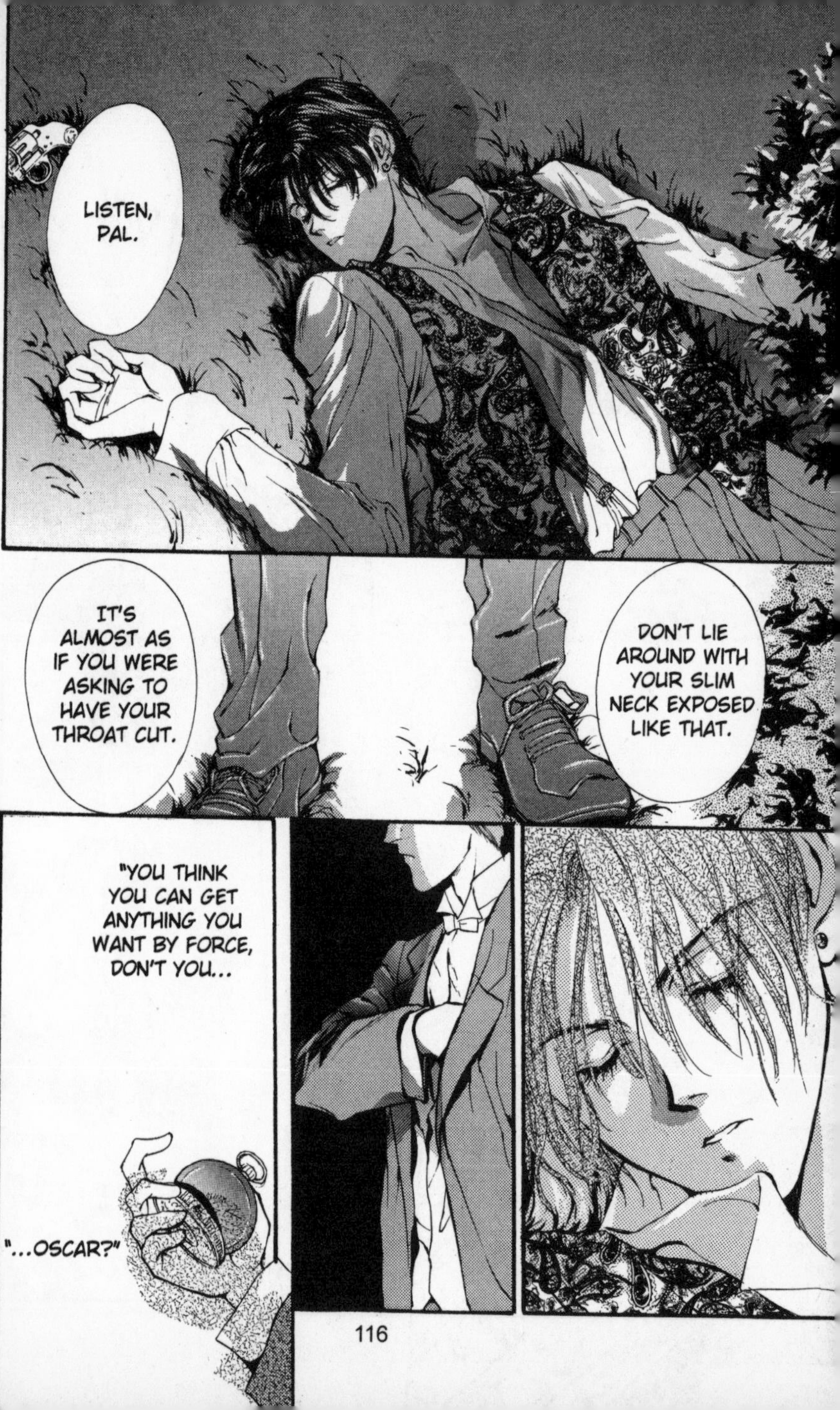
LISTEN, PAL.
DON'T LIE AROUND WITH YOUR SLIM NECK EXPOSED LIKE THAT.
IT'S ALMOST AS IF YOU WERE ASKING TO HAVE YOUR THROAT CUT.
"YOU THINK YOU CAN GET ANYTHING YOU WANT BY FORCE, DON'T YOU...
"...OSCAR?"

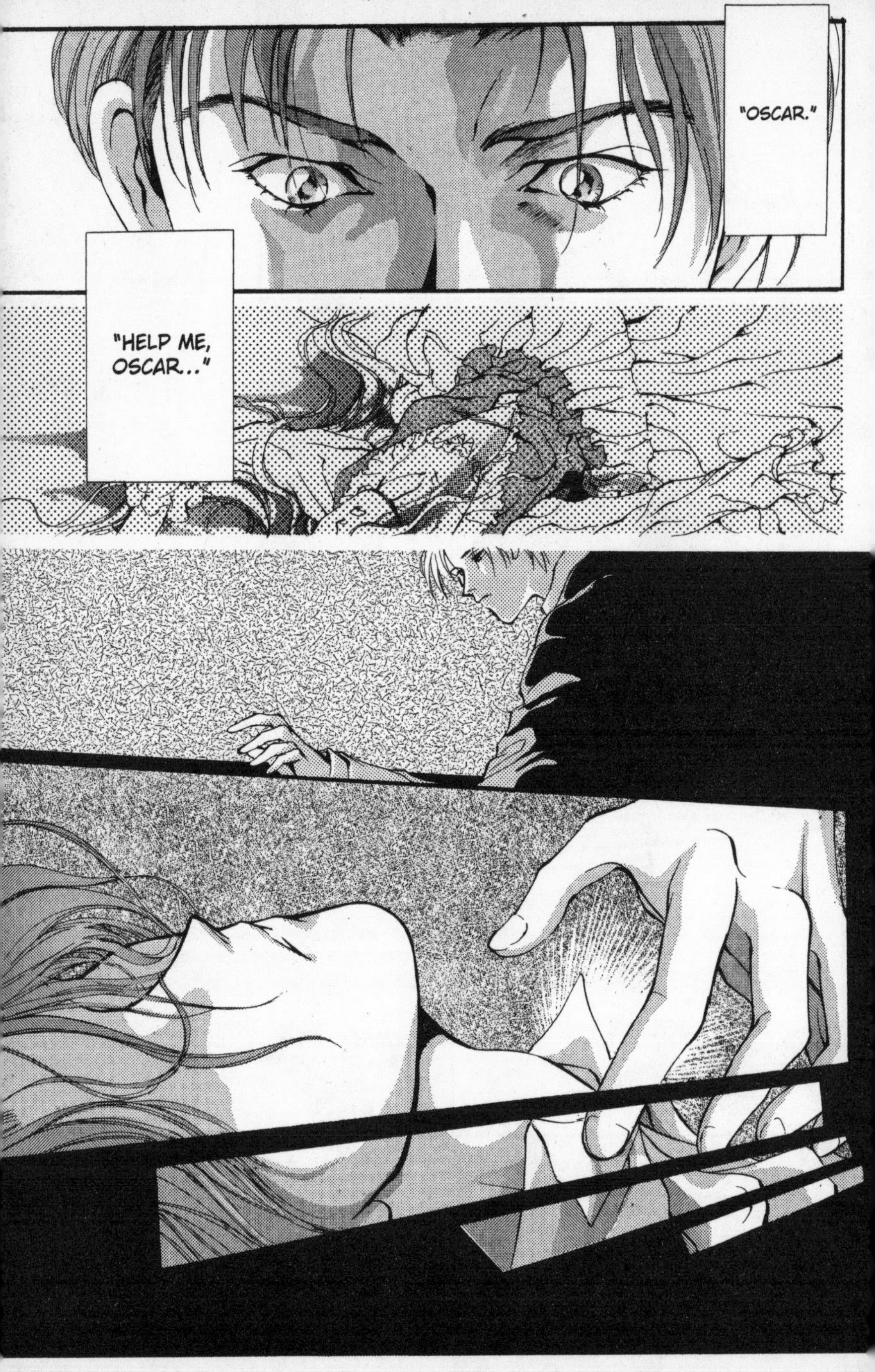
"OSCAR."
"HELP ME, OSCAR..."

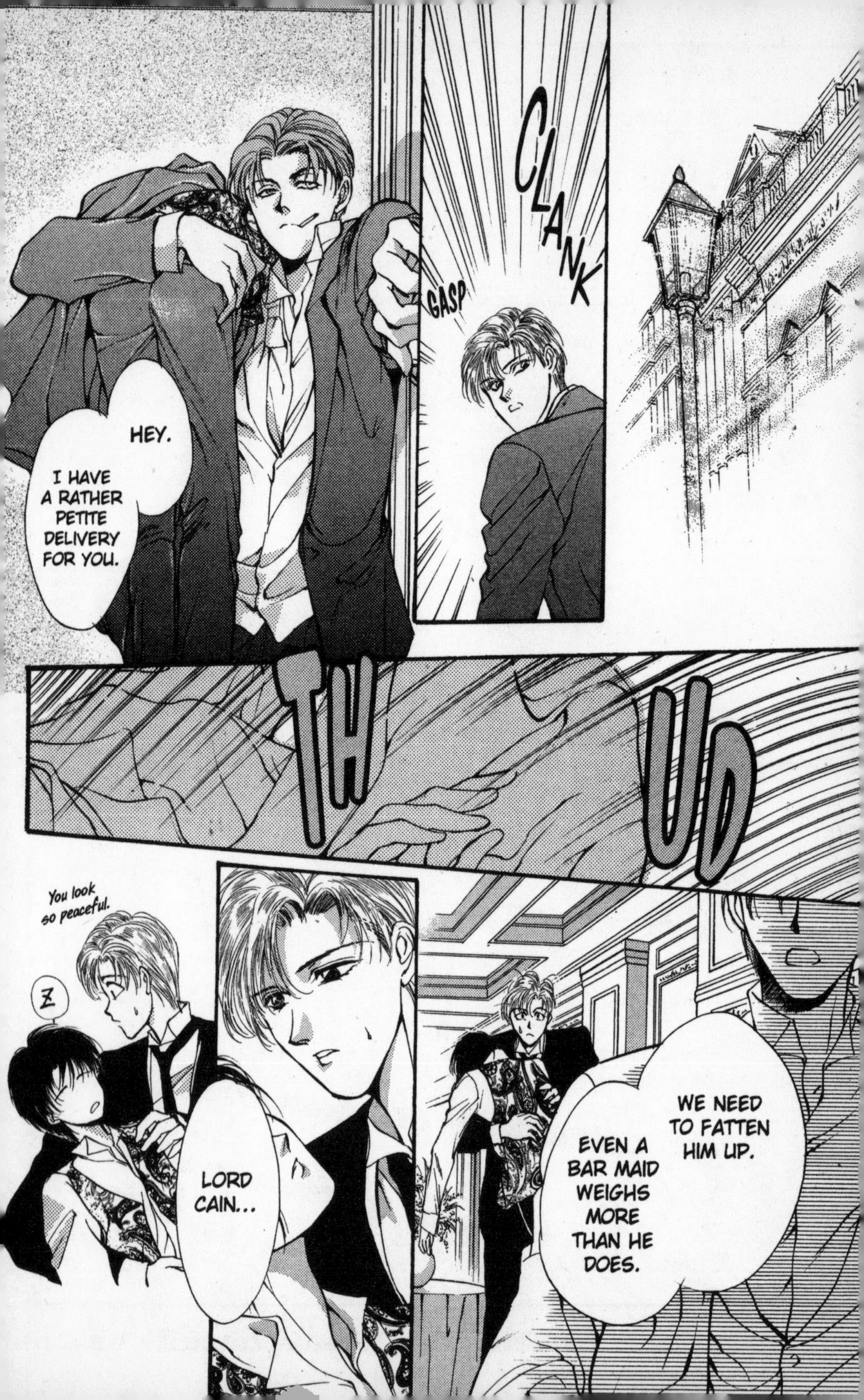
CLANK
GASP
HEY.
I HAVE A RATHER PETITE DELIVERY FOR YOU.
THUD
WE NEED TO FATTEN HIM UP.
EVEN A BAR MAID WEIGHS MORE THAN HE DOES.
LORD CAIN...
You look so peaceful.
Z

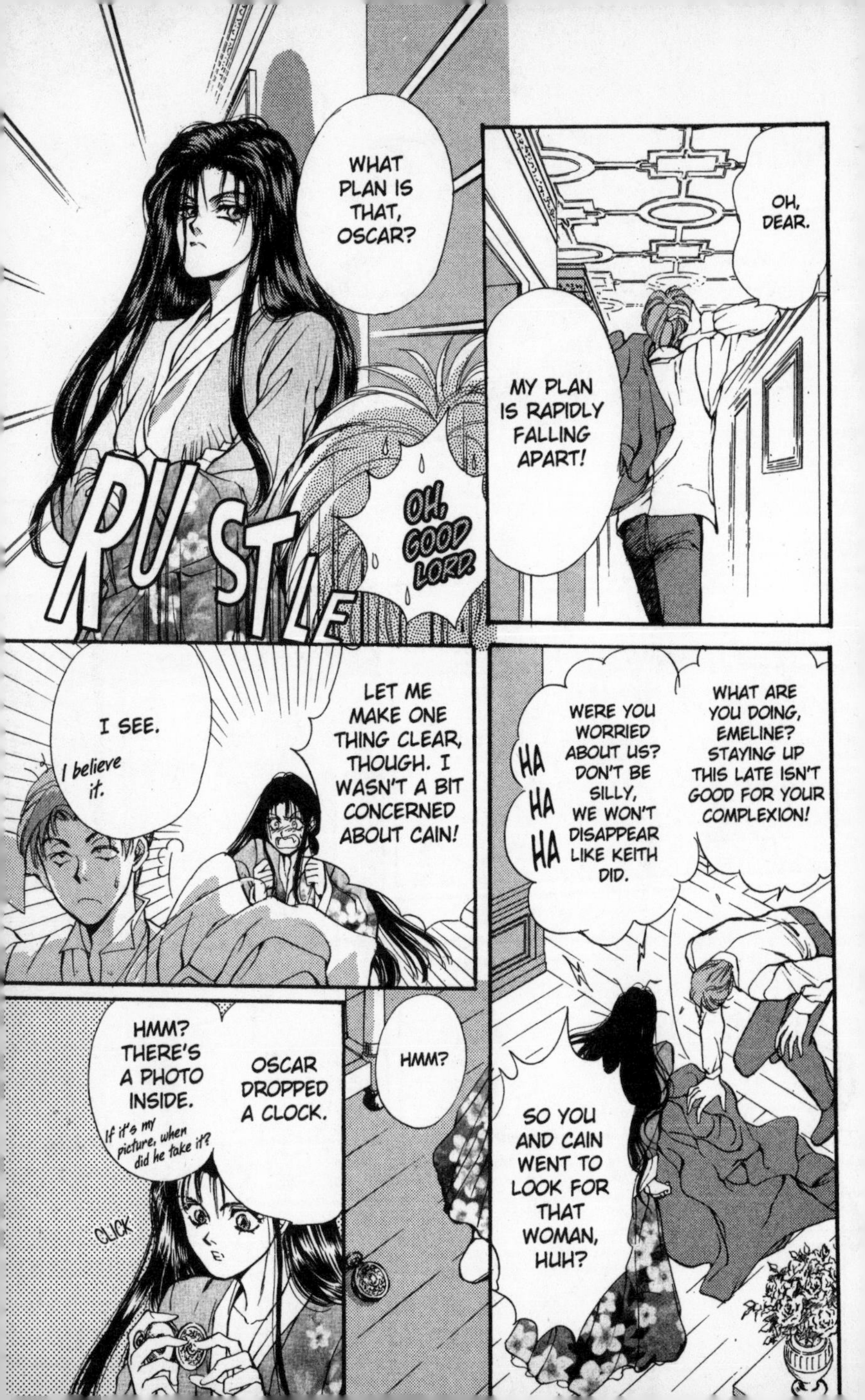
OH, DEAR.
MY PLAN IS RAPIDLY FALLING APART!
WHAT PLAN IS THAT, OSCAR?
RUSTLE
OH, GOOD LORD.
WHAT ARE YOU DOING, EMELINE? STAYING UP THIS LATE ISN'T GOOD FOR YOUR COMPLEXION!
WERE YOU WORRIED ABOUT US? DON'T BE SILLY, WE WON'T DISAPPEAR LIKE KEITH DID.
HA HA HA
SO YOU AND CAIN WENT TO LOOK FOR THAT WOMAN, HUH?
LET ME MAKE ONE THING CLEAR, THOUGH. I WASN'T A BIT CONCERNED ABOUT CAIN!
I SEE.
I believe it.
HMM?
OSCAR DROPPED A CLOCK.
HMM? THERE'S A PHOTO INSIDE.
If it's my picture, when did he take it?
CLICK

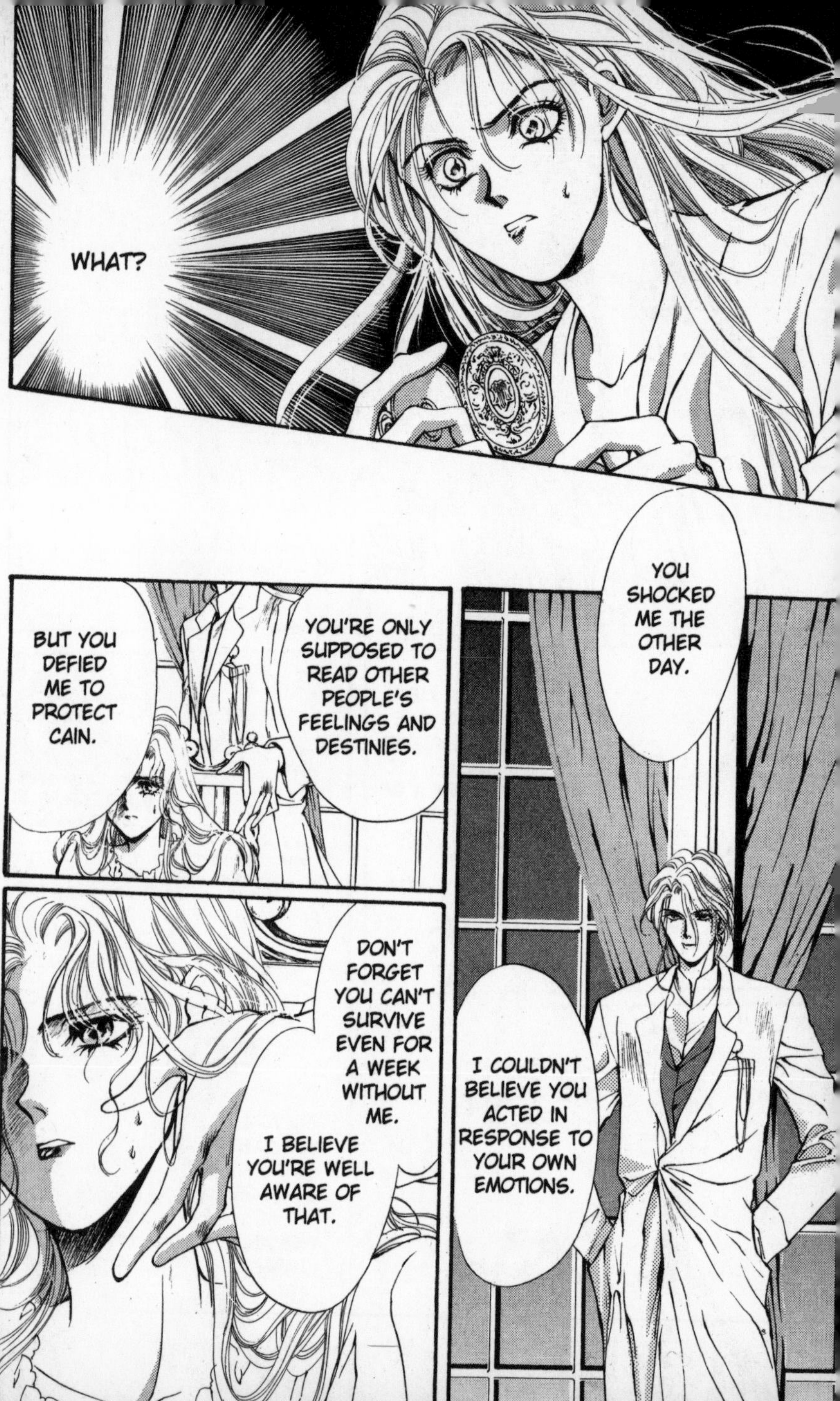
WHAT?
YOU SHOCKED ME THE OTHER DAY.
I COULDN'T BELIEVE YOU ACTED IN RESPONSE TO YOUR OWN EMOTIONS.
YOU'RE ONLY SUPPOSED TO READ OTHER PEOPLE'S FEELINGS AND DESTINIES.
BUT YOU DEFIED ME TO PROTECT CAIN.
DON'T FORGET YOU CAN'T SURVIVE EVEN FOR A WEEK WITHOUT ME.
I BELIEVE YOU'RE WELL AWARE OF THAT.

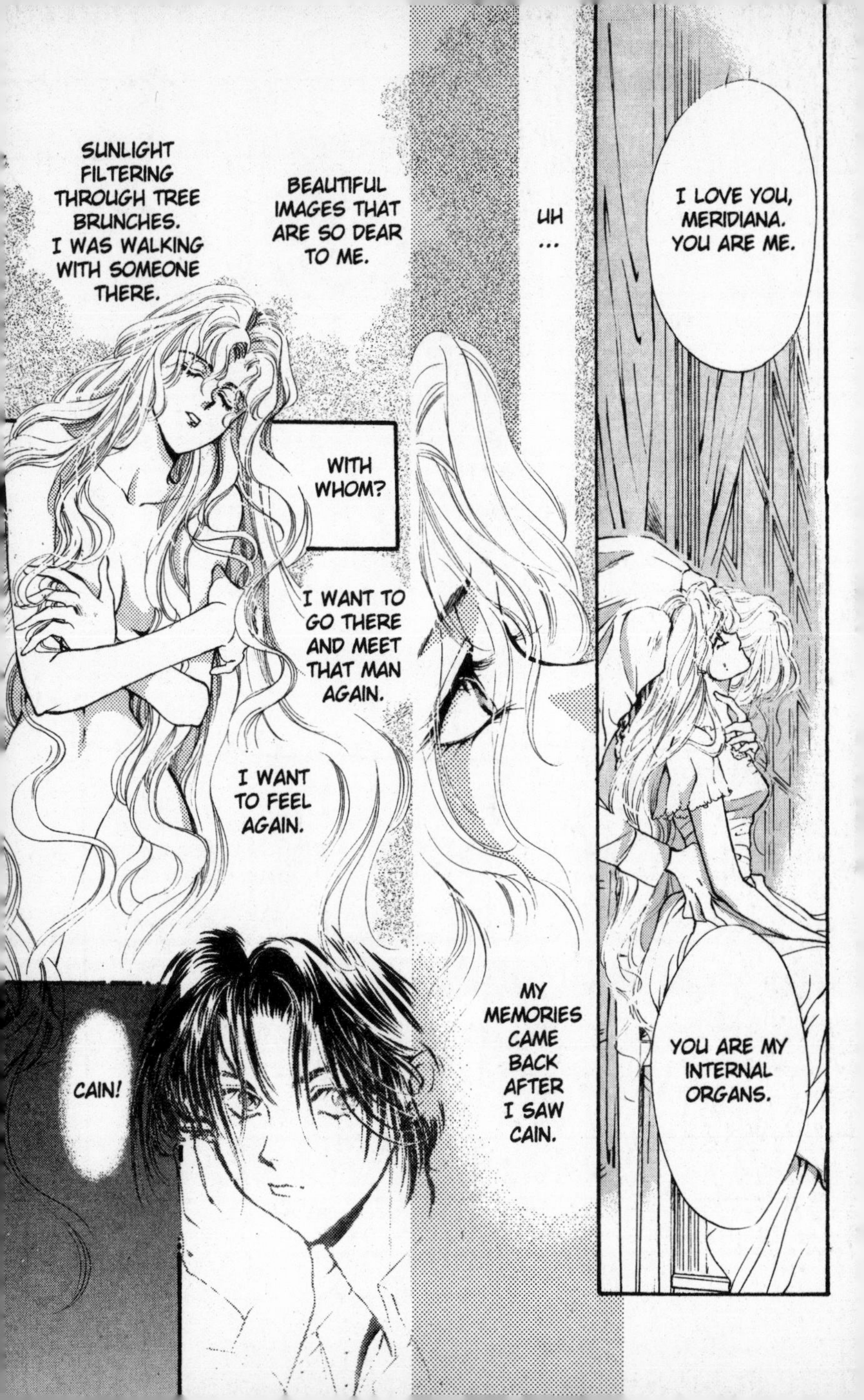
I LOVE YOU, MERIDIANA. YOU ARE ME.
YOU ARE MY INTERNAL ORGANS.
UH ...
MY MEMORIES CAME BACK AFTER I SAW CAIN.
SUNLIGHT FILTERING THROUGH TREE BRUNCHES. I WAS WALKING WITH SOMEONE THERE.
BEAUTIFUL IMAGES THAT ARE SO DEAR TO ME.
WITH WHOM?
I WANT TO GO THERE AND MEET THAT MAN AGAIN.
I WANT TO FEEL AGAIN.
CAIN!

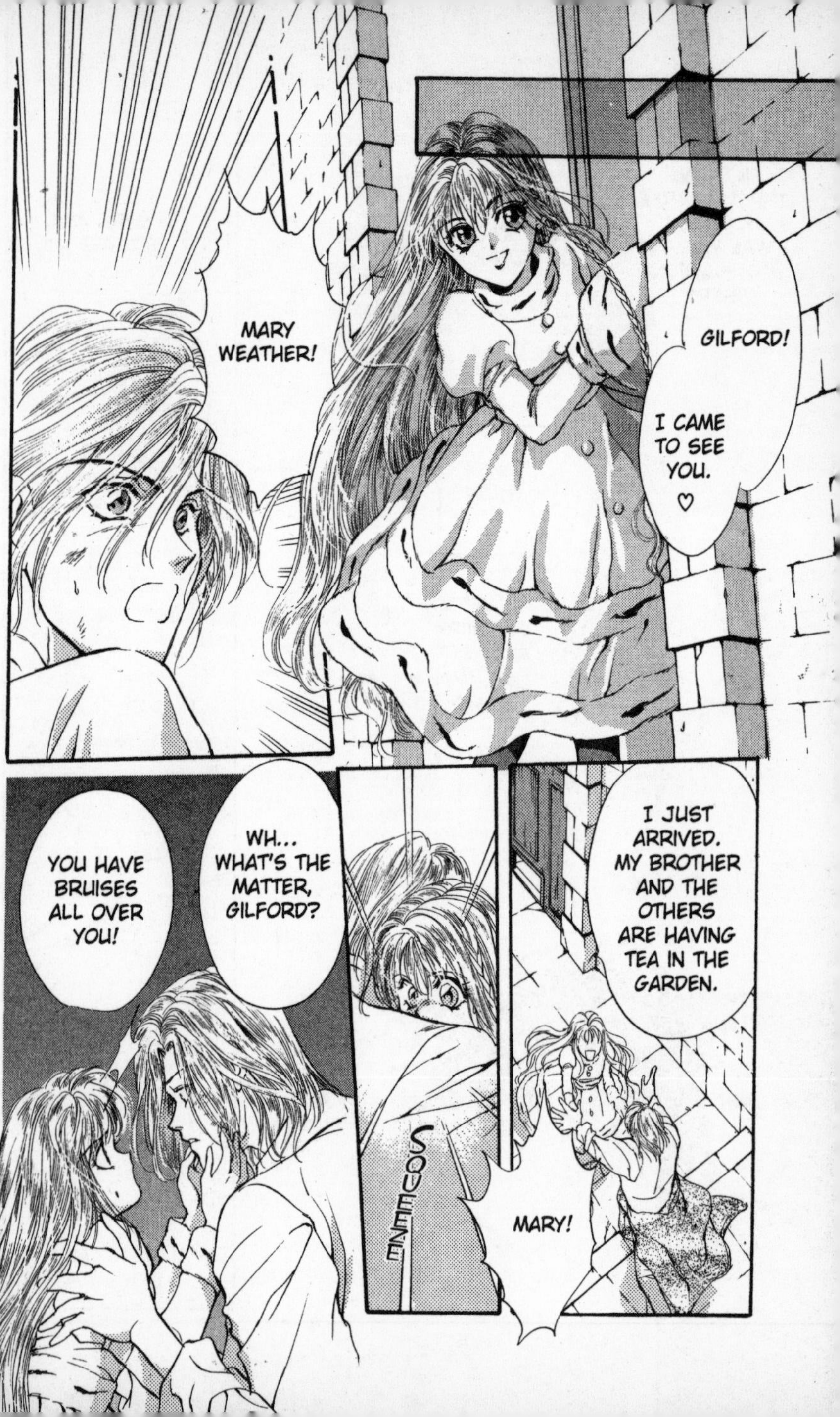
GILFORD!
I CAME TO SEE YOU. ♥
MARY WEATHER!
I JUST ARRIVED. MY BROTHER AND THE OTHERS ARE HAVING TEA IN THE GARDEN.
MARY!
SQUEEEE
WH... WHAT'S THE MATTER, GILFORD?
YOU HAVE BRUISES ALL OVER YOU!

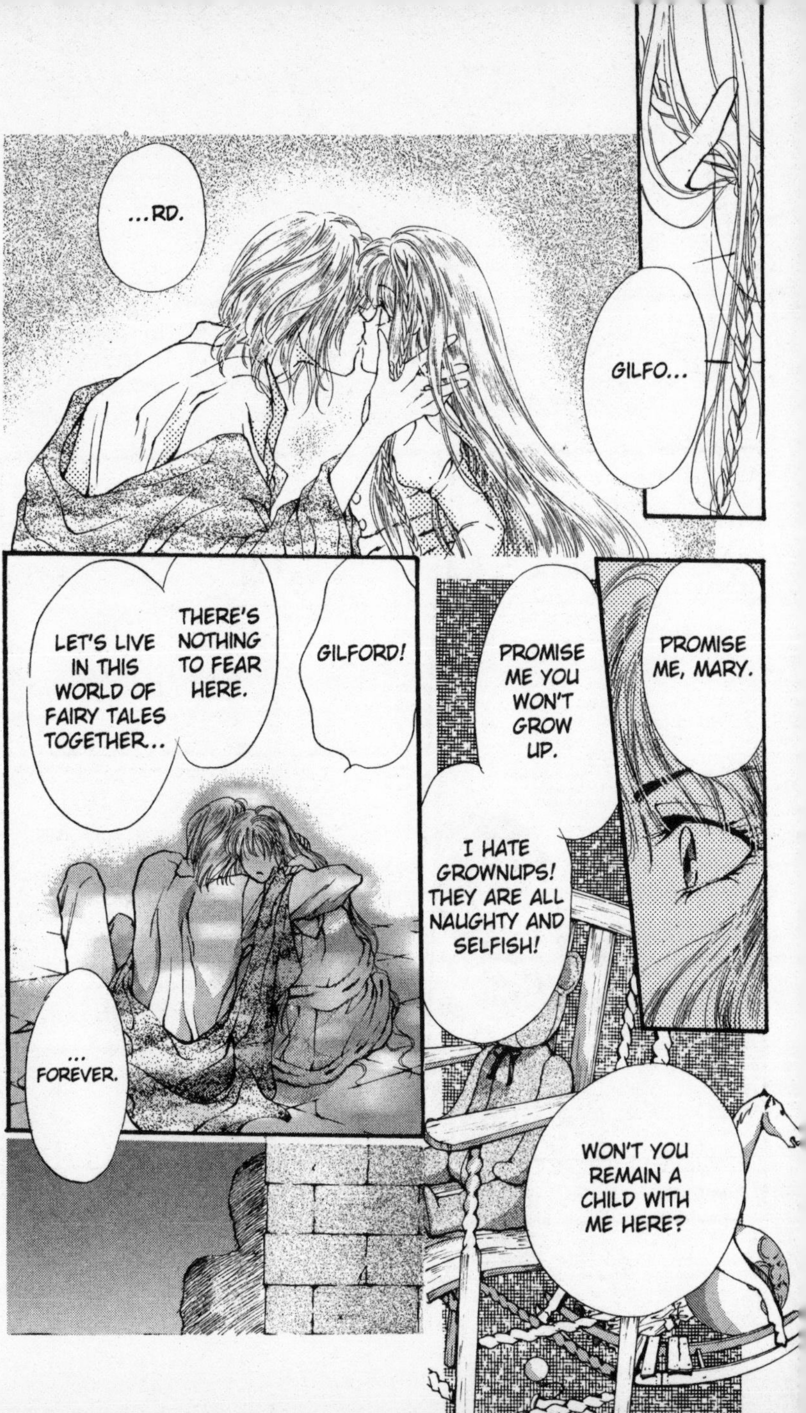
GILFO...
...RD.
PROMISE ME, MARY.
PROMISE ME YOU WON'T GROW UP.
I HATE GROWNUPS! THEY ARE ALL NAUGHTY AND SELFISH!
WON'T YOU REMAIN A CHILD WITH ME HERE?
GILFORD!
THERE'S NOTHING TO FEAR HERE.
LET'S LIVE IN THIS WORLD OF FAIRY TALES TOGETHER...
... FOREVER.

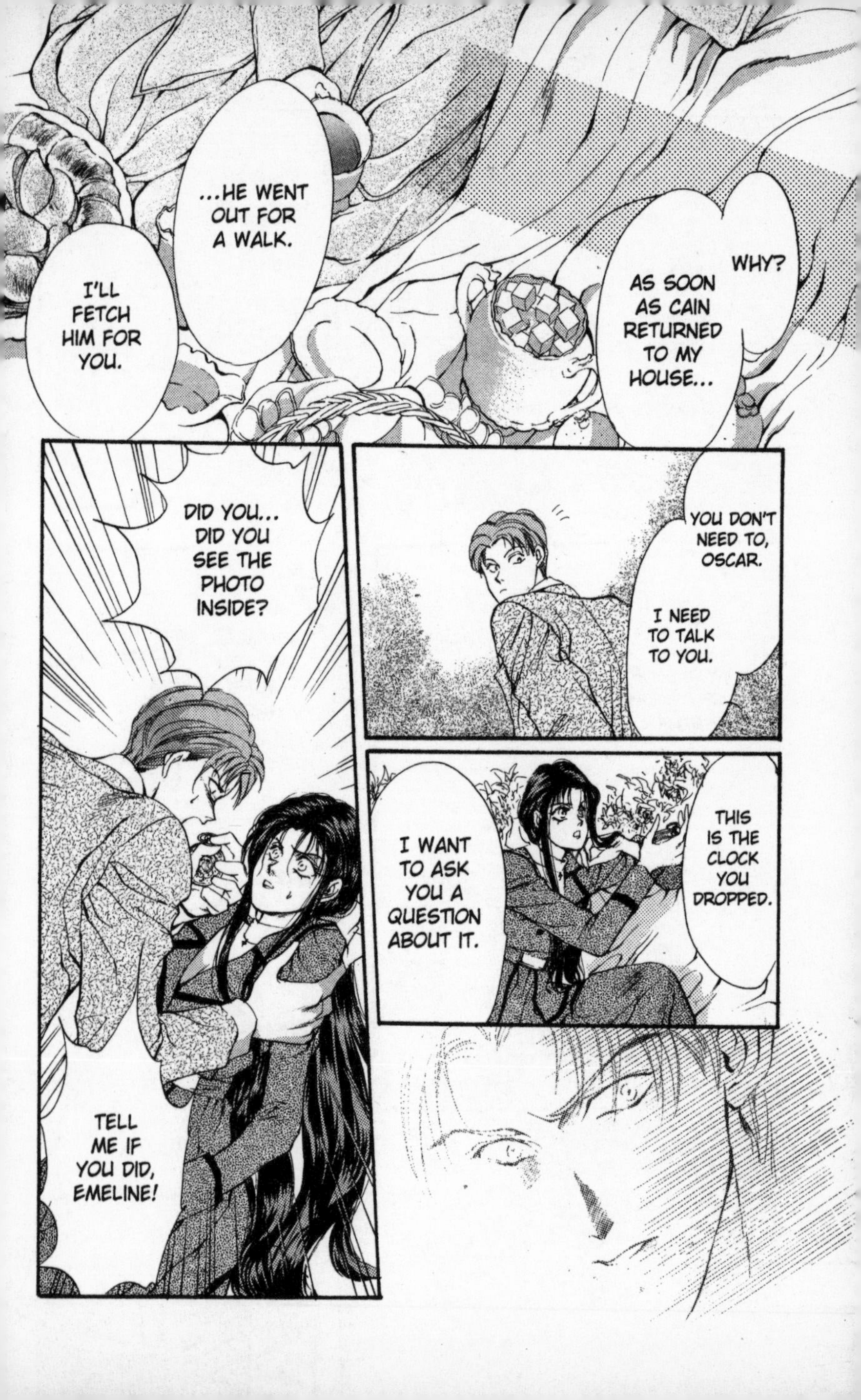
WHY?
AS SOON AS CAIN RETURNED TO MY HOUSE...
...HE WENT OUT FOR A WALK.
I'LL FETCH HIM FOR YOU.
YOU DON'T NEED TO, OSCAR.
I NEED TO TALK TO YOU.
THIS IS THE CLOCK YOU DROPPED.
I WANT TO ASK YOU A QUESTION ABOUT IT.
DID YOU... DID YOU SEE THE PHOTO INSIDE?
TELL ME IF YOU DID, EMELINE!

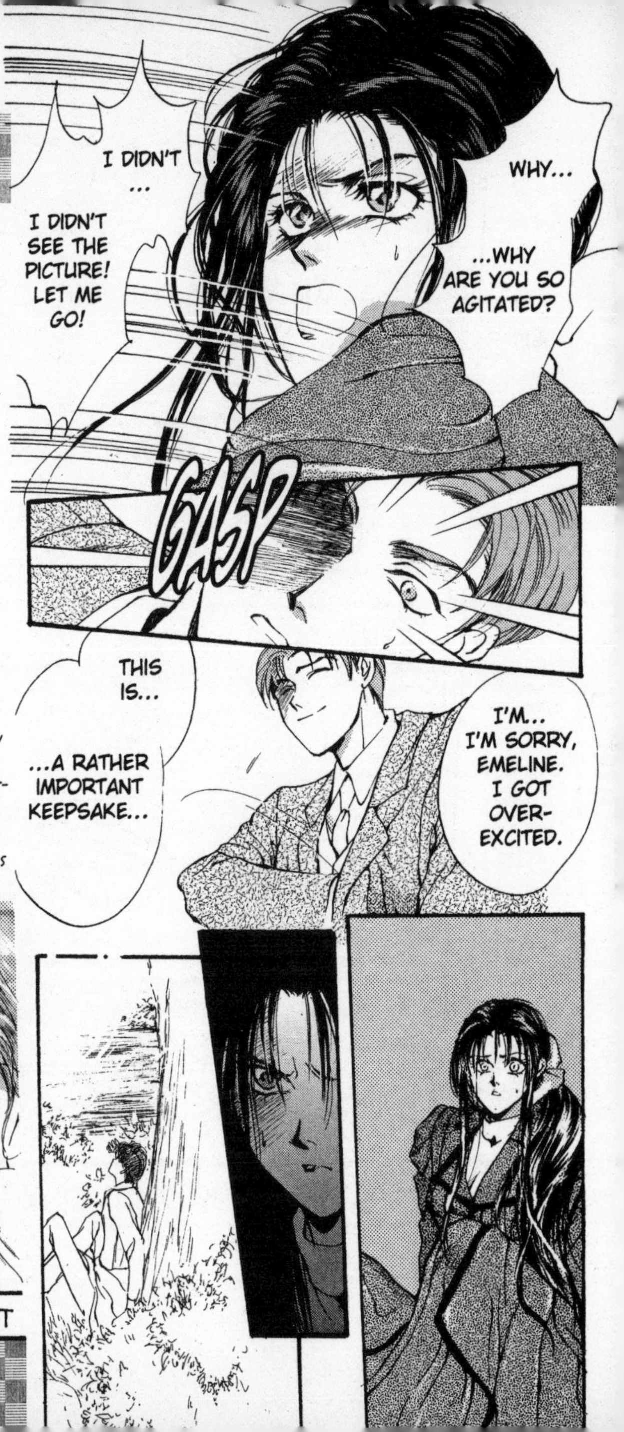
WHY...
...WHY ARE YOU SO AGITATED?
I DIDN'T ...
I DIDN'T SEE THE PICTURE! LET ME GO!
GASP
I'M.. I'M SORRY, EMELINE. I GOT OVER-EXCITED.
THIS IS...
...A RATHER IMPORTANT KEEPSAKE...

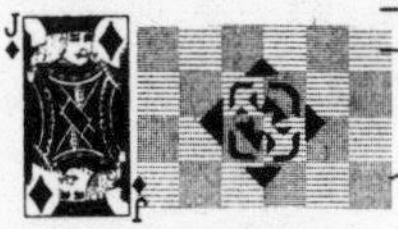

I've been receiving an increasing number of fan letters saying, "Emeline struggles with her inability to show her feelings and that makes her lovable. On the other hand, I don't like Meridiana at all!" This reaction on the part of the readers was unexpected. I basically like both characters equally. However, when I put myself in Cain's position, I can't help thinking that Emeline barks at him too much. On the other hand, Meridiana's way of overreacting to things can be exhausting. By the way, one fan wrote to me that she believes Emeline is Jack the Ripper!

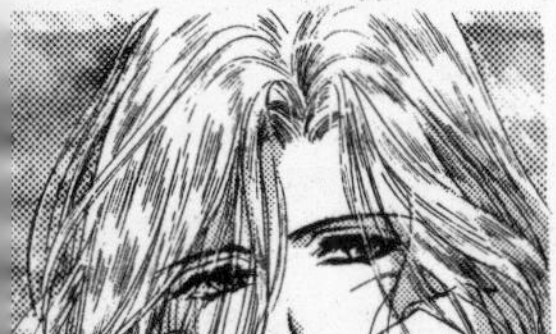

IX - THE HERMIT

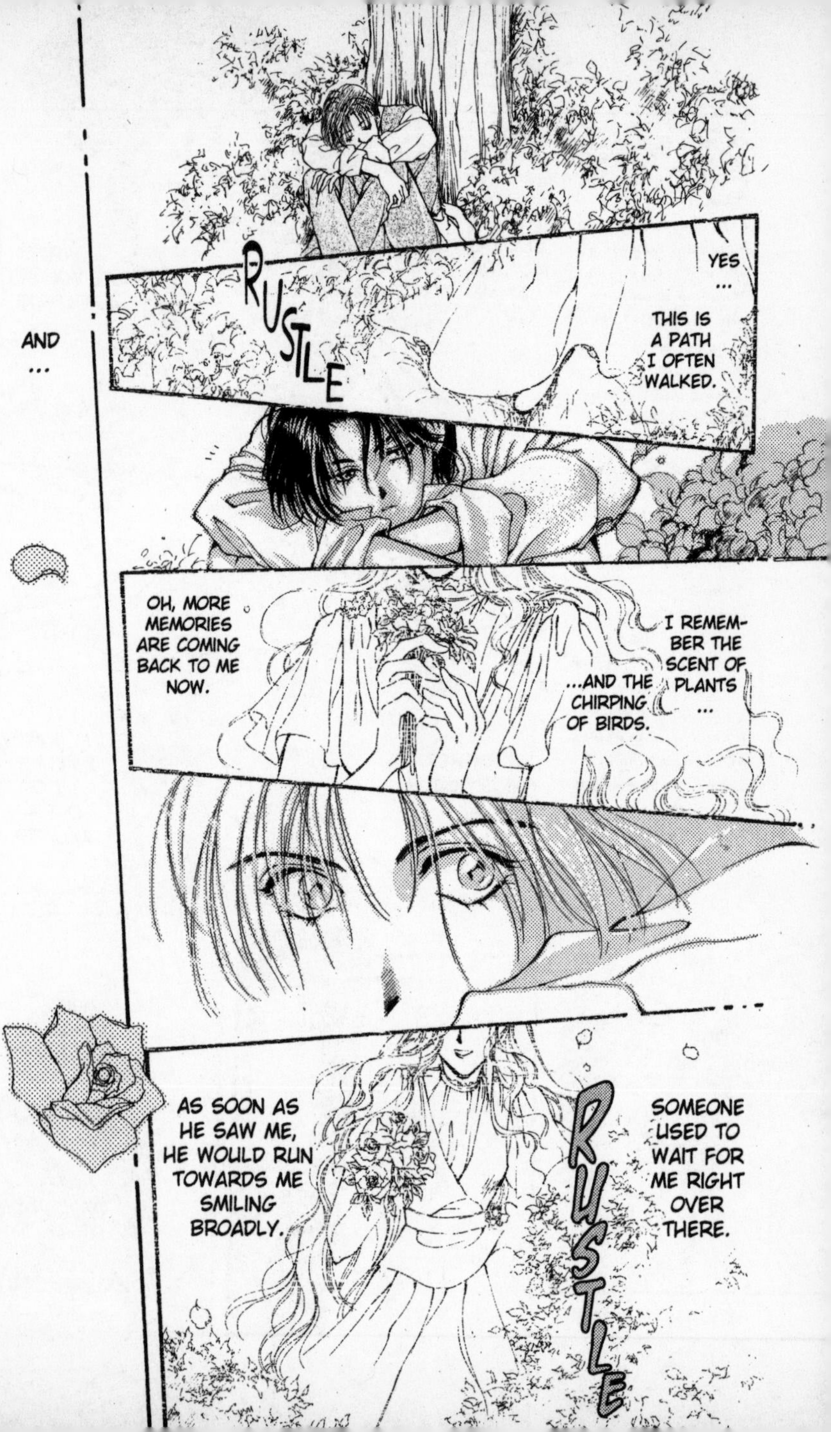
YES ...
THIS IS A PATH I OFTEN WALKED.
RUSTLE
AND ...
I REMEMBER THE SCENT OF PLANTS ...
...AND THE CHIRPING OF BIRDS.
OH, MORE MEMORIES ARE COMING BACK TO ME NOW.
SOMEONE USED TO WAIT FOR ME RIGHT OVER THERE.
RUSTLE
AS SOON AS HE SAW ME, HE WOULD RUN TOWARDS ME SMILING BROADLY.

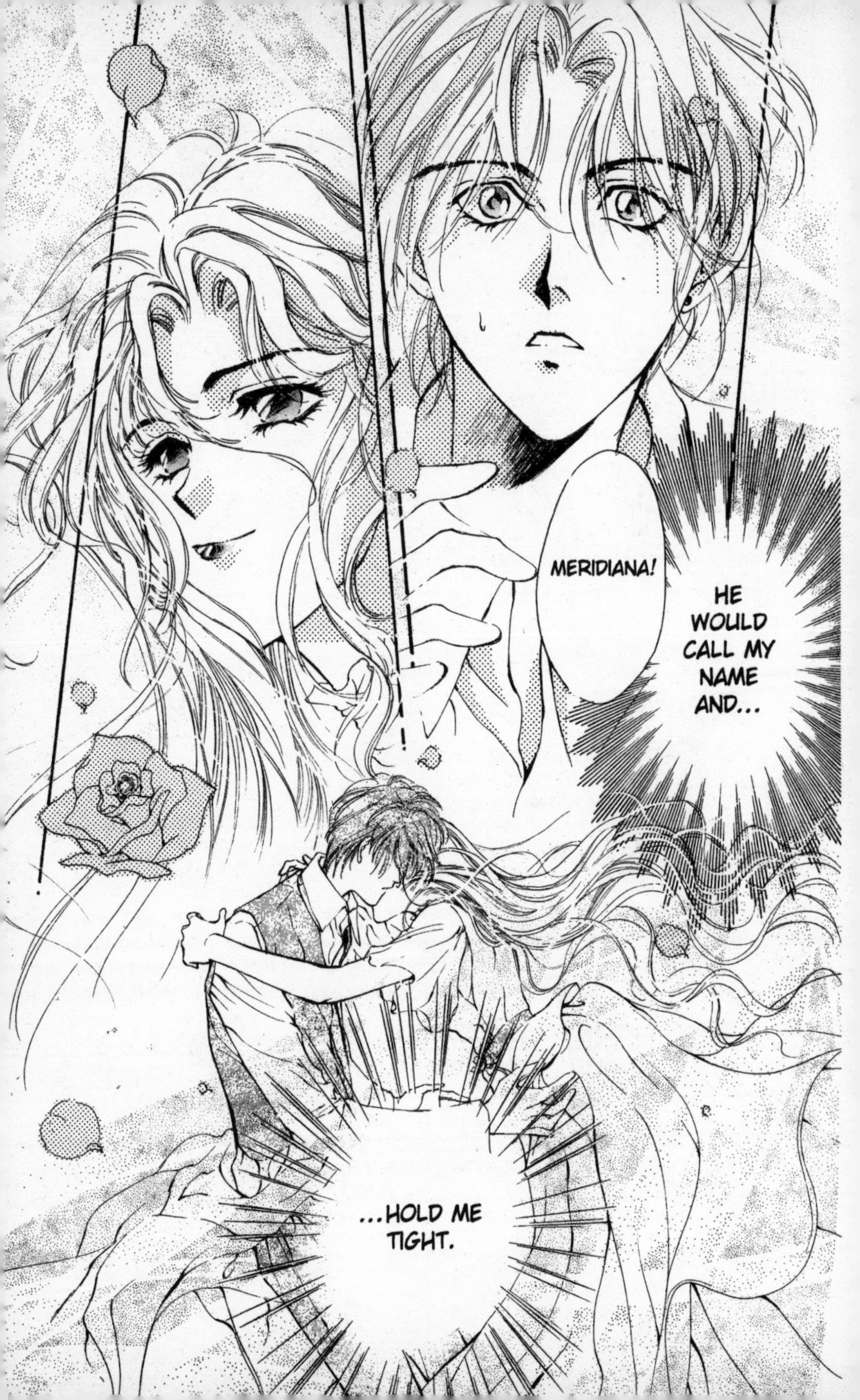
MERIDIANA!
HE WOULD CALL MY NAME AND...
...HOLD ME TIGHT.

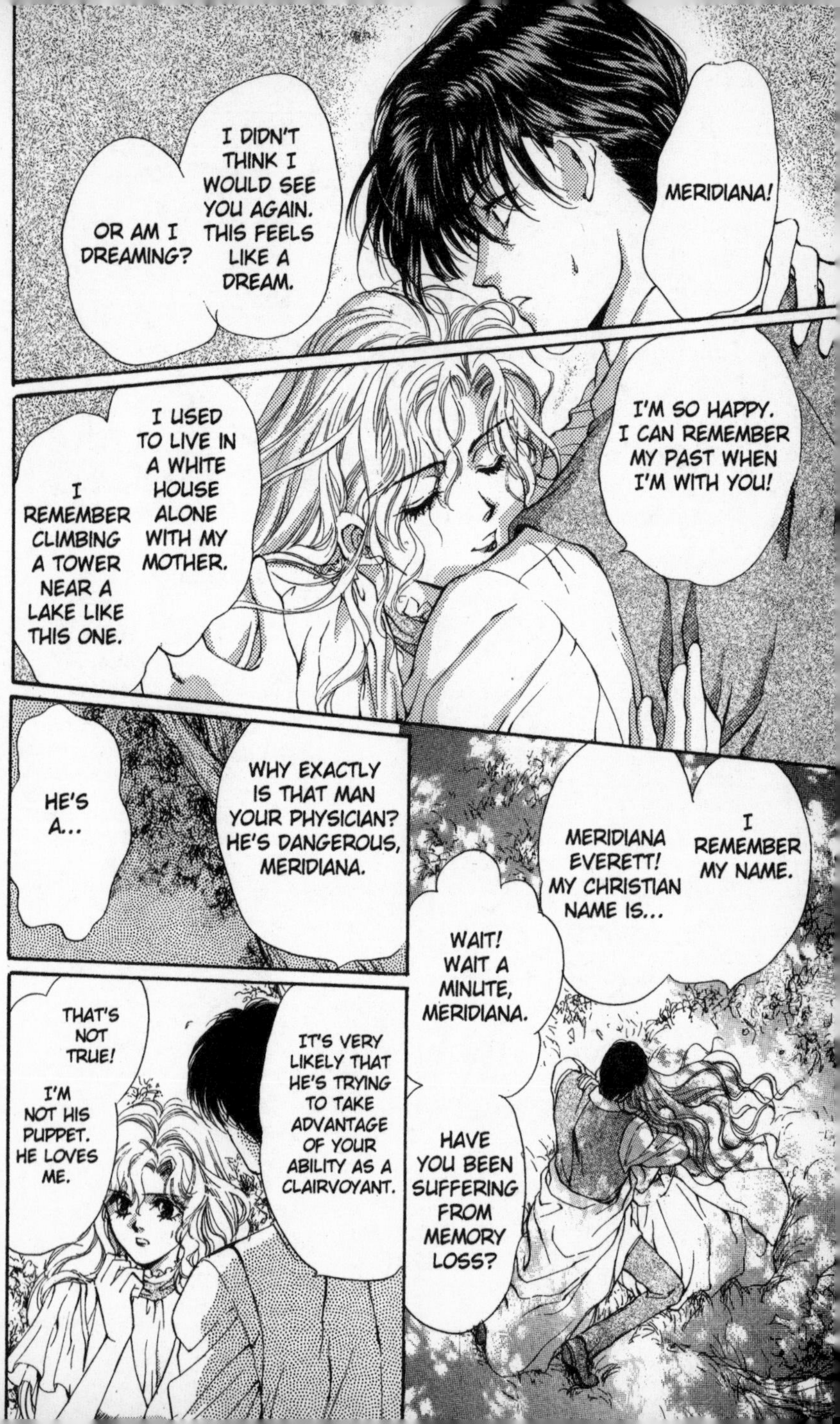
MERIDIANA!
I DIDN'T THINK I WOULD SEE YOU AGAIN. THIS FEELS LIKE A DREAM.
OR AM I DREAMING?
I'M SO HAPPY. I CAN REMEMBER MY PAST WHEN I'M WITH YOU!
I USED TO LIVE IN A WHITE HOUSE ALONE WITH MY MOTHER.
I REMEMBER CLIMBING A TOWER NEAR A LAKE LIKE THIS ONE.
I REMEMBER MY NAME.
MERIDIANA EVERETT! MY CHRISTIAN NAME IS...
WAIT! WAIT A MINUTE, MERIDIANA.
HAVE YOU BEEN SUFFERING FROM MEMORY LOSS?
WHY EXACTLY IS THAT MAN YOUR PHYSICIAN? HE'S DANGEROUS, MERIDIANA.
HE'S A...
IT'S VERY LIKELY THAT HE'S TRYING TO TAKE ADVANTAGE OF YOUR ABILITY AS A CLAIRVOYANT.
THAT'S NOT TRUE!
I'M NOT HIS PUPPET. HE LOVES ME.

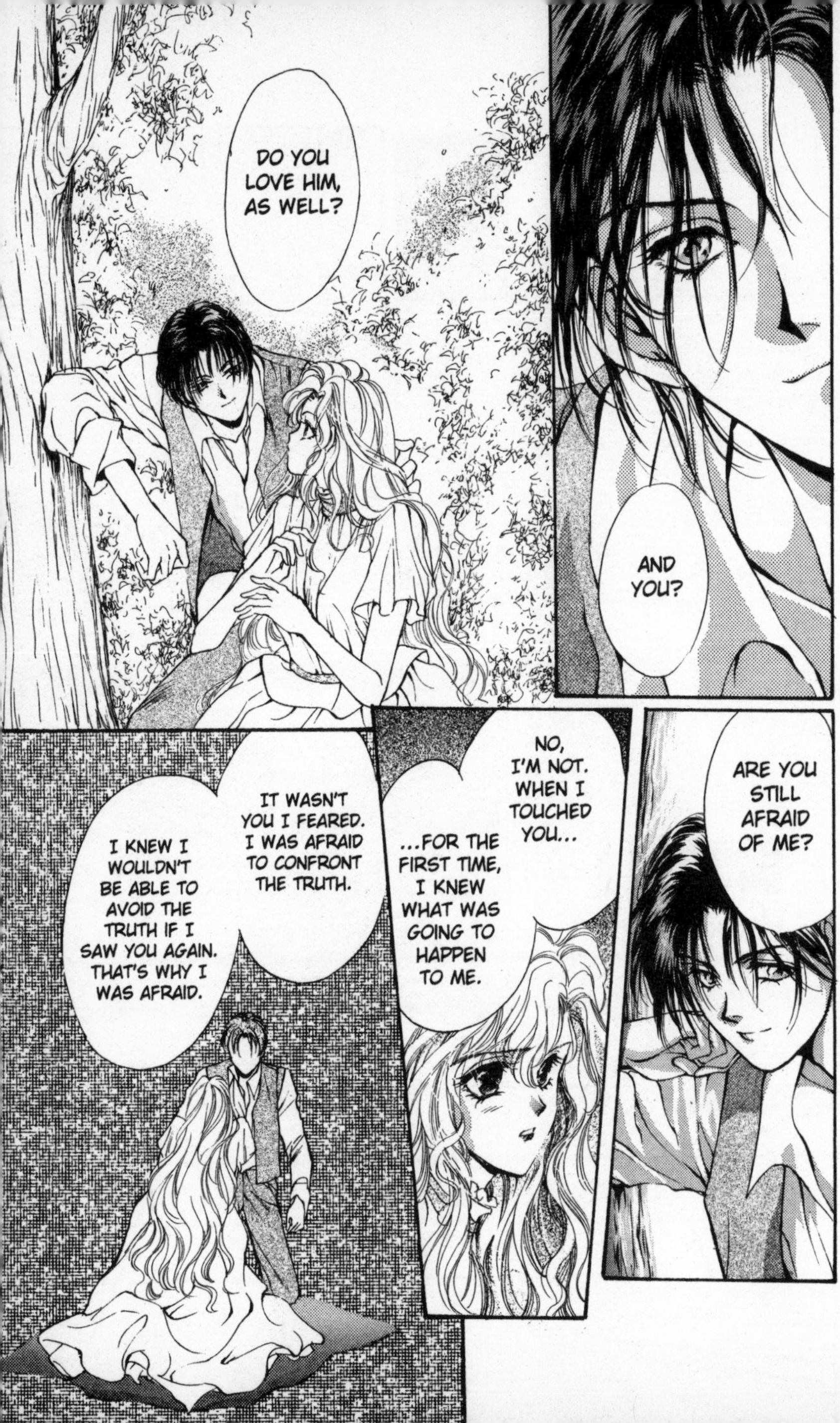
AND YOU?
DO YOU LOVE HIM, AS WELL?
ARE YOU STILL AFRAID OF ME?
NO, I'M NOT. WHEN I TOUCHED YOU...
...FOR THE FIRST TIME, I KNEW WHAT WAS GOING TO HAPPEN TO ME.
IT WASN'T YOU I FEARED. I WAS AFRAID TO CONFRONT THE TRUTH.
I KNEW I WOULDN'T BE ABLE TO AVOID THE TRUTH IF I SAW YOU AGAIN. THAT'S WHY I WAS AFRAID.

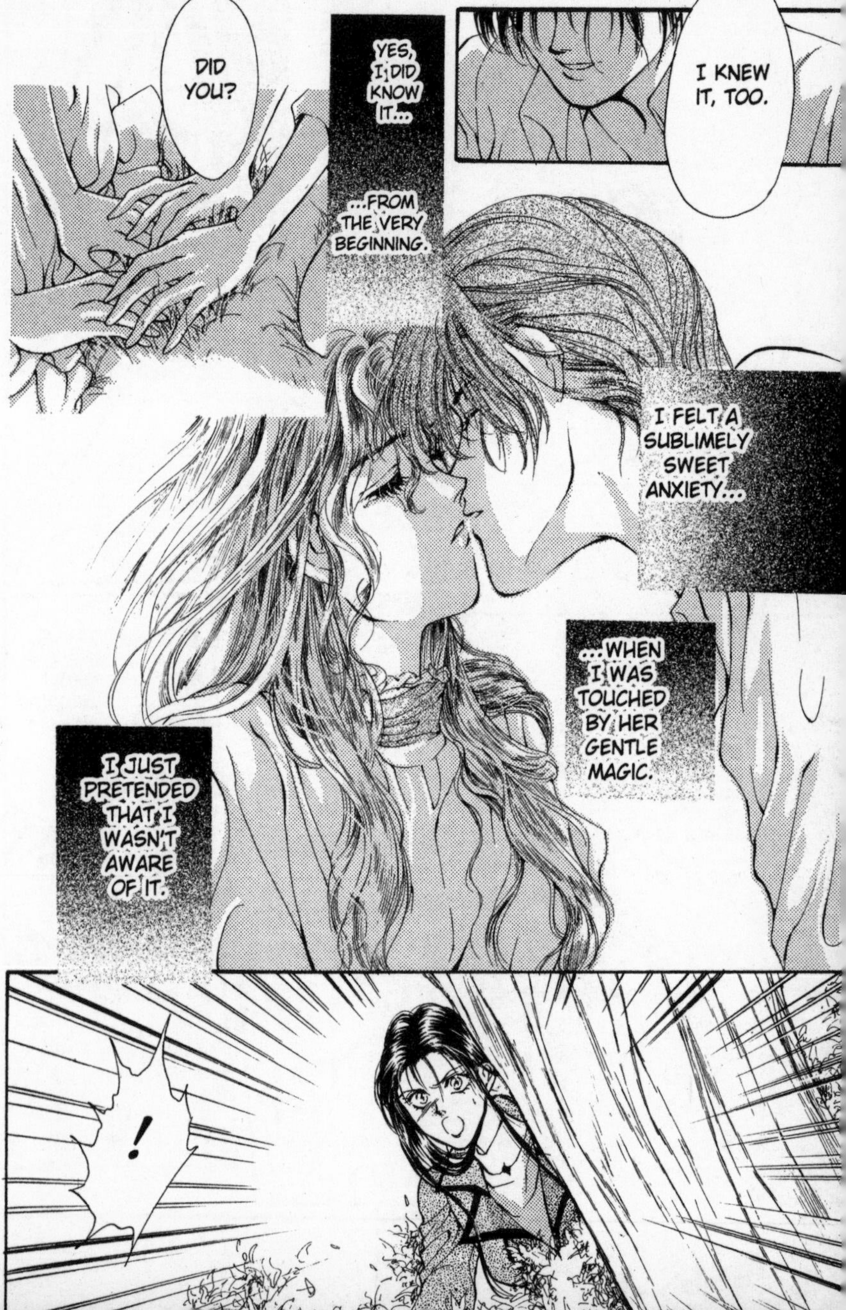
I KNEW IT, TOO.
YES, I DID KNOW IT...
...FROM THE VERY BEGINNING.
DID YOU?
I FELT A SUBLIMELY SWEET ANXIETY...
...WHEN I WAS TOUCHED BY HER GENTLE MAGIC.
I JUST PRETENDED THAT I WASN'T AWARE OF IT.
!

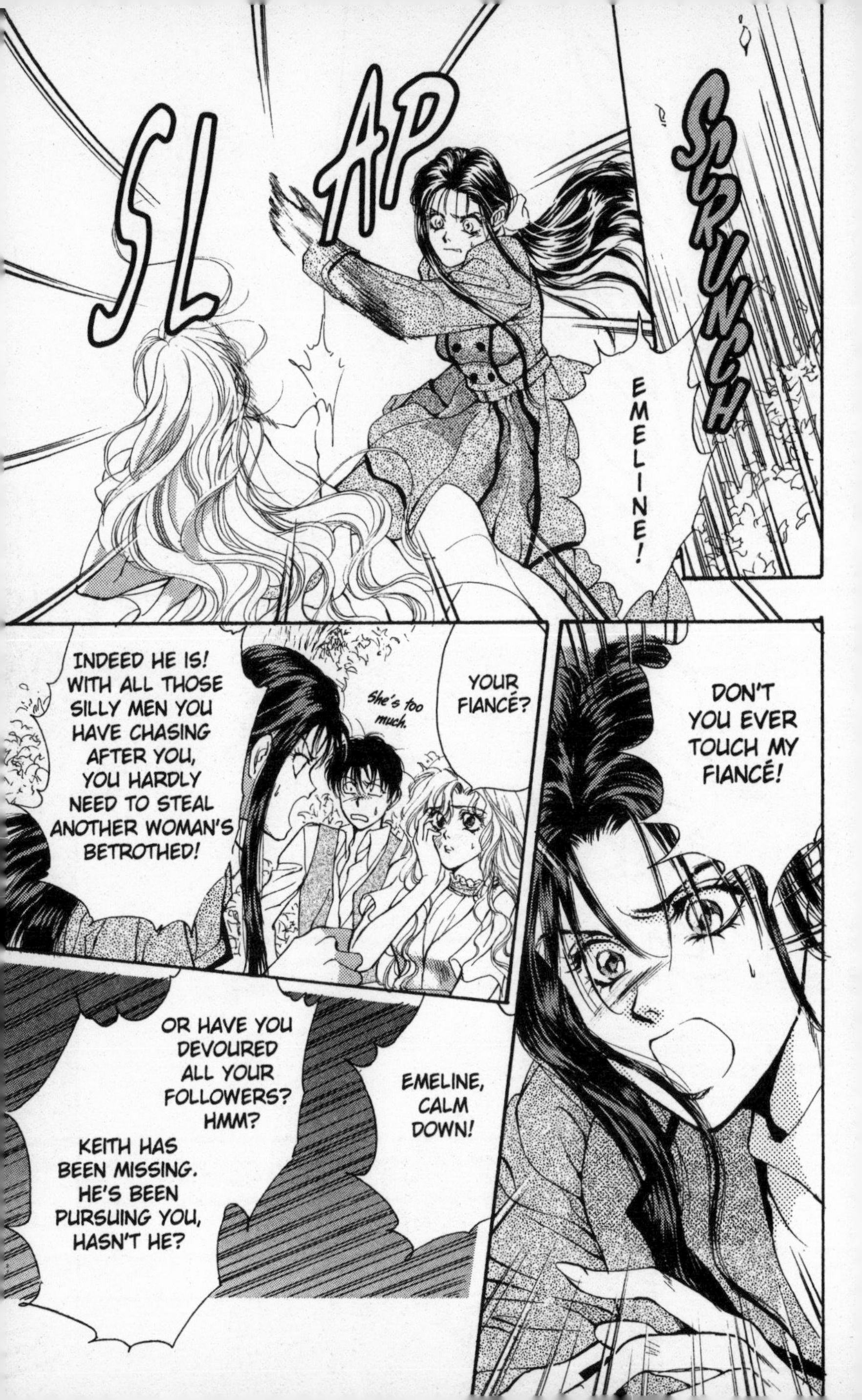
SCRUNCH
EMELINE!
SLAP
DON'T YOU EVER TOUCH MY FIANCÉ!
YOUR FIANCÉ?
She's too much.
INDEED HE IS! WITH ALL THOSE SILLY MEN YOU HAVE CHASING AFTER YOU, YOU HARDLY NEED TO STEAL ANOTHER WOMAN'S BETROTHED!
EMELINE, CALM DOWN!
OR HAVE YOU DEVOURED ALL YOUR FOLLOWERS? HMM?
KEITH HAS BEEN MISSING. HE'S BEEN PURSUING YOU, HASN'T HE?

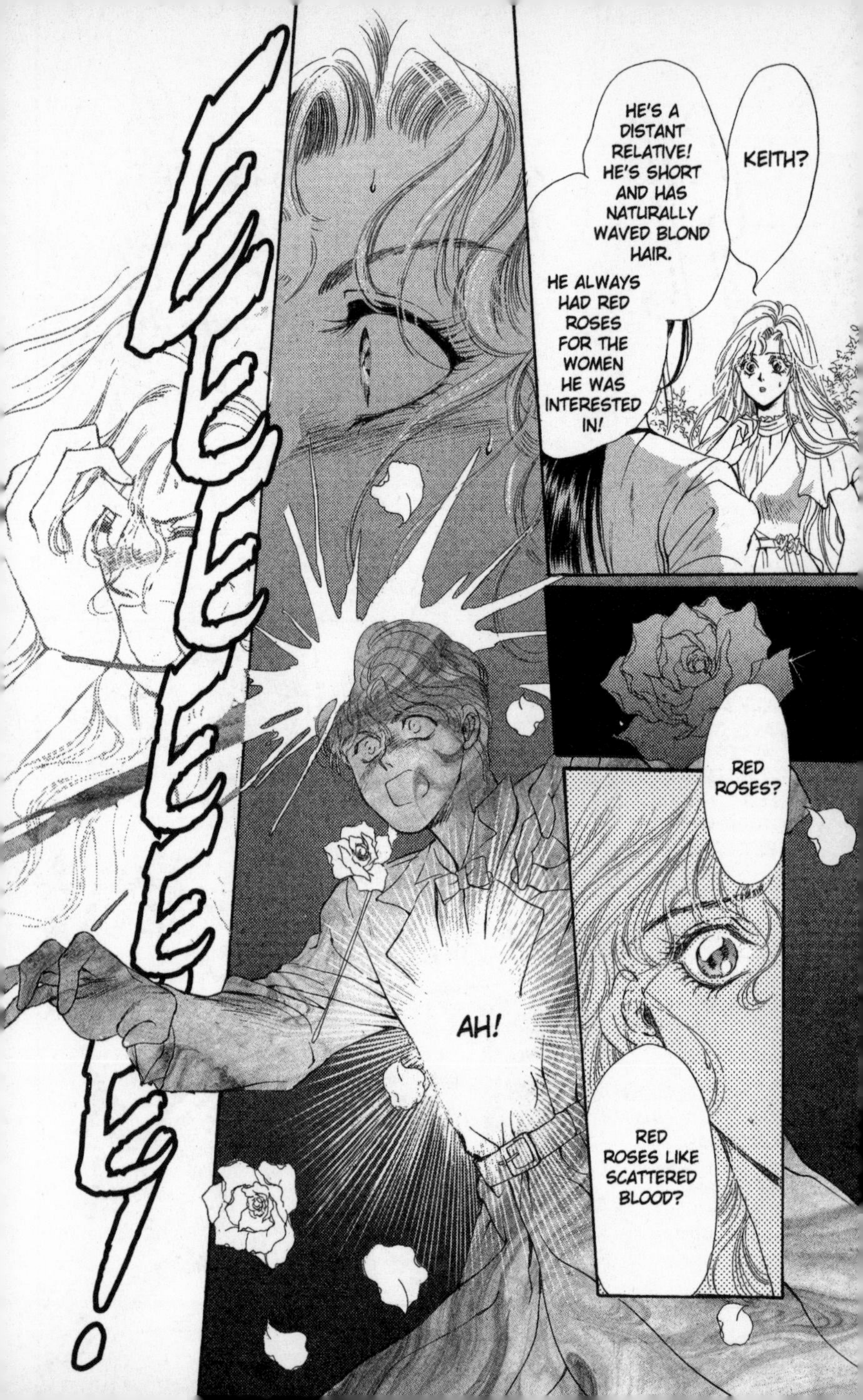
KEITH?
HE'S A DISTANT RELATIVE! HE'S SHORT AND HAS NATURALLY WAVED BLOND HAIR.
HE ALWAYS HAD RED ROSES FOR THE WOMEN HE WAS INTERESTED IN!
RED ROSES?
RED ROSES LIKE SCATTERED BLOOD?
AH!

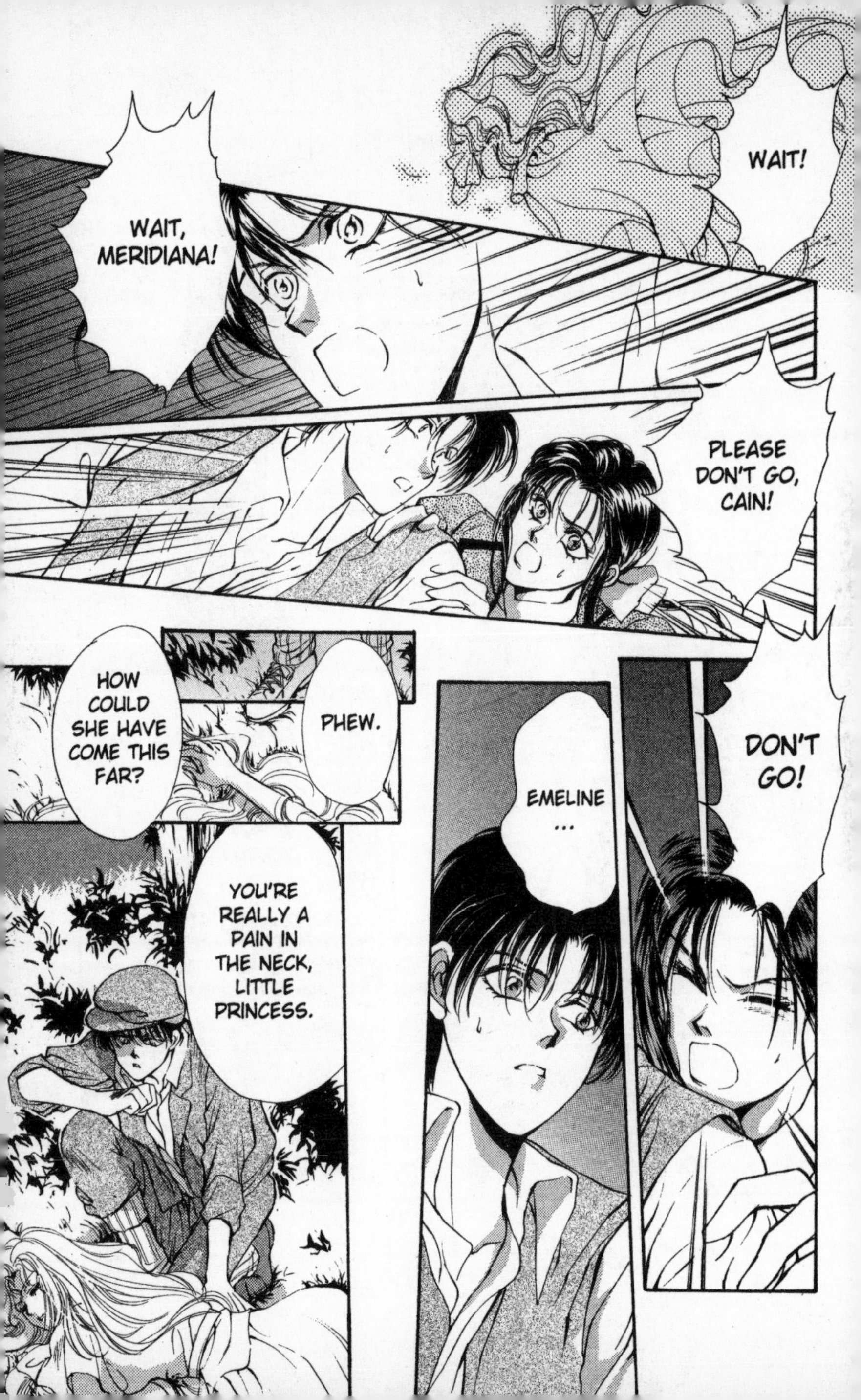
WAIT!
WAIT, MERIDIANA!
PLEASE DON'T GO, CAIN!
DON'T GO!
EMELINE ...
PHEW.
HOW COULD SHE HAVE COME THIS FAR?
YOU'RE REALLY A PAIN IN THE NECK, LITTLE PRINCESS.

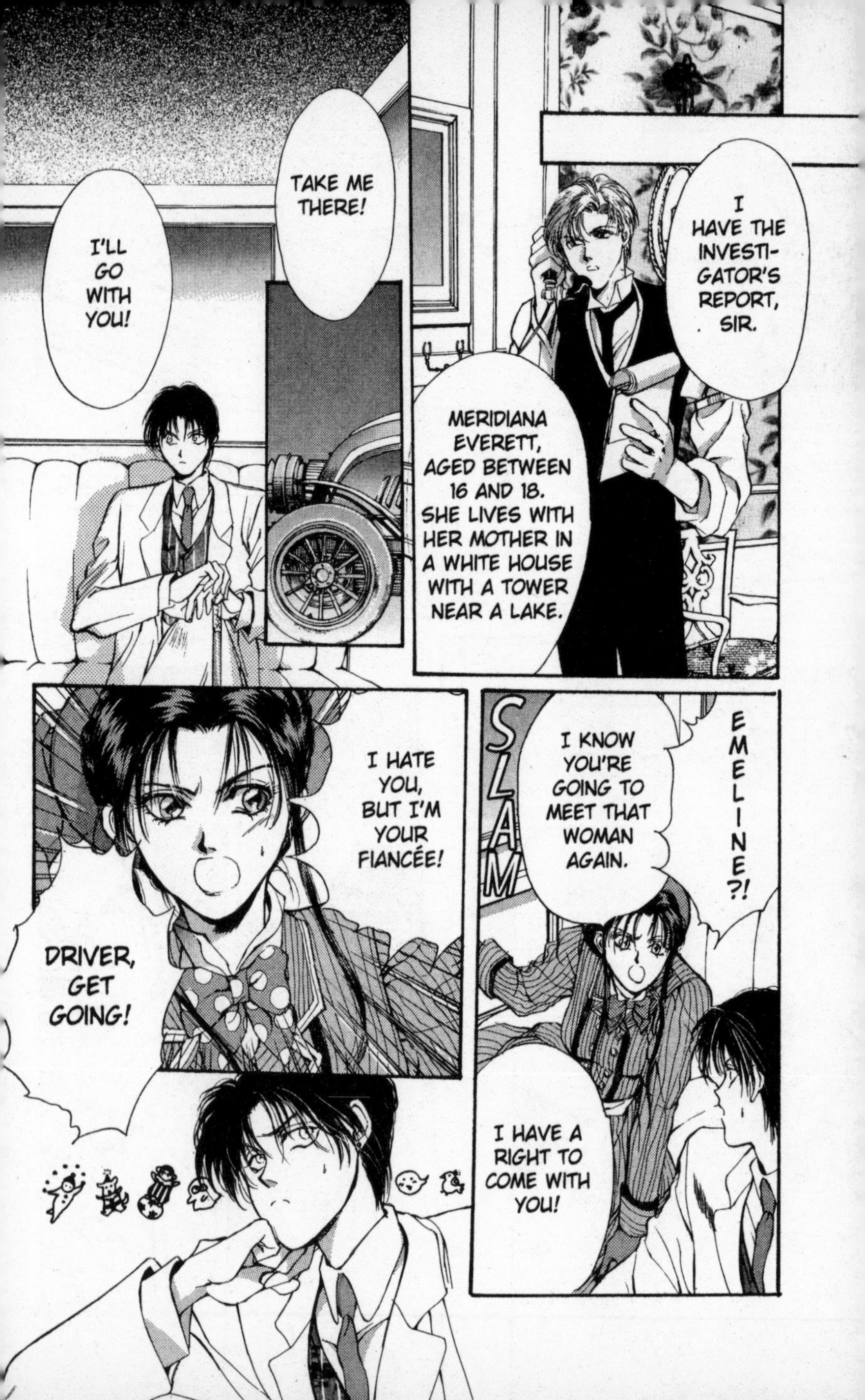
I HAVE THE INVESTIGATOR'S REPORT, SIR.
MERIDIANA EVERETT, AGED BETWEEN 16 AND 18. SHE LIVES WITH HER MOTHER IN A WHITE HOUSE WITH A TOWER NEAR A LAKE.
TAKE ME THERE!
I'LL GO WITH YOU!
EMELINE?!
I KNOW YOU'RE GOING TO MEET THAT WOMAN AGAIN.
SLAM
I HAVE A RIGHT TO COME WITH YOU!
I HATE YOU, BUT I'M YOUR FIANCÉE!
DRIVER, GET GOING!

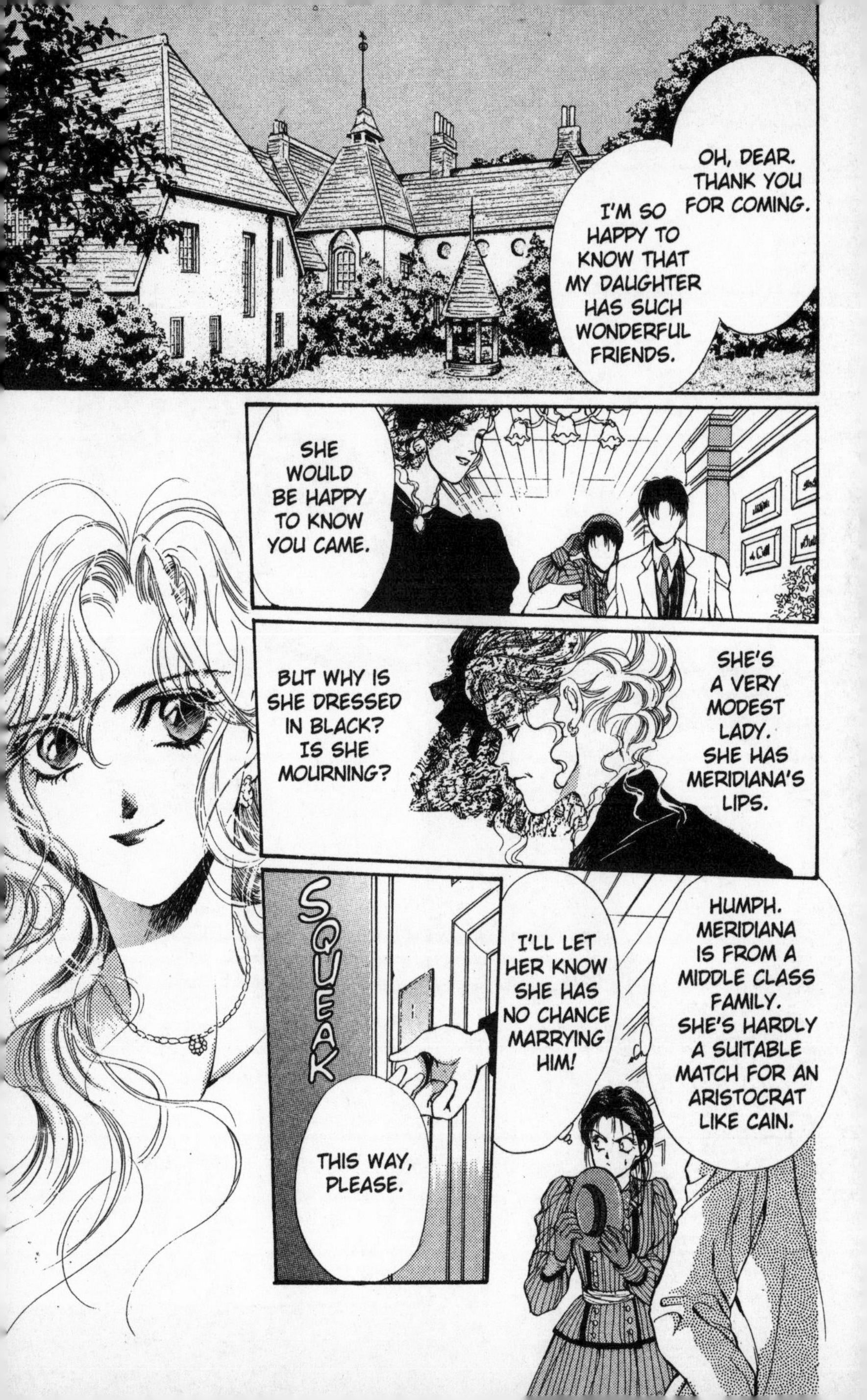

OH, DEAR. THANK YOU FOR COMING.
I'M SO HAPPY TO KNOW THAT MY DAUGHTER HAS SUCH WONDERFUL FRIENDS.
SHE WOULD BE HAPPY TO KNOW YOU CAME.
SHE'S A VERY MODEST LADY. SHE HAS MERIDIANA'S LIPS.
BUT WHY IS SHE DRESSED IN BLACK? IS SHE MOURNING?
HUMPH. MERIDIANA IS FROM A MIDDLE CLASS FAMILY. SHE'S HARDLY A SUITABLE MATCH FOR AN ARISTOCRAT LIKE CAIN.
I'LL LET HER KNOW SHE HAS NO CHANCE MARRYING HIM!
SQUEAK
THIS WAY, PLEASE.

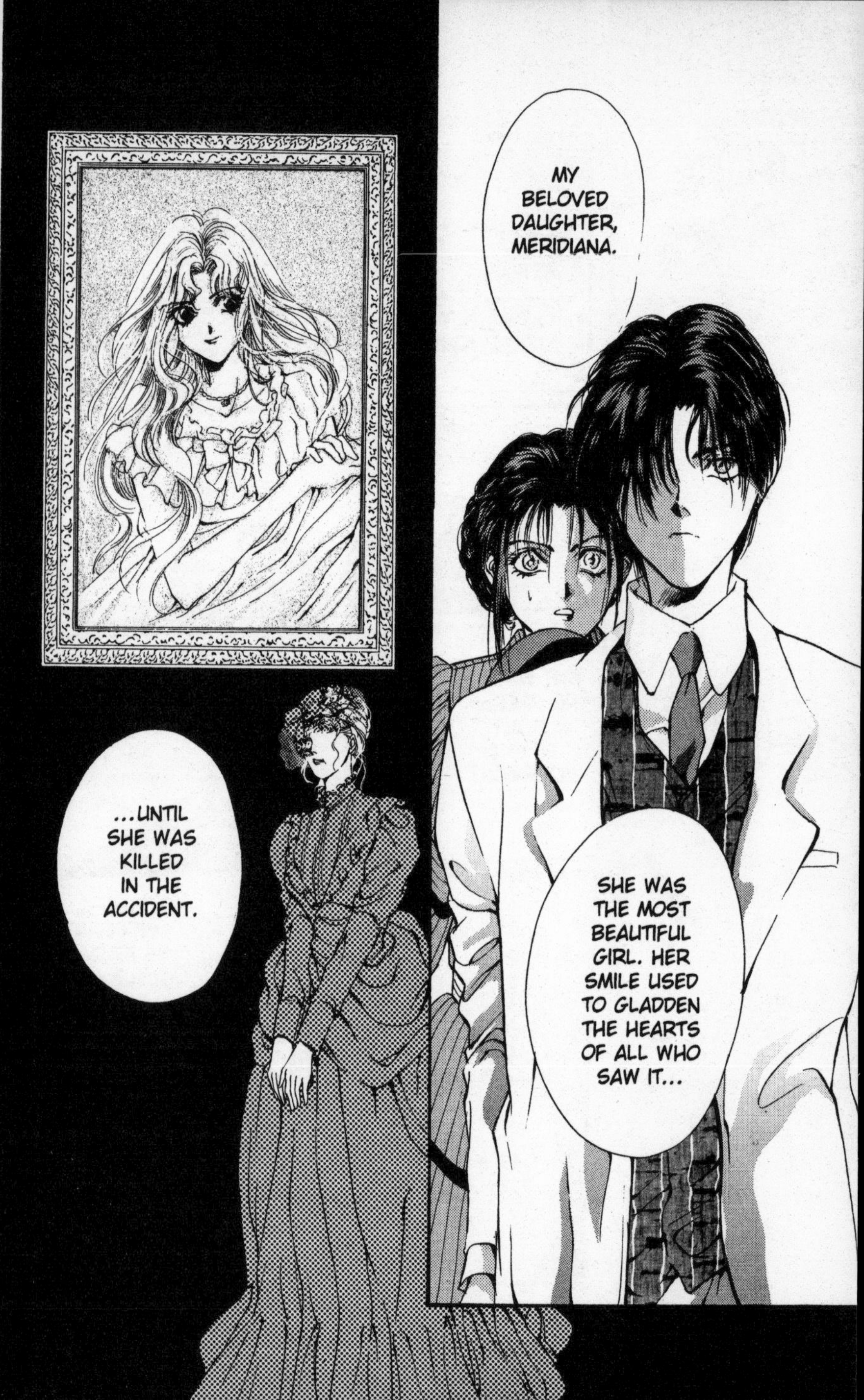
MY BELOVED DAUGHTER, MERIDIANA.
SHE WAS THE MOST BEAUTIFUL GIRL. HER SMILE USED TO GLADDEN THE HEARTS OF ALL WHO SAW IT...
...UNTIL SHE WAS KILLED IN THE ACCIDENT.

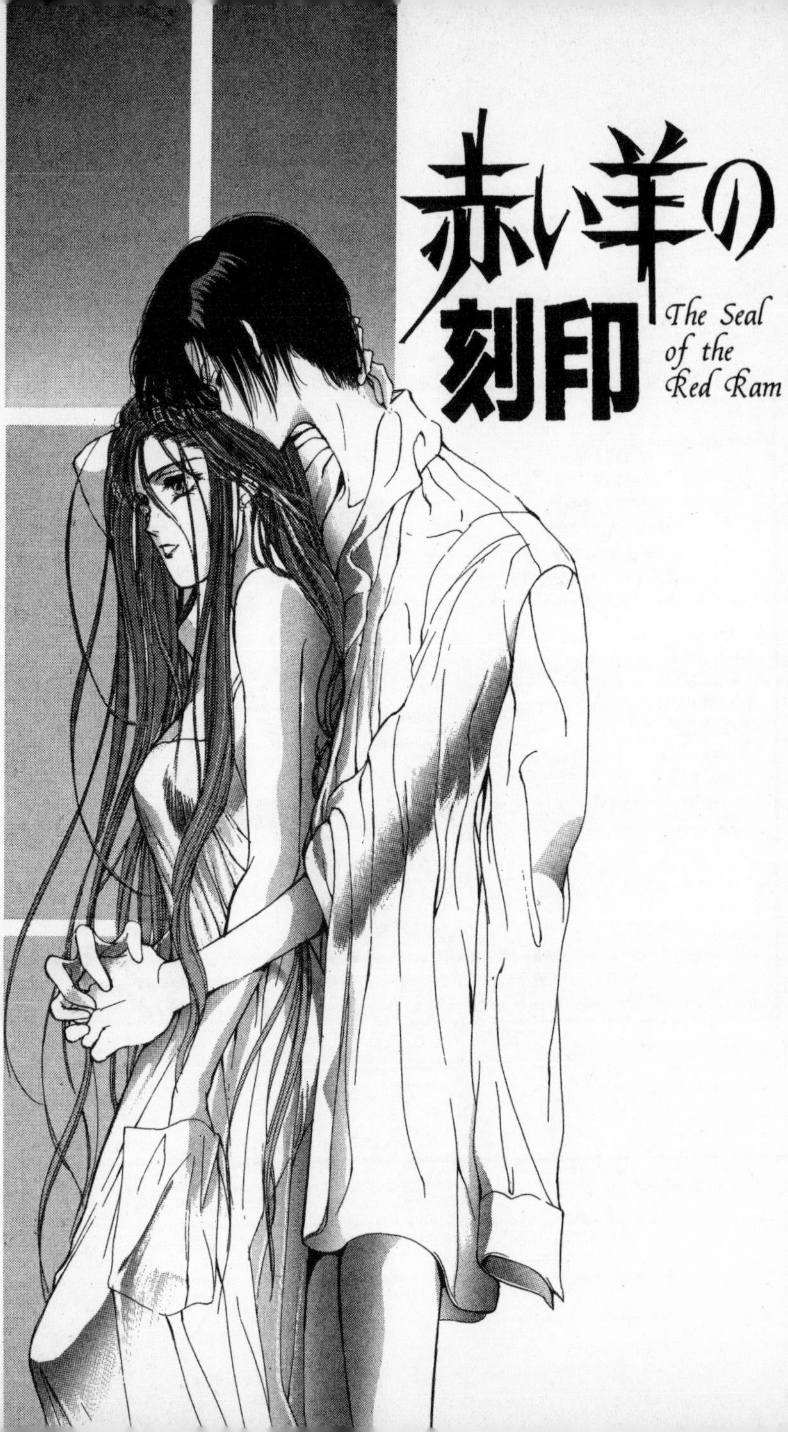
赤い羊の刻印
The Seal of the Red Ram

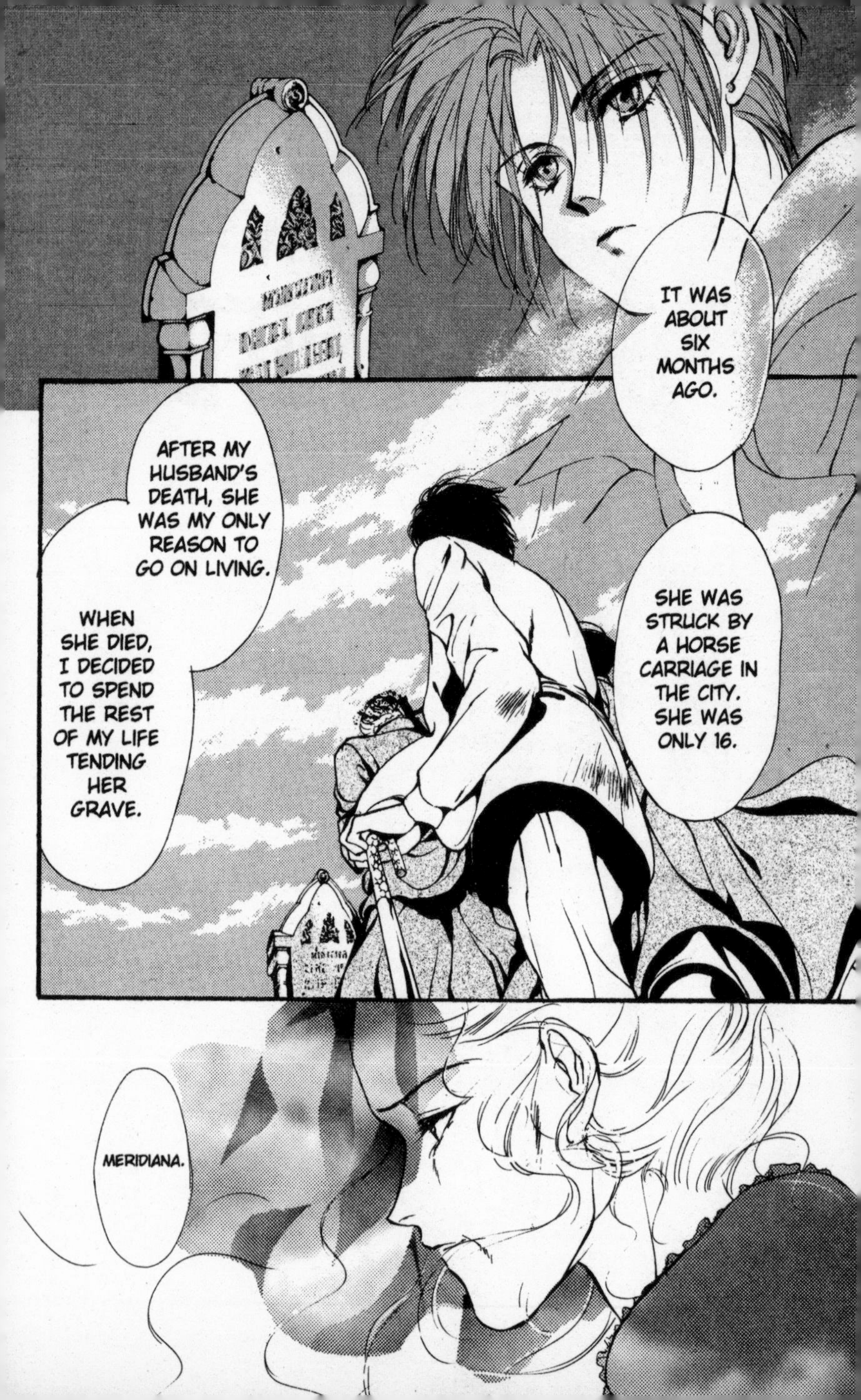
IT WAS ABOUT SIX MONTHS AGO.
SHE WAS STRUCK BY A HORSE CARRIAGE IN THE CITY. SHE WAS ONLY 16.
AFTER MY HUSBAND'S DEATH, SHE WAS MY ONLY REASON TO GO ON LIVING.
WHEN SHE DIED, I DECIDED TO SPEND THE REST OF MY LIFE TENDING HER GRAVE.
MERIDIANA.

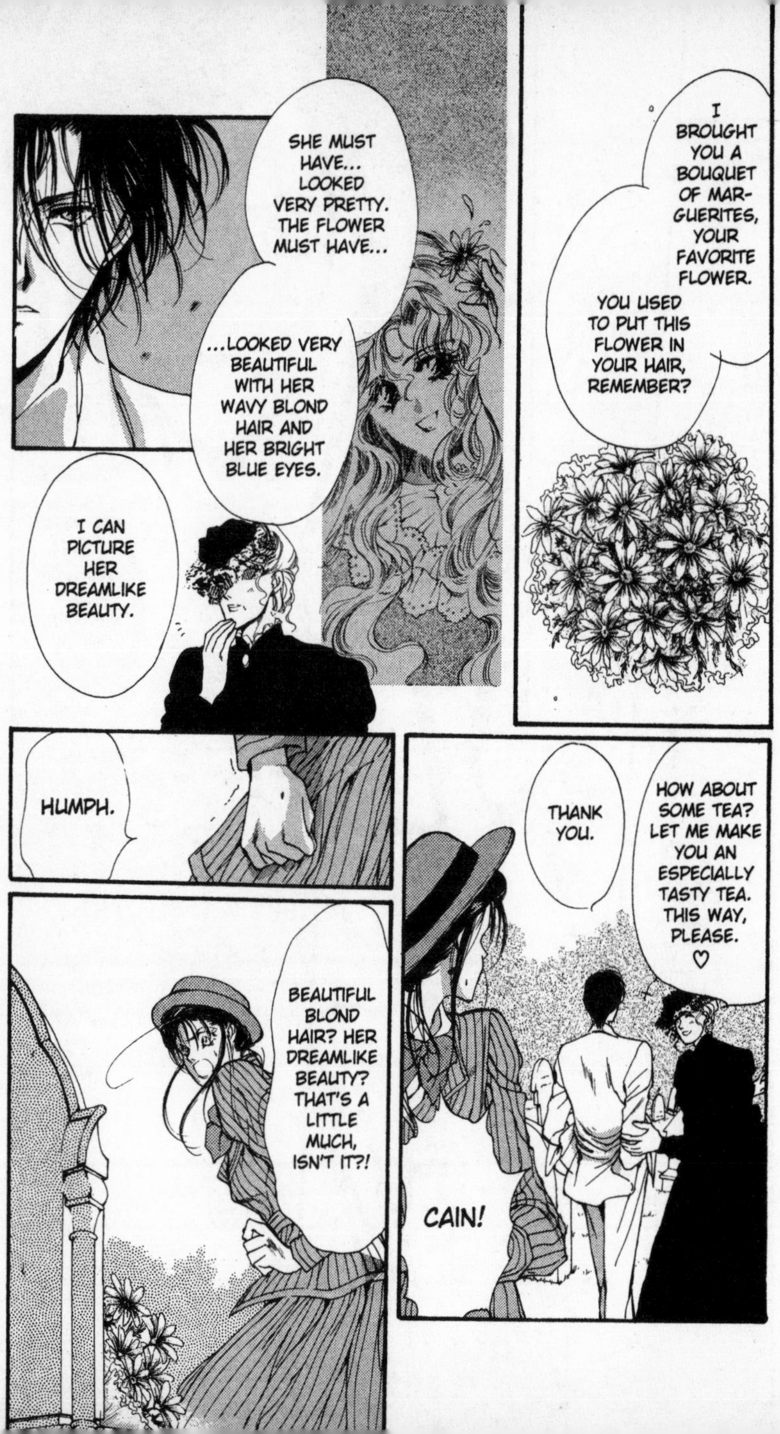
I BROUGHT YOU A BOUQUET OF MAR-GUERITES, YOUR FAVORITE FLOWER.
YOU USED TO PUT THIS FLOWER IN YOUR HAIR, REMEMBER?
SHE MUST HAVE... LOOKED VERY PRETTY. THE FLOWER MUST HAVE...
...LOOKED VERY BEAUTIFUL WITH HER WAVY BLOND HAIR AND HER BRIGHT BLUE EYES.
I CAN PICTURE HER DREAMLIKE BEAUTY.
HOW ABOUT SOME TEA? LET ME MAKE YOU AN ESPECIALLY TASTY TEA. THIS WAY, PLEASE. ♡
THANK YOU.
CAIN!
HUMPH.
BEAUTIFUL BLOND HAIR? HER DREAMLIKE BEAUTY? THAT'S A LITTLE MUCH, ISN'T IT?!

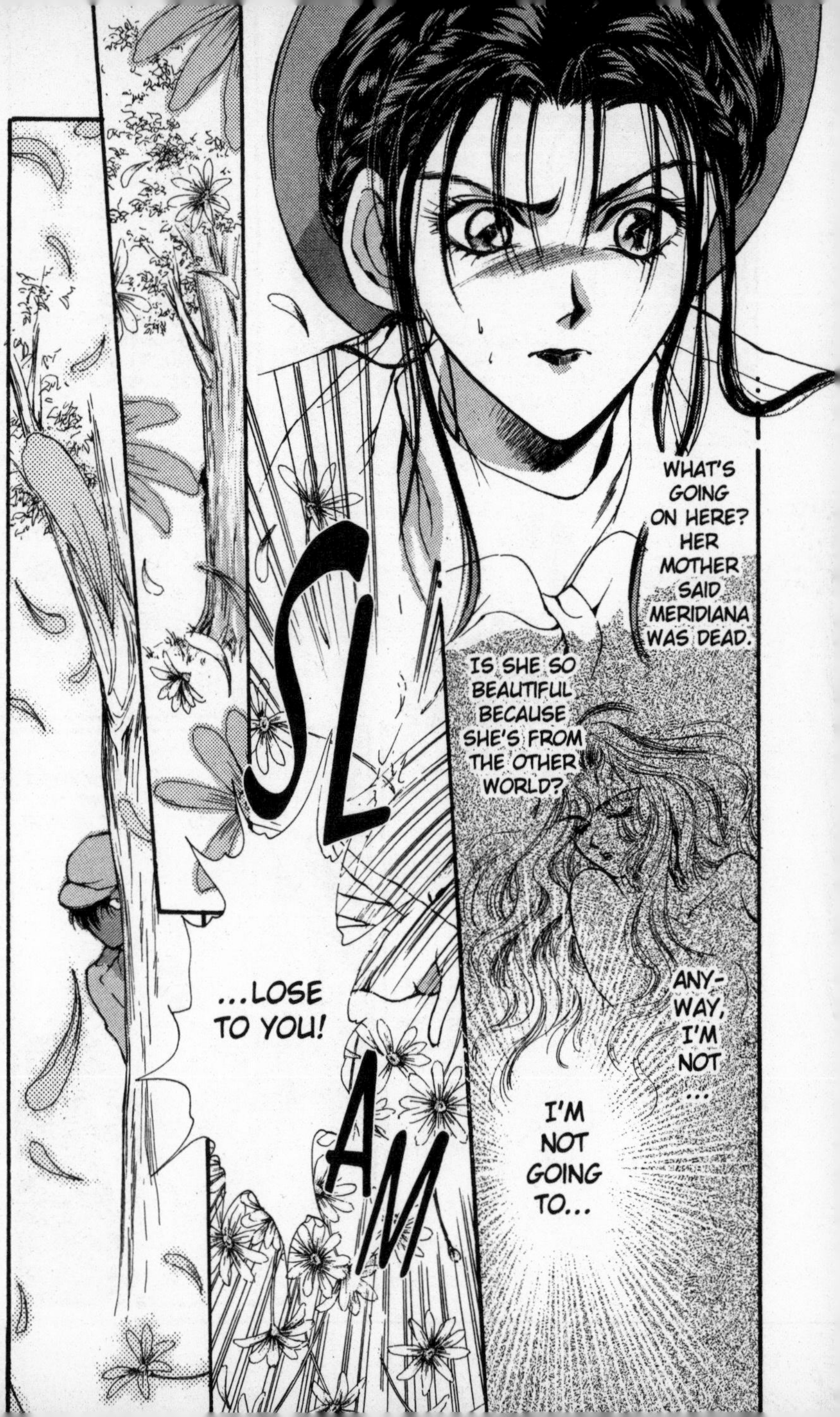
WHAT'S GOING ON HERE? HER MOTHER SAID MERIDIANA WAS DEAD.
IS SHE SO BEAUTIFUL BECAUSE SHE'S FROM THE OTHER WORLD?
ANY-WAY, I'M NOT...
I'M NOT GOING TO...
SLAM
...LOSE TO YOU!

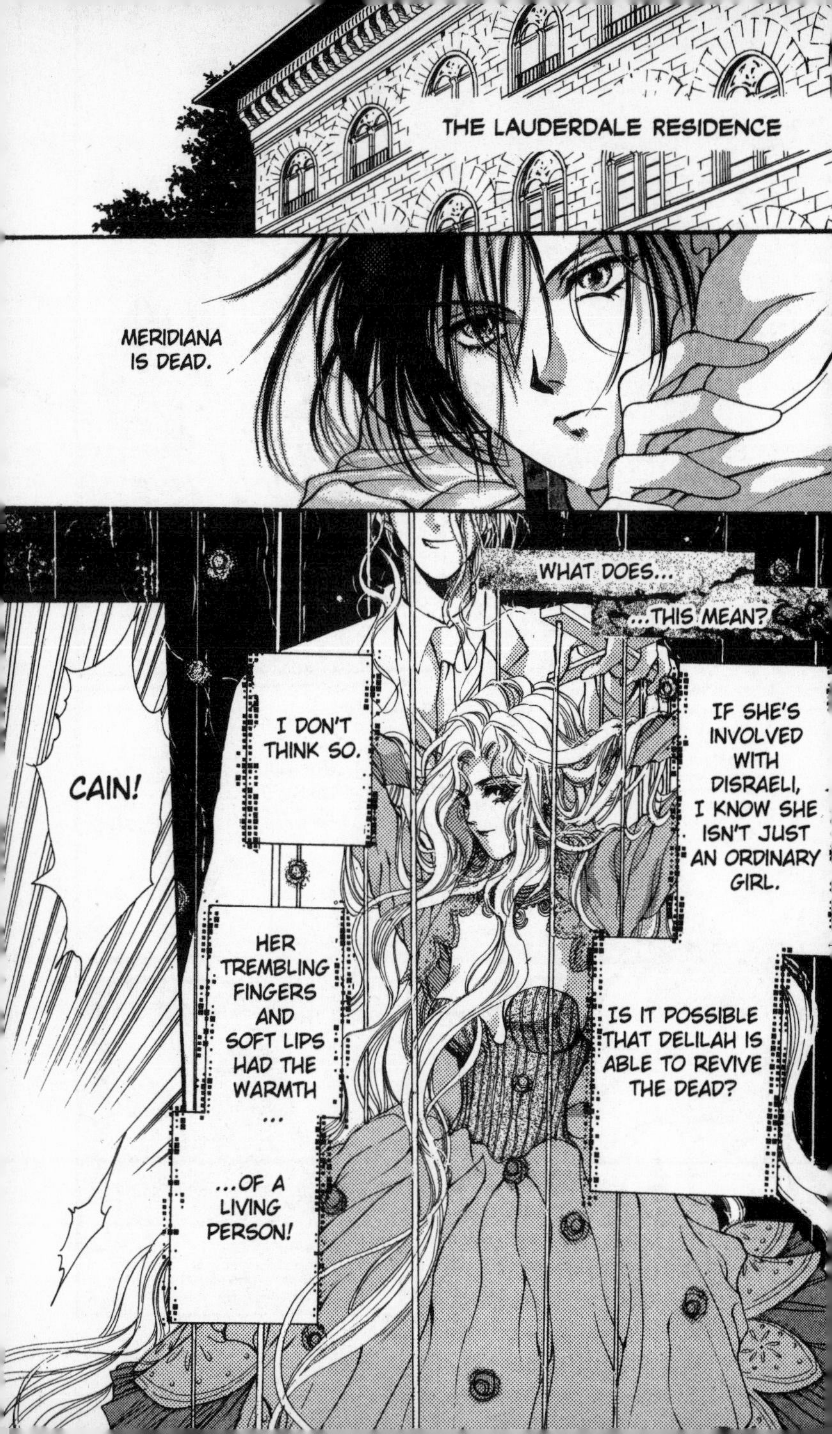
THE LAUDERDALE RESIDENCE
MERIDIANA IS DEAD.
WHAT DOES...
...THIS MEAN?
IF SHE'S INVOLVED WITH DISRAELI, I KNOW SHE ISN'T JUST AN ORDINARY GIRL.
IS IT POSSIBLE THAT DELILAH IS ABLE TO REVIVE THE DEAD?
I DON'T THINK SO.
HER TREMBLING FINGERS AND SOFT LIPS HAD THE WARMTH ...
...OF A LIVING PERSON!
CAIN!

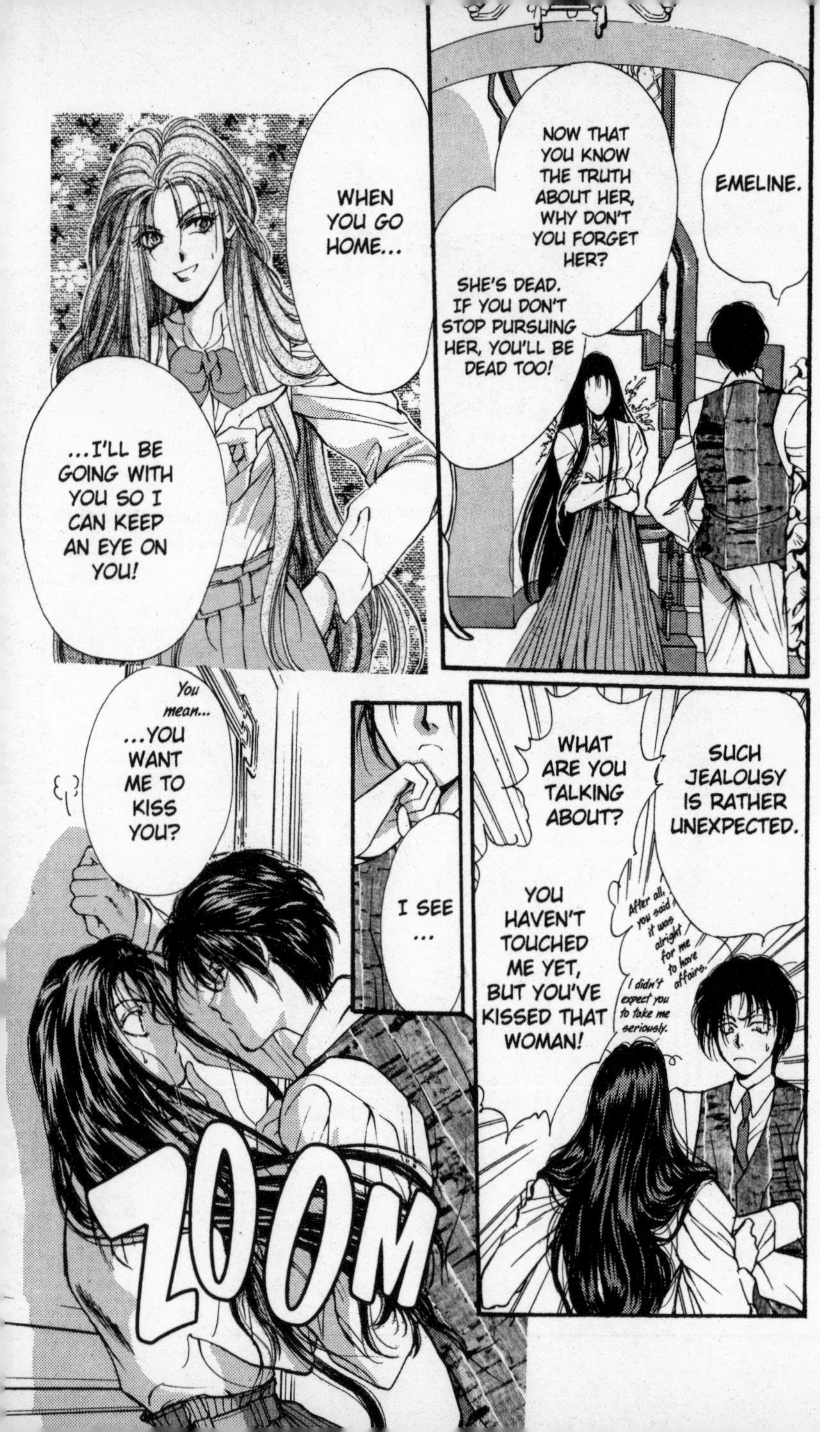
EMELINE.
NOW THAT YOU KNOW THE TRUTH ABOUT HER, WHY DON'T YOU FORGET HER?
SHE'S DEAD. IF YOU DON'T STOP PURSUING HER, YOU'LL BE DEAD TOO!
WHEN YOU GO HOME...
...I'LL BE GOING WITH YOU SO I CAN KEEP AN EYE ON YOU!
SUCH JEALOUSY IS RATHER UNEXPECTED.
WHAT ARE YOU TALKING ABOUT?
After all, you said it was alright for me to have affairs.
I didn't expect you to take me seriously.
YOU HAVEN'T TOUCHED ME YET, BUT YOU'VE KISSED THAT WOMAN!
I SEE ...
You mean...
...YOU WANT ME TO KISS YOU?
ZOOM

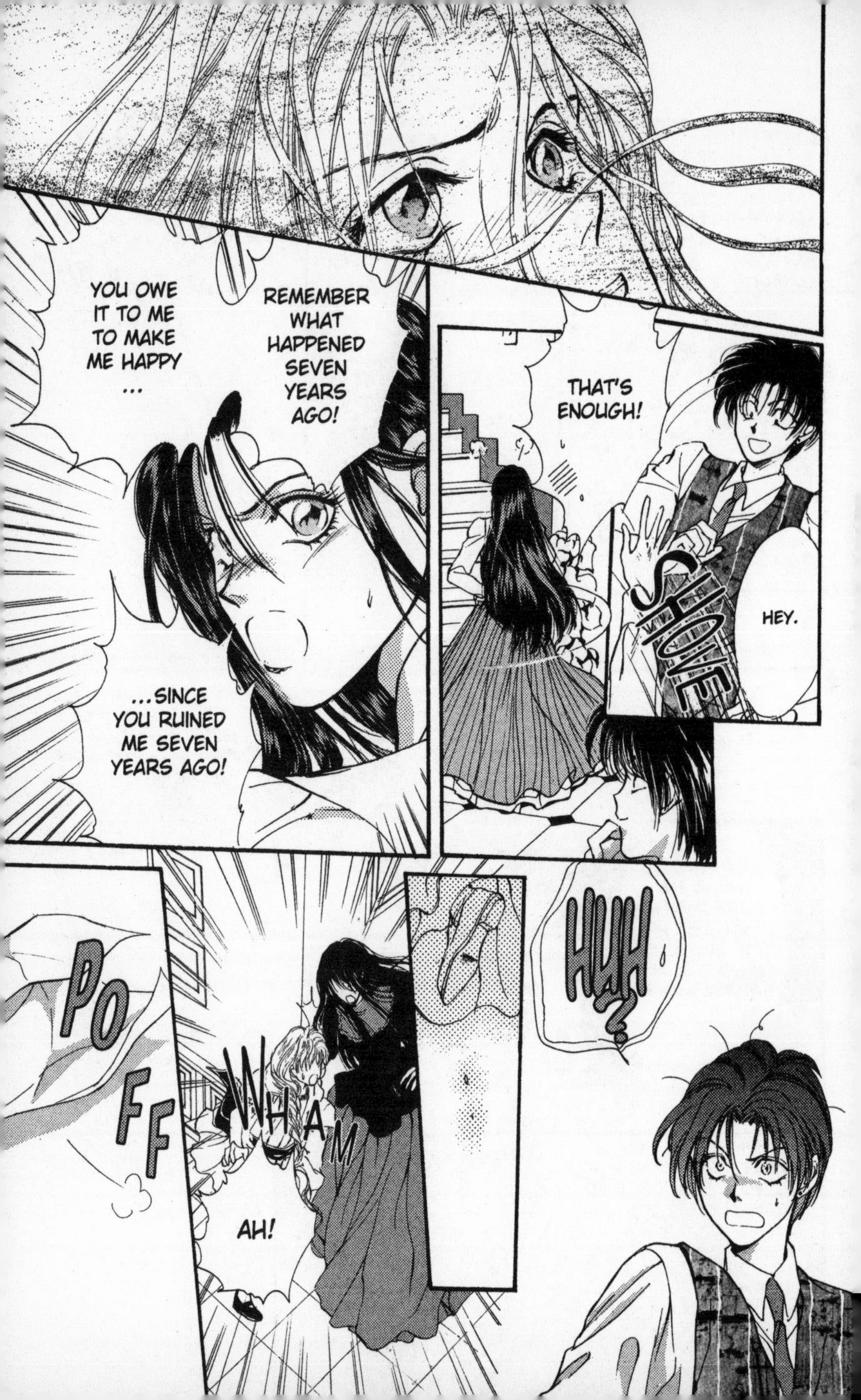
THAT'S ENOUGH!
SHOVE
HEY.
REMEMBER WHAT HAPPENED SEVEN YEARS AGO!
YOU OWE IT TO ME TO MAKE ME HAPPY ...
...SINCE YOU RUINED ME SEVEN YEARS AGO!
HUH?
WHAM
AH!
POFF

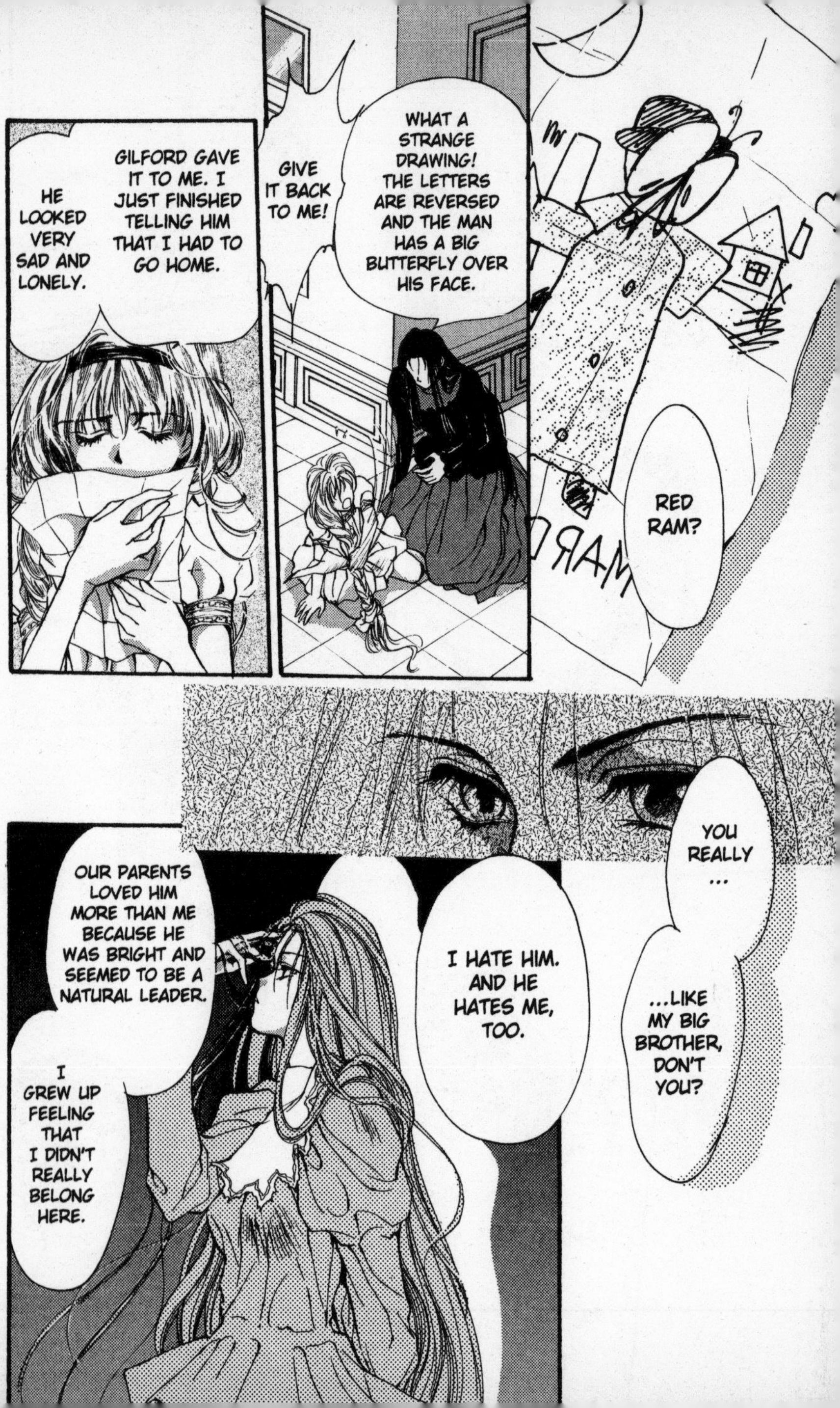
RED RAM?
WHAT A STRANGE DRAWING! THE LETTERS ARE REVERSED AND THE MAN HAS A BIG BUTTERFLY OVER HIS FACE.
GIVE IT BACK TO ME!
GILFORD GAVE IT TO ME. I JUST FINISHED TELLING HIM THAT I HAD TO GO HOME.
HE LOOKED VERY SAD AND LONELY.
YOU REALLY ...
...LIKE MY BIG BROTHER, DON'T YOU?
I HATE HIM. AND HE HATES ME, TOO.
OUR PARENTS LOVED HIM MORE THAN ME BECAUSE HE WAS BRIGHT AND SEEMED TO BE A NATURAL LEADER.
I GREW UP FEELING THAT I DIDN'T REALLY BELONG HERE.

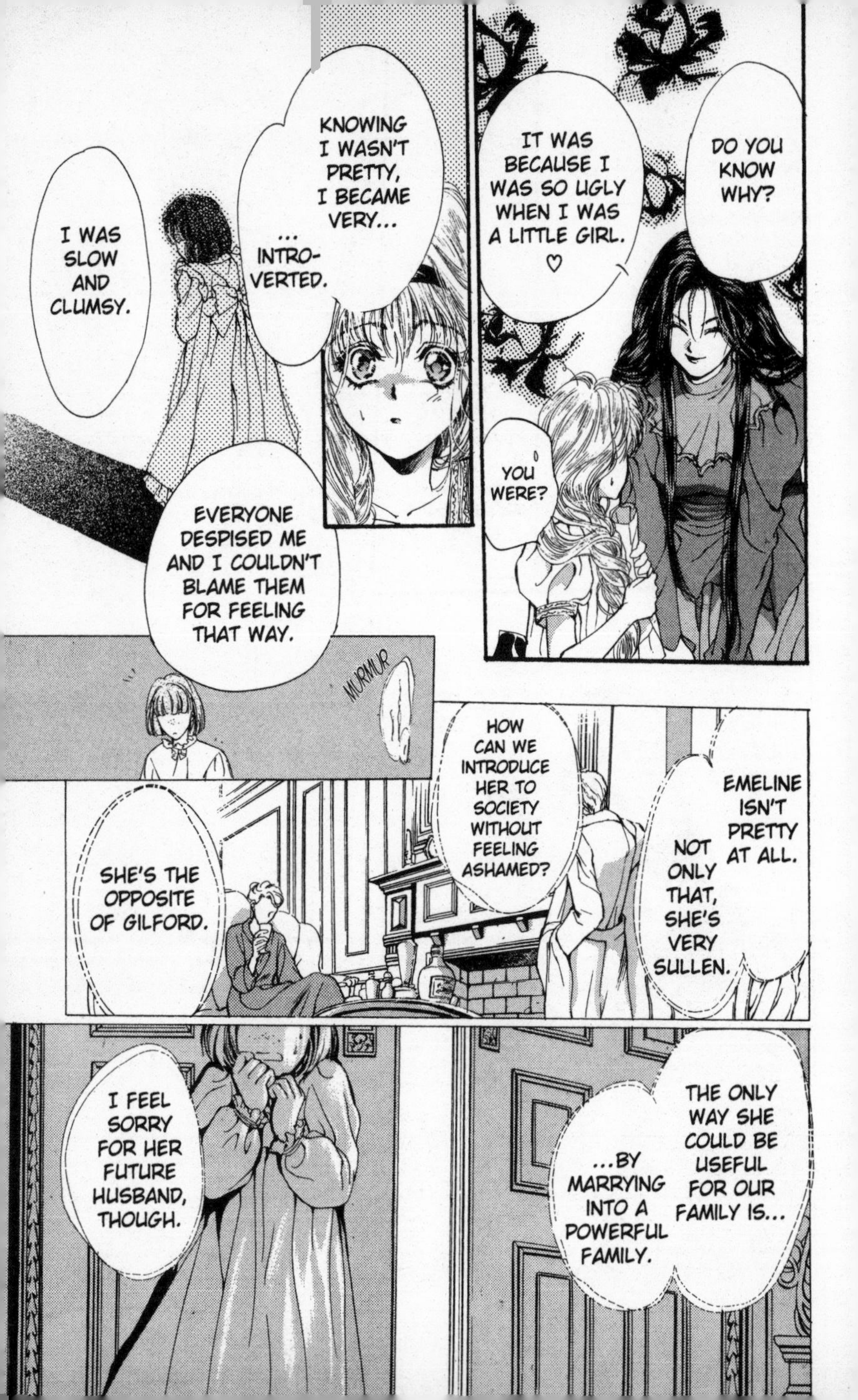
DO YOU KNOW WHY?
IT WAS BECAUSE I WAS SO UGLY WHEN I WAS A LITTLE GIRL. ♡
YOU WERE?
KNOWING I WASN'T PRETTY, I BECAME VERY...
...INTROVERTED.
I WAS SLOW AND CLUMSY.
EVERYONE DESPISED ME AND I COULDN'T BLAME THEM FOR FEELING THAT WAY.
MURMUR
EMELINE ISN'T PRETTY AT ALL.
NOT ONLY THAT, SHE'S VERY SULLEN.
HOW CAN WE INTRODUCE HER TO SOCIETY WITHOUT FEELING ASHAMED?
SHE'S THE OPPOSITE OF GILFORD.
THE ONLY WAY SHE COULD BE USEFUL FOR OUR FAMILY IS...
...BY MARRYING INTO A POWERFUL FAMILY.
I FEEL SORRY FOR HER FUTURE HUSBAND, THOUGH.

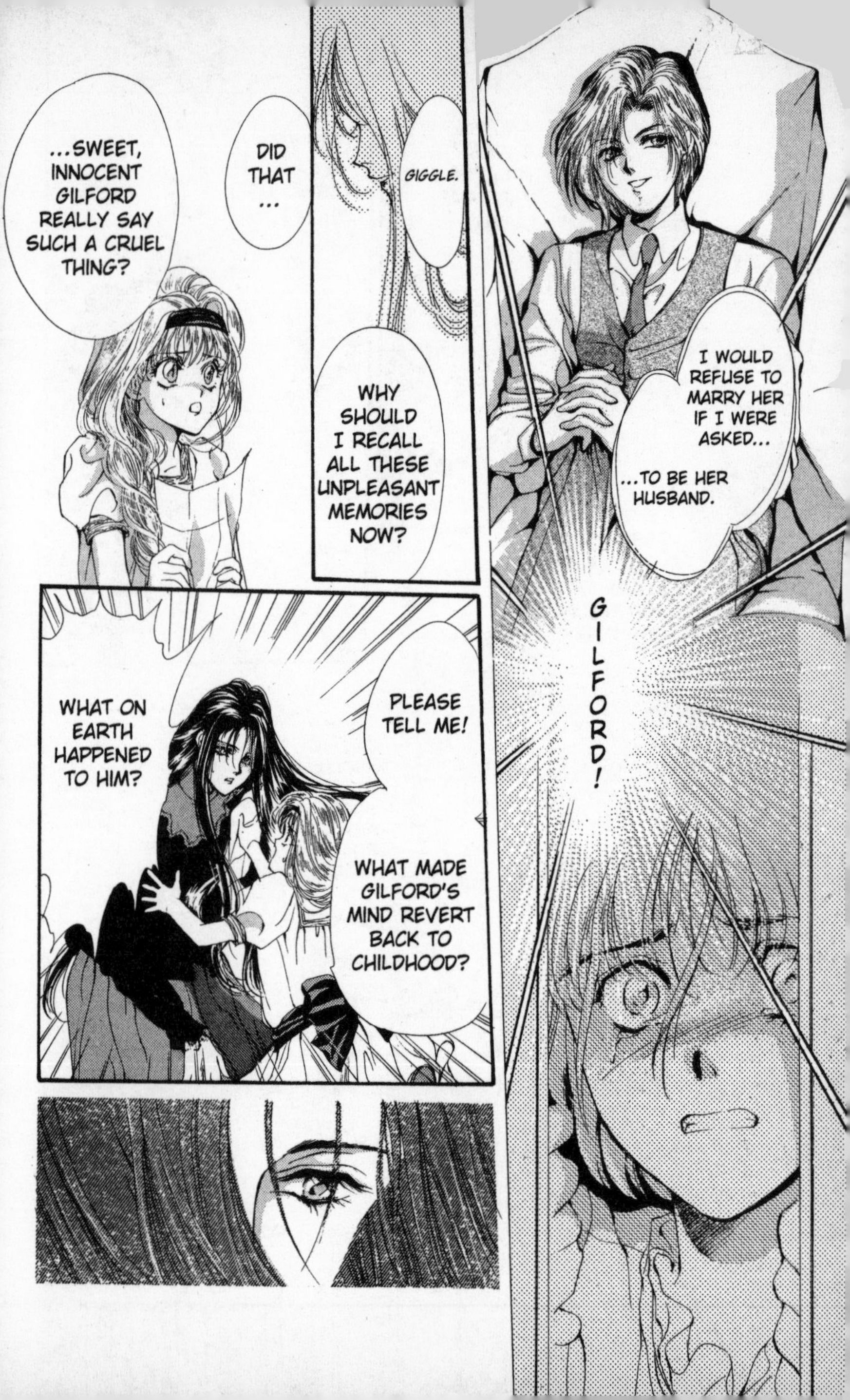
I WOULD REFUSE TO MARRY HER IF I WERE ASKED...
...TO BE HER HUSBAND.
GILFORD!
GIGGLE.
WHY SHOULD I RECALL ALL THESE UNPLEASANT MEMORIES NOW?
DID THAT...
...SWEET, INNOCENT GILFORD REALLY SAY SUCH A CRUEL THING?
PLEASE TELL ME!
WHAT ON EARTH HAPPENED TO HIM?
WHAT MADE GILFORD'S MIND REVERT BACK TO CHILDHOOD?

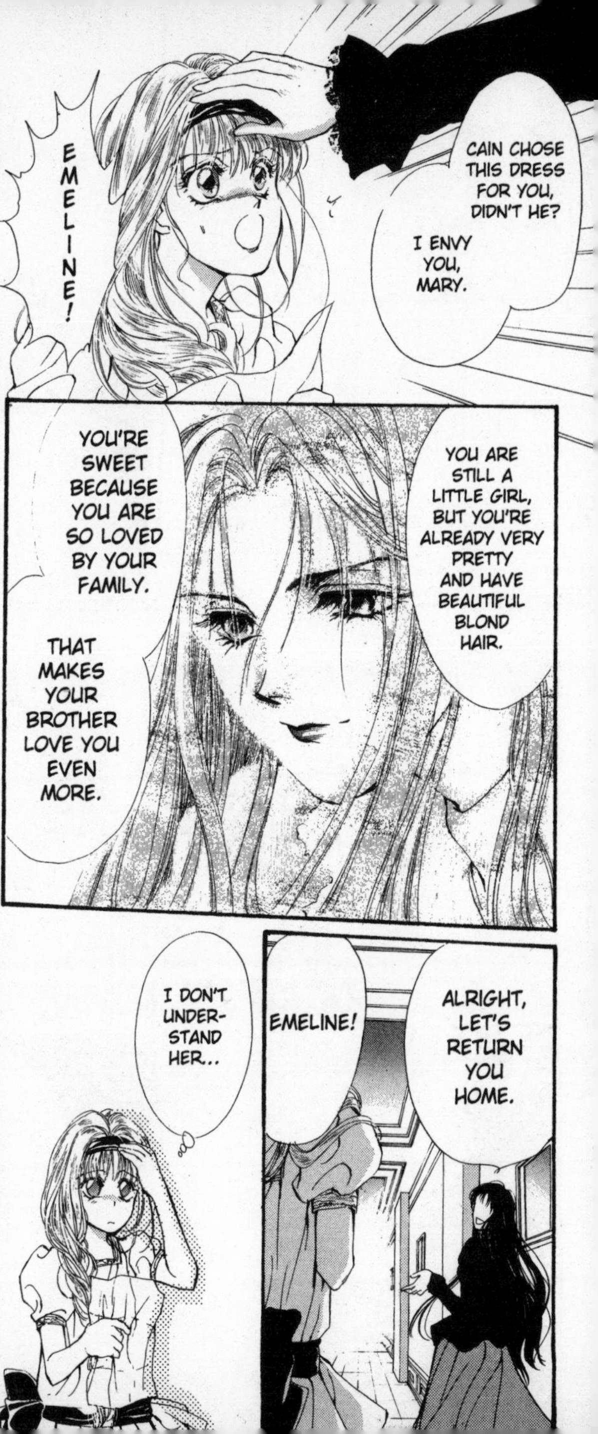
CAIN CHOSE THIS DRESS FOR YOU, DIDN'T HE?
I ENVY YOU, MARY.
EMELINE!
YOU ARE STILL A LITTLE GIRL, BUT YOU'RE ALREADY VERY PRETTY AND HAVE BEAUTIFUL BLOND HAIR.
YOU'RE SWEET BECAUSE YOU ARE SO LOVED BY YOUR FAMILY.
THAT MAKES YOUR BROTHER LOVE YOU EVEN MORE.
ALRIGHT, LET'S RETURN YOU HOME.
EMELINE!
I DON'T UNDER-STAND HER...

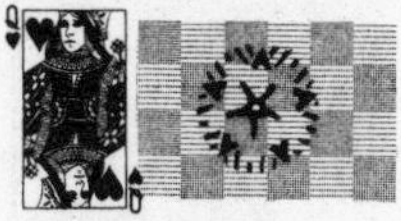

Emeline is becoming more and more popular among the readers! An increasing number of readers are feeling sympathy for her and some have grown to hate not only Meridiana but also Cain because of the way he treats Emeline! I'm a little perplexed by this trend... Anyway, it's now clear that Emeline isn't the killer. (Those who thought she was Jack the Ripper overinterpreted my story.) At any rate, I regret that I wasn't able to do a better job of depicting Emeline on horseback. [Note: the picture the author refers to probably appears on the cover of the magazine in which the story was first published.] I like the way an equestrian looks because it symbolizes for me the part of British culture I most admire. In the cover page I did for this issue, it looks like Emeline is about to fall from her horse, doesn't it? Meanwhile, Cain is digging a grave on the cover page. He must be thinking of Suzette as he digs. He's really a complicated man. I'd like to ask him, "Why can't you fall in love with a normal woman, Cain?"

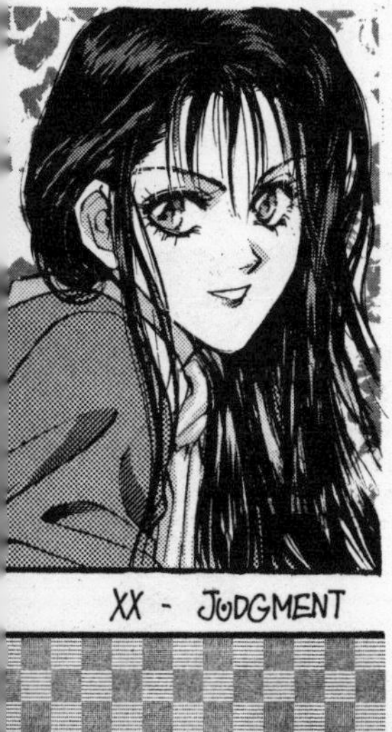

XX - JUDGMENT

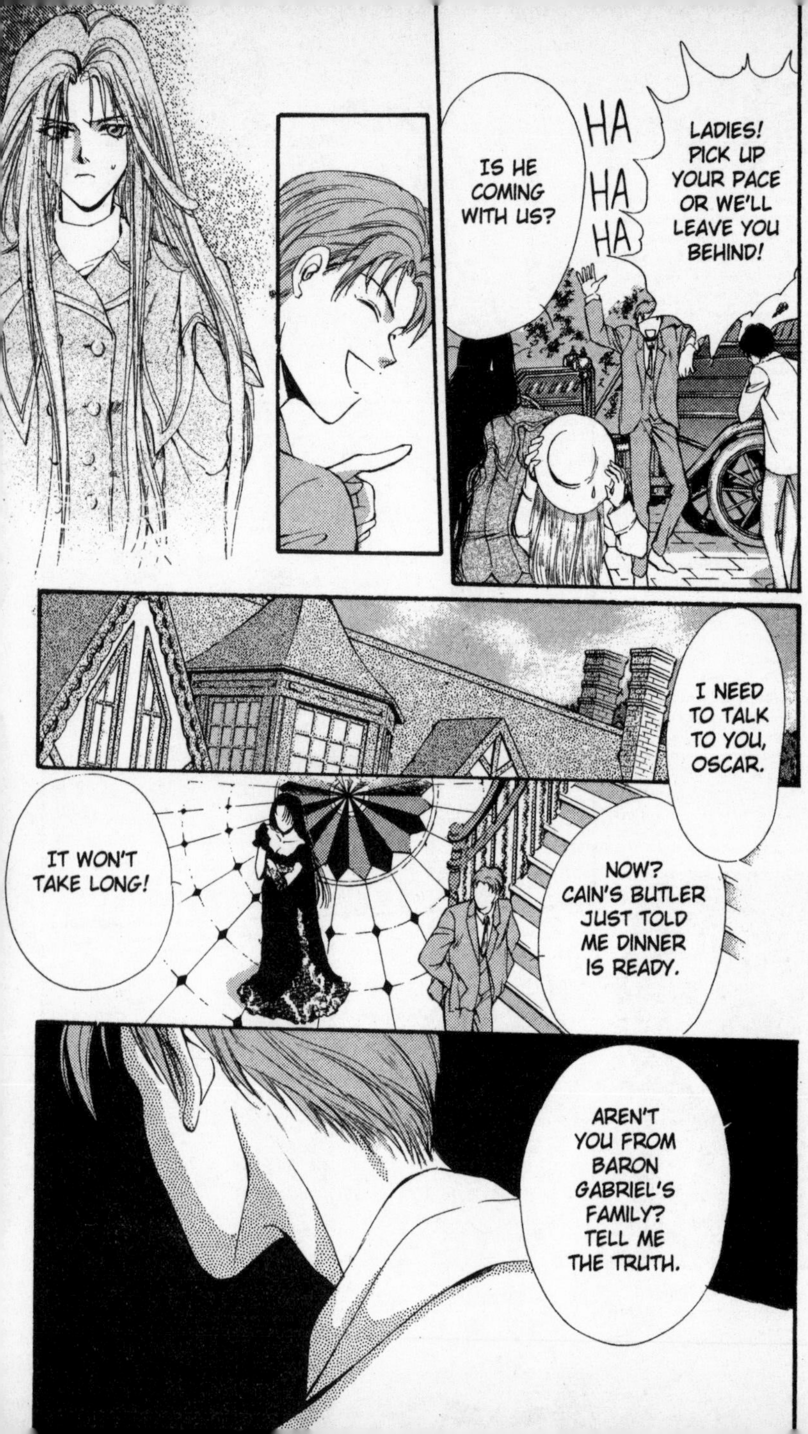
LADIES! PICK UP YOUR PACE OR WE'LL LEAVE YOU BEHIND!
HA HA HA
IS HE COMING WITH US?
I NEED TO TALK TO YOU, OSCAR.
NOW? CAIN'S BUTLER JUST TOLD ME DINNER IS READY.
IT WON'T TAKE LONG!
AREN'T YOU FROM BARON GABRIEL'S FAMILY? TELL ME THE TRUTH.

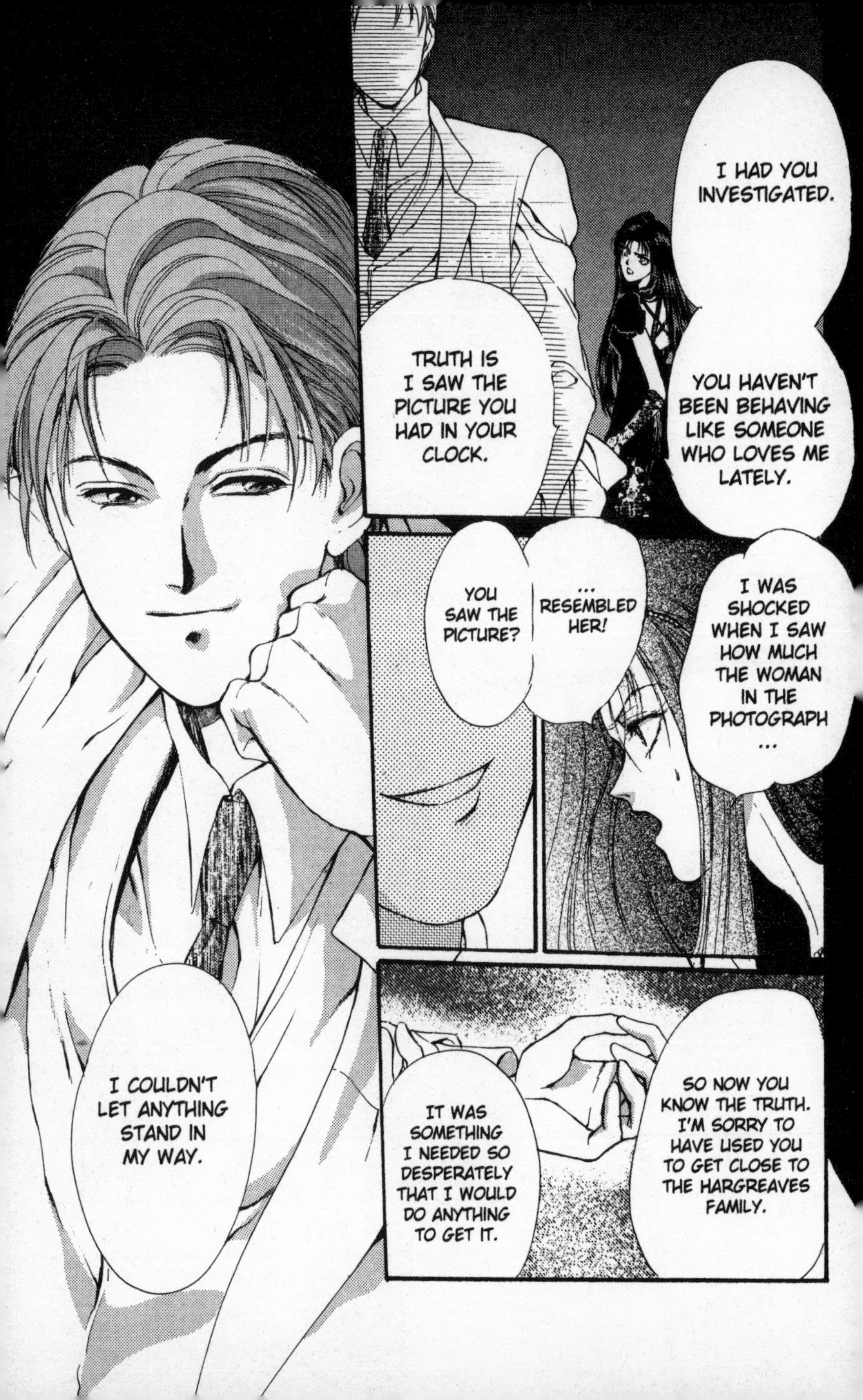
I HAD YOU INVESTIGATED.
YOU HAVEN'T BEEN BEHAVING LIKE SOMEONE WHO LOVES ME LATELY.
TRUTH IS I SAW THE PICTURE YOU HAD IN YOUR CLOCK.
I WAS SHOCKED WHEN I SAW HOW MUCH THE WOMAN IN THE PHOTOGRAPH ...
... RESEMBLED HER!
YOU SAW THE PICTURE?
SO NOW YOU KNOW THE TRUTH. I'M SORRY TO HAVE USED YOU TO GET CLOSE TO THE HARGREAVES FAMILY.
IT WAS SOMETHING I NEEDED SO DESPERATELY THAT I WOULD DO ANYTHING TO GET IT.
I COULDN'T LET ANYTHING STAND IN MY WAY.

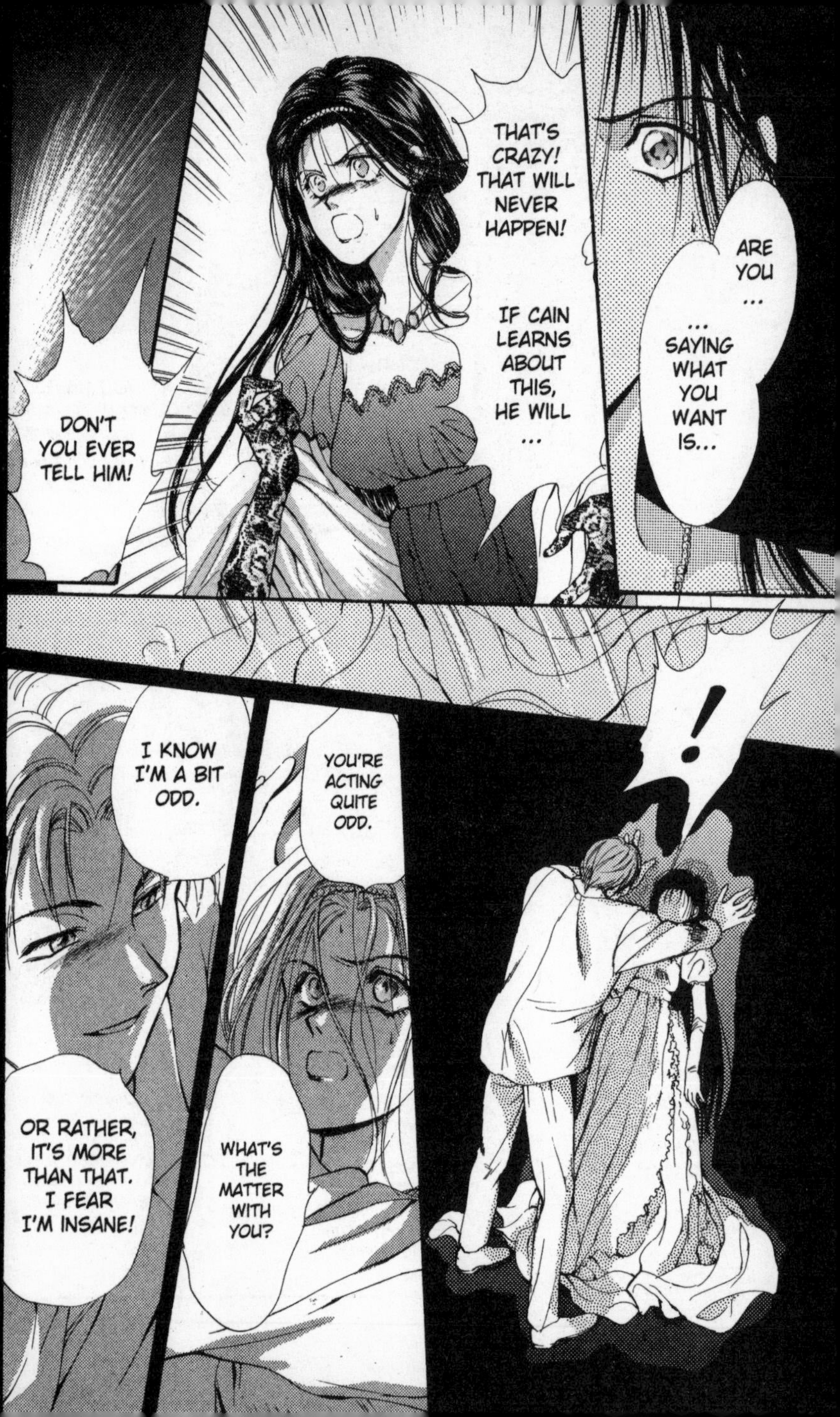
ARE YOU ...
... SAYING WHAT YOU WANT IS...
THAT'S CRAZY! THAT WILL NEVER HAPPEN!
IF CAIN LEARNS ABOUT THIS, HE WILL ...
DON'T YOU EVER TELL HIM!
!
YOU'RE ACTING QUITE ODD.
WHAT'S THE MATTER WITH YOU?
I KNOW I'M A BIT ODD.
OR RATHER, IT'S MORE THAN THAT. I FEAR I'M INSANE!

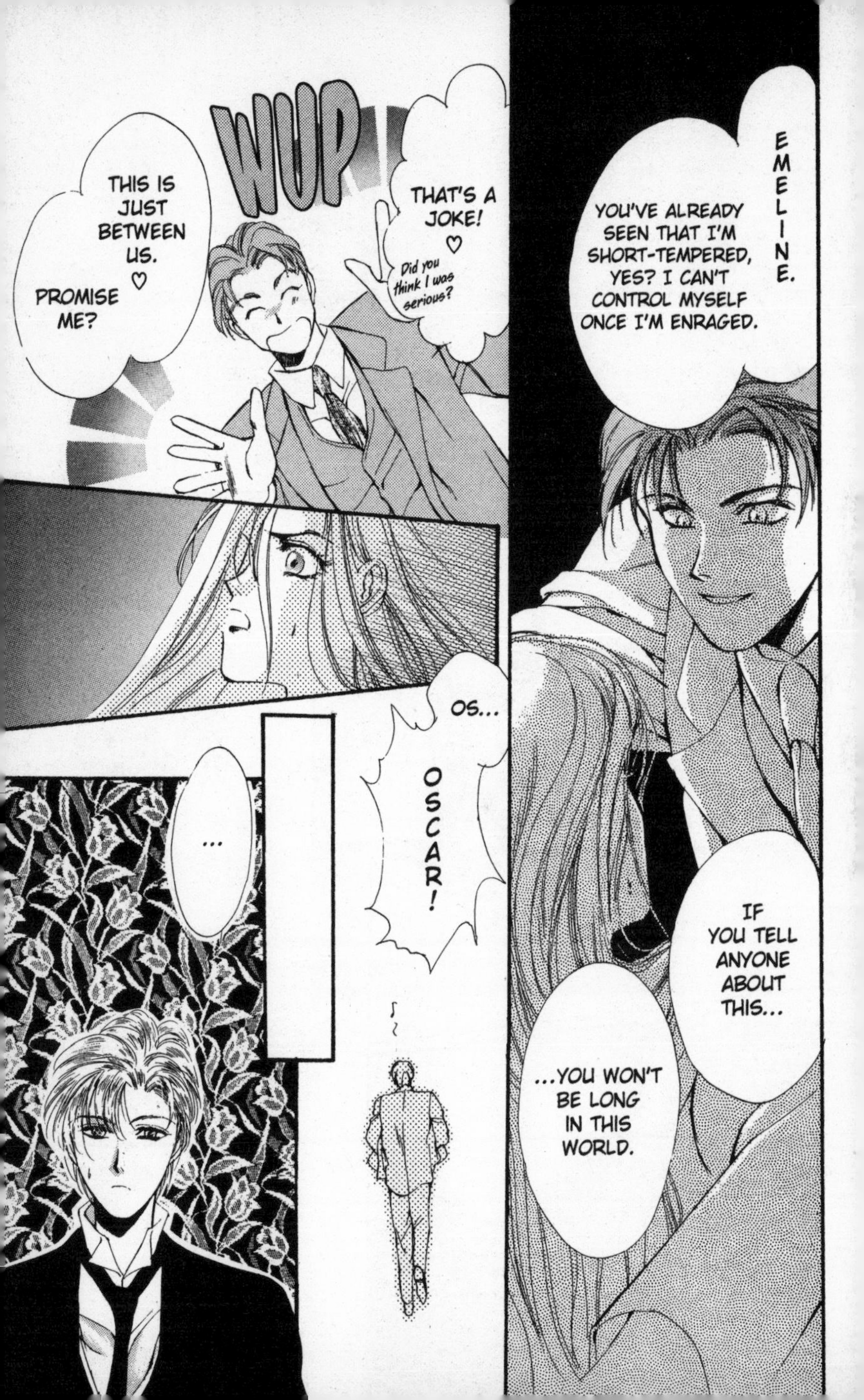
EMELINE.
YOU'VE ALREADY SEEN THAT I'M SHORT-TEMPERED, YES? I CAN'T CONTROL MYSELF ONCE I'M ENRAGED.
IF YOU TELL ANYONE ABOUT THIS...
...YOU WON'T BE LONG IN THIS WORLD.
THAT'S A JOKE! ♡
Did you think I was serious?
WUP
THIS IS JUST BETWEEN US. ♡
PROMISE ME?
OS...
OSCAR!
...

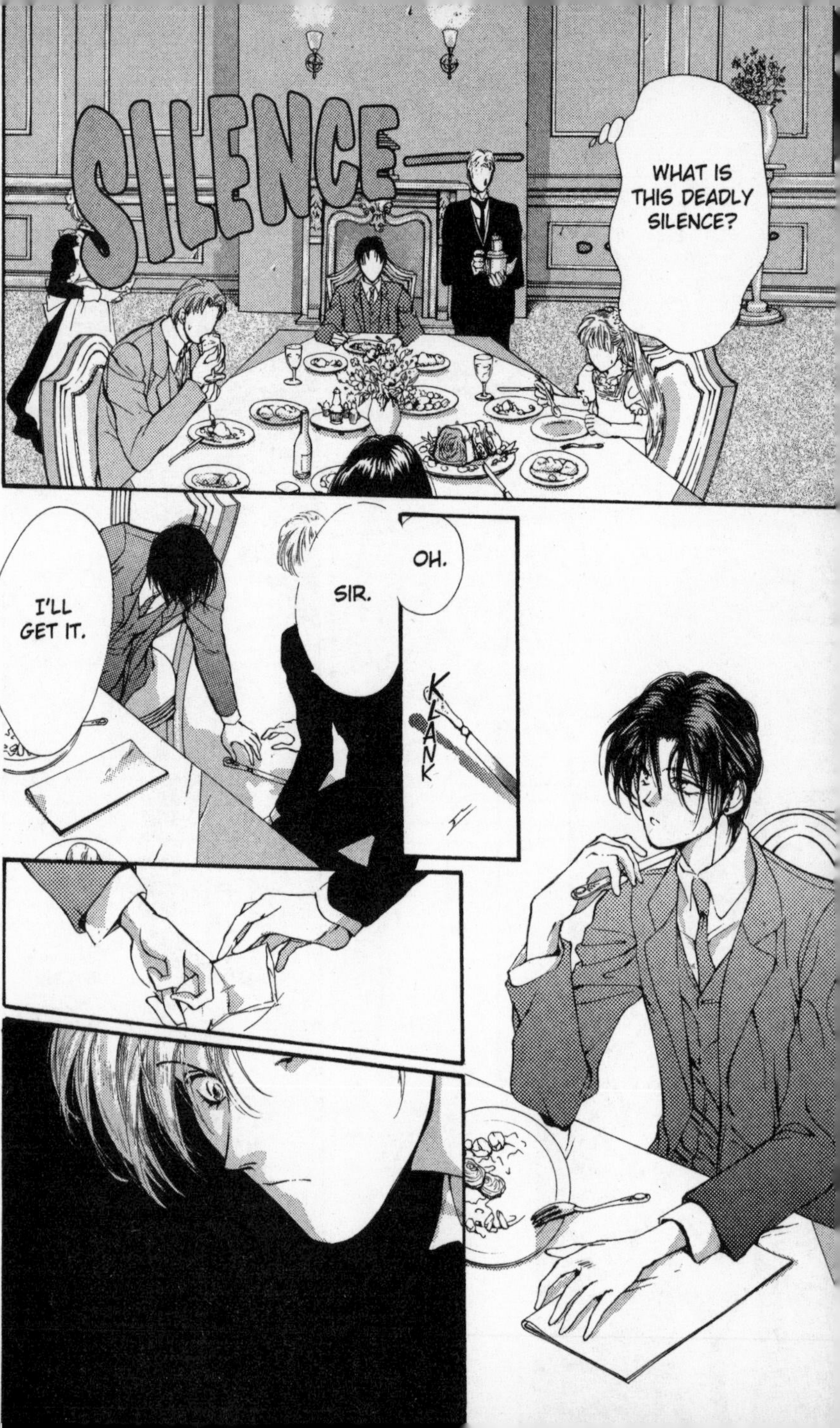
WHAT IS THIS DEADLY SILENCE?
SILENCE—
KLANK
OH.
SIR.
I'LL GET IT.

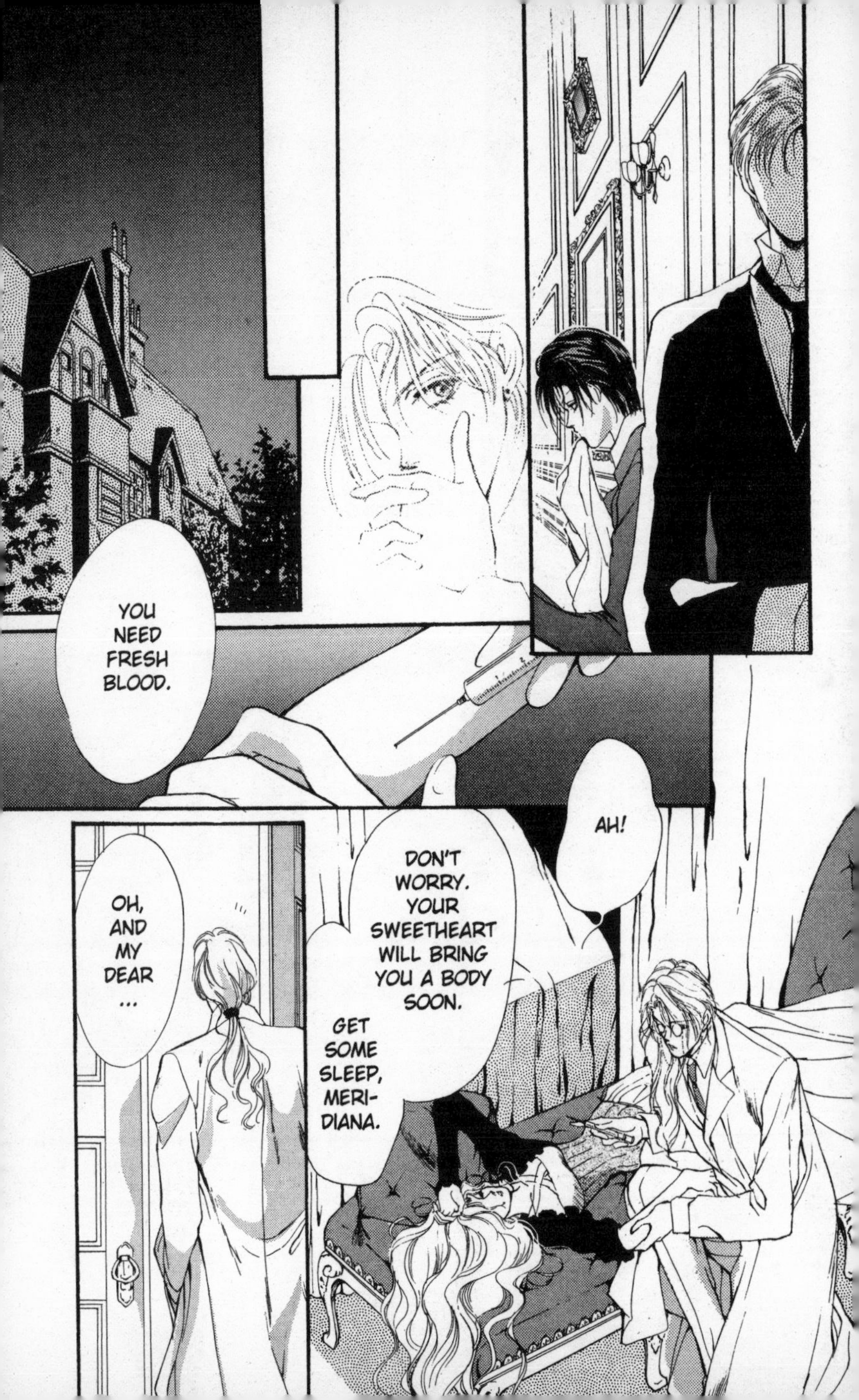
YOU NEED FRESH BLOOD.
AH!
DON'T WORRY. YOUR SWEETHEART WILL BRING YOU A BODY SOON.
GET SOME SLEEP, MERI-DIANA.
OH, AND MY DEAR ...

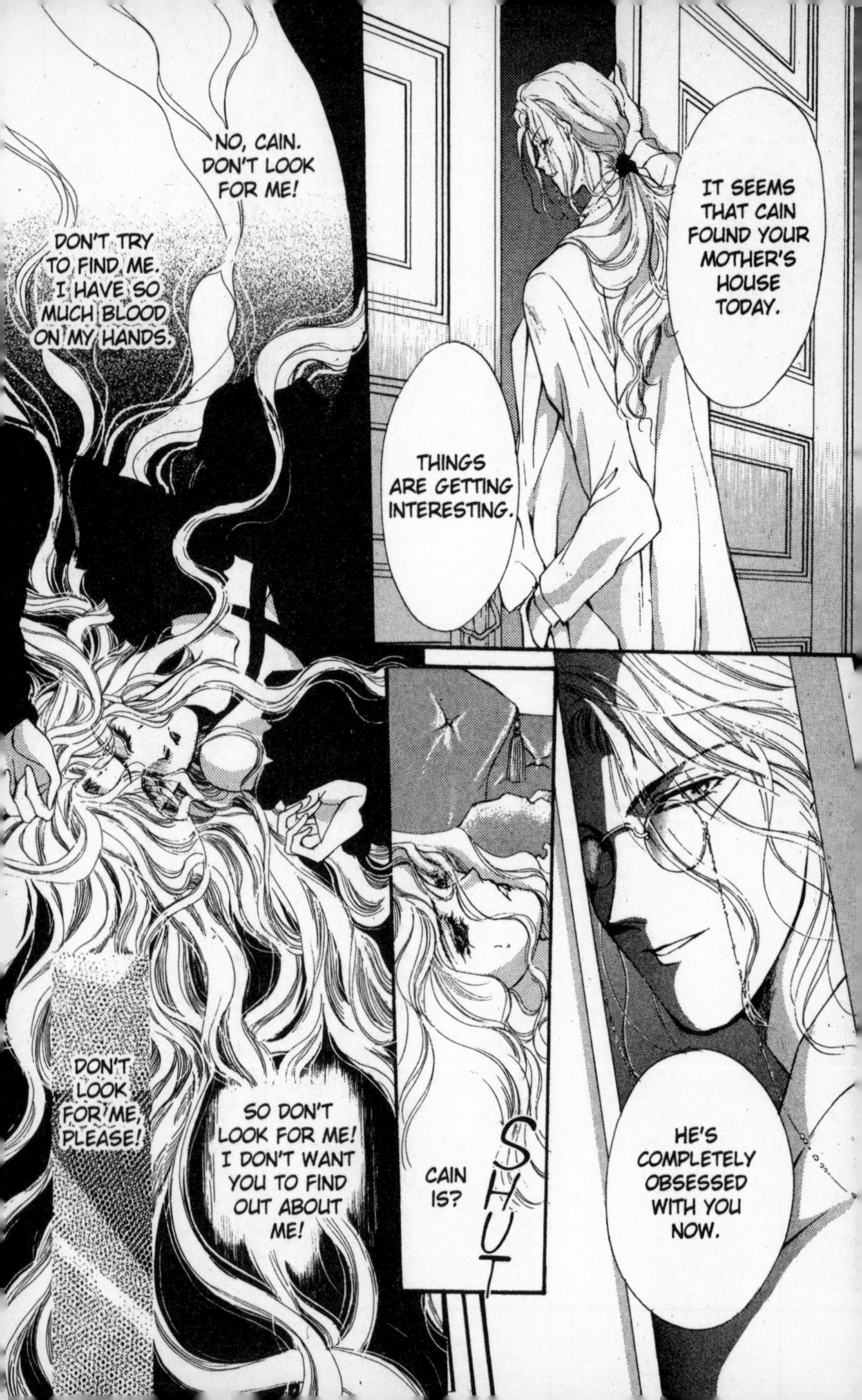
IT SEEMS THAT CAIN FOUND YOUR MOTHER'S HOUSE TODAY.
THINGS ARE GETTING INTERESTING.
HE'S COMPLETELY OBSESSED WITH YOU NOW.
SHUT
CAIN IS?
NO, CAIN. DON'T LOOK FOR ME!
DON'T TRY TO FIND ME. I HAVE SO MUCH BLOOD ON MY HANDS.
SO DON'T LOOK FOR ME! I DON'T WANT YOU TO FIND OUT ABOUT ME!
DON'T LOOK FOR ME, PLEASE!

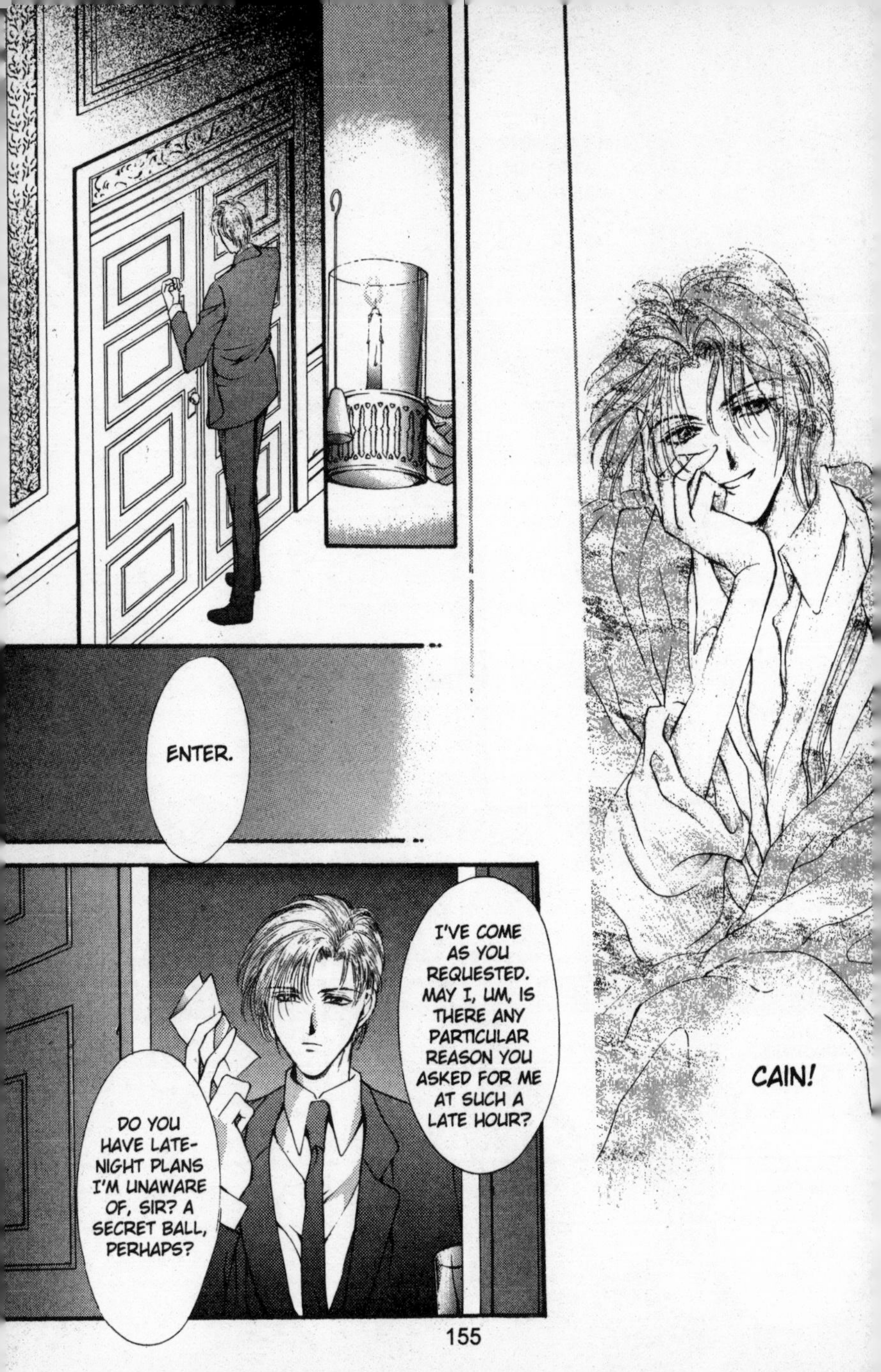
CAIN!
ENTER.
I'VE COME AS YOU REQUESTED. MAY I, UM, IS THERE ANY PARTICULAR REASON YOU ASKED FOR ME AT SUCH A LATE HOUR?
DO YOU HAVE LATE-NIGHT PLANS I'M UNAWARE OF, SIR? A SECRET BALL, PERHAPS?

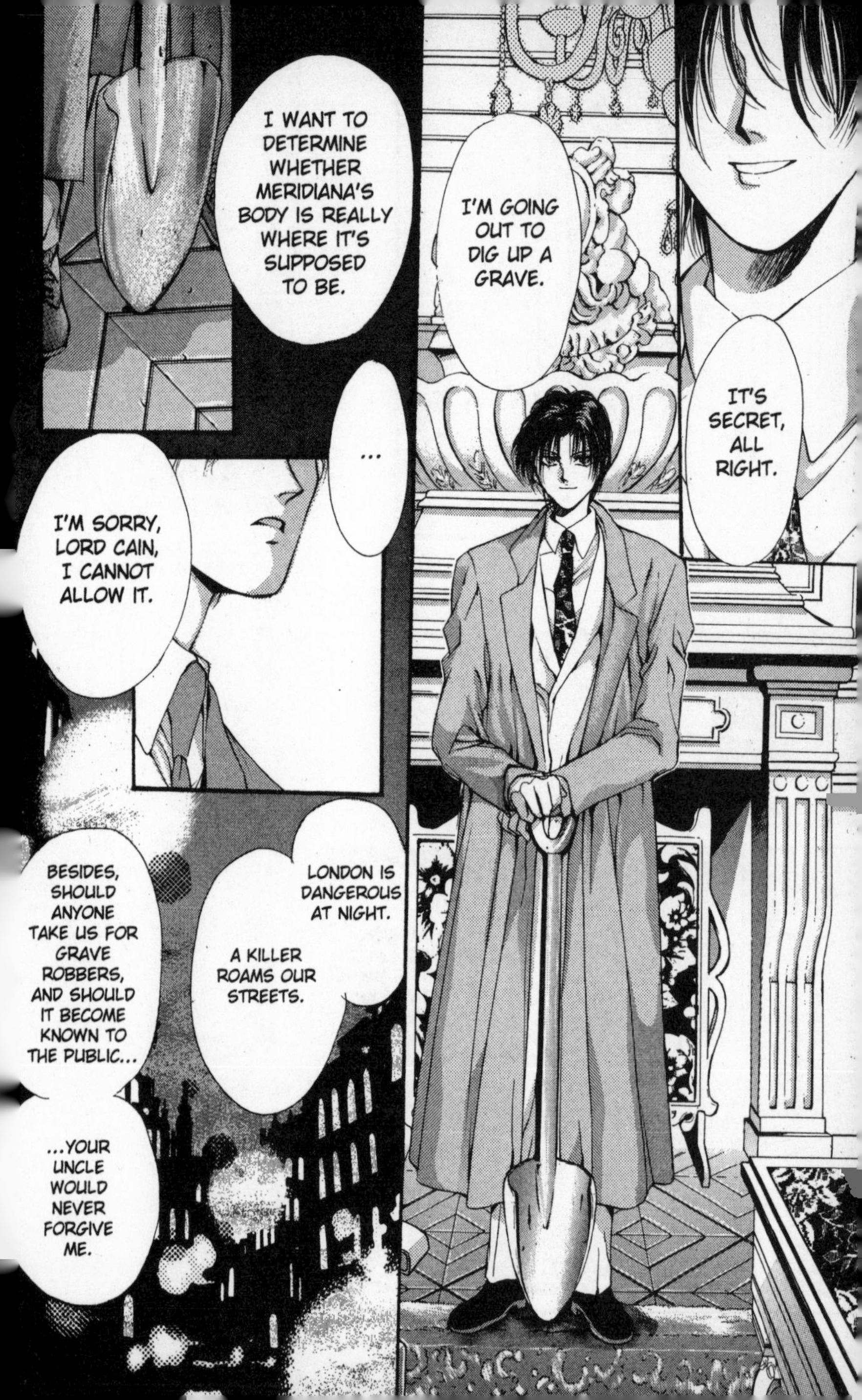
IT'S SECRET, ALL RIGHT.
I'M GOING OUT TO DIG UP A GRAVE.
I WANT TO DETERMINE WHETHER MERIDIANA'S BODY IS REALLY WHERE IT'S SUPPOSED TO BE.
...
I'M SORRY, LORD CAIN, I CANNOT ALLOW IT.
LONDON IS DANGEROUS AT NIGHT.
A KILLER ROAMS OUR STREETS.
BESIDES, SHOULD ANYONE TAKE US FOR GRAVE ROBBERS, AND SHOULD IT BECOME KNOWN TO THE PUBLIC...
...YOUR UNCLE WOULD NEVER FORGIVE ME.

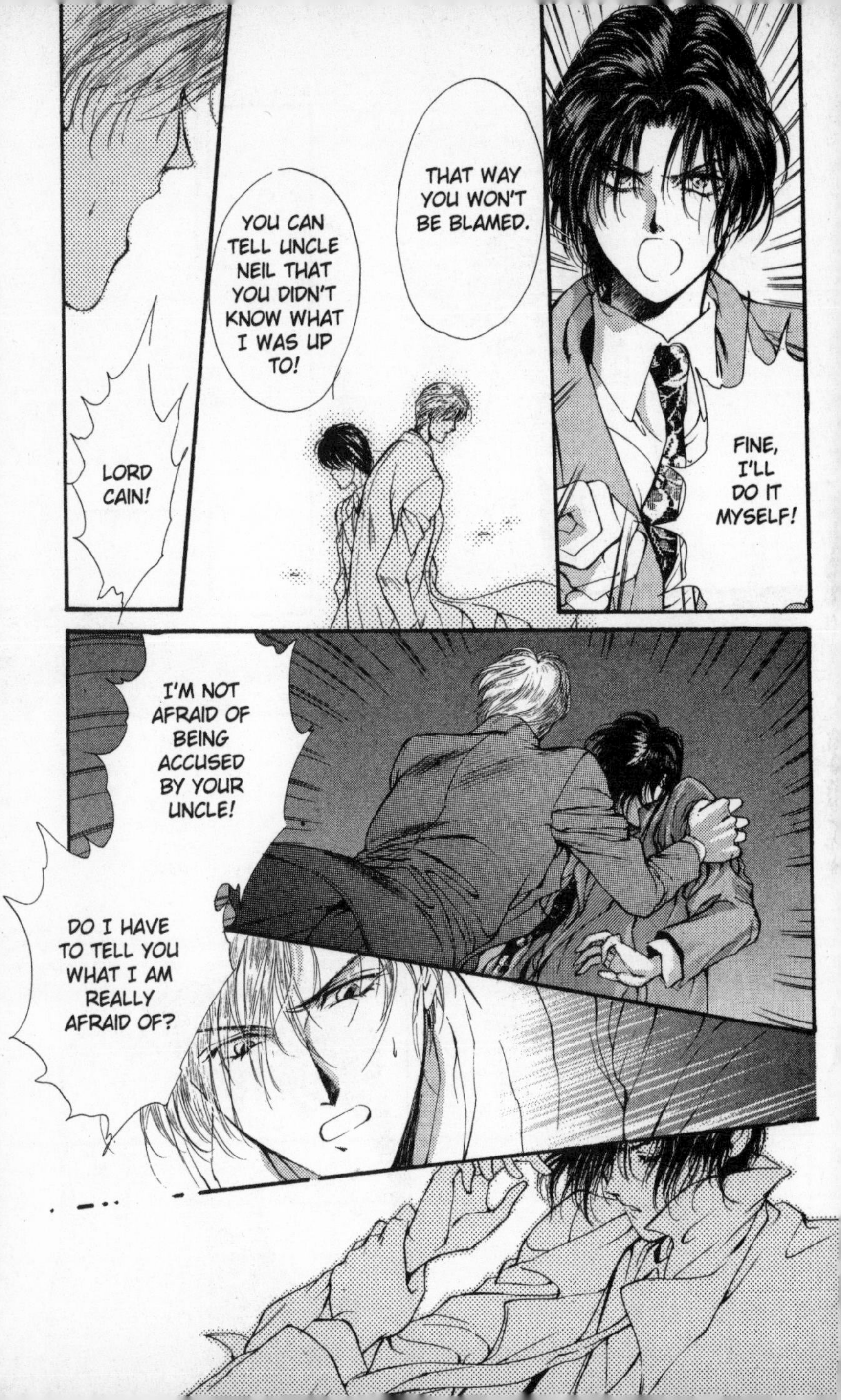
FINE, I'LL DO IT MYSELF!
THAT WAY YOU WON'T BE BLAMED.
YOU CAN TELL UNCLE NEIL THAT YOU DIDN'T KNOW WHAT I WAS UP TO!
LORD CAIN!
I'M NOT AFRAID OF BEING ACCUSED BY YOUR UNCLE!
DO I HAVE TO TELL YOU WHAT I AM REALLY AFRAID OF?
...

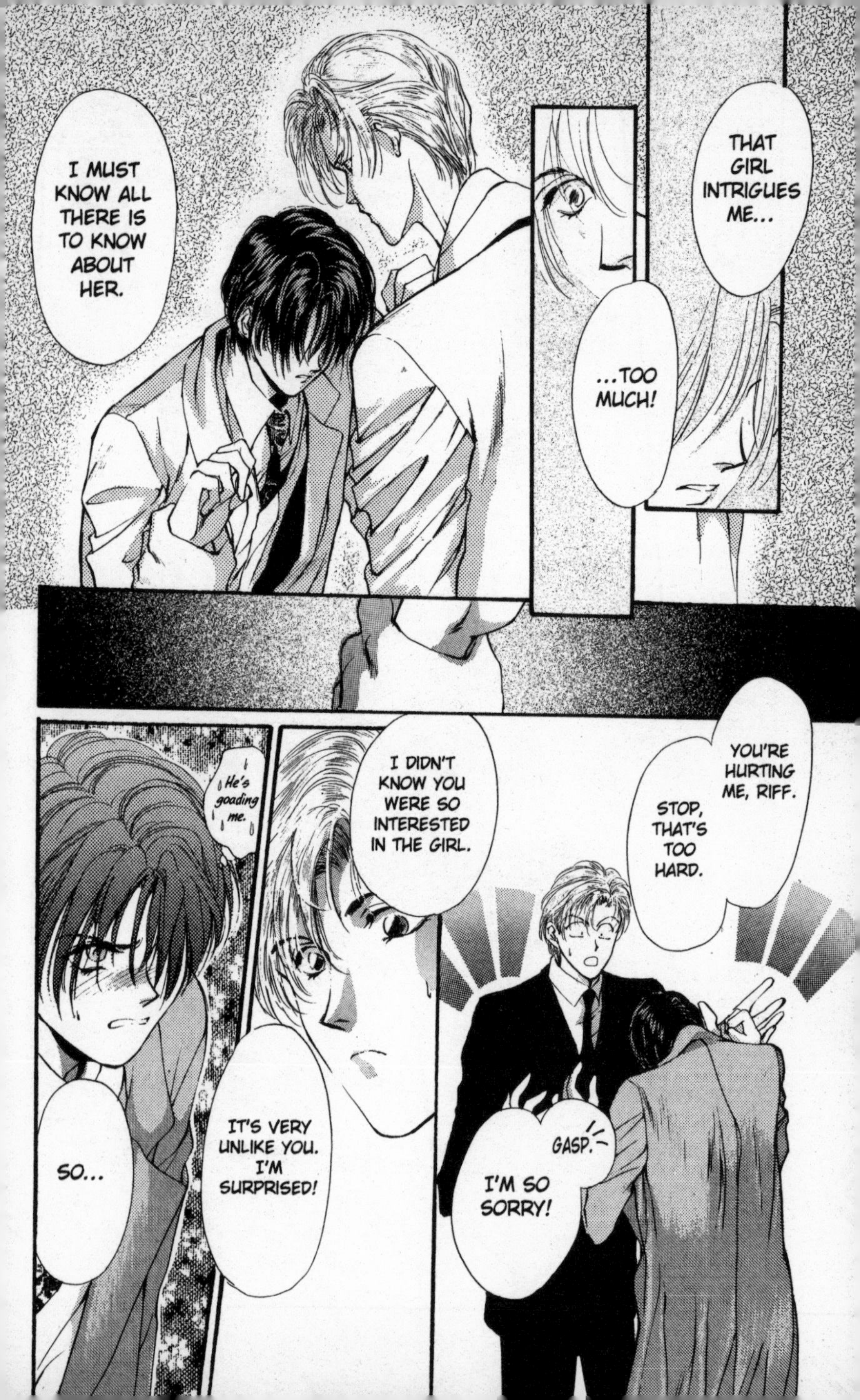
THAT GIRL INTRIGUES ME...
...TOO MUCH!
I MUST KNOW ALL THERE IS TO KNOW ABOUT HER.
YOU'RE HURTING ME, RIFF.
STOP, THAT'S TOO HARD.
GASP.
I'M SO SORRY!
I DIDN'T KNOW YOU WERE SO INTERESTED IN THE GIRL.
IT'S VERY UNLIKE YOU. I'M SURPRISED!
He's goading me.
SO...

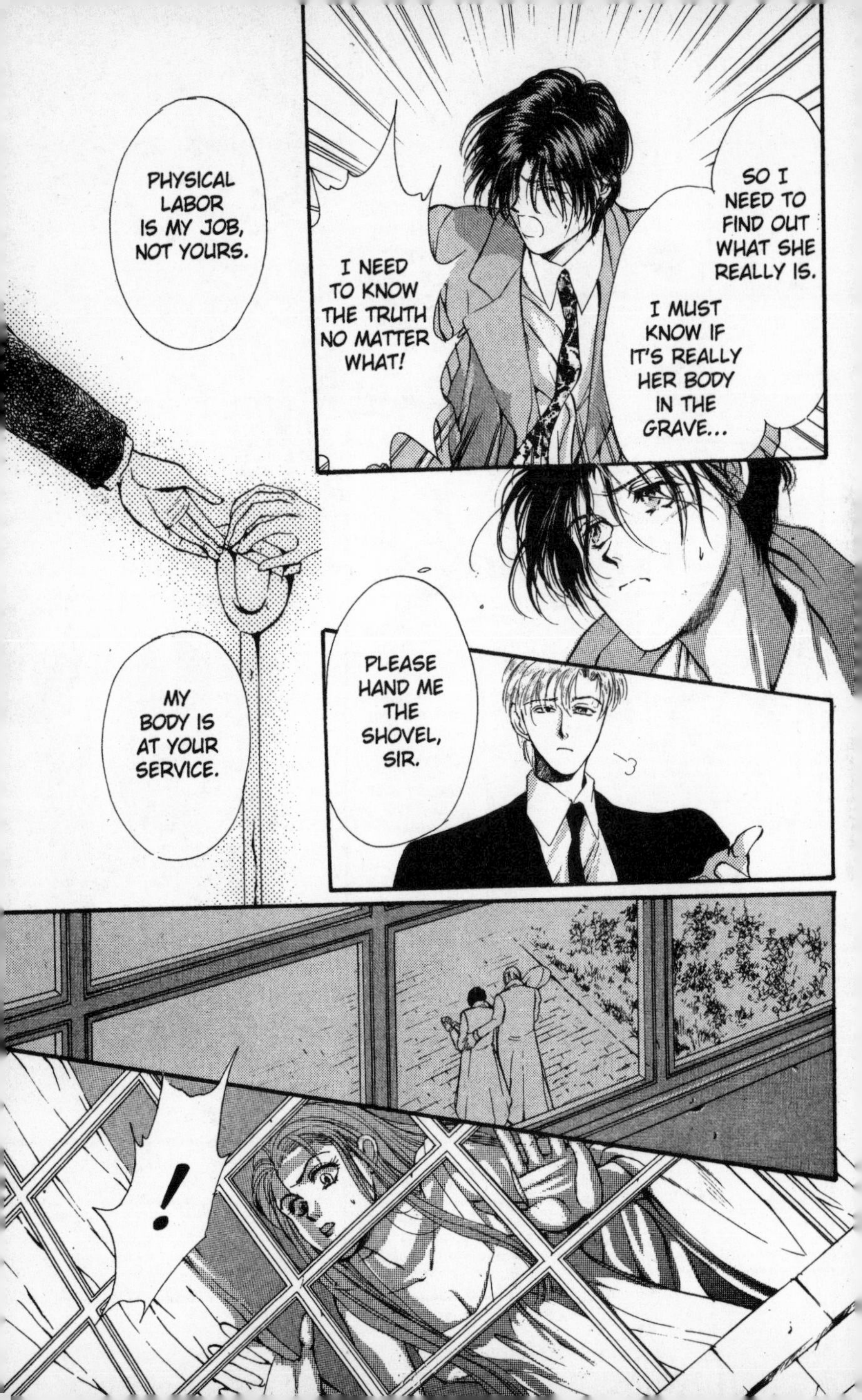
SO I NEED TO FIND OUT WHAT SHE REALLY IS.
I MUST KNOW IF IT'S REALLY HER BODY IN THE GRAVE...
I NEED TO KNOW THE TRUTH NO MATTER WHAT!
PLEASE HAND ME THE SHOVEL, SIR.
PHYSICAL LABOR IS MY JOB, NOT YOURS.
MY BODY IS AT YOUR SERVICE.
!

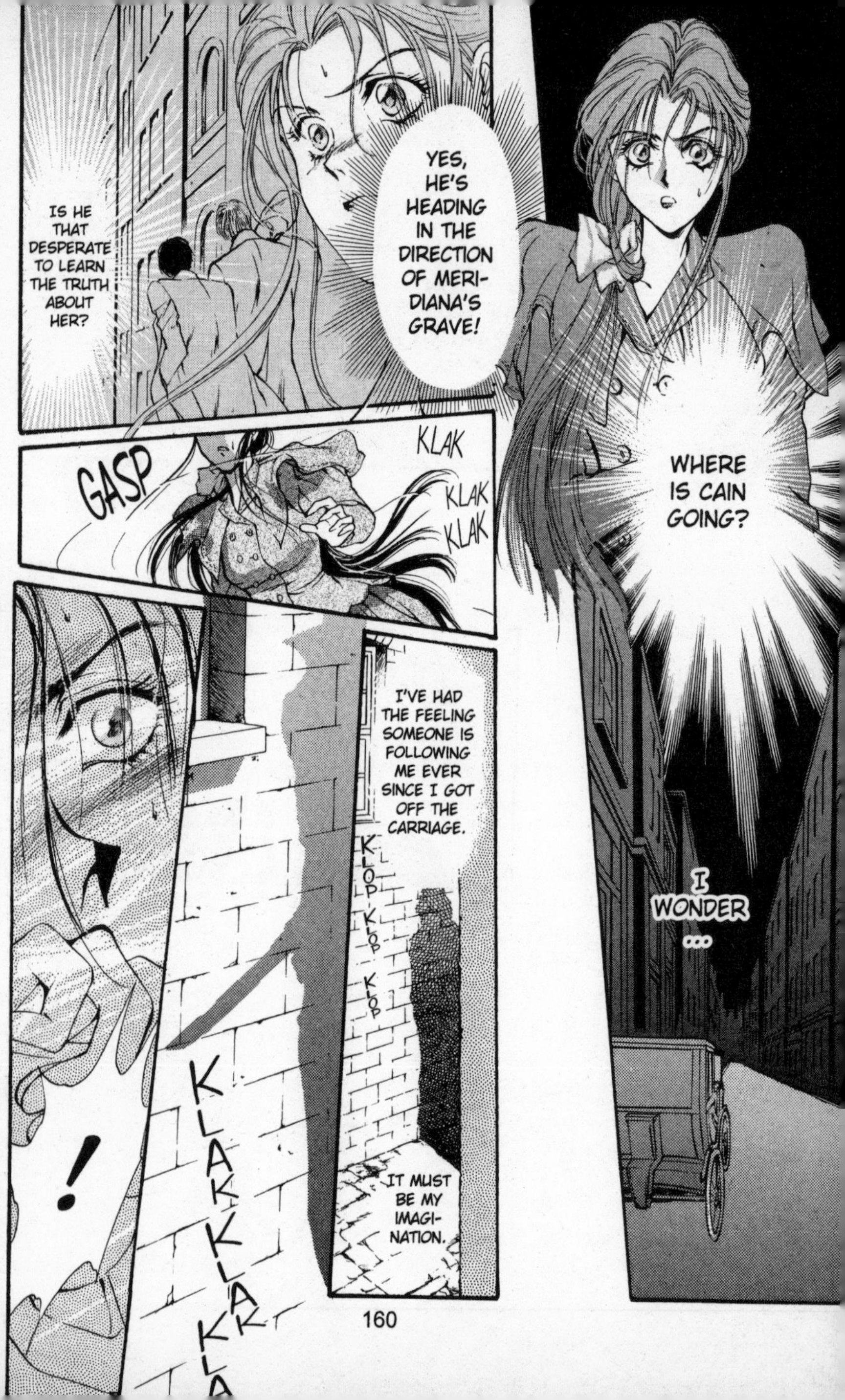
WHERE IS CAIN GOING?
I WONDER...
YES, HE'S HEADING IN THE DIRECTION OF MERI-DIANA'S GRAVE!
IS HE THAT DESPERATE TO LEARN THE TRUTH ABOUT HER?
KLAK
KLAK KLAK
GASP
I'VE HAD THE FEELING SOMEONE IS FOLLOWING ME EVER SINCE I GOT OFF THE CARRIAGE.
KLOP KLOP KLOP KLOP
IT MUST BE MY IMAGINATION.
!
KLAK KLAK KLAK KLA

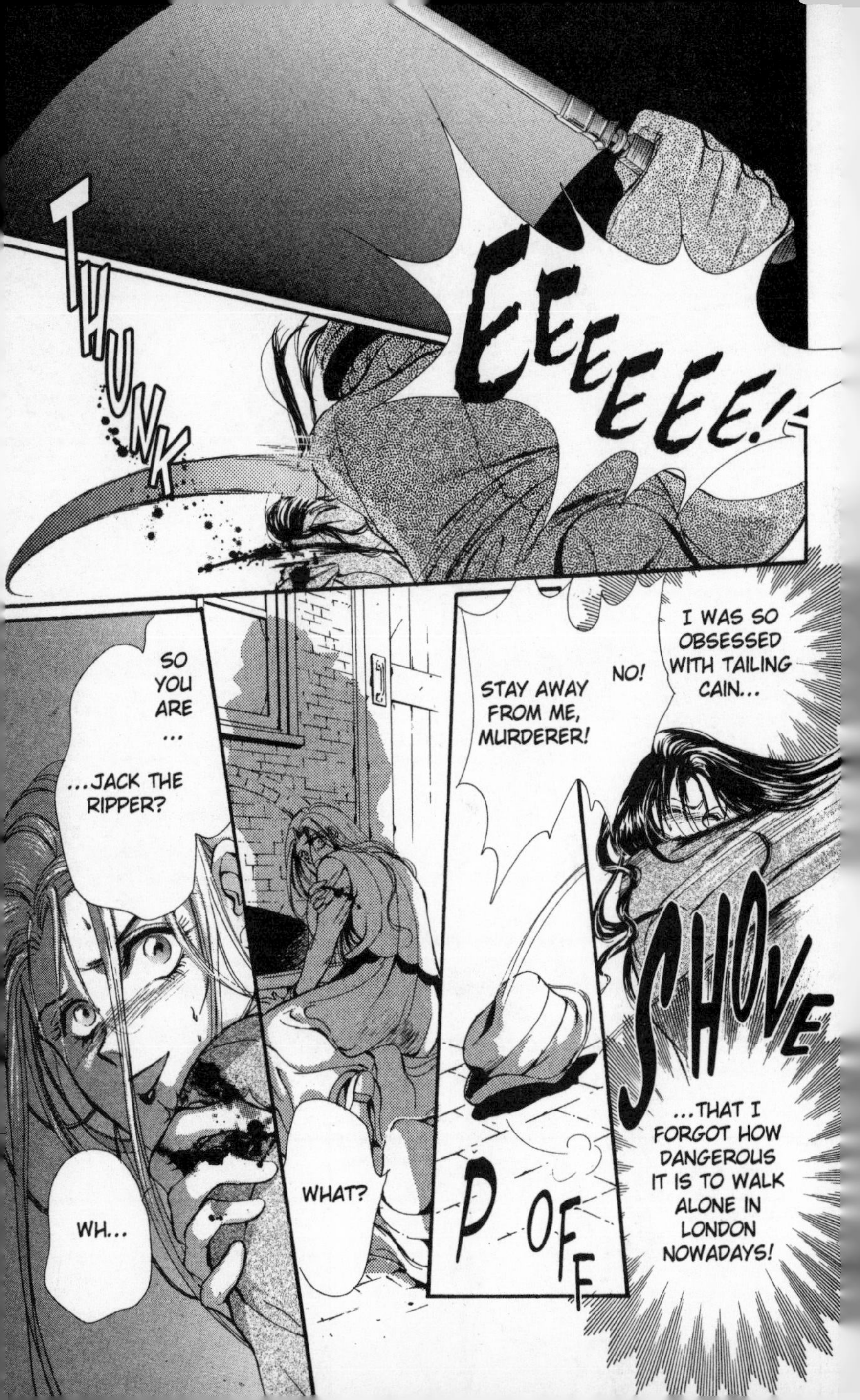
EEEEEE!
THUNK
I WAS SO OBSESSED WITH TAILING CAIN...
NO!
STAY AWAY FROM ME, MURDERER!
SHOVE
...THAT I FORGOT HOW DANGEROUS IT IS TO WALK ALONE IN LONDON NOWADAYS!
POFF
SO YOU ARE ...
...JACK THE RIPPER?
WHAT?
WH...

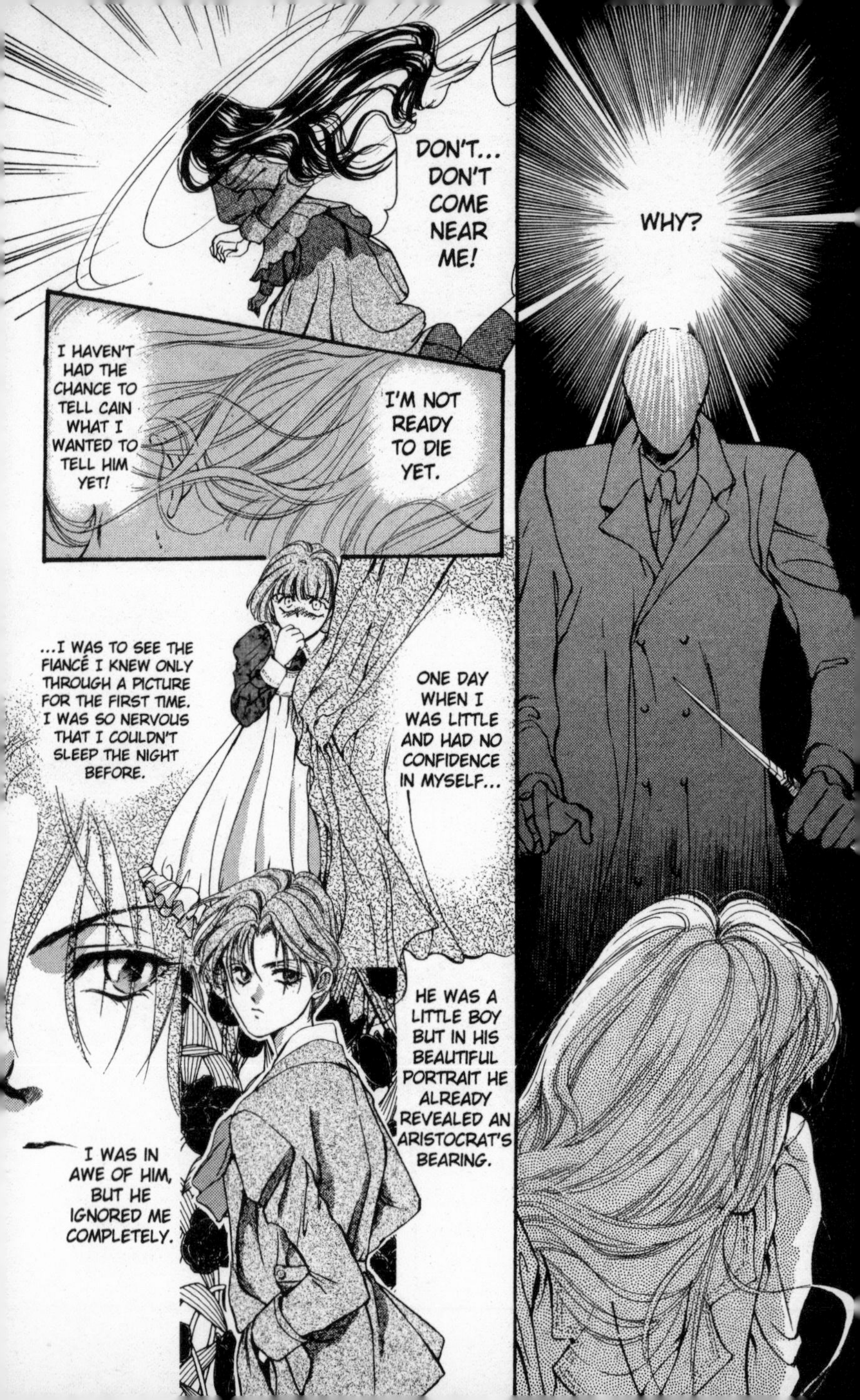
WHY?
DON'T... DON'T COME NEAR ME!
I'M NOT READY TO DIE YET.
I HAVEN'T HAD THE CHANCE TO TELL CAIN WHAT I WANTED TO TELL HIM YET!
ONE DAY WHEN I WAS LITTLE AND HAD NO CONFIDENCE IN MYSELF...
...I WAS TO SEE THE FIANCÉ I KNEW ONLY THROUGH A PICTURE FOR THE FIRST TIME. I WAS SO NERVOUS THAT I COULDN'T SLEEP THE NIGHT BEFORE.
HE WAS A LITTLE BOY BUT IN HIS BEAUTIFUL PORTRAIT HE ALREADY REVEALED AN ARISTOCRAT'S BEARING.
I WAS IN AWE OF HIM, BUT HE IGNORED ME COMPLETELY.

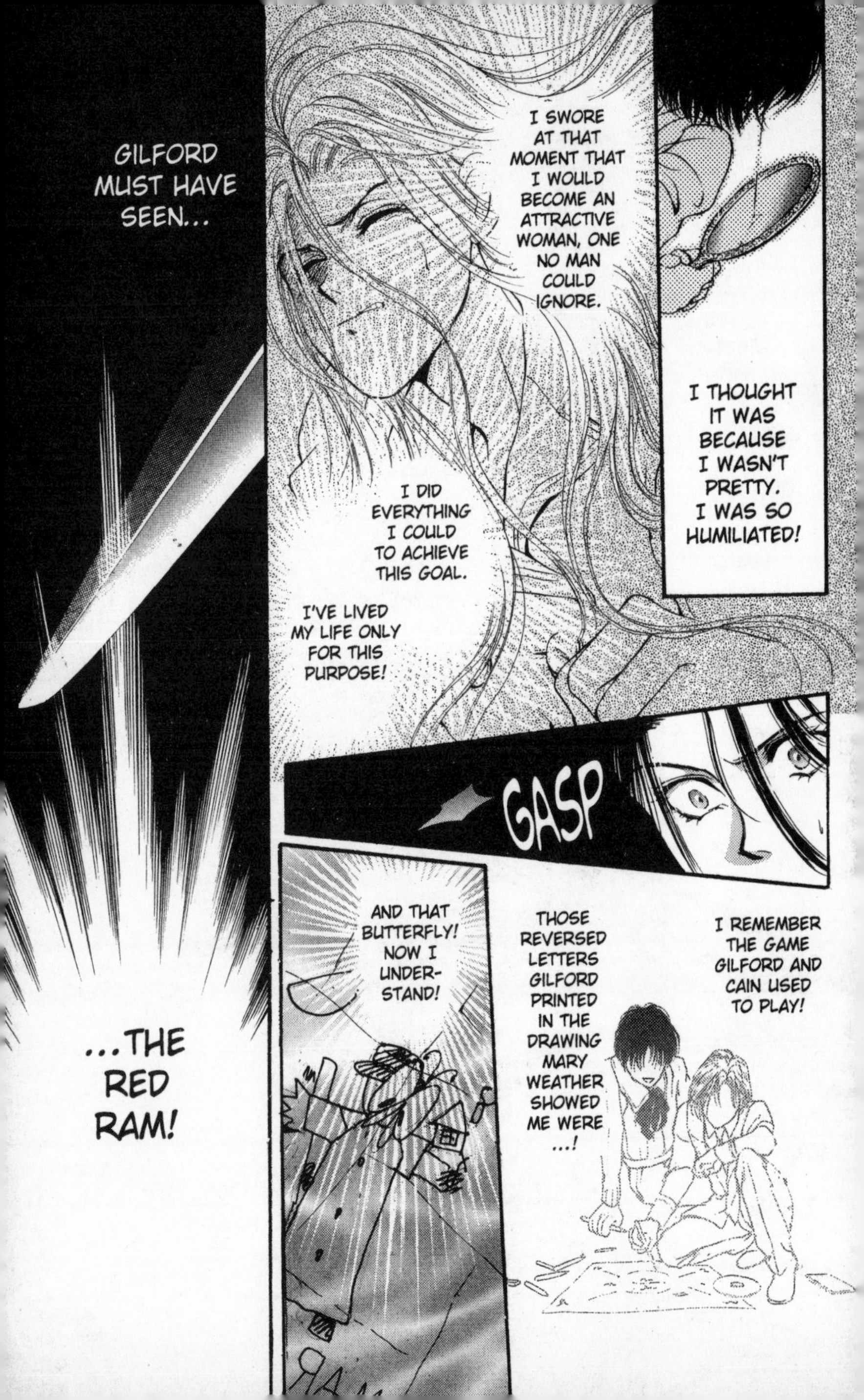
I SWORE AT THAT MOMENT THAT I WOULD BECOME AN ATTRACTIVE WOMAN, ONE NO MAN COULD IGNORE.
I THOUGHT IT WAS BECAUSE I WASN'T PRETTY. I WAS SO HUMILIATED!
I DID EVERYTHING I COULD TO ACHIEVE THIS GOAL.
I'VE LIVED MY LIFE ONLY FOR THIS PURPOSE!
GASP
I REMEMBER THE GAME GILFORD AND CAIN USED TO PLAY!
THOSE REVERSED LETTERS GILFORD PRINTED IN THE DRAWING MARY WEATHER SHOWED ME WERE ...!
AND THAT BUTTERFLY! NOW I UNDER-STAND!
GILFORD MUST HAVE SEEN...
...THE RED RAM!

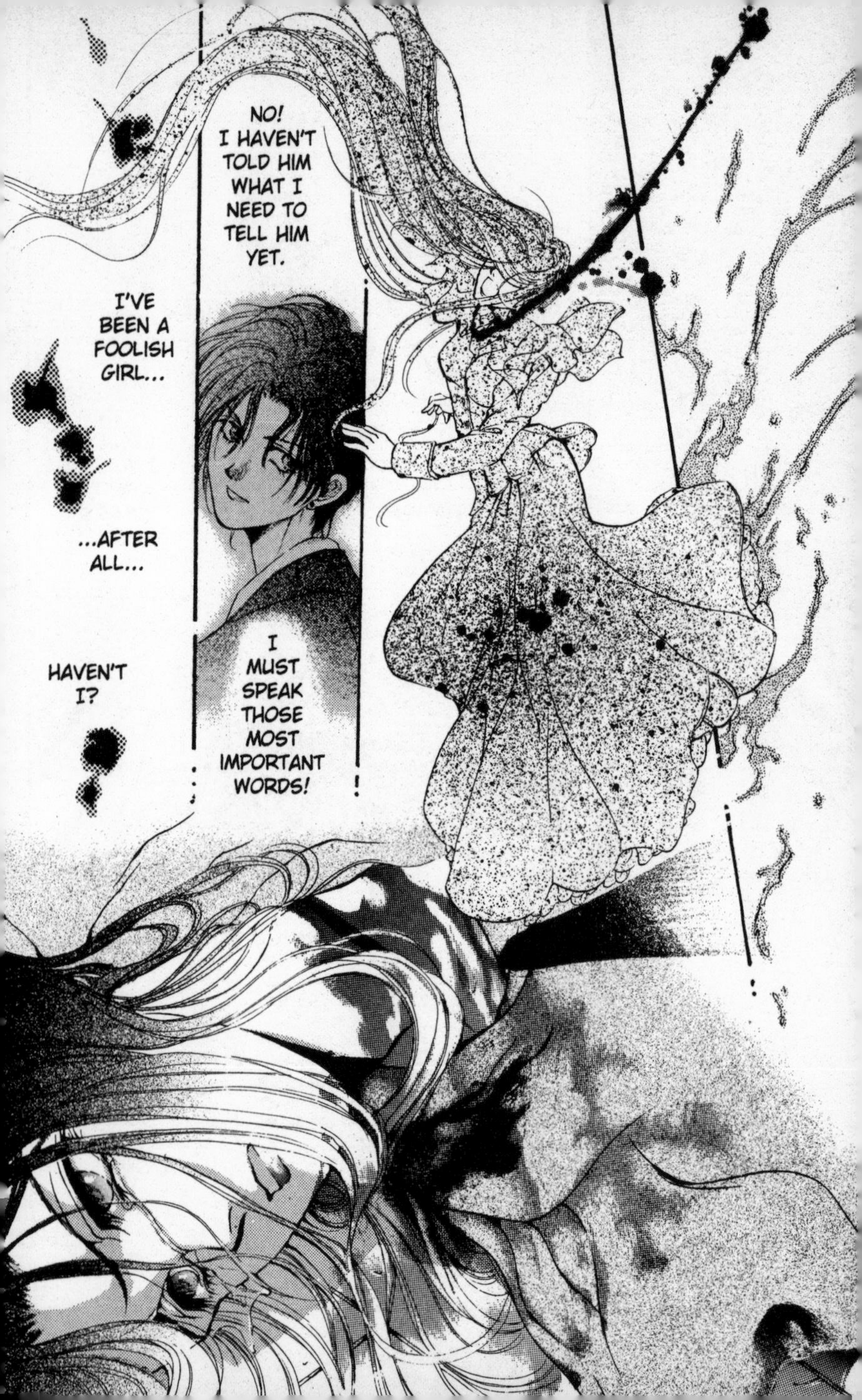
NO! I HAVEN'T TOLD HIM WHAT I NEED TO TELL HIM YET.
I MUST SPEAK THOSE MOST IMPORTANT WORDS!
I'VE BEEN A FOOLISH GIRL...
...AFTER ALL...
HAVEN'T I?

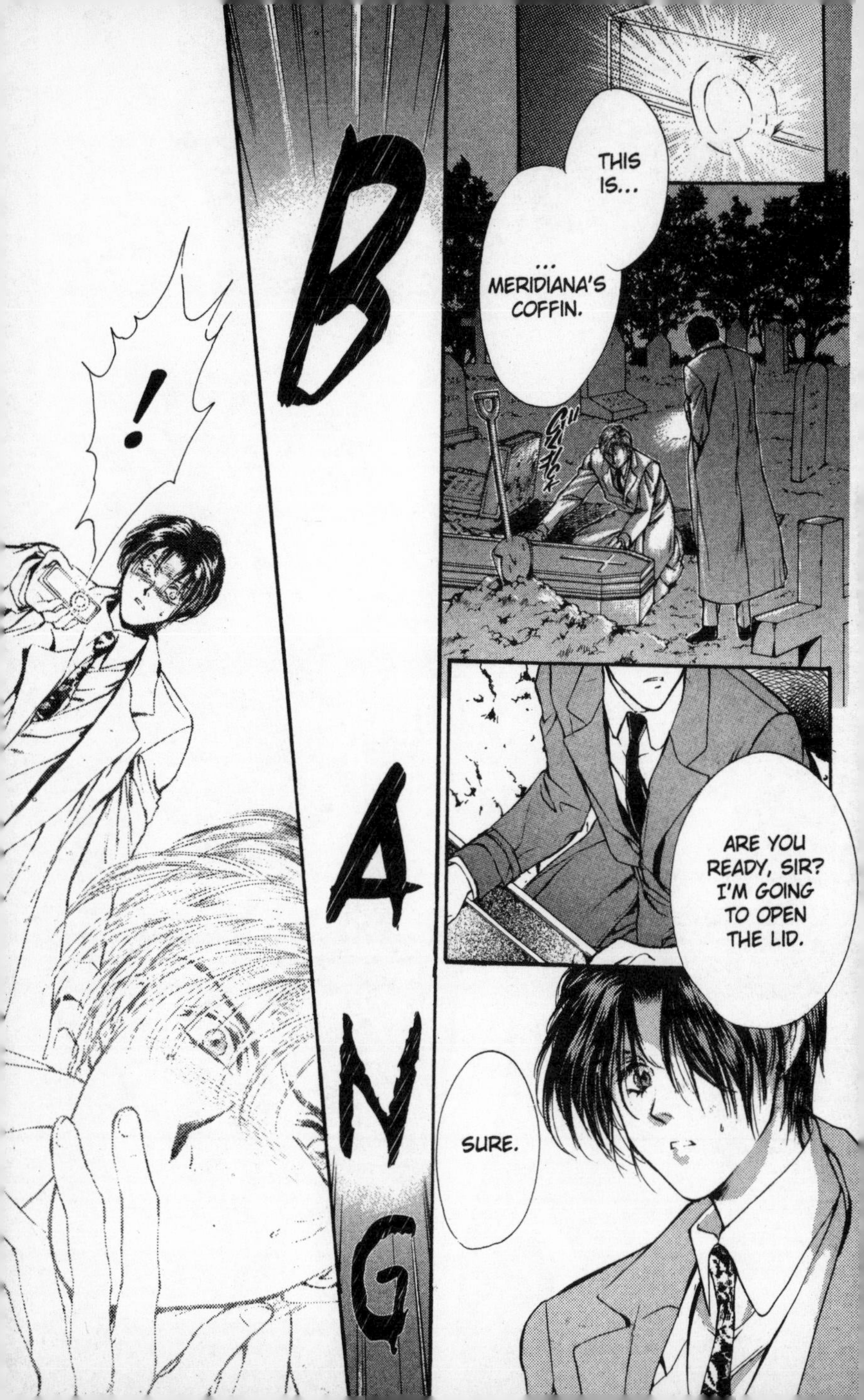
THIS IS...
...MERIDIANA'S COFFIN.
ARE YOU READY, SIR? I'M GOING TO OPEN THE LID.
SURE.
BANG
!

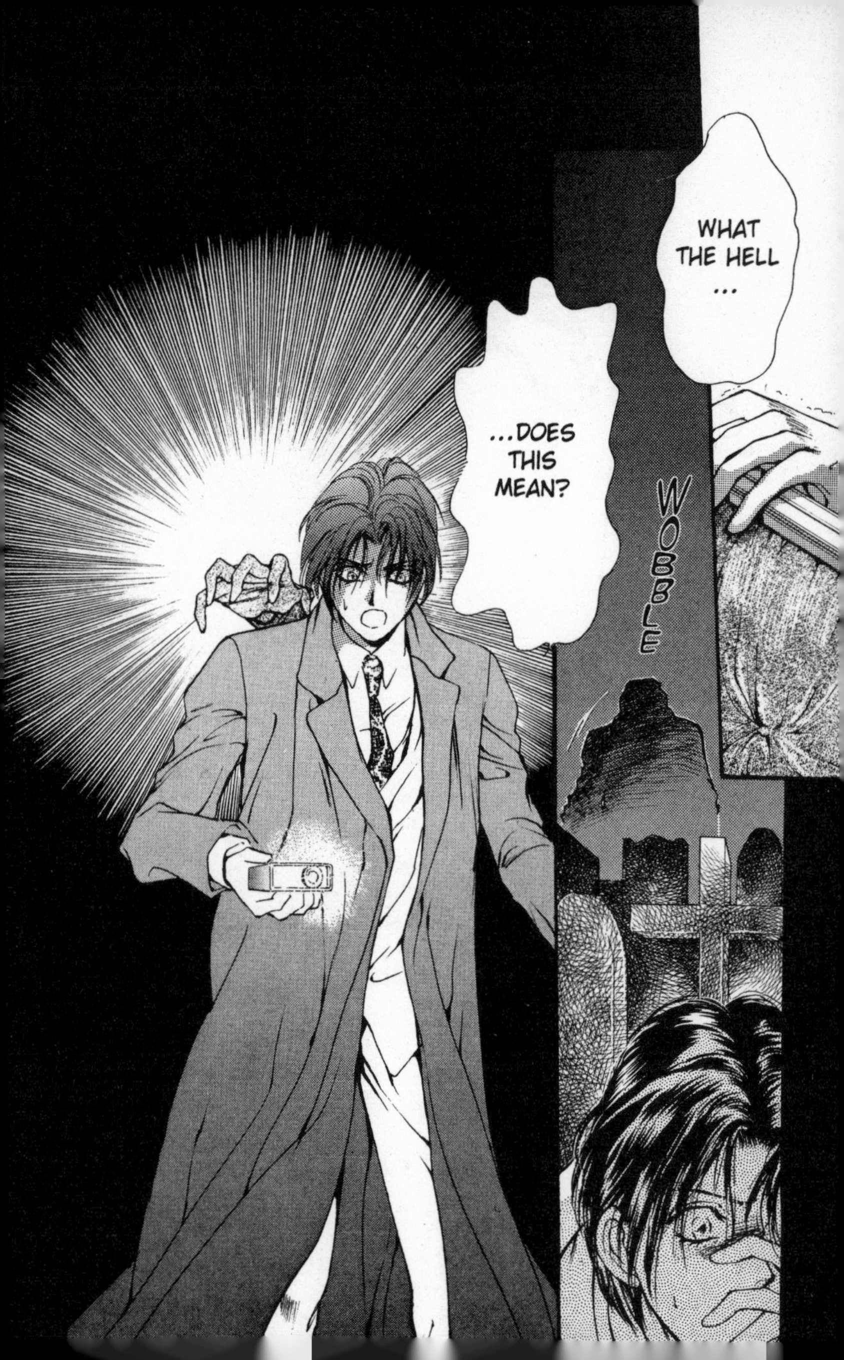
WHAT THE HELL ...
WOBBLE
...DOES THIS MEAN?

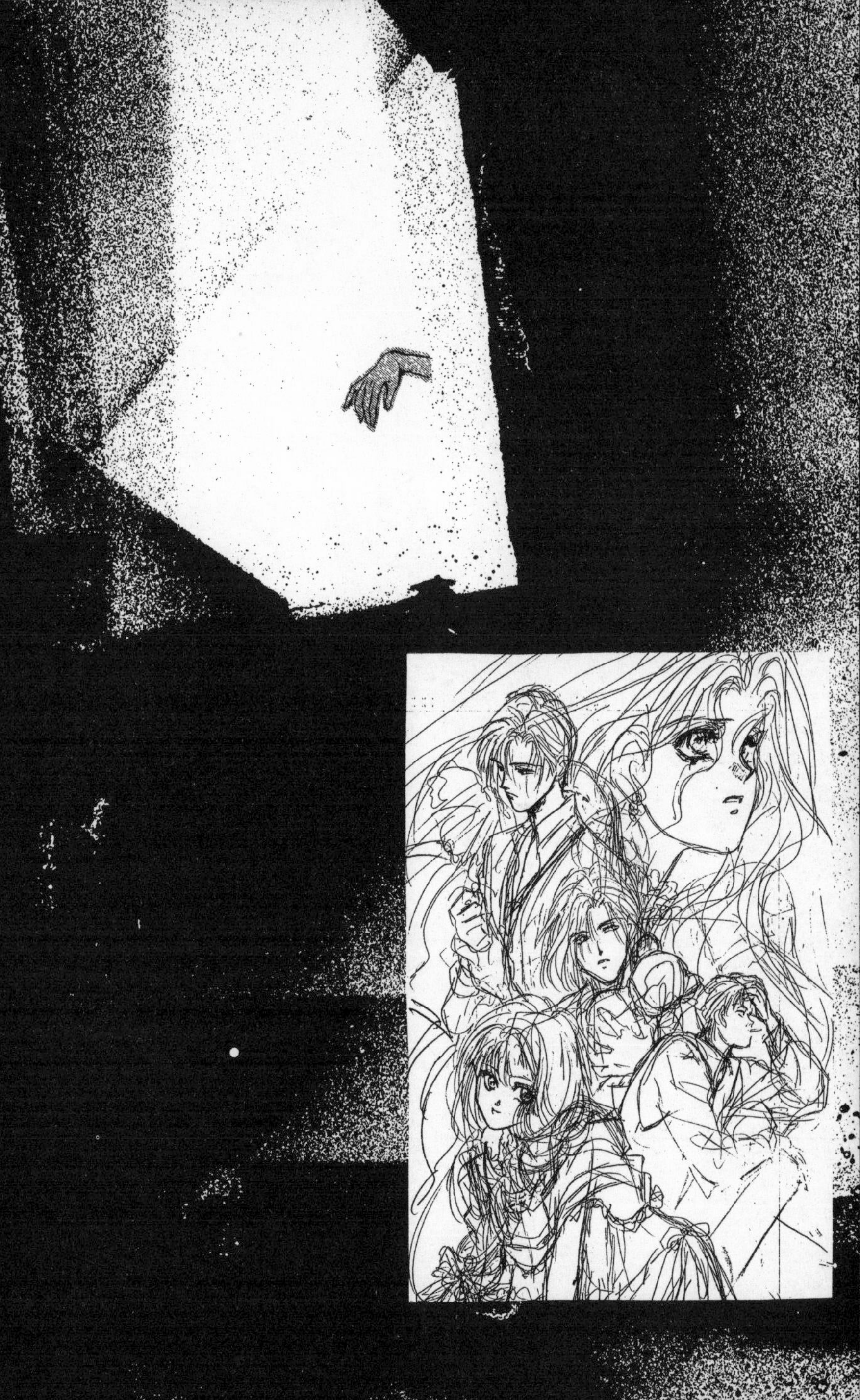

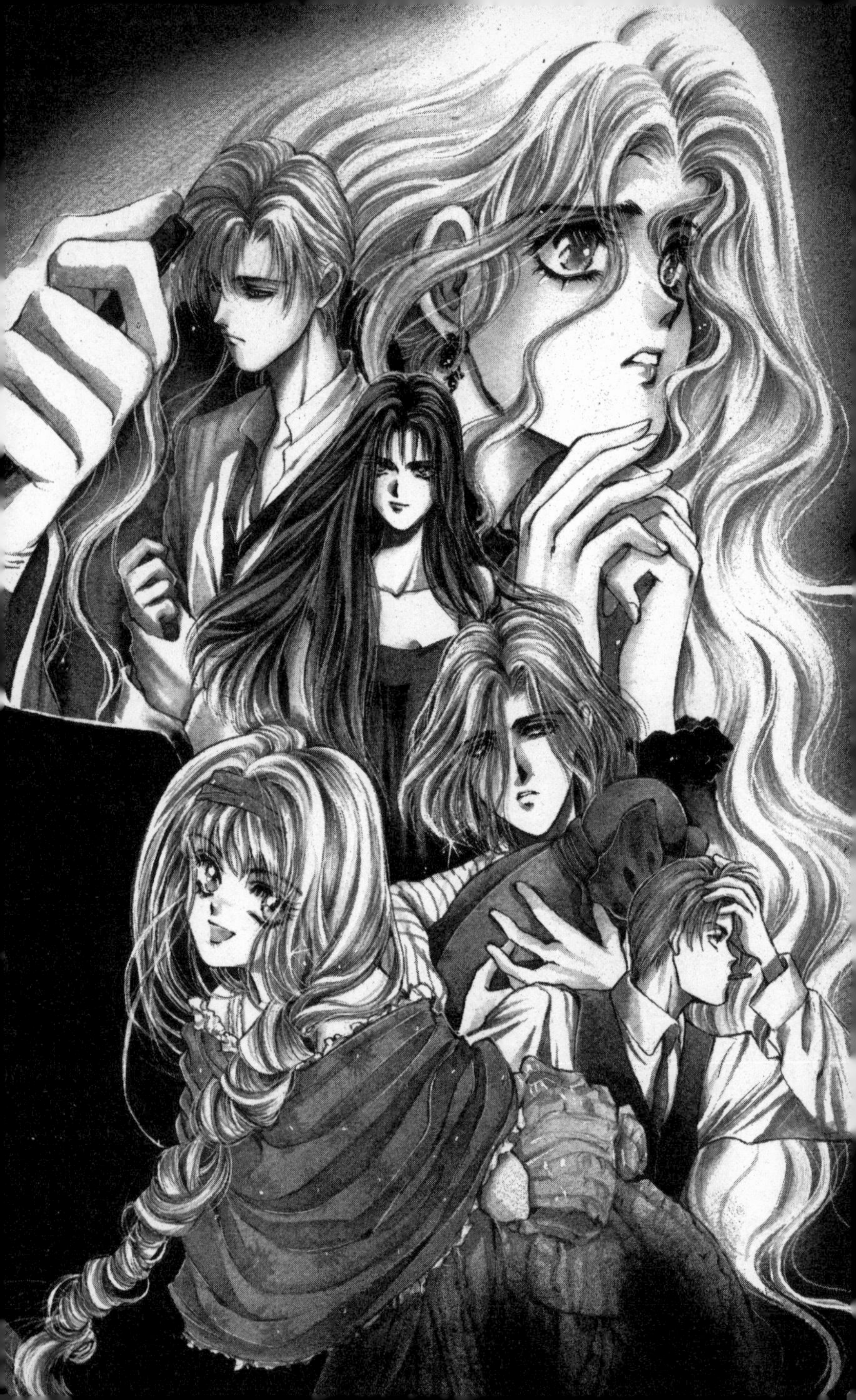

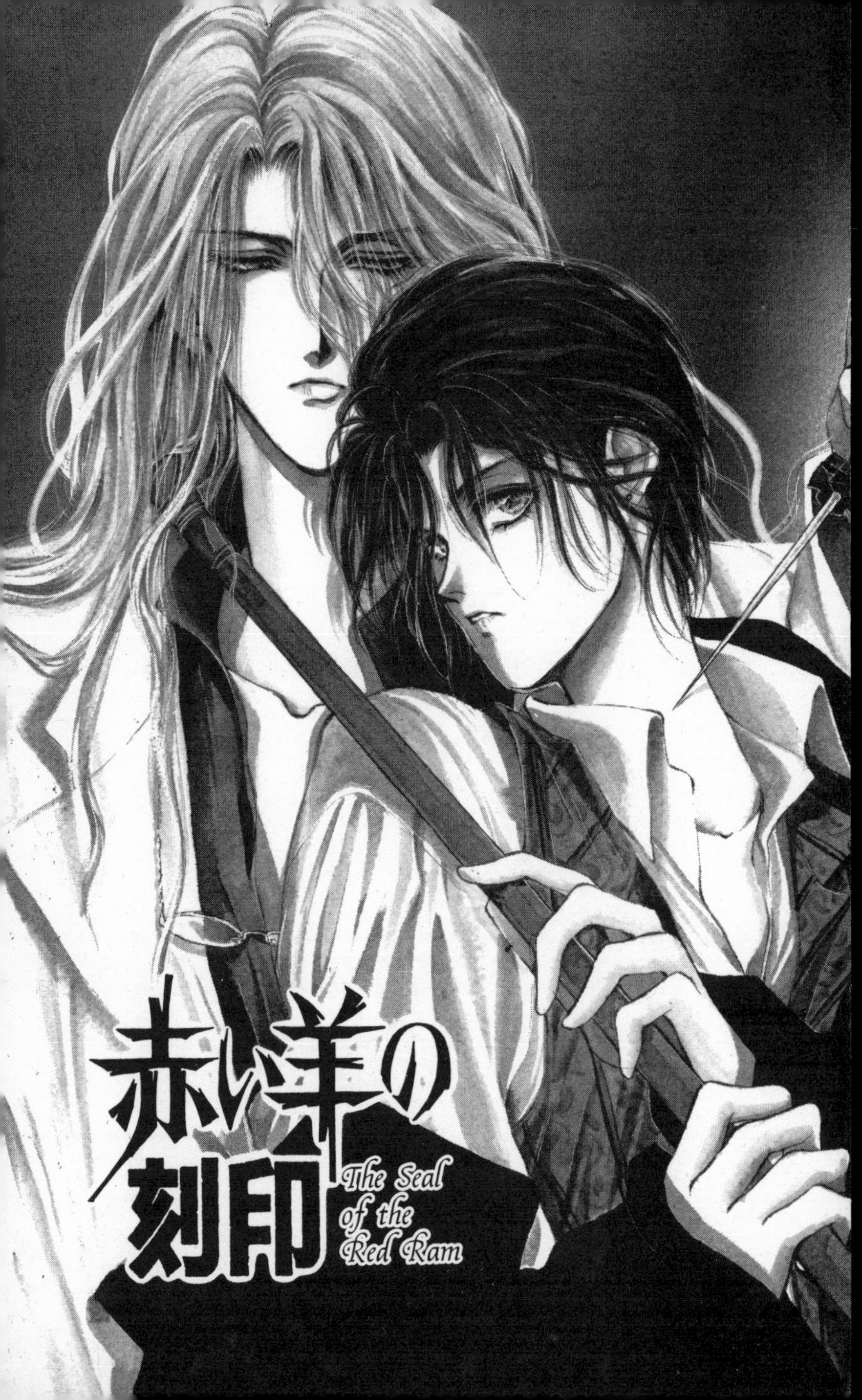
赤い羊の刻印
The Seal of the Red Ram

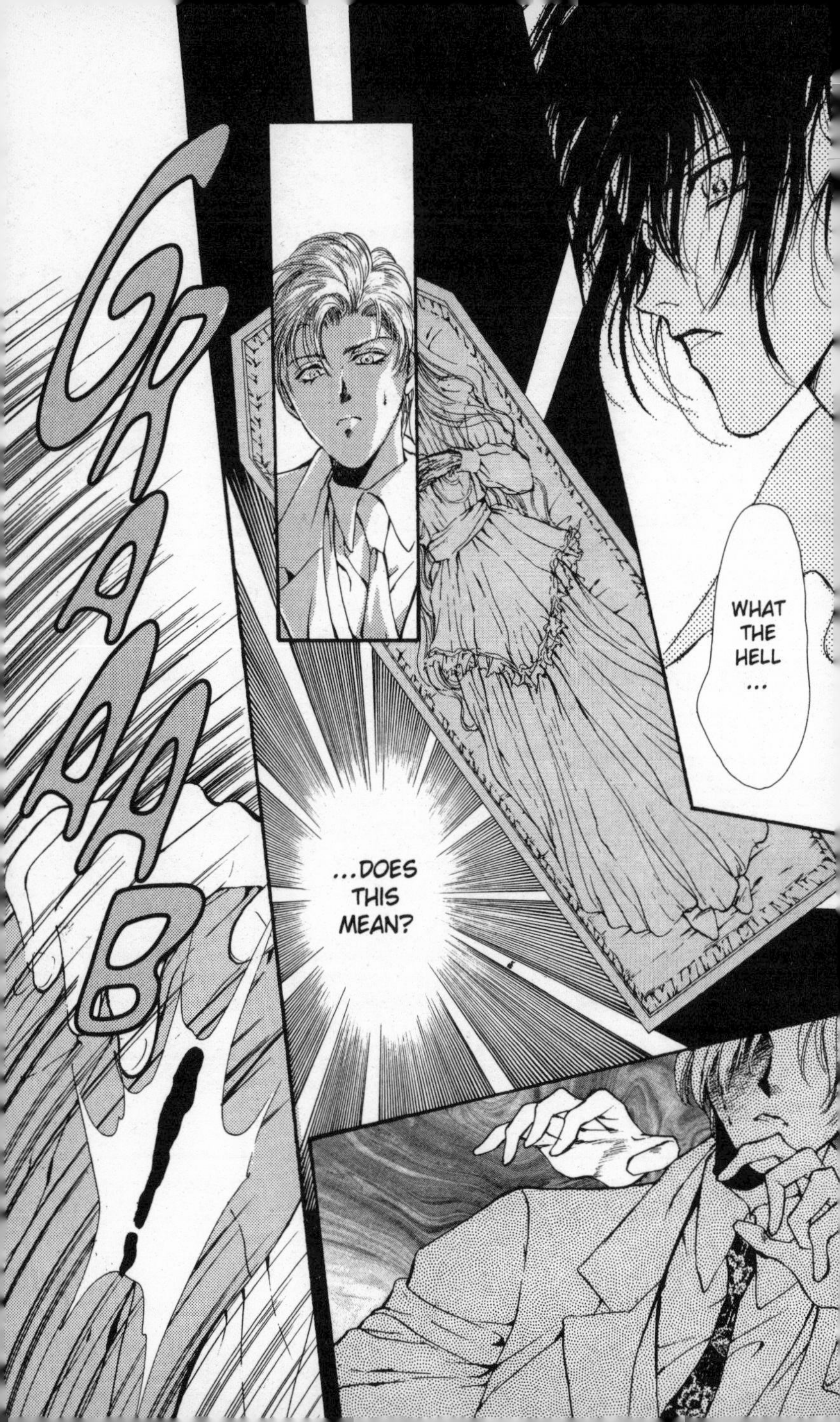
WHAT THE HELL ...
...DOES THIS MEAN?
GRAAAB
!

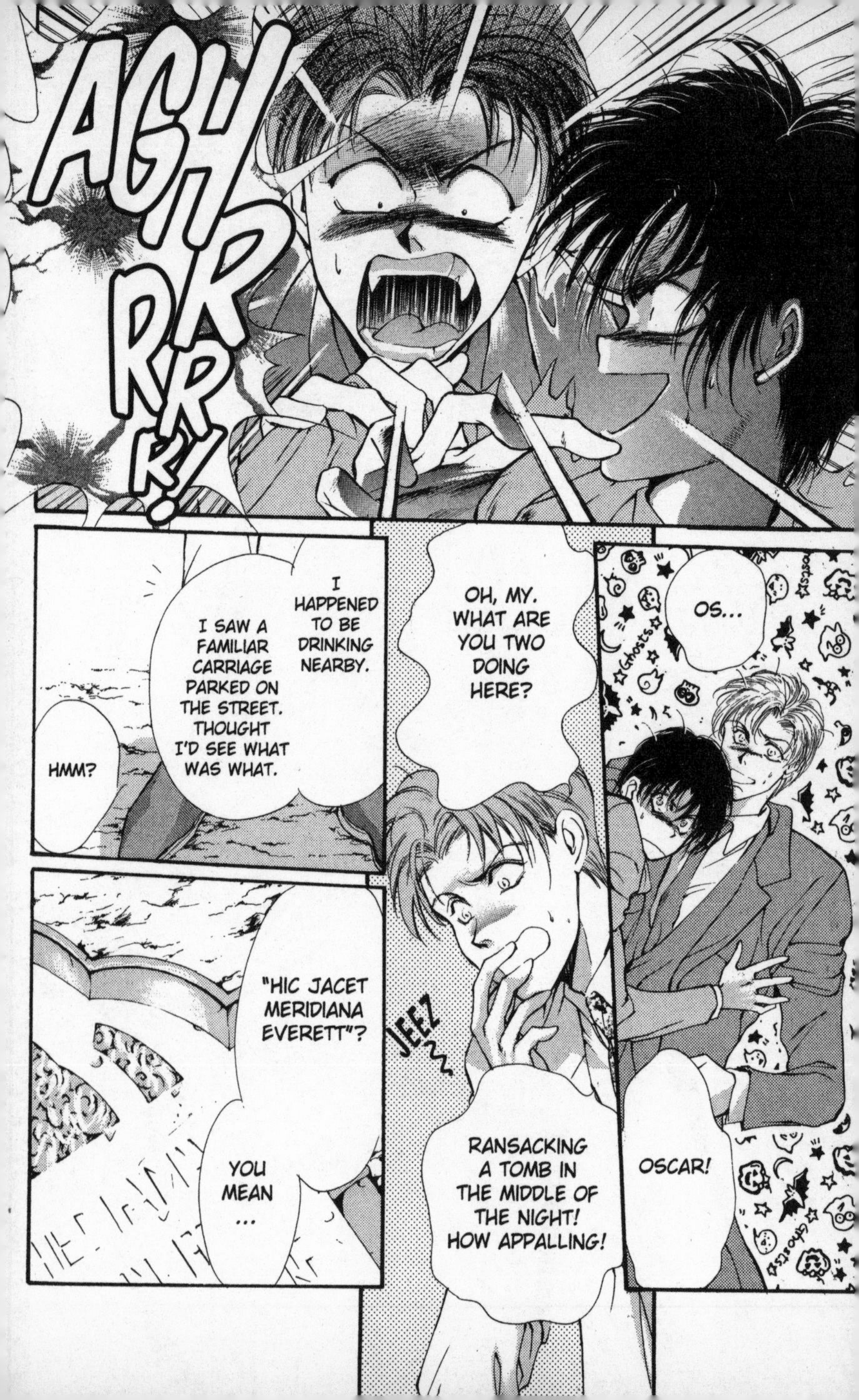
AGHRRRRK!
OS...
OSCAR!
OH, MY. WHAT ARE YOU TWO DOING HERE?
JEEZ
RANSACKING A TOMB IN THE MIDDLE OF THE NIGHT! HOW APPALLING!
I HAPPENED TO BE DRINKING NEARBY.
I SAW A FAMILIAR CARRIAGE PARKED ON THE STREET. THOUGHT I'D SEE WHAT WAS WHAT.
HMM?
"HIC JACET MERIDIANA EVERETT"?
YOU MEAN ...

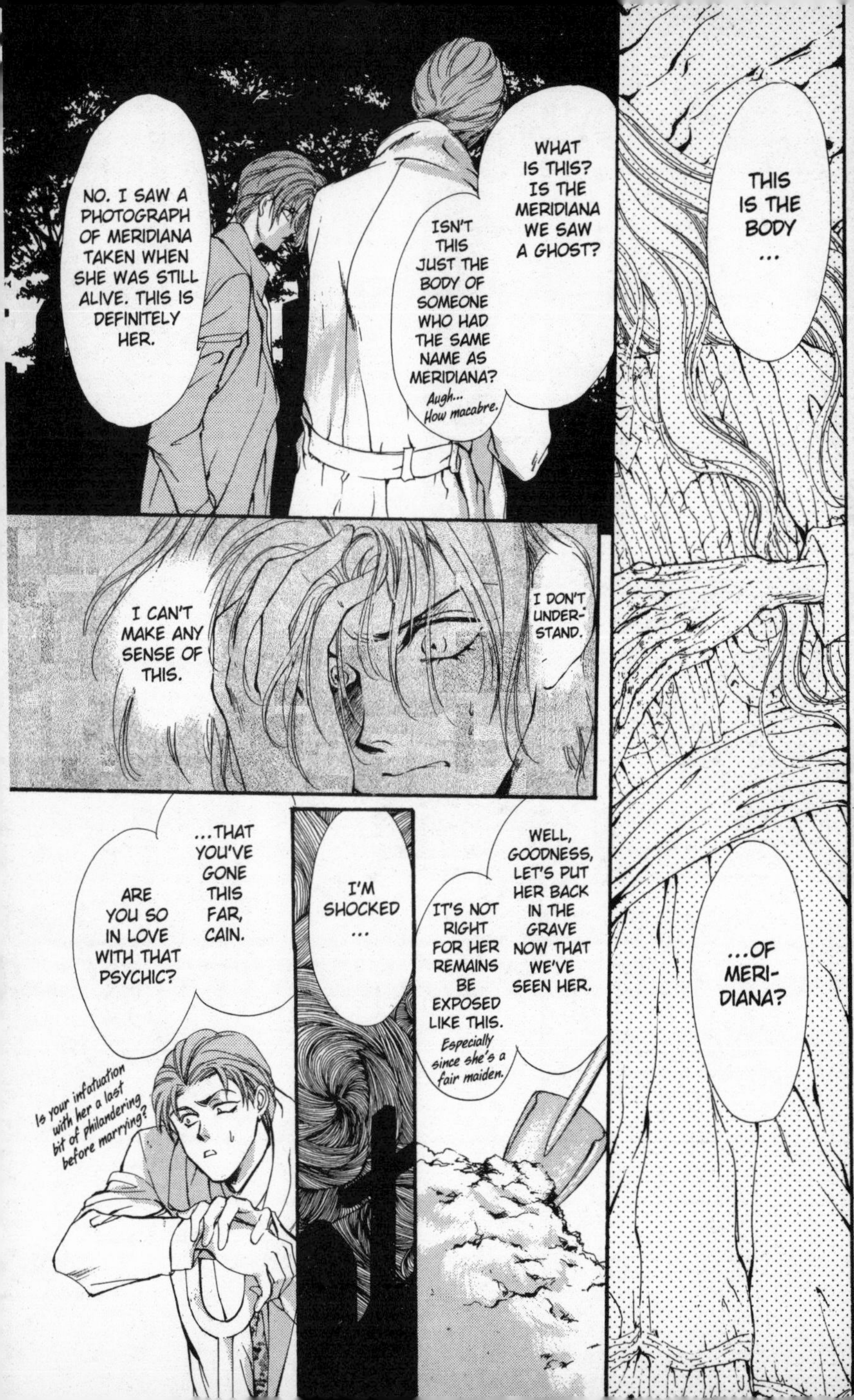
THIS IS THE BODY ...
...OF MERI-DIANA?
WHAT IS THIS? IS THE MERIDIANA WE SAW A GHOST?
ISN'T THIS JUST THE BODY OF SOMEONE WHO HAD THE SAME NAME AS MERIDIANA?
Augh... How macabre.
NO. I SAW A PHOTOGRAPH OF MERIDIANA TAKEN WHEN SHE WAS STILL ALIVE. THIS IS DEFINITELY HER.
I DON'T UNDER-STAND.
I CAN'T MAKE ANY SENSE OF THIS.
WELL, GOODNESS, LET'S PUT HER BACK IN THE GRAVE NOW THAT WE'VE SEEN HER.
IT'S NOT RIGHT FOR HER REMAINS BE EXPOSED LIKE THIS.
Especially since she's a fair maiden.
I'M SHOCKED ...
...THAT YOU'VE GONE THIS FAR, CAIN.
ARE YOU SO IN LOVE WITH THAT PSYCHIC?
Is your infatuation with her a last bit of philandering before marrying?

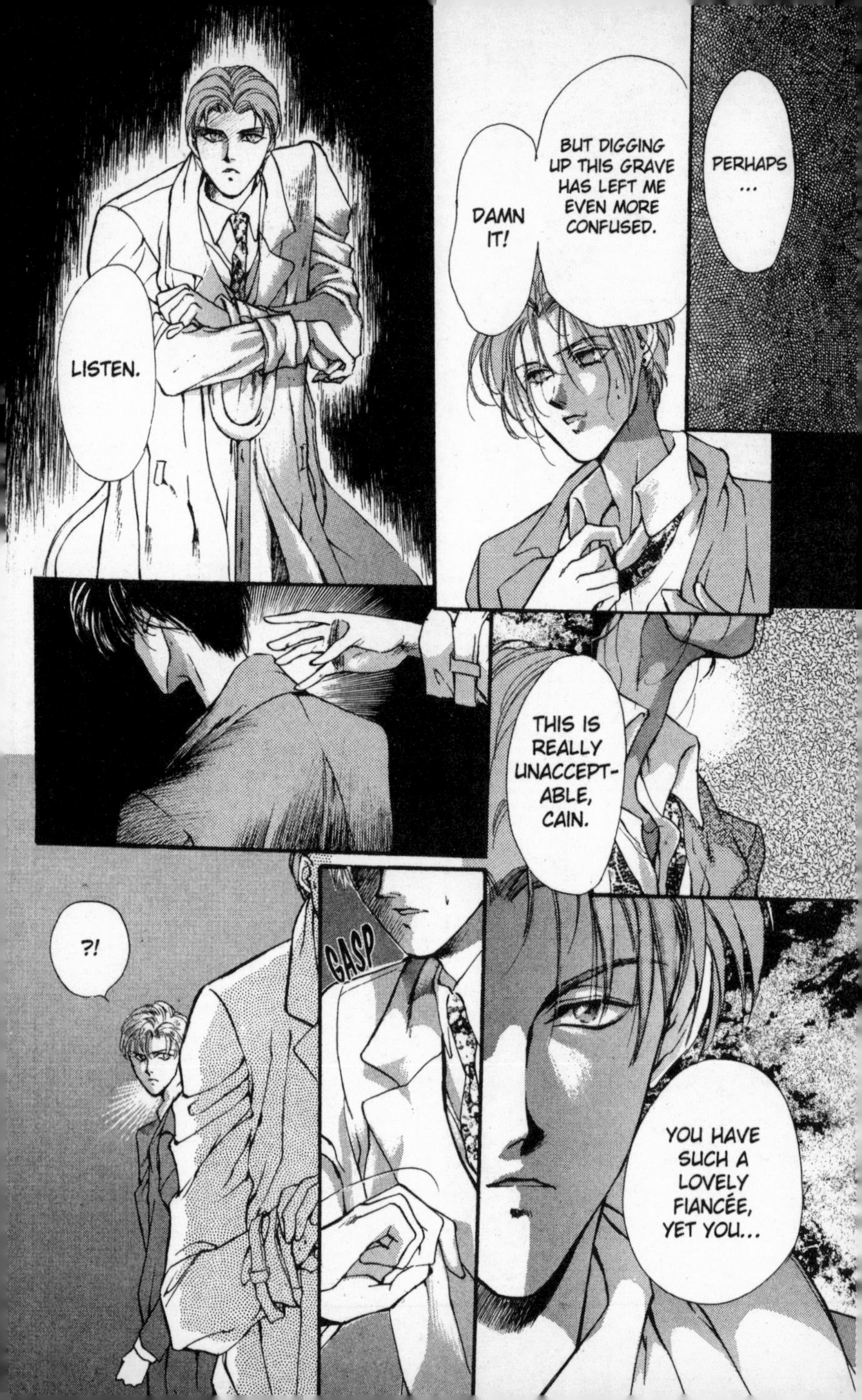
PERHAPS...
BUT DIGGING UP THIS GRAVE HAS LEFT ME EVEN MORE CONFUSED.
DAMN IT!
LISTEN.
THIS IS REALLY UNACCEPT-ABLE, CAIN.
YOU HAVE SUCH A LOVELY FIANCÉE, YET YOU...
GASP
?!

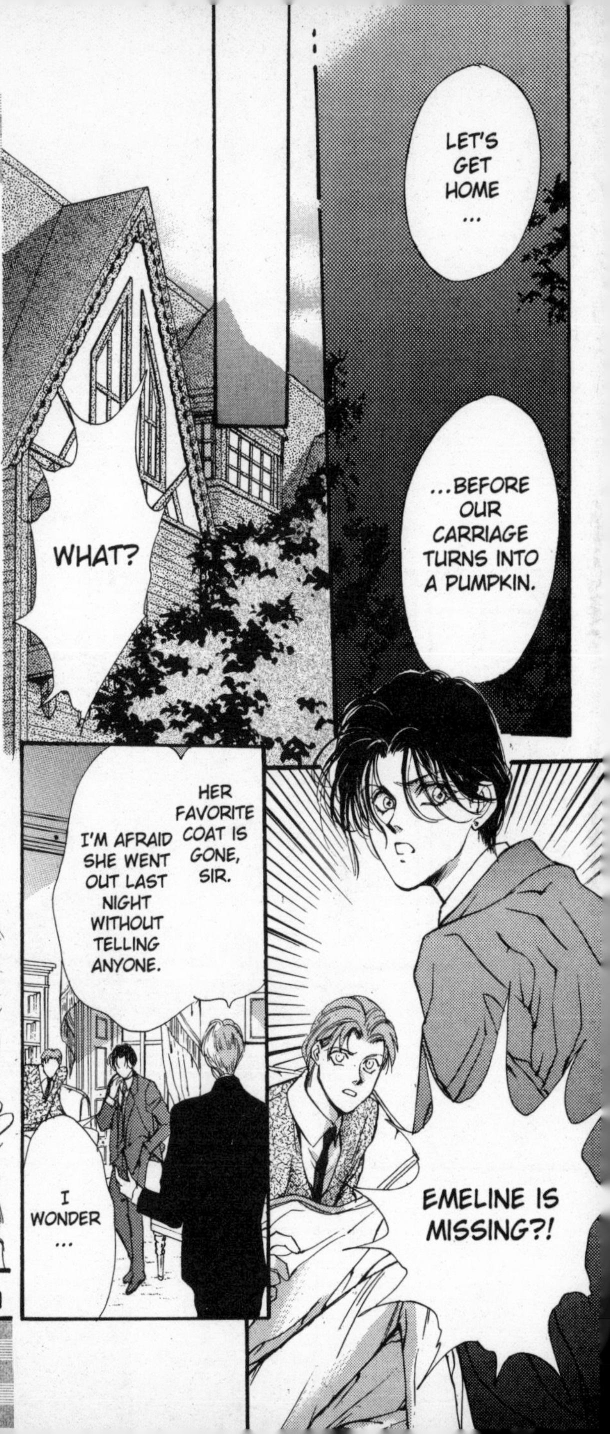
LET'S GET HOME ...
...BEFORE OUR CARRIAGE TURNS INTO A PUMPKIN.
WHAT?
EMELINE IS MISSING?!
HER FAVORITE COAT IS GONE, SIR.
I'M AFRAID SHE WENT OUT LAST NIGHT WITHOUT TELLING ANYONE.
I WONDER ...

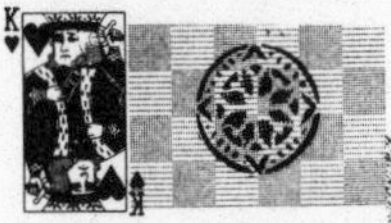

I kind of like Oscar. He is a very simple man and his face is easy to draw. I got the idea of Oscar's character from a Japanese boxer-turned-actor, Hidexxxx Akai, but he no longer has much in common with Akai. You'll see Oscar punched by Riff in a later page, but don't think that means that Oscar is not tough as he looks. As Riff says, Oscar needed to be calmed down since he was overexcited like a bull in an arena. That's why Riff punched him. Cain, on the other hand, is a total wimp when it comes to physical strength. That's why some people think he could be xxx. (Riff could easily kill Cain with a slap if he wanted to.)

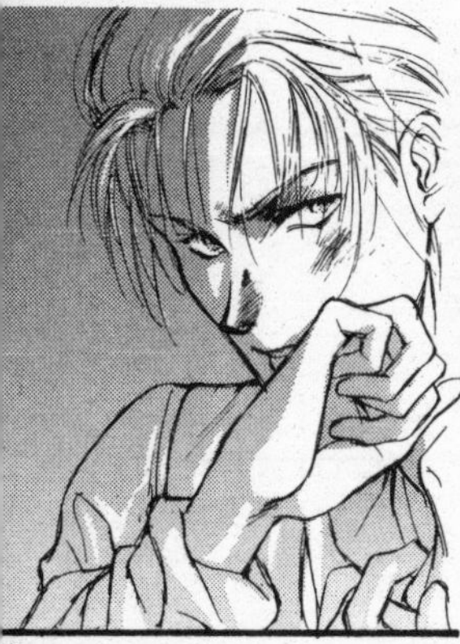

XII-THE HANGED MAN

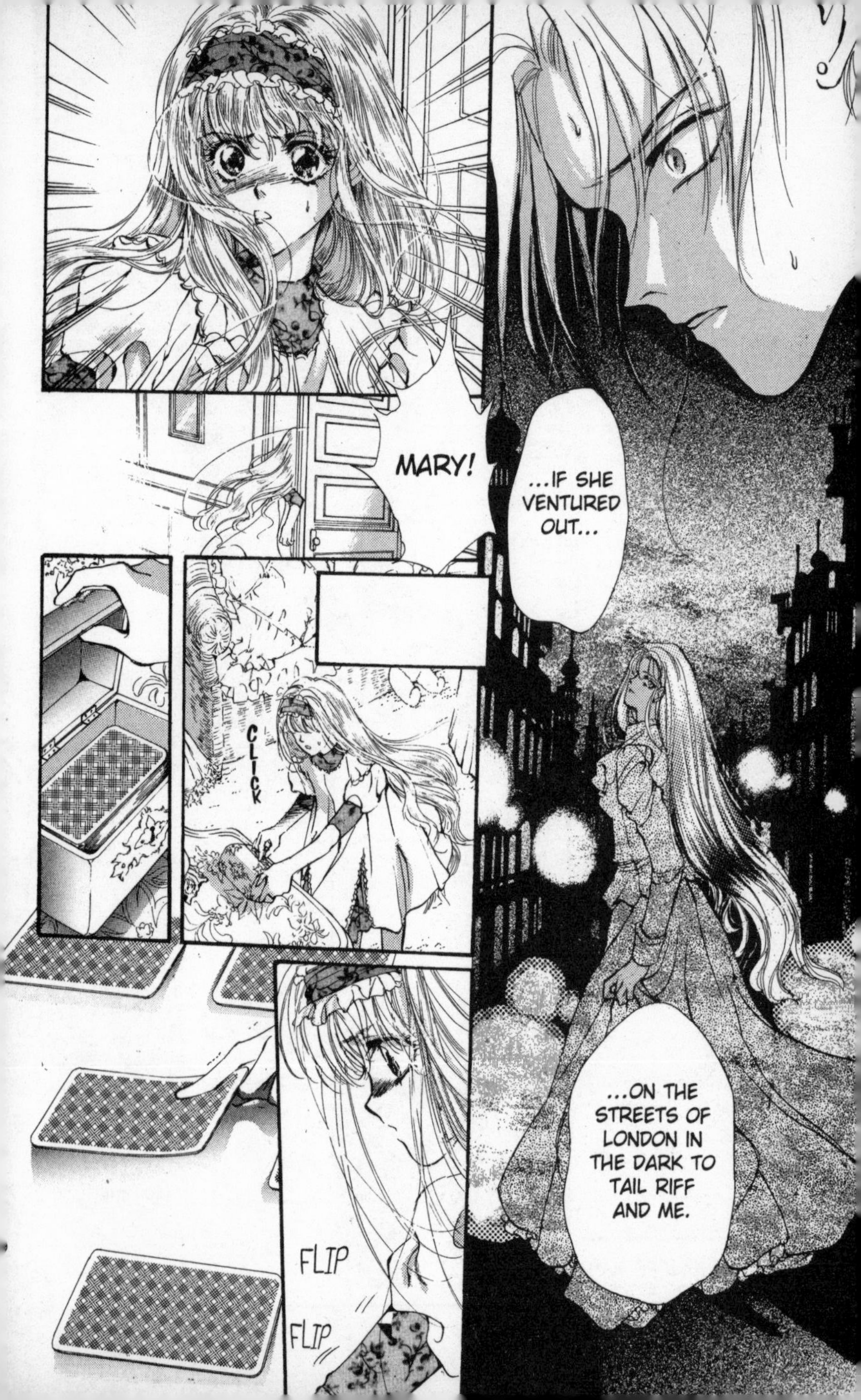
...IF SHE VENTURED OUT...
...ON THE STREETS OF LONDON IN THE DARK TO TAIL RIFF AND ME.
MARY!
CLICK
FLIP
FLIP

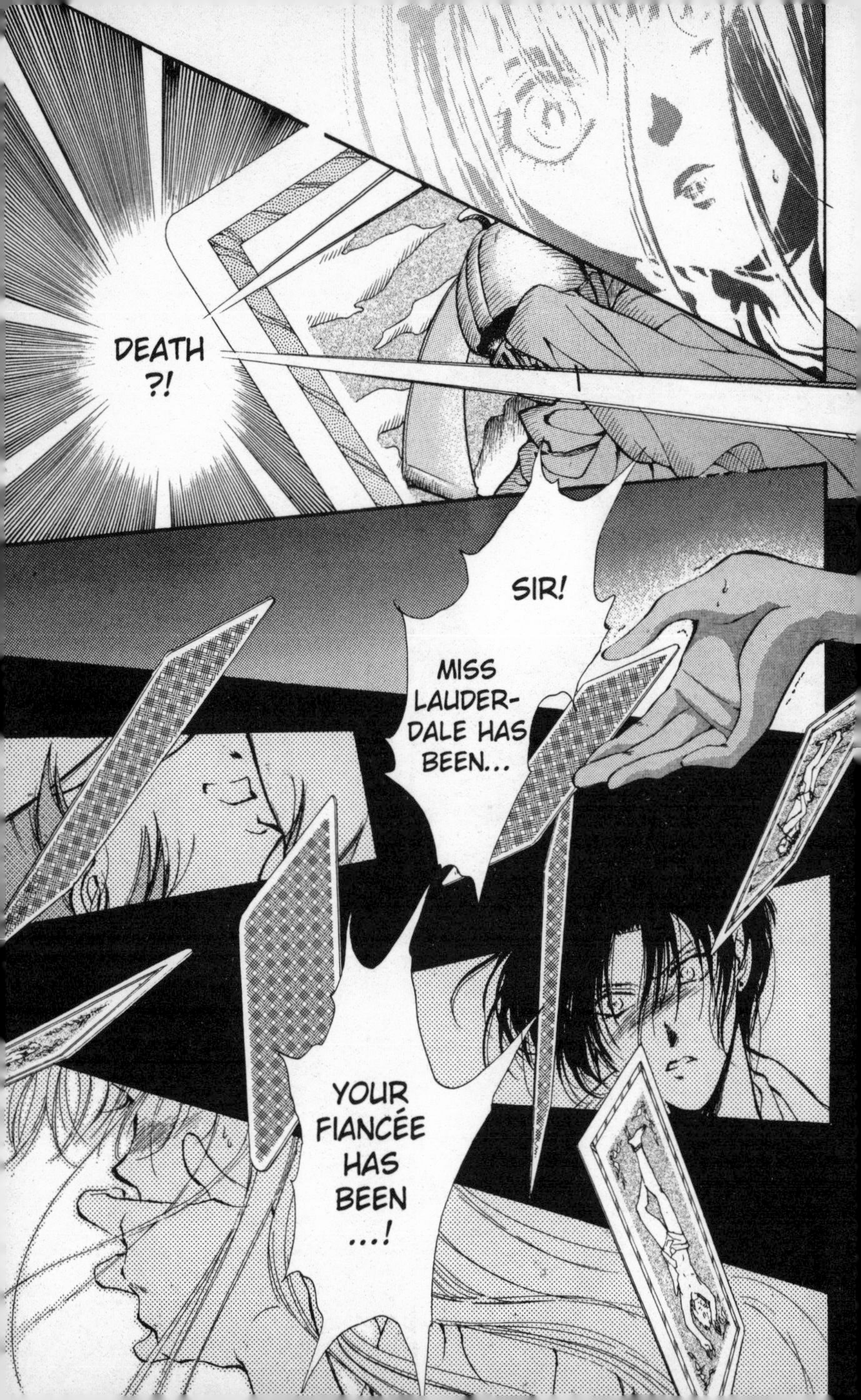
DEATH ?!
SIR!
MISS LAUDER-DALE HAS BEEN...
YOUR FIANCÉE HAS BEEN ...!

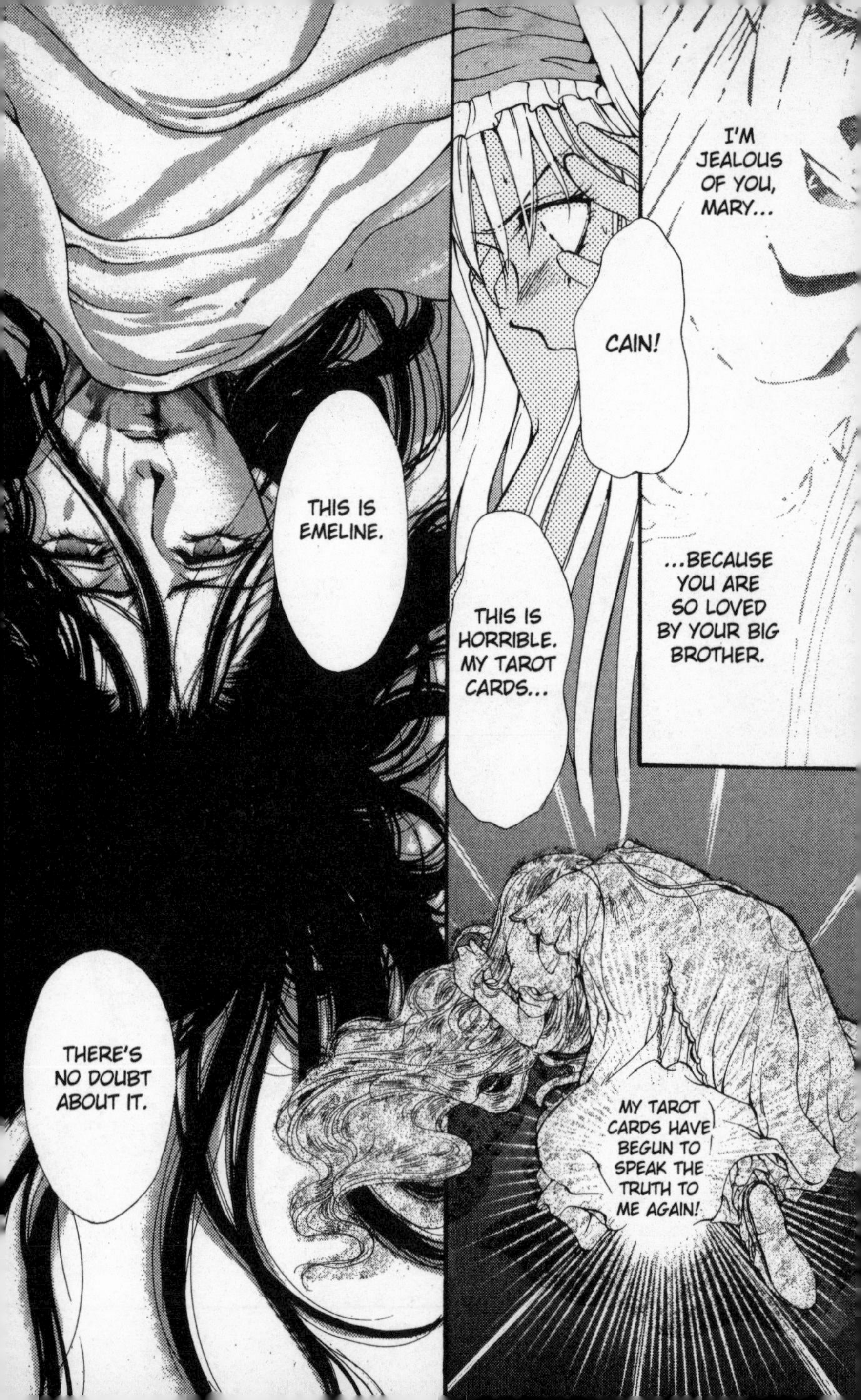
I'M JEALOUS OF YOU, MARY...
...BECAUSE YOU ARE SO LOVED BY YOUR BIG BROTHER.
CAIN!
THIS IS HORRIBLE. MY TAROT CARDS...
MY TAROT CARDS HAVE BEGUN TO SPEAK THE TRUTH TO ME AGAIN!
THIS IS EMELINE.
THERE'S NO DOUBT ABOUT IT.

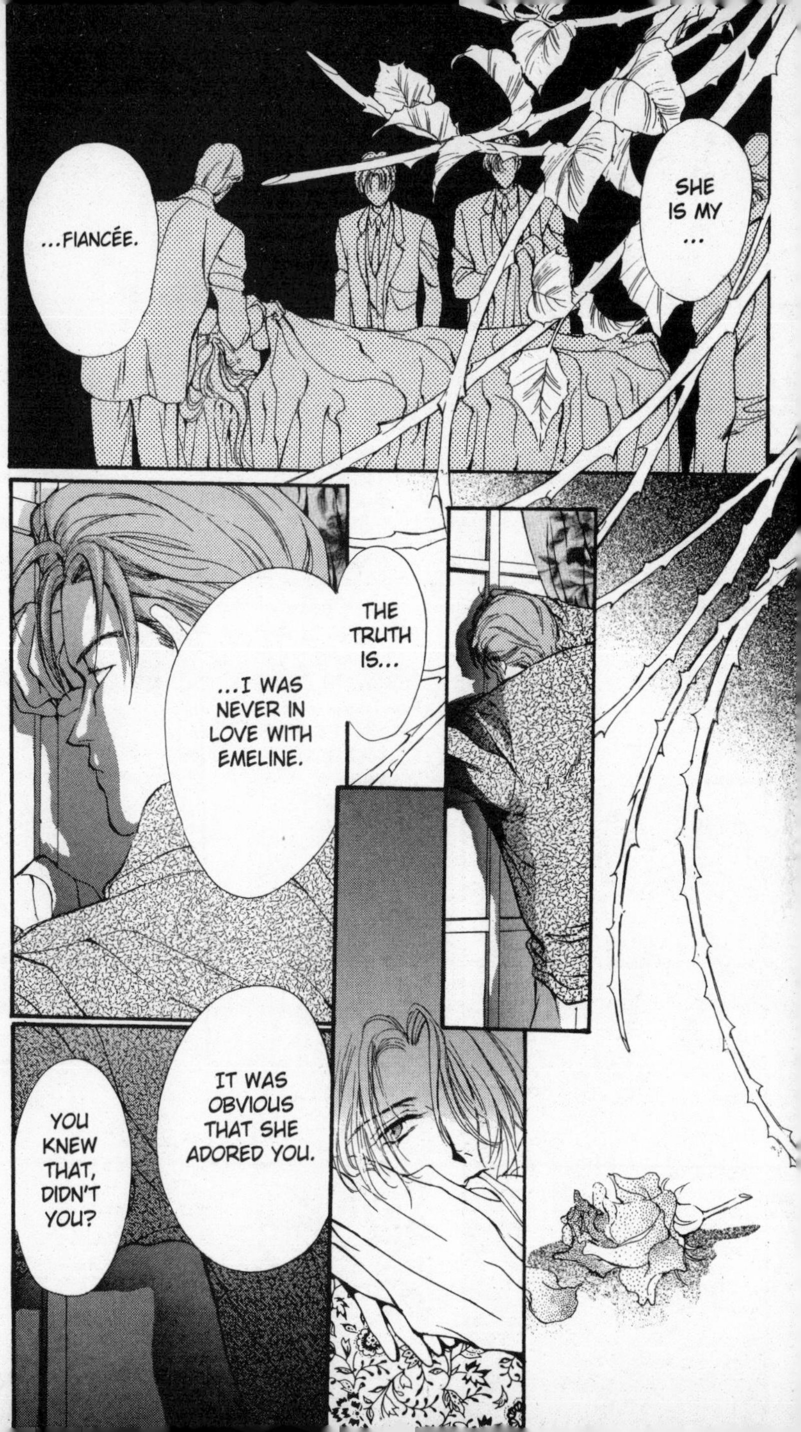
SHE IS MY ...
...FIANCÉE.
THE TRUTH IS...
...I WAS NEVER IN LOVE WITH EMELINE.
IT WAS OBVIOUS THAT SHE ADORED YOU.
YOU KNEW THAT, DIDN'T YOU?

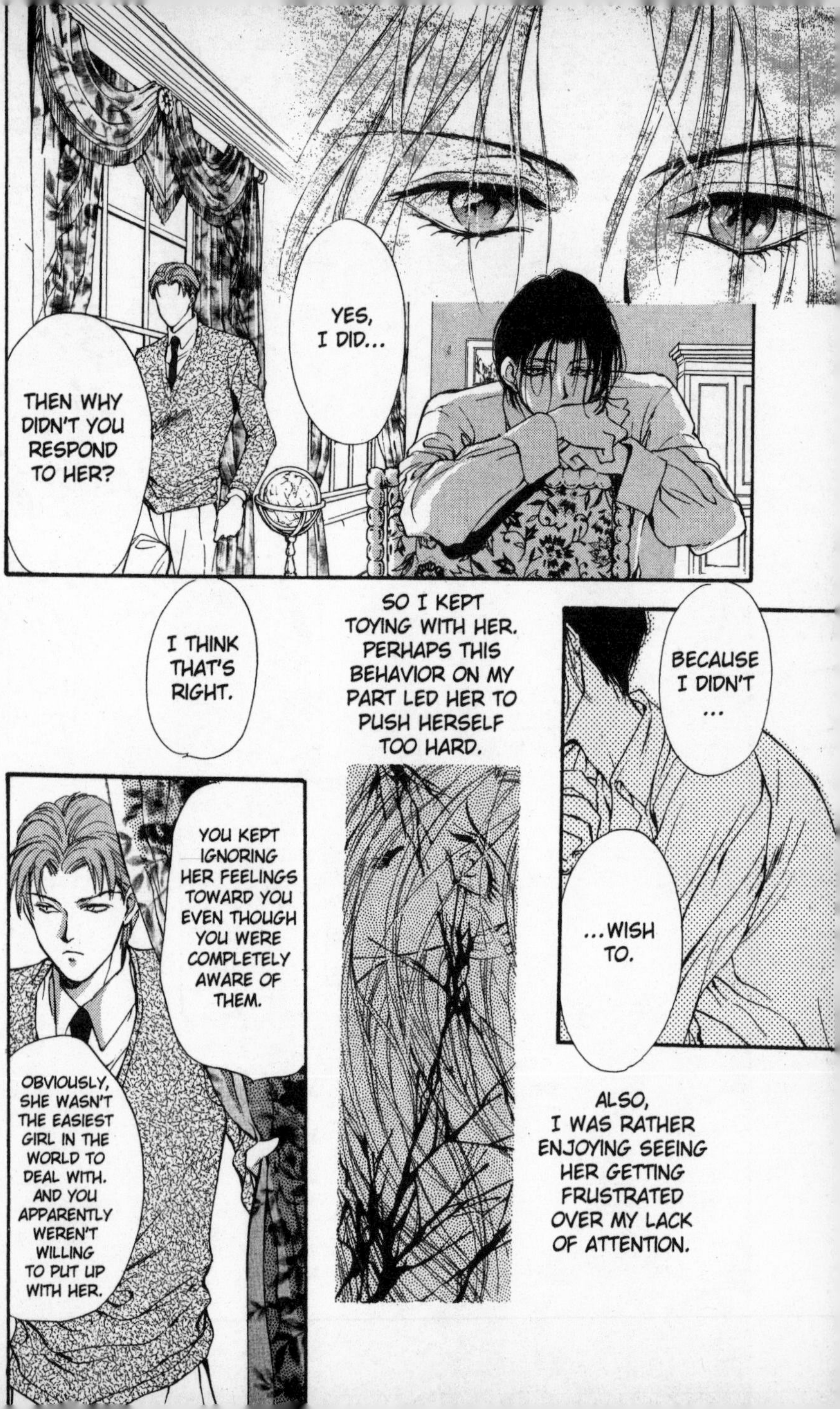
YES, I DID...
THEN WHY DIDN'T YOU RESPOND TO HER?
BECAUSE I DIDN'T ...
...WISH TO.
ALSO, I WAS RATHER ENJOYING SEEING HER GETTING FRUSTRATED OVER MY LACK OF ATTENTION.
SO I KEPT TOYING WITH HER. PERHAPS THIS BEHAVIOR ON MY PART LED HER TO PUSH HERSELF TOO HARD.
I THINK THAT'S RIGHT.
YOU KEPT IGNORING HER FEELINGS TOWARD YOU EVEN THOUGH YOU WERE COMPLETELY AWARE OF THEM.
OBVIOUSLY, SHE WASN'T THE EASIEST GIRL IN THE WORLD TO DEAL WITH. AND YOU APPARENTLY WEREN'T WILLING TO PUT UP WITH HER.

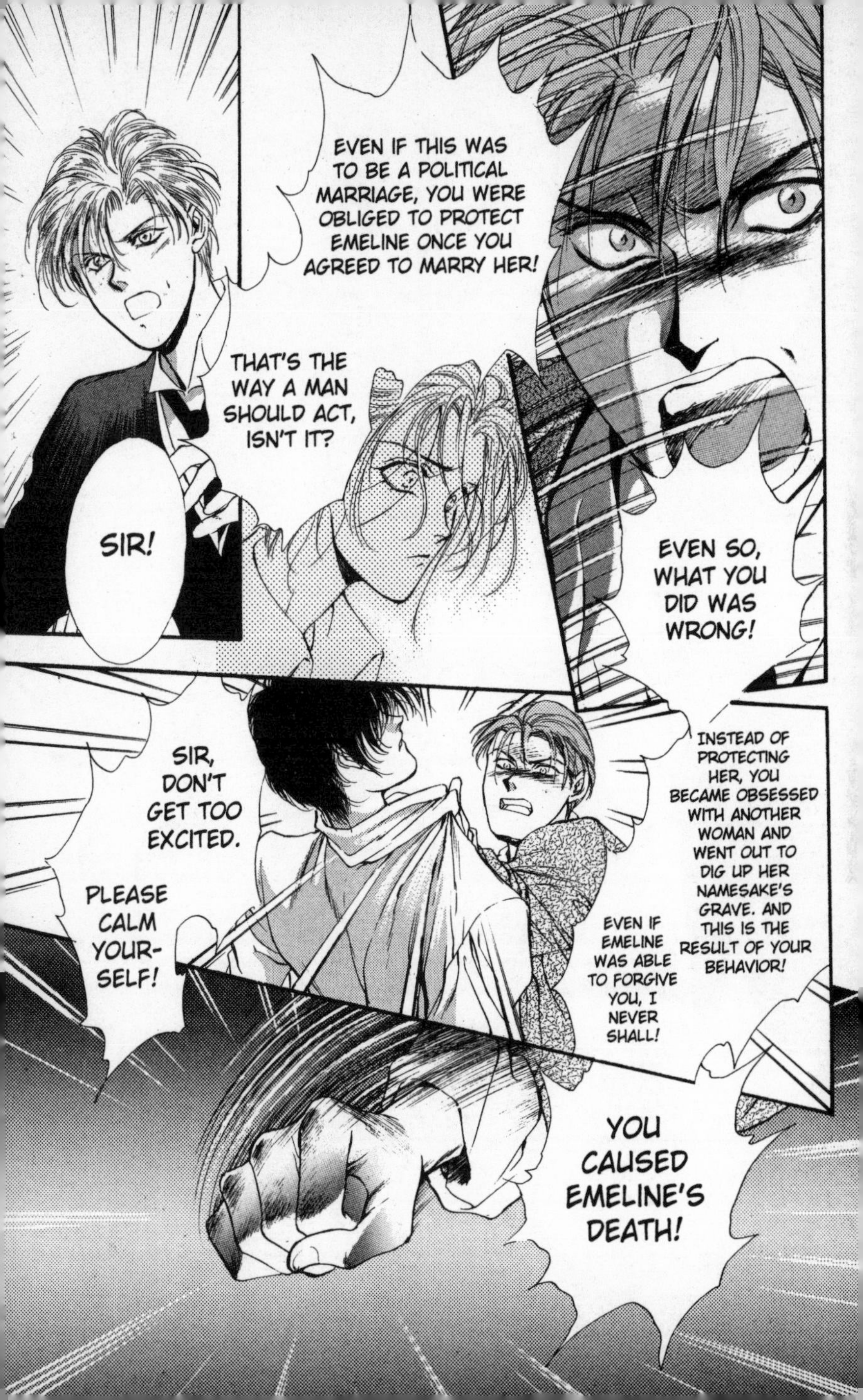
EVEN IF THIS WAS TO BE A POLITICAL MARRIAGE, YOU WERE OBLIGED TO PROTECT EMELINE ONCE YOU AGREED TO MARRY HER!
THAT'S THE WAY A MAN SHOULD ACT, ISN'T IT?
EVEN SO, WHAT YOU DID WAS WRONG!
SIR!
INSTEAD OF PROTECTING HER, YOU BECAME OBSESSED WITH ANOTHER WOMAN AND WENT OUT TO DIG UP HER NAMESAKE'S GRAVE. AND THIS IS THE RESULT OF YOUR BEHAVIOR!
EVEN IF EMELINE WAS ABLE TO FORGIVE YOU, I NEVER SHALL!
SIR, DON'T GET TOO EXCITED.
PLEASE CALM YOUR-SELF!
YOU CAUSED EMELINE'S DEATH!

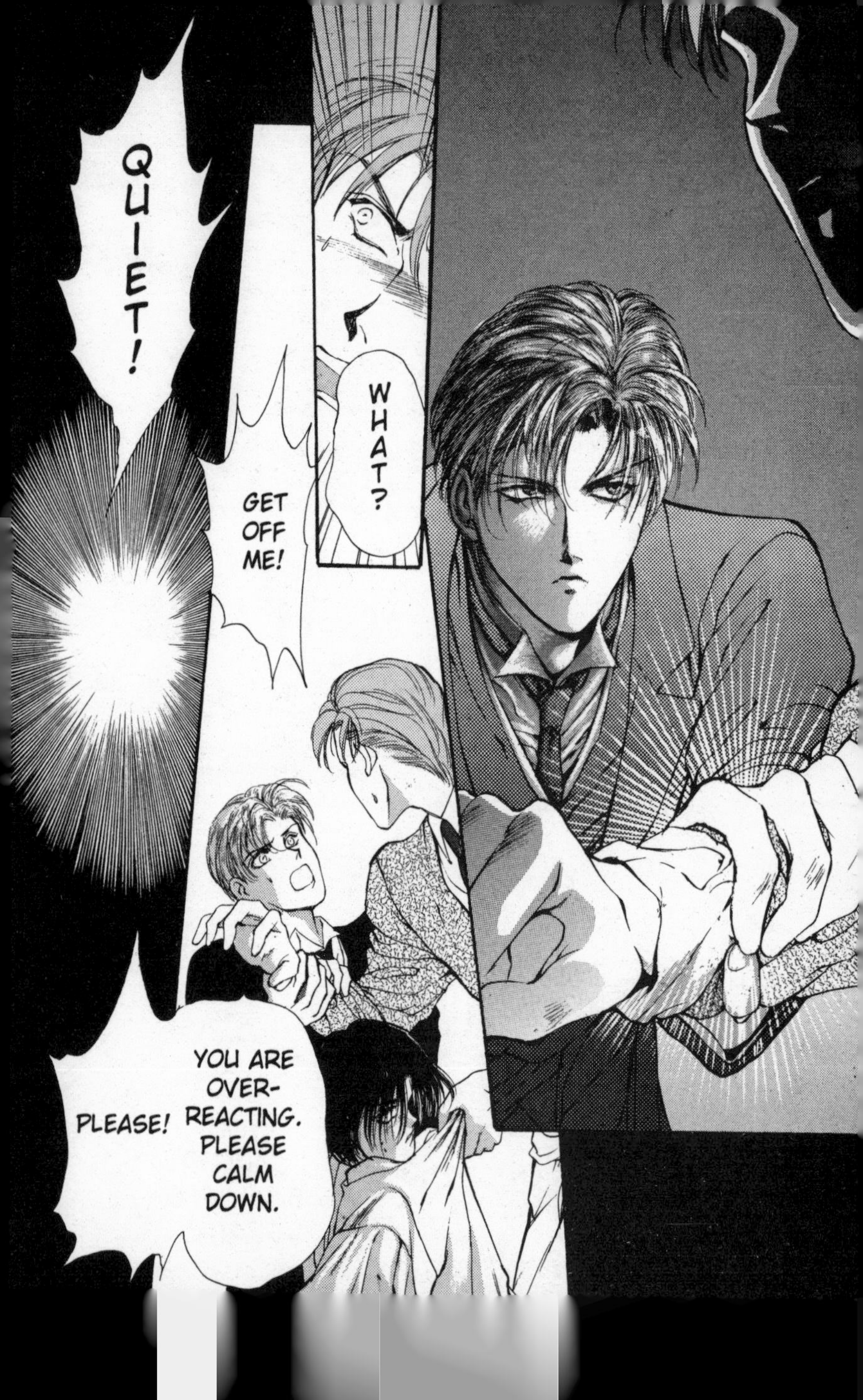
WHAT?
GET OFF ME!
QUIET!
YOU ARE OVER-REACTING. PLEASE CALM DOWN.
PLEASE!

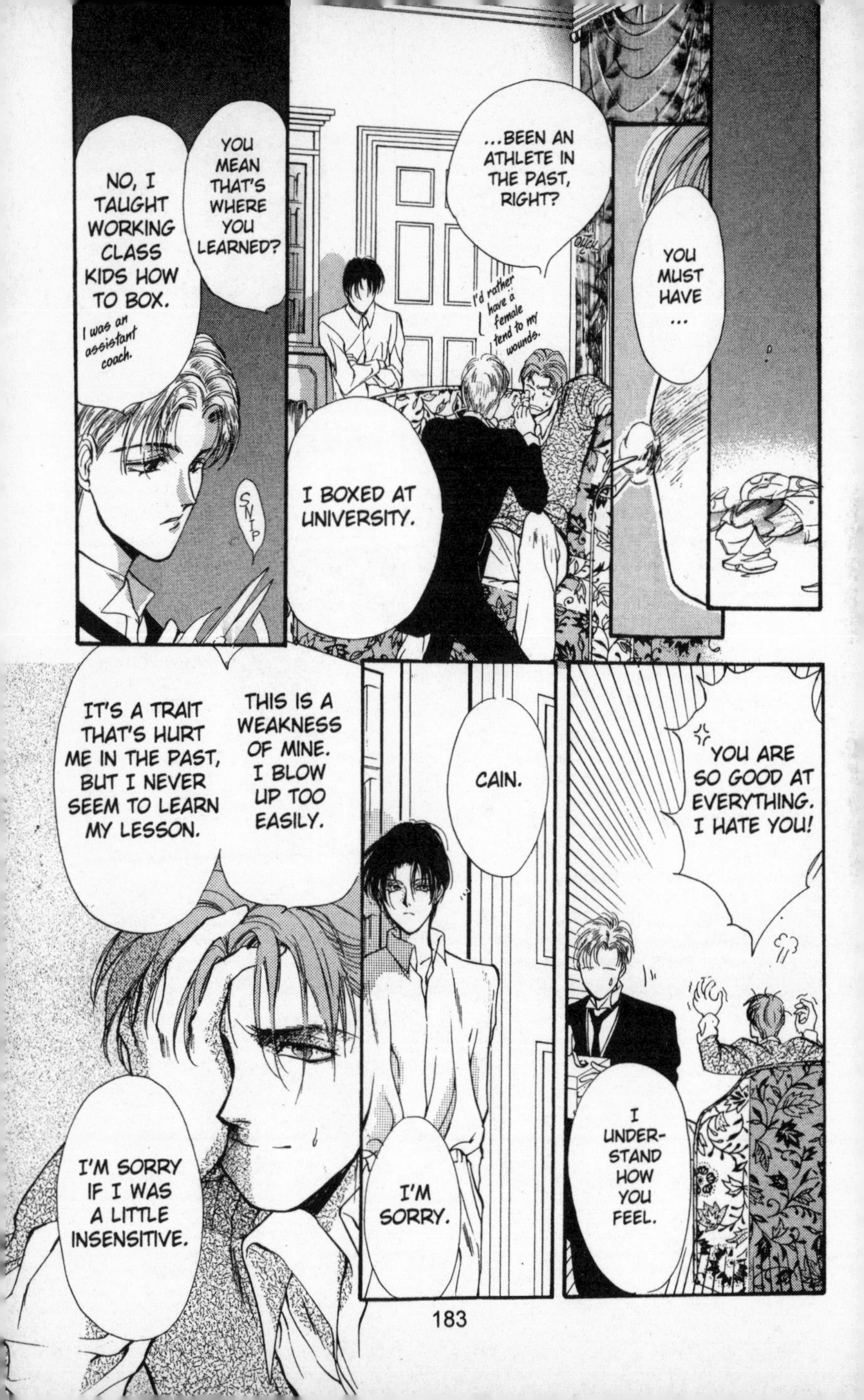
YOU MUST HAVE ...
...BEEN AN ATHLETE IN THE PAST, RIGHT?
OUCH
I'd rather have a female tend to my wounds.
I BOXED AT UNIVERSITY.
YOU MEAN THAT'S WHERE YOU LEARNED?
NO, I TAUGHT WORKING CLASS KIDS HOW TO BOX.
I was an assistant coach.
SNIP
YOU ARE SO GOOD AT EVERYTHING. I HATE YOU!
I UNDERSTAND HOW YOU FEEL.
CAIN.
I'M SORRY.
THIS IS A WEAKNESS OF MINE. I BLOW UP TOO EASILY.
IT'S A TRAIT THAT'S HURT ME IN THE PAST, BUT I NEVER SEEM TO LEARN MY LESSON.
I'M SORRY IF I WAS A LITTLE INSENSITIVE.

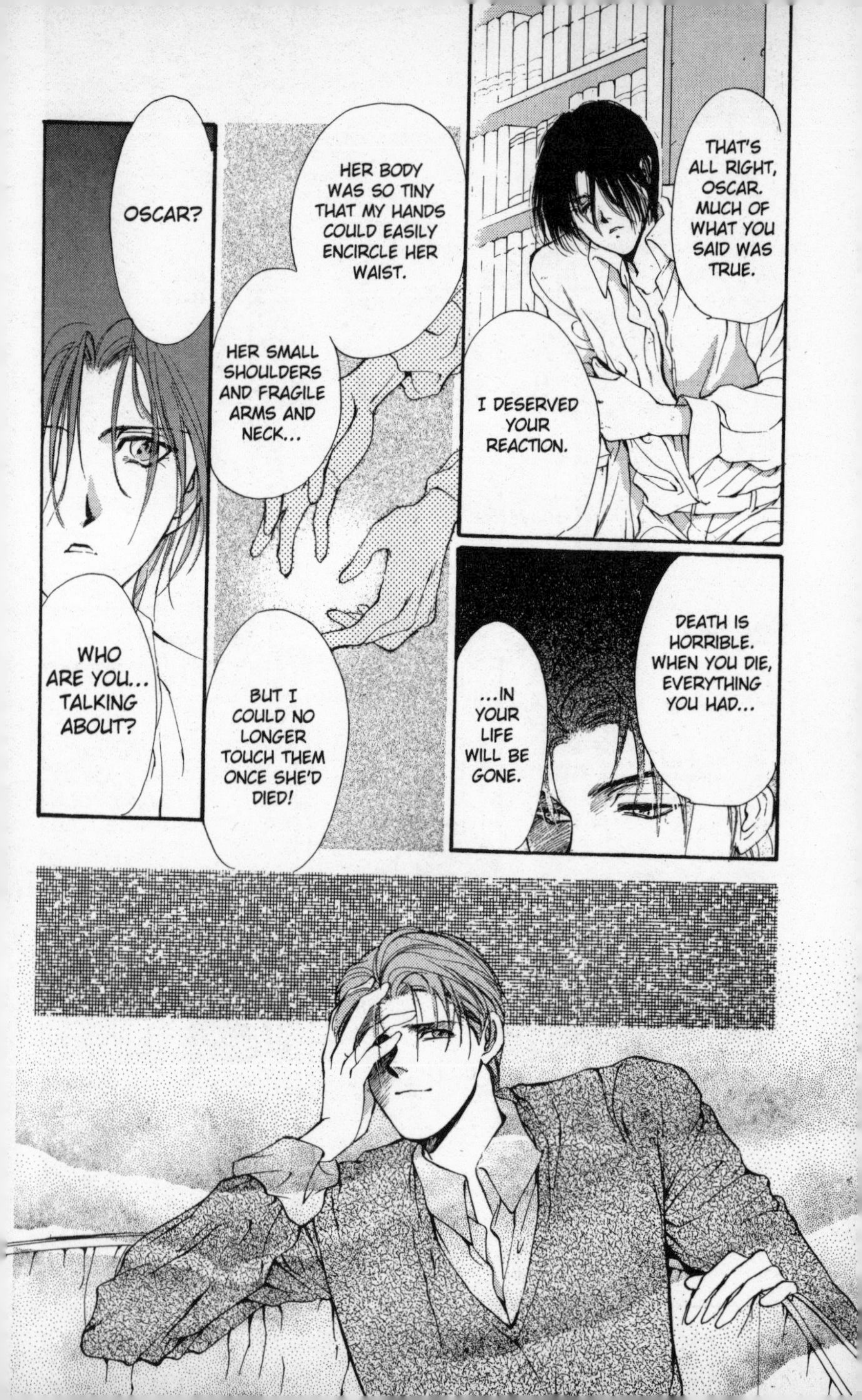
THAT'S ALL RIGHT, OSCAR. MUCH OF WHAT YOU SAID WAS TRUE.
I DESERVED YOUR REACTION.
DEATH IS HORRIBLE. WHEN YOU DIE, EVERYTHING YOU HAD...
...IN YOUR LIFE WILL BE GONE.
HER BODY WAS SO TINY THAT MY HANDS COULD EASILY ENCIRCLE HER WAIST.
HER SMALL SHOULDERS AND FRAGILE ARMS AND NECK...
BUT I COULD NO LONGER TOUCH THEM ONCE SHE'D DIED!
OSCAR?
WHO ARE YOU... TALKING ABOUT?

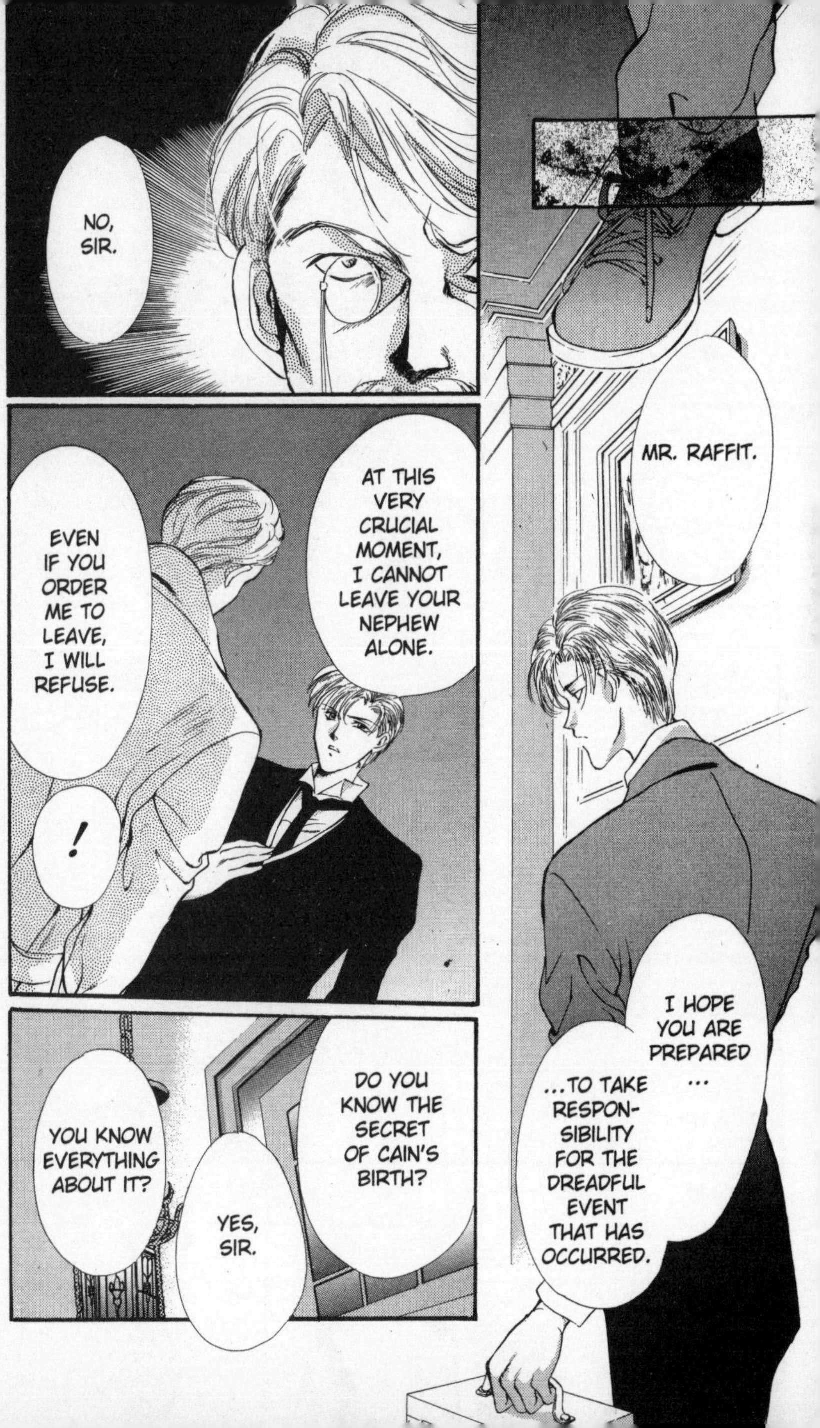
MR. RAFFIT.
I HOPE YOU ARE PREPARED ...
...TO TAKE RESPON-SIBILITY FOR THE DREADFUL EVENT THAT HAS OCCURRED.
NO, SIR.
AT THIS VERY CRUCIAL MOMENT, I CANNOT LEAVE YOUR NEPHEW ALONE.
EVEN IF YOU ORDER ME TO LEAVE, I WILL REFUSE.
!
DO YOU KNOW THE SECRET OF CAIN'S BIRTH?
YOU KNOW EVERYTHING ABOUT IT?
YES, SIR.

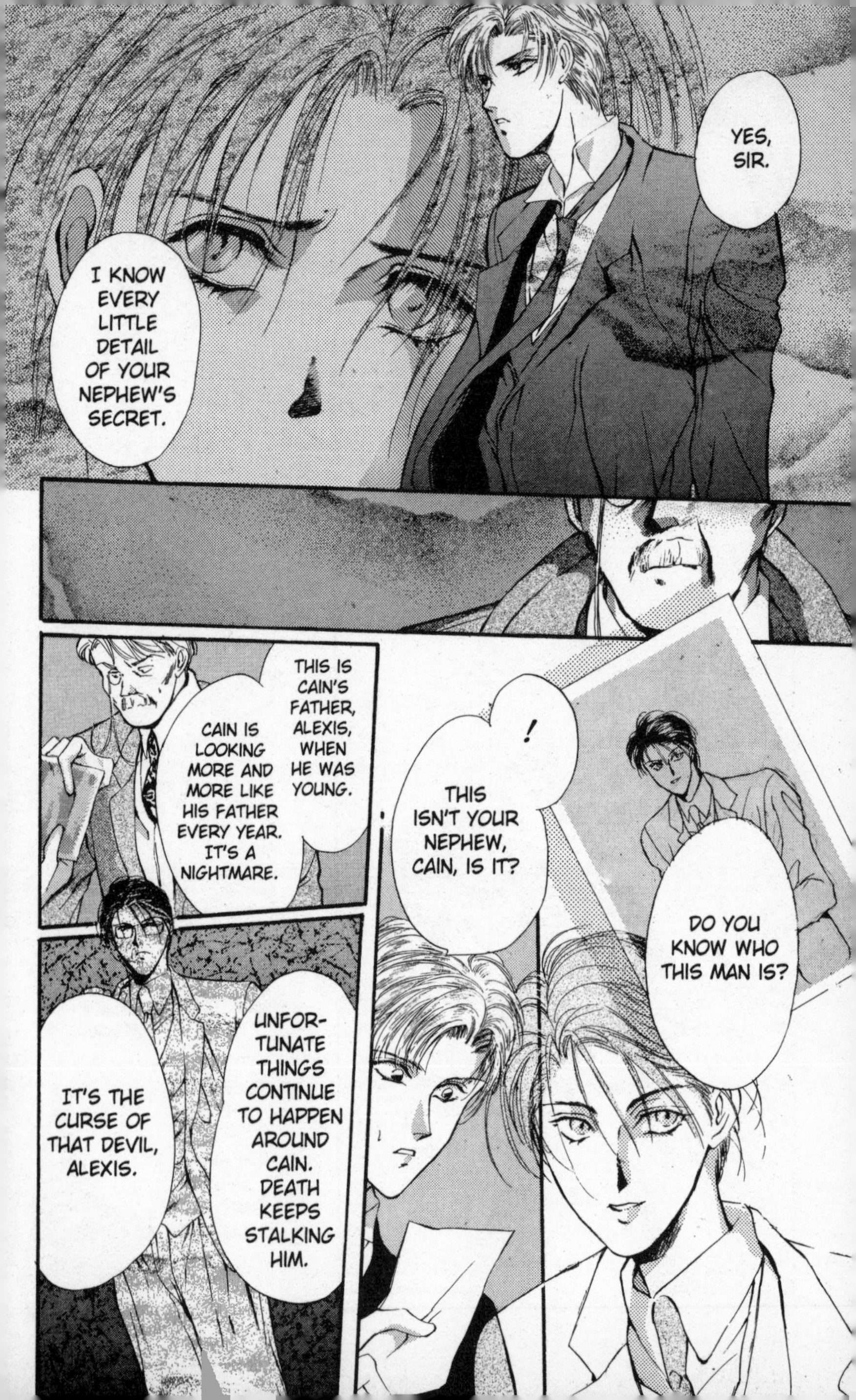
YES, SIR.
I KNOW EVERY LITTLE DETAIL OF YOUR NEPHEW'S SECRET.
DO YOU KNOW WHO THIS MAN IS?
!
THIS ISN'T YOUR NEPHEW, CAIN, IS IT?
THIS IS CAIN'S FATHER, ALEXIS, WHEN HE WAS YOUNG.
CAIN IS LOOKING MORE AND MORE LIKE HIS FATHER EVERY YEAR. IT'S A NIGHTMARE.
UNFOR-TUNATE THINGS CONTINUE TO HAPPEN AROUND CAIN. DEATH KEEPS STALKING HIM.
IT'S THE CURSE OF THAT DEVIL, ALEXIS.

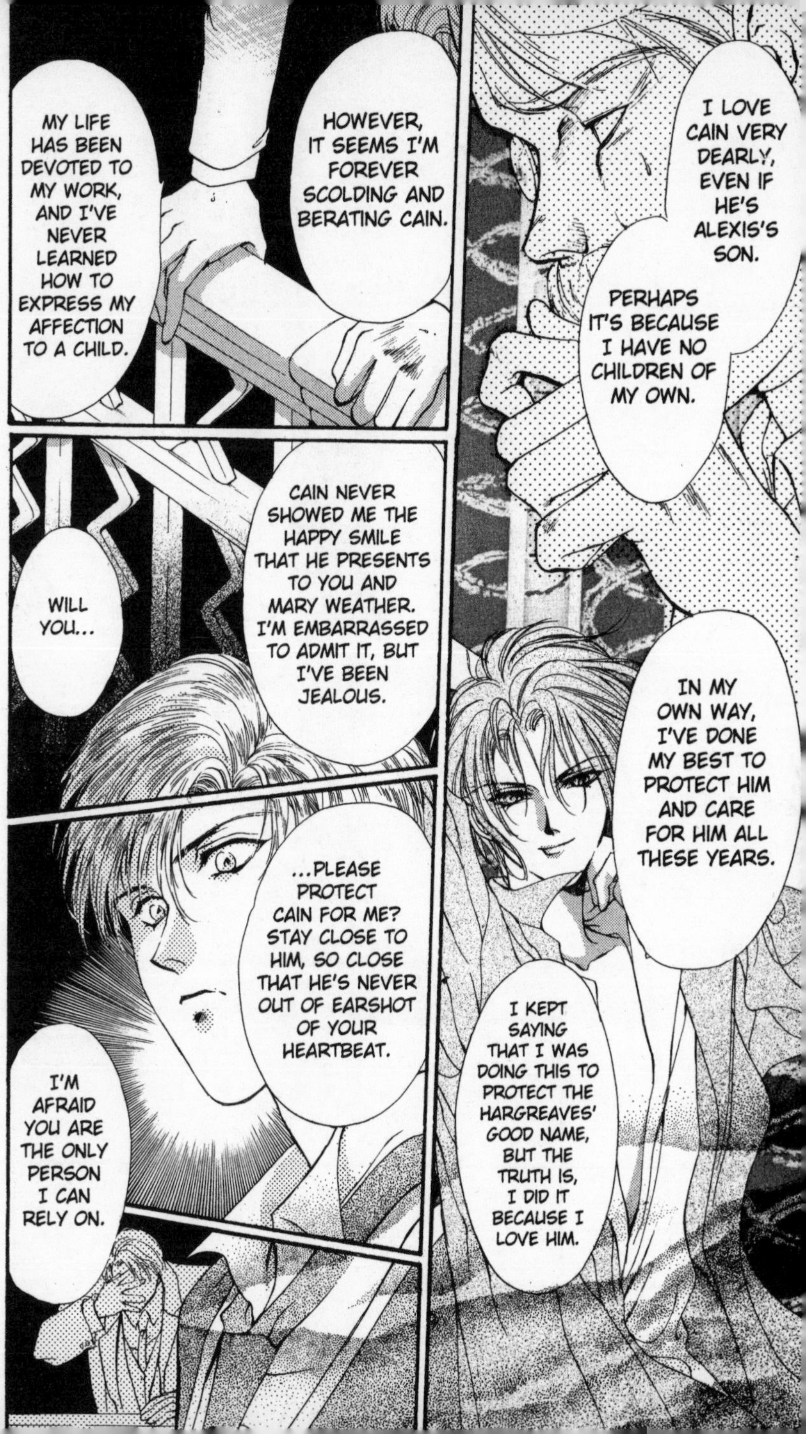
I LOVE CAIN VERY DEARLY, EVEN IF HE'S ALEXIS'S SON.
PERHAPS IT'S BECAUSE I HAVE NO CHILDREN OF MY OWN.
HOWEVER, IT SEEMS I'M FOREVER SCOLDING AND BERATING CAIN.
MY LIFE HAS BEEN DEVOTED TO MY WORK, AND I'VE NEVER LEARNED HOW TO EXPRESS MY AFFECTION TO A CHILD.
IN MY OWN WAY, I'VE DONE MY BEST TO PROTECT HIM AND CARE FOR HIM ALL THESE YEARS.
I KEPT SAYING THAT I WAS DOING THIS TO PROTECT THE HARGREAVES' GOOD NAME, BUT THE TRUTH IS, I DID IT BECAUSE I LOVE HIM.
CAIN NEVER SHOWED ME THE HAPPY SMILE THAT HE PRESENTS TO YOU AND MARY WEATHER. I'M EMBARRASSED TO ADMIT IT, BUT I'VE BEEN JEALOUS.
WILL YOU...
...PLEASE PROTECT CAIN FOR ME? STAY CLOSE TO HIM, SO CLOSE THAT HE'S NEVER OUT OF EARSHOT OF YOUR HEARTBEAT.
I'M AFRAID YOU ARE THE ONLY PERSON I CAN RELY ON.

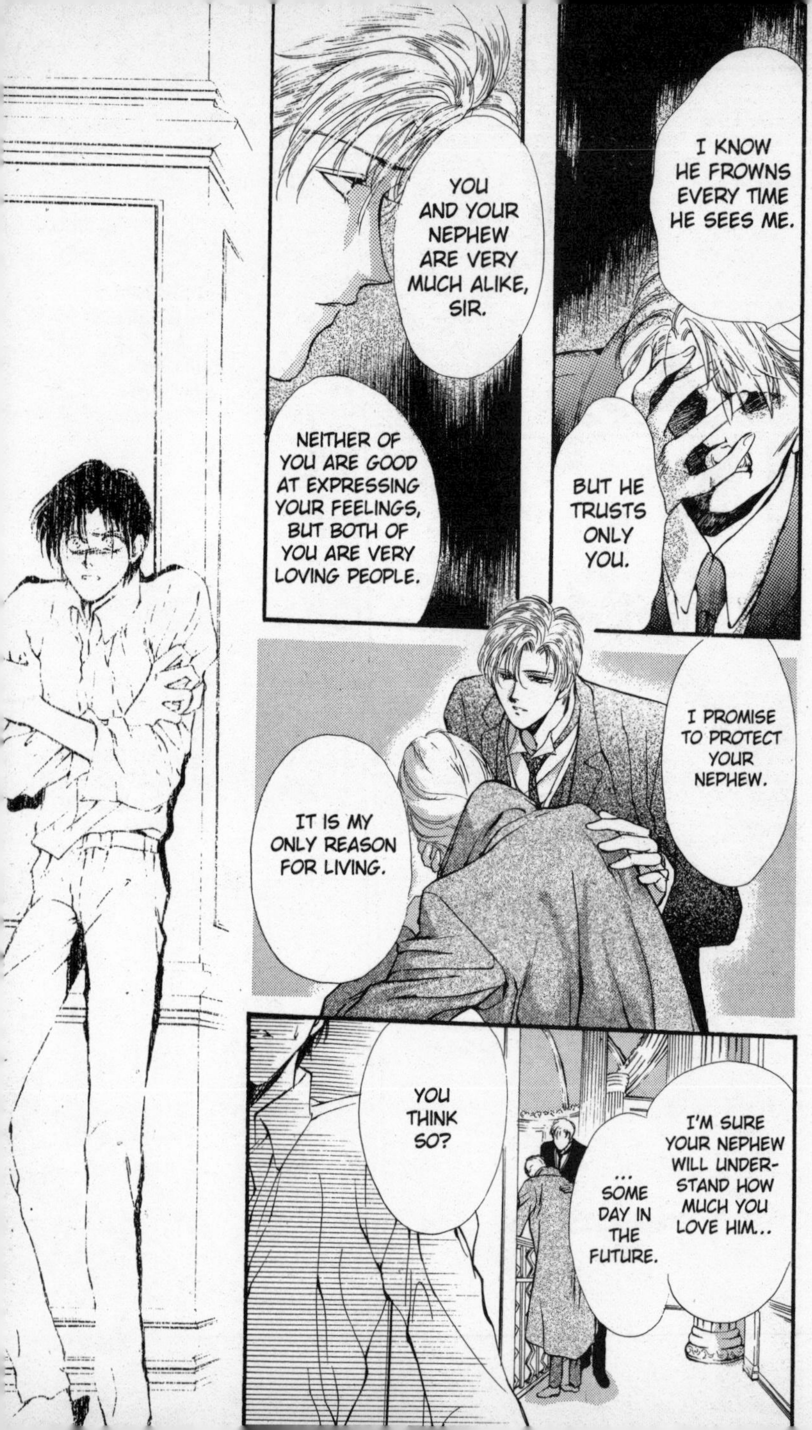
I KNOW HE FROWNS EVERY TIME HE SEES ME.
BUT HE TRUSTS ONLY YOU.
YOU AND YOUR NEPHEW ARE VERY MUCH ALIKE, SIR.
NEITHER OF YOU ARE GOOD AT EXPRESSING YOUR FEELINGS, BUT BOTH OF YOU ARE VERY LOVING PEOPLE.
I PROMISE TO PROTECT YOUR NEPHEW.
IT IS MY ONLY REASON FOR LIVING.
I'M SURE YOUR NEPHEW WILL UNDER-STAND HOW MUCH YOU LOVE HIM..
... SOME DAY IN THE FUTURE.
YOU THINK SO?

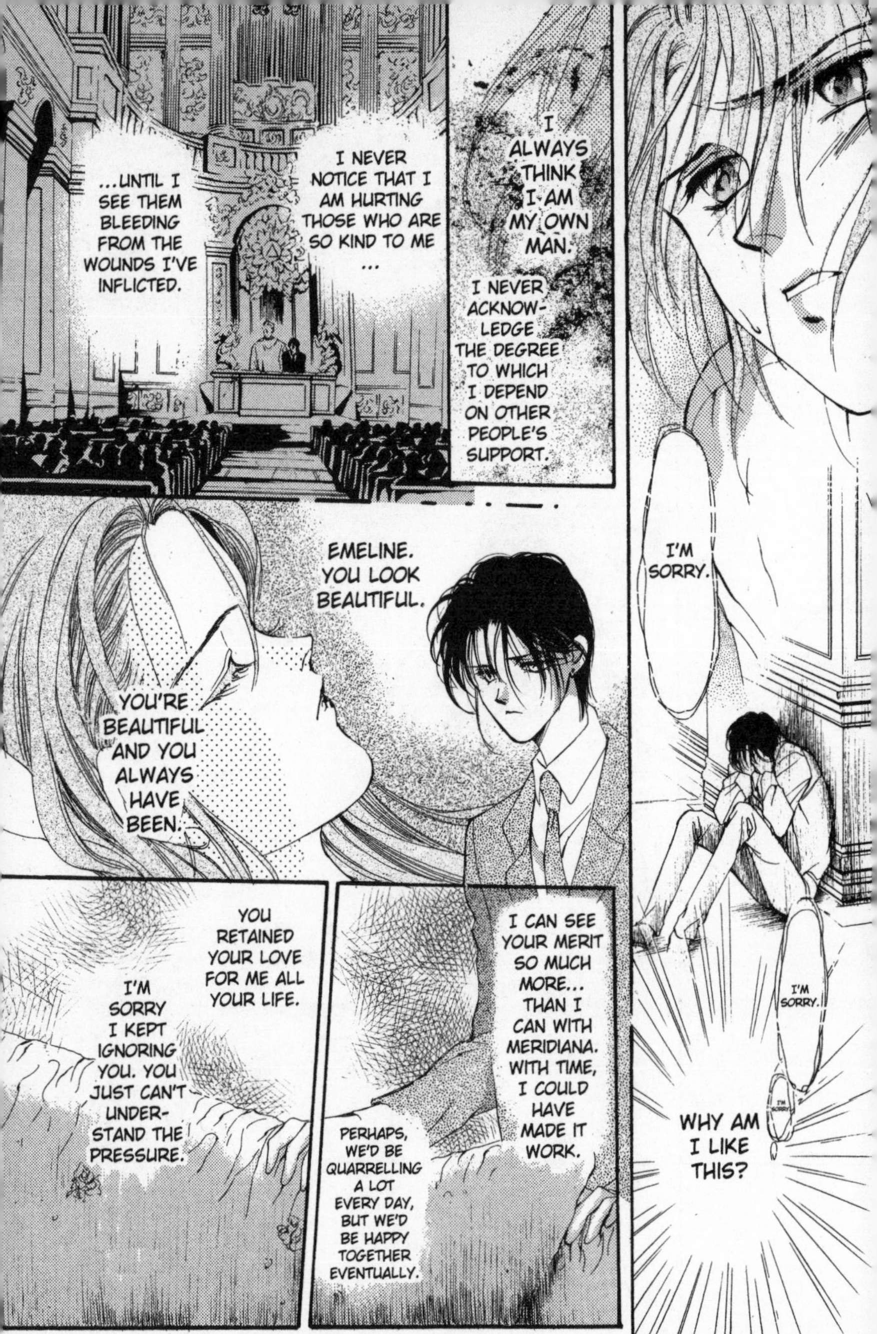
I'M SORRY.
I'M SORRY.
I'M SORRY
WHY AM I LIKE THIS?
I ALWAYS THINK I AM MY OWN MAN.
I NEVER ACKNOWLEDGE THE DEGREE TO WHICH I DEPEND ON OTHER PEOPLE'S SUPPORT.
I NEVER NOTICE THAT I AM HURTING THOSE WHO ARE SO KIND TO ME ...
...UNTIL I SEE THEM BLEEDING FROM THE WOUNDS I'VE INFLICTED.
EMELINE. YOU LOOK BEAUTIFUL.
YOU'RE BEAUTIFUL AND YOU ALWAYS HAVE BEEN.
I CAN SEE YOUR MERIT SO MUCH MORE... THAN I CAN WITH MERIDIANA. WITH TIME, I COULD HAVE MADE IT WORK.
PERHAPS, WE'D BE QUARRELLING A LOT EVERY DAY, BUT WE'D BE HAPPY TOGETHER EVENTUALLY.
YOU RETAINED YOUR LOVE FOR ME ALL YOUR LIFE.
I'M SORRY I KEPT IGNORING YOU. YOU JUST CAN'T UNDERSTAND THE PRESSURE.

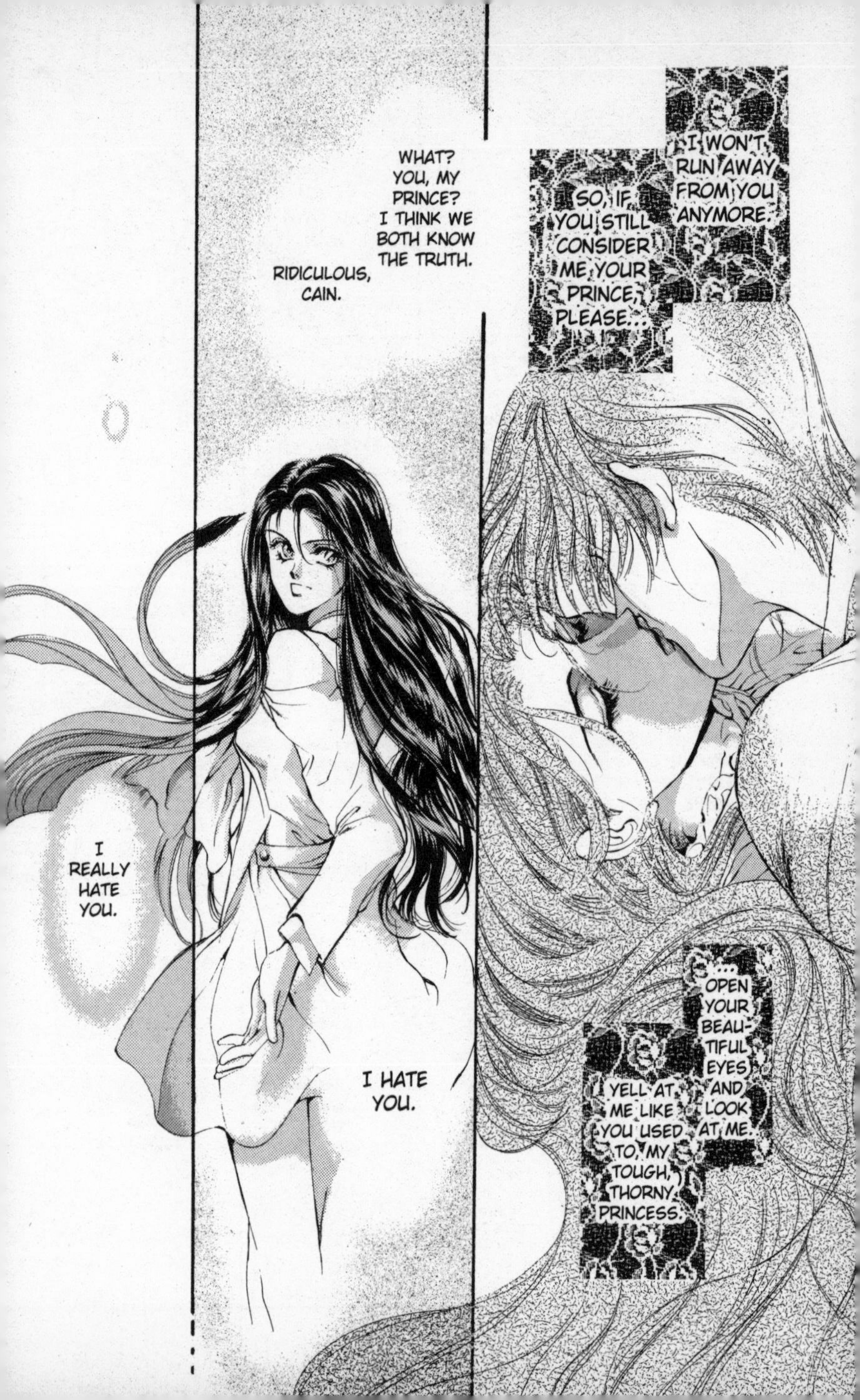
I WON'T RUN AWAY FROM YOU ANYMORE.
SO, IF YOU STILL CONSIDER ME YOUR PRINCE, PLEASE...
...OPEN YOUR BEAU-TIFUL EYES AND LOOK AT ME.
YELL AT ME LIKE YOU USED TO, MY TOUGH, THORNY PRINCESS.
WHAT? YOU, MY PRINCE? I THINK WE BOTH KNOW THE TRUTH.
RIDICULOUS, CAIN.
I HATE YOU.
I REALLY HATE YOU.

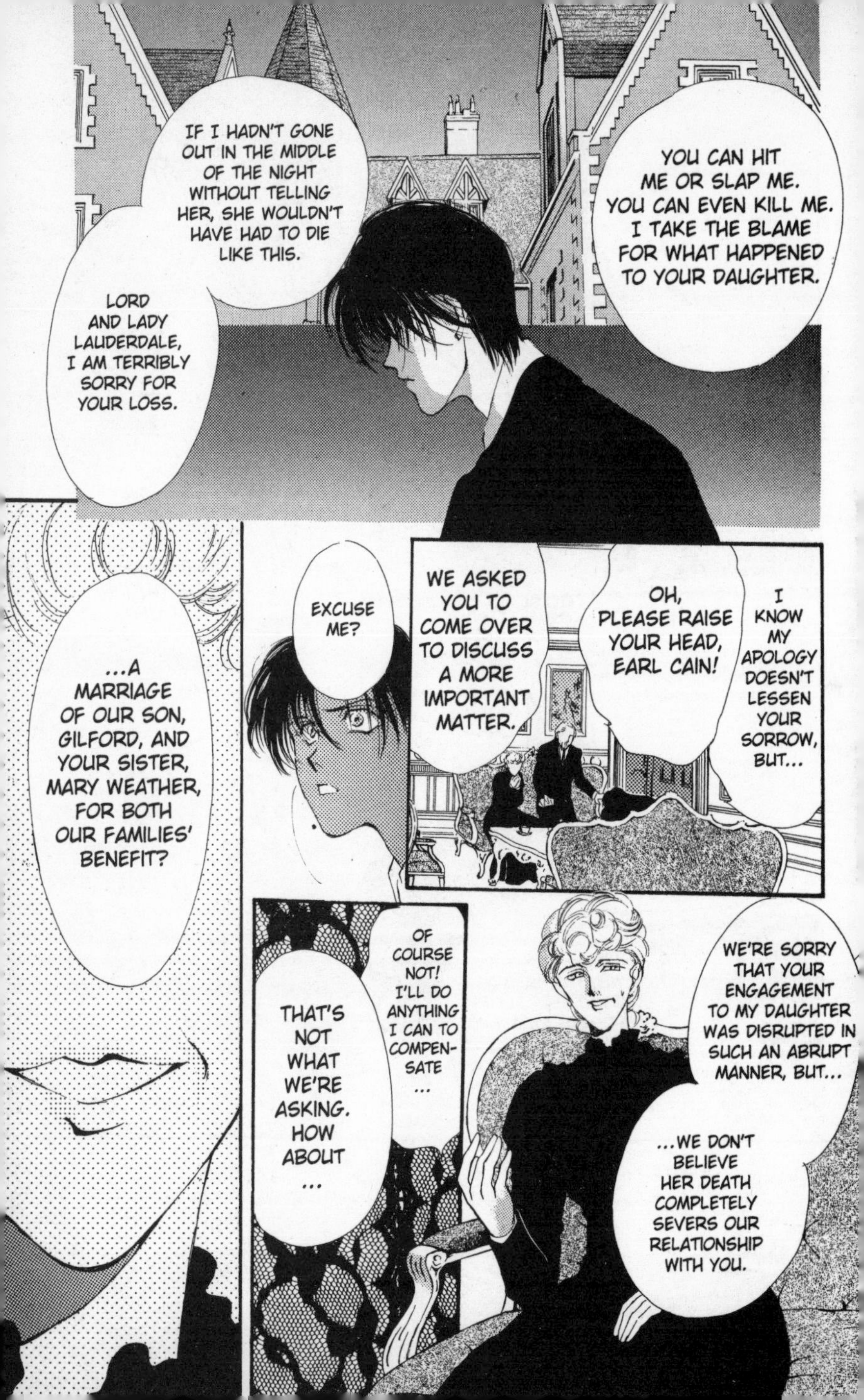
YOU CAN HIT ME OR SLAP ME. YOU CAN EVEN KILL ME. I TAKE THE BLAME FOR WHAT HAPPENED TO YOUR DAUGHTER.
IF I HADN'T GONE OUT IN THE MIDDLE OF THE NIGHT WITHOUT TELLING HER, SHE WOULDN'T HAVE HAD TO DIE LIKE THIS.
LORD AND LADY LAUDERDALE, I AM TERRIBLY SORRY FOR YOUR LOSS.
I KNOW MY APOLOGY DOESN'T LESSEN YOUR SORROW, BUT...
OH, PLEASE RAISE YOUR HEAD, EARL CAIN!
WE ASKED YOU TO COME OVER TO DISCUSS A MORE IMPORTANT MATTER.
EXCUSE ME?
WE'RE SORRY THAT YOUR ENGAGEMENT TO MY DAUGHTER WAS DISRUPTED IN SUCH AN ABRUPT MANNER, BUT...
...WE DON'T BELIEVE HER DEATH COMPLETELY SEVERS OUR RELATIONSHIP WITH YOU.
OF COURSE NOT! I'LL DO ANYTHING I CAN TO COMPEN-SATE ...
THAT'S NOT WHAT WE'RE ASKING. HOW ABOUT ...
...A MARRIAGE OF OUR SON, GILFORD, AND YOUR SISTER, MARY WEATHER, FOR BOTH OUR FAMILIES' BENEFIT?

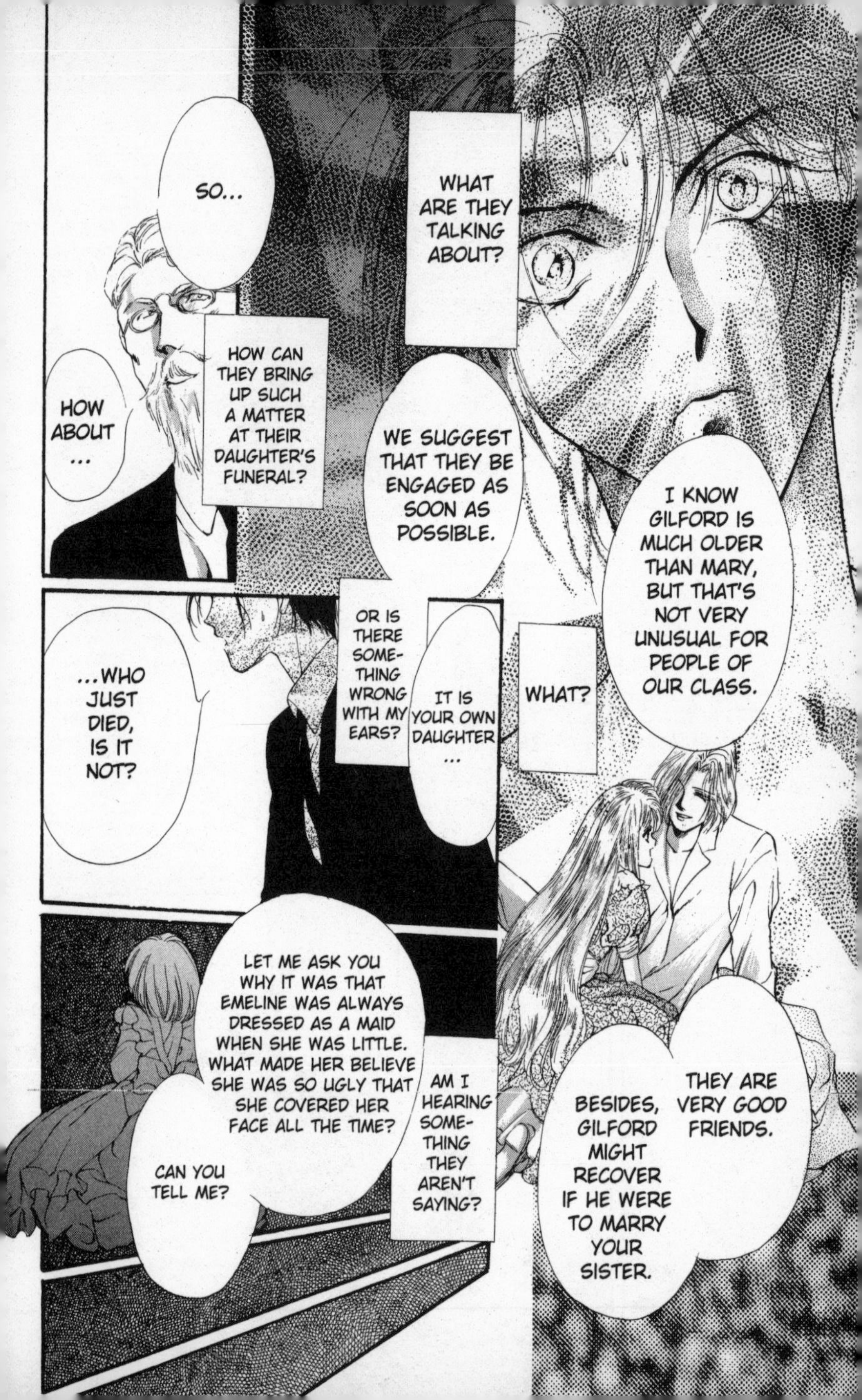
WHAT ARE THEY TALKING ABOUT?
SO...
HOW CAN THEY BRING UP SUCH A MATTER AT THEIR DAUGHTER'S FUNERAL?
HOW ABOUT ...
WE SUGGEST THAT THEY BE ENGAGED AS SOON AS POSSIBLE.
I KNOW GILFORD IS MUCH OLDER THAN MARY, BUT THAT'S NOT VERY UNUSUAL FOR PEOPLE OF OUR CLASS.
WHAT?
IT IS YOUR OWN DAUGHTER ...
OR IS THERE SOME-THING WRONG WITH MY EARS?
...WHO JUST DIED, IS IT NOT?
THEY ARE VERY GOOD FRIENDS.
BESIDES, GILFORD MIGHT RECOVER IF HE WERE TO MARRY YOUR SISTER.
AM I HEARING SOME-THING THEY AREN'T SAYING?
LET ME ASK YOU WHY IT WAS THAT EMELINE WAS ALWAYS DRESSED AS A MAID WHEN SHE WAS LITTLE. WHAT MADE HER BELIEVE SHE WAS SO UGLY THAT SHE COVERED HER FACE ALL THE TIME?
CAN YOU TELL ME?

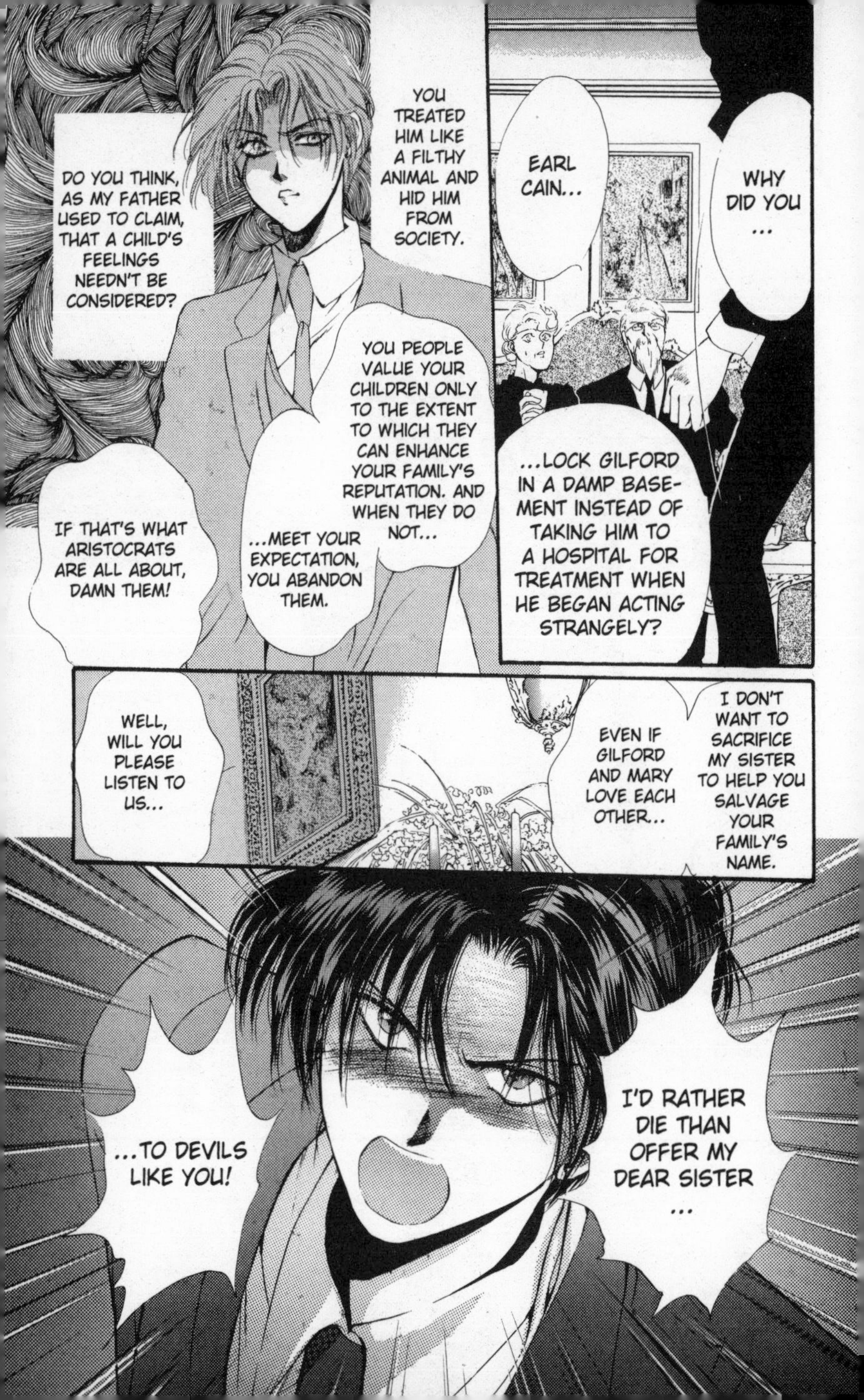

WHY DID YOU ...
EARL CAIN...
...LOCK GILFORD IN A DAMP BASE-MENT INSTEAD OF TAKING HIM TO A HOSPITAL FOR TREATMENT WHEN HE BEGAN ACTING STRANGELY?
YOU TREATED HIM LIKE A FILTHY ANIMAL AND HID HIM FROM SOCIETY.
DO YOU THINK, AS MY FATHER USED TO CLAIM, THAT A CHILD'S FEELINGS NEEDN'T BE CONSIDERED?
YOU PEOPLE VALUE YOUR CHILDREN ONLY TO THE EXTENT TO WHICH THEY CAN ENHANCE YOUR FAMILY'S REPUTATION. AND WHEN THEY DO NOT...
...MEET YOUR EXPECTATION, YOU ABANDON THEM.
IF THAT'S WHAT ARISTOCRATS ARE ALL ABOUT, DAMN THEM!
I DON'T WANT TO SACRIFICE MY SISTER TO HELP YOU SALVAGE YOUR FAMILY'S NAME.
EVEN IF GILFORD AND MARY LOVE EACH OTHER...
WELL, WILL YOU PLEASE LISTEN TO US...
I'D RATHER DIE THAN OFFER MY DEAR SISTER ...
...TO DEVILS LIKE YOU!

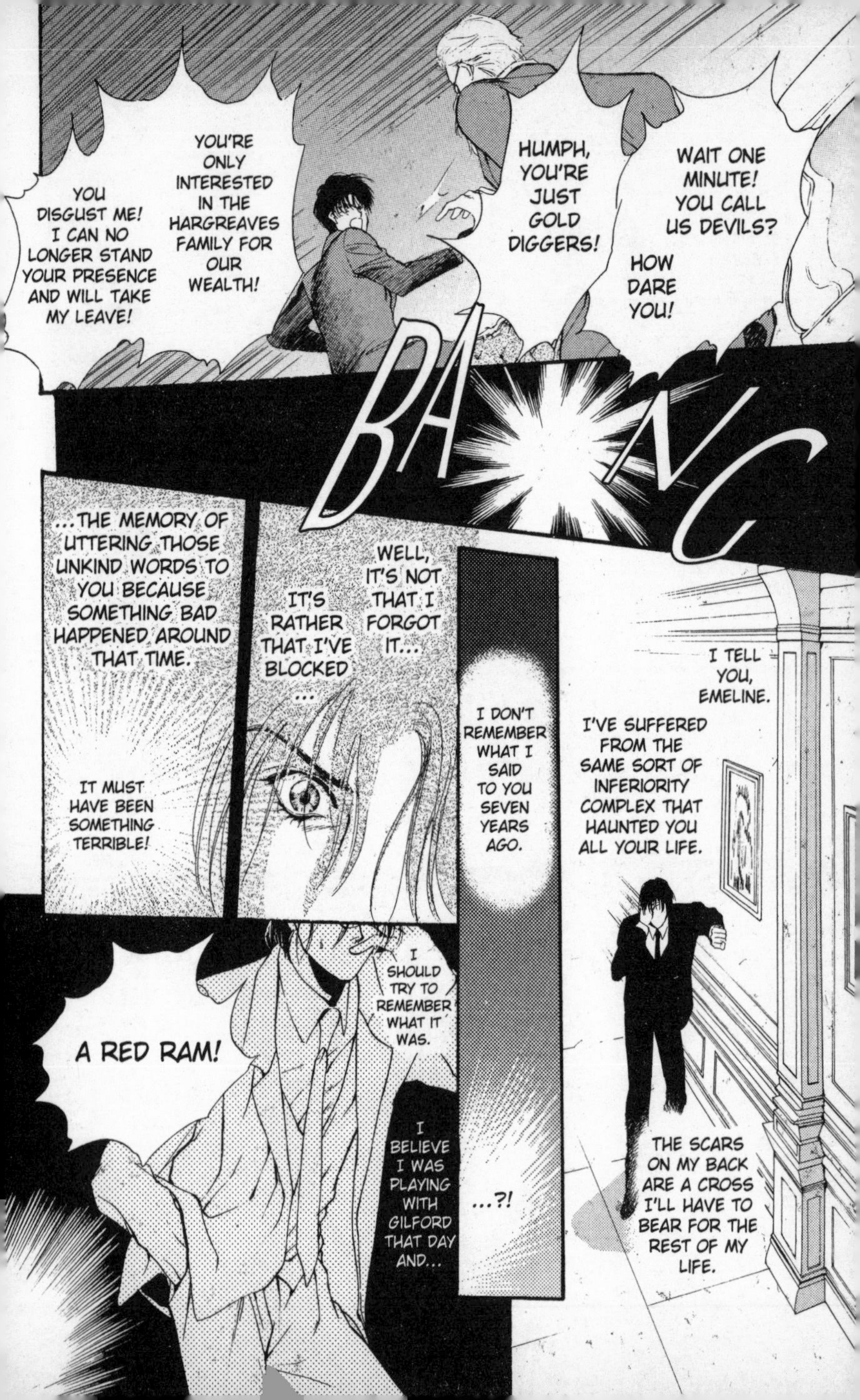

WAIT ONE MINUTE! YOU CALL US DEVILS?
HOW DARE YOU!
HUMPH, YOU'RE JUST GOLD DIGGERS!
YOU'RE ONLY INTERESTED IN THE HARGREAVES FAMILY FOR OUR WEALTH!
YOU DISGUST ME! I CAN NO LONGER STAND YOUR PRESENCE AND WILL TAKE MY LEAVE!
BANG
I TELL YOU, EMELINE.
I'VE SUFFERED FROM THE SAME SORT OF INFERIORITY COMPLEX THAT HAUNTED YOU ALL YOUR LIFE.
THE SCARS ON MY BACK ARE A CROSS I'LL HAVE TO BEAR FOR THE REST OF MY LIFE.
I DON'T REMEMBER WHAT I SAID TO YOU SEVEN YEARS AGO.
...?!
WELL, IT'S NOT THAT I FORGOT IT...
IT'S RATHER THAT I'VE BLOCKED ...
...THE MEMORY OF UTTERING THOSE UNKIND WORDS TO YOU BECAUSE SOMETHING BAD HAPPENED AROUND THAT TIME.
IT MUST HAVE BEEN SOMETHING TERRIBLE!
I SHOULD TRY TO REMEMBER WHAT IT WAS.
I BELIEVE I WAS PLAYING WITH GILFORD THAT DAY AND...
A RED RAM!

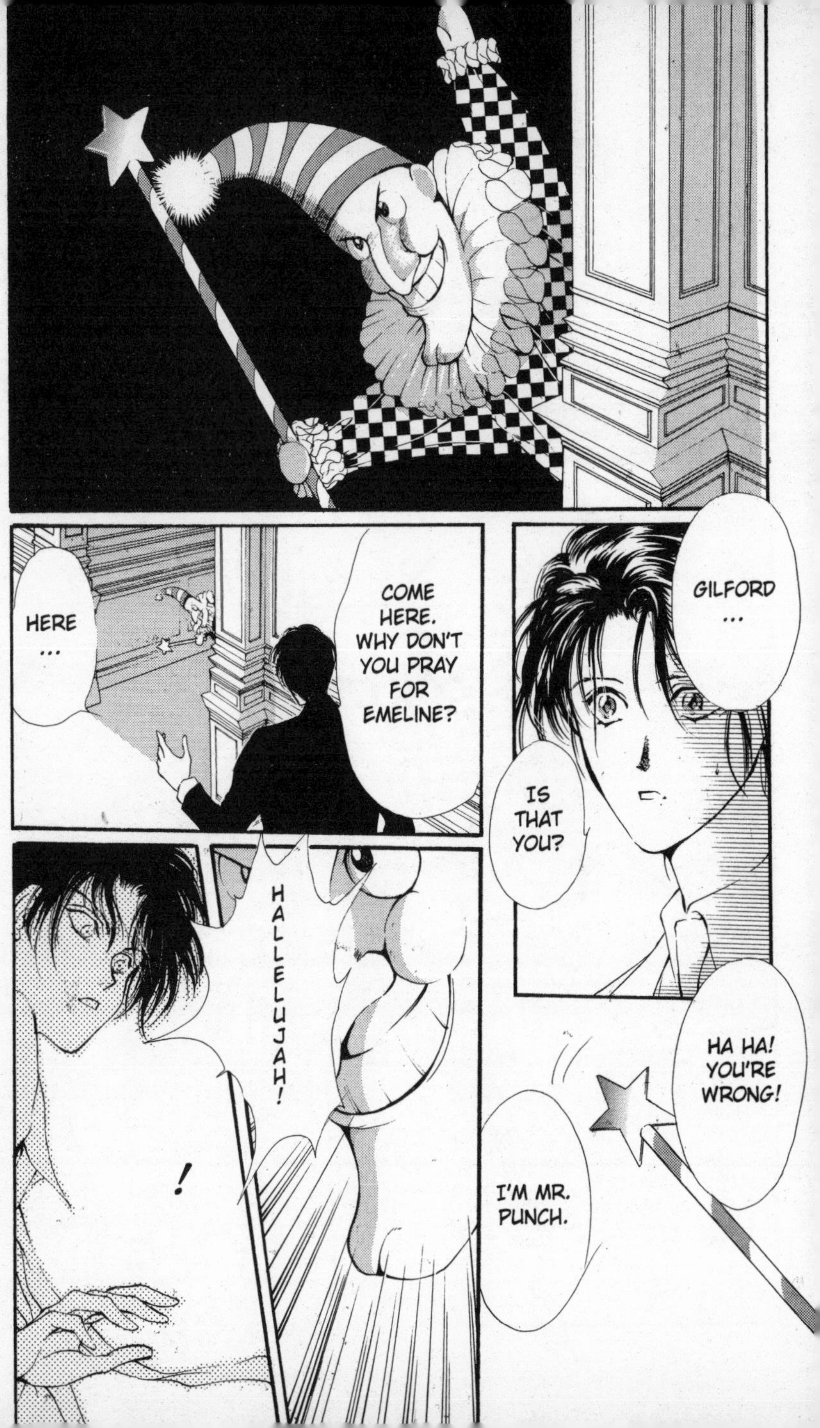
GILFORD ...
IS THAT YOU?
COME HERE. WHY DON'T YOU PRAY FOR EMELINE?
HERE ...
HA HA! YOU'RE WRONG!
I'M MR. PUNCH.
HALLELUJAH!
!

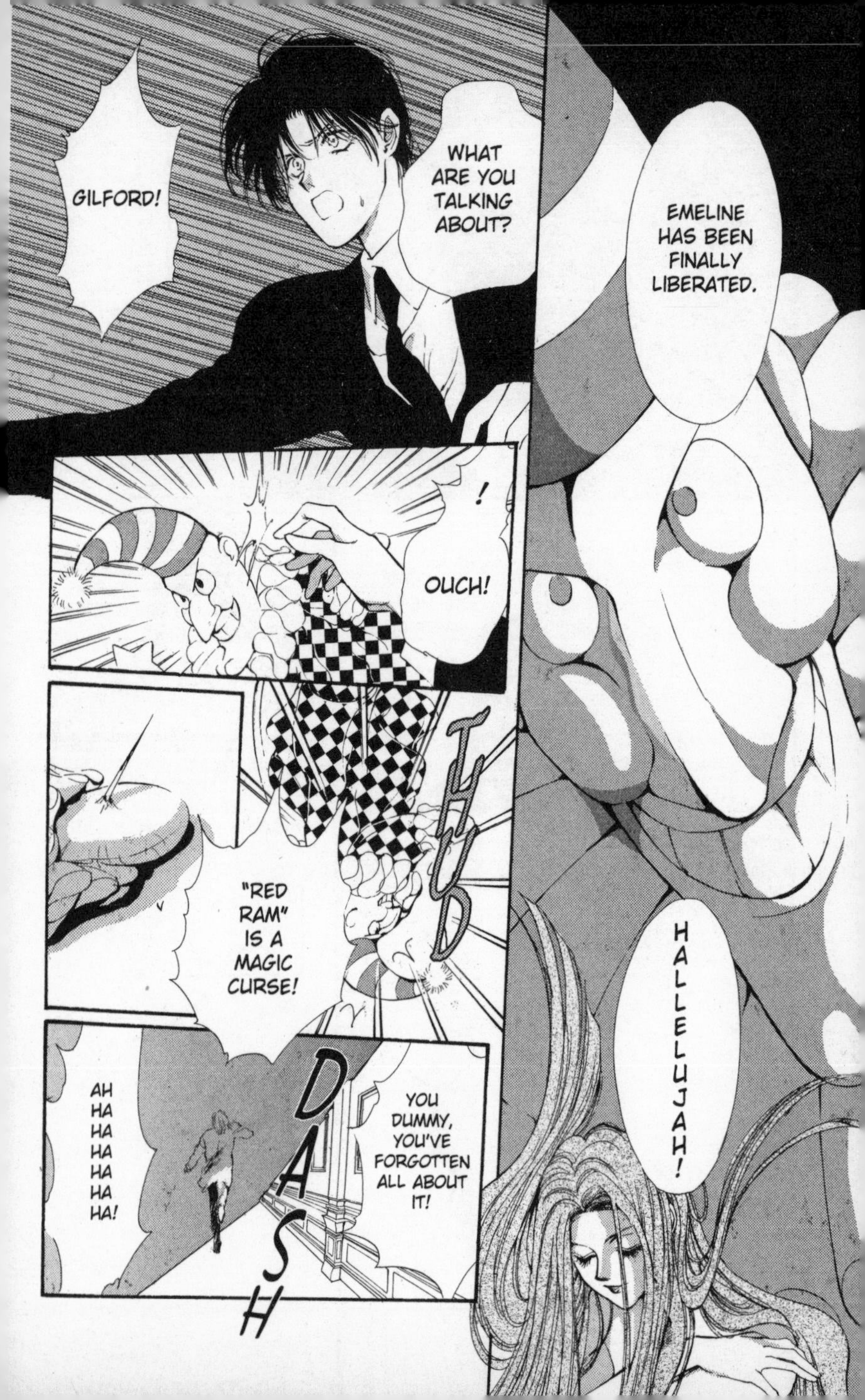
EMELINE HAS BEEN FINALLY LIBERATED.
HALLELUJAH!
WHAT ARE YOU TALKING ABOUT?
GILFORD!
!
OUCH!
THUD
"RED RAM" IS A MAGIC CURSE!
YOU DUMMY, YOU'VE FORGOTTEN ALL ABOUT IT!
DASH
AH HA HA HA HA HA HA!

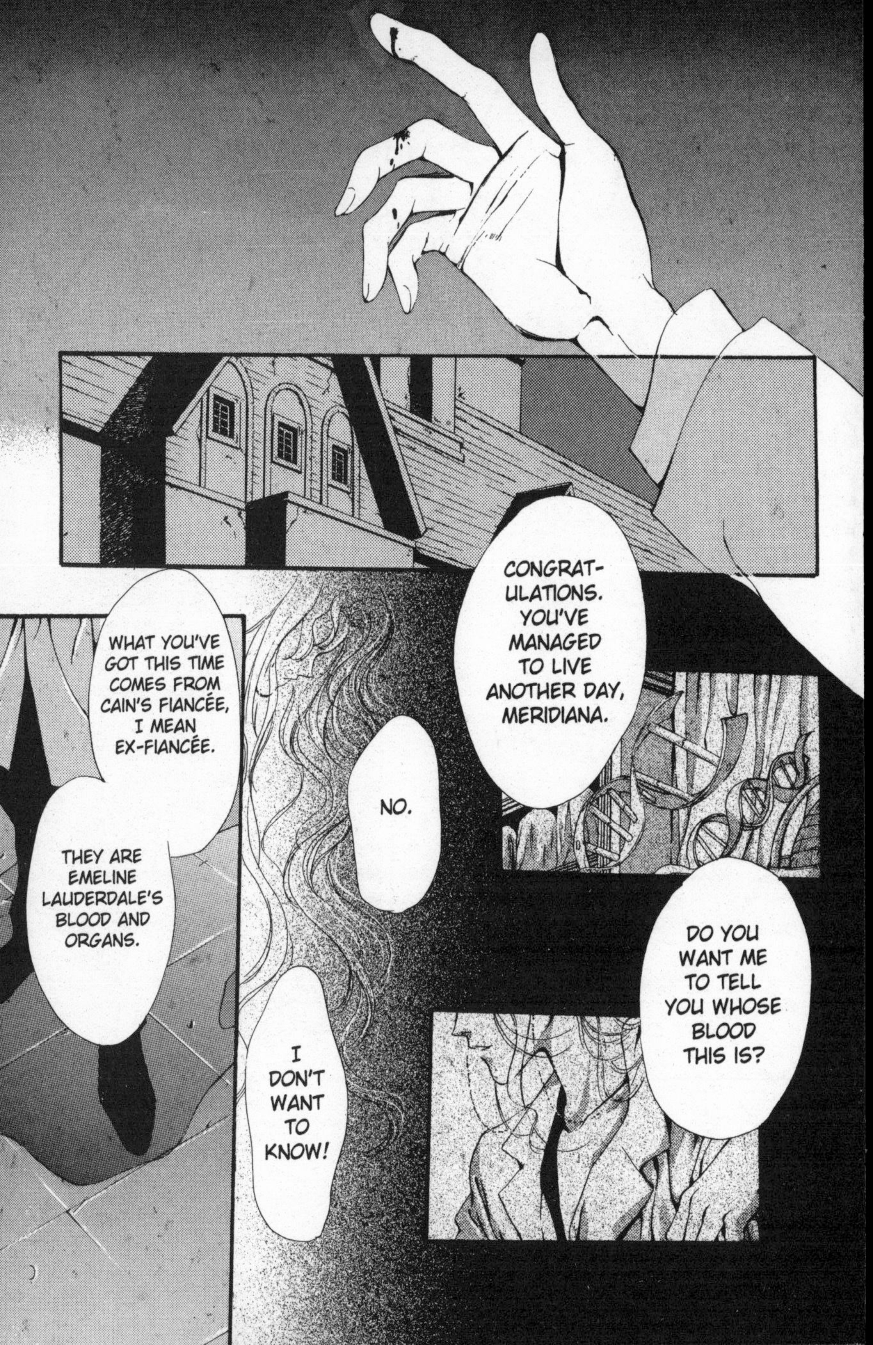
CONGRAT-ULATIONS. YOU'VE MANAGED TO LIVE ANOTHER DAY, MERIDIANA.
WHAT YOU'VE GOT THIS TIME COMES FROM CAIN'S FIANCÉE, I MEAN EX-FIANCÉE.
THEY ARE EMELINE LAUDERDALE'S BLOOD AND ORGANS.
NO.
DO YOU WANT ME TO TELL YOU WHOSE BLOOD THIS IS?
I DON'T WANT TO KNOW!

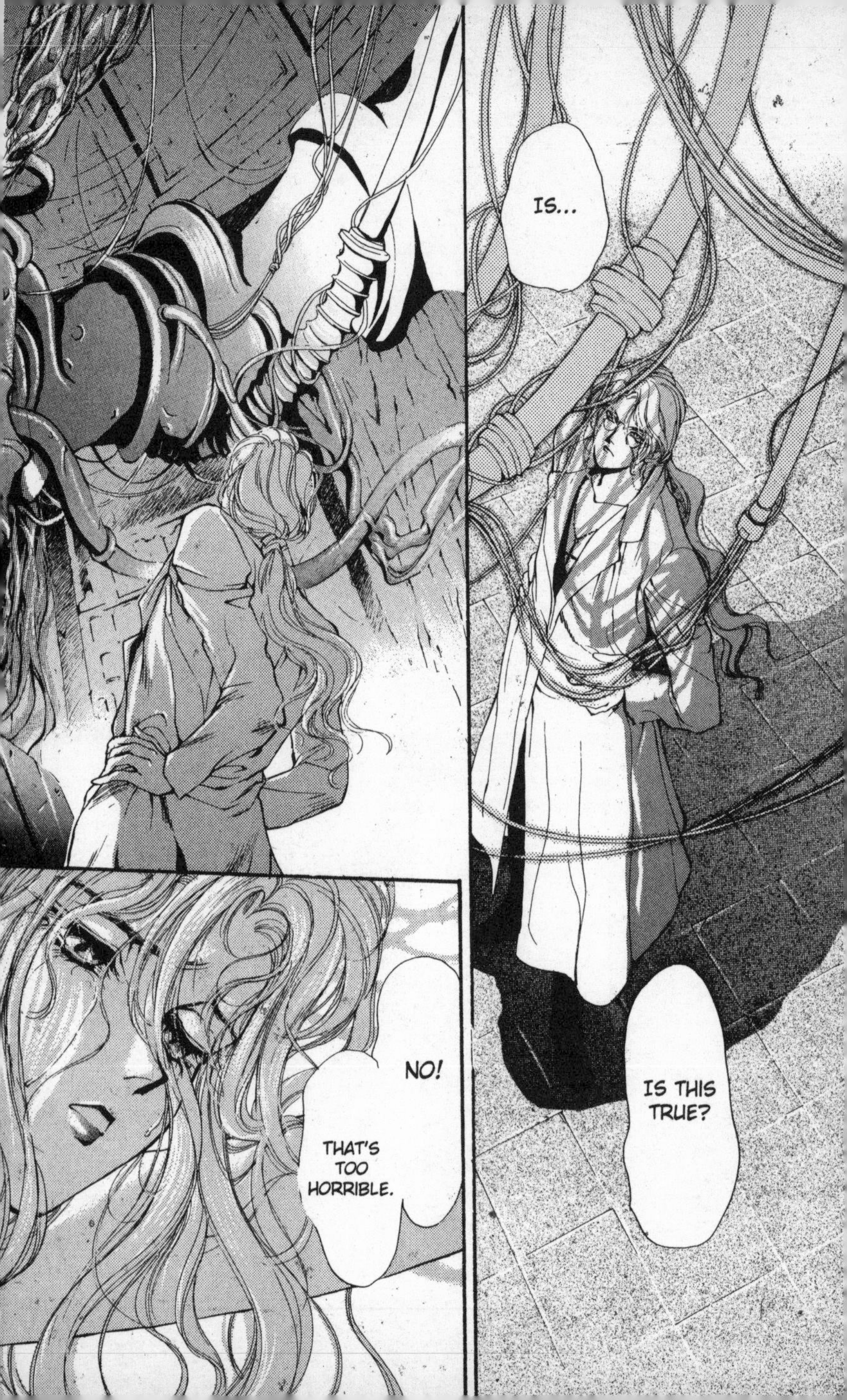
IS...
IS THIS TRUE?
NO!
THAT'S TOO HORRIBLE.

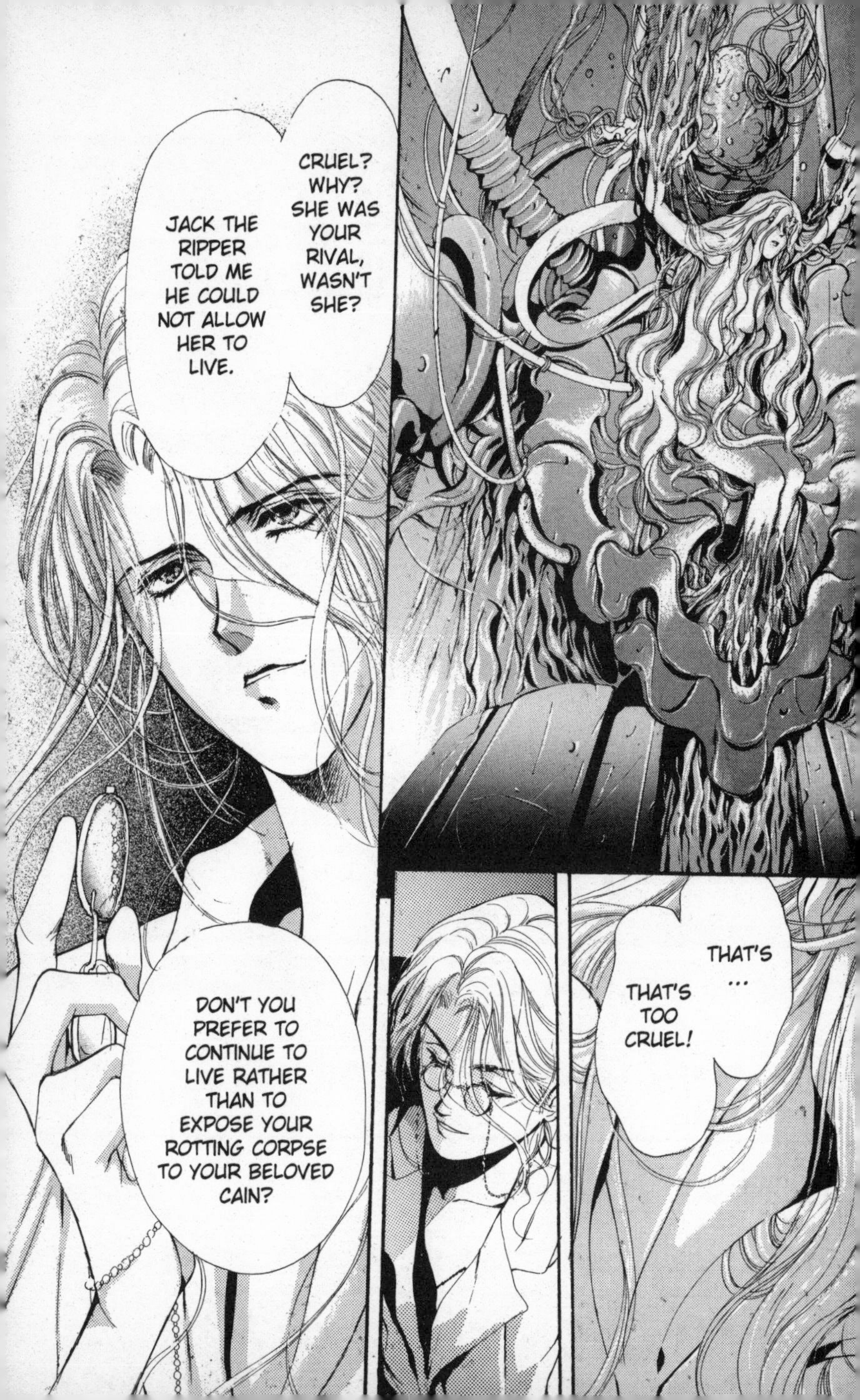
THAT'S ...
THAT'S TOO CRUEL!
CRUEL? WHY? SHE WAS YOUR RIVAL, WASN'T SHE?
JACK THE RIPPER TOLD ME HE COULD NOT ALLOW HER TO LIVE.
DON'T YOU PREFER TO CONTINUE TO LIVE RATHER THAN TO EXPOSE YOUR ROTTING CORPSE TO YOUR BELOVED CAIN?

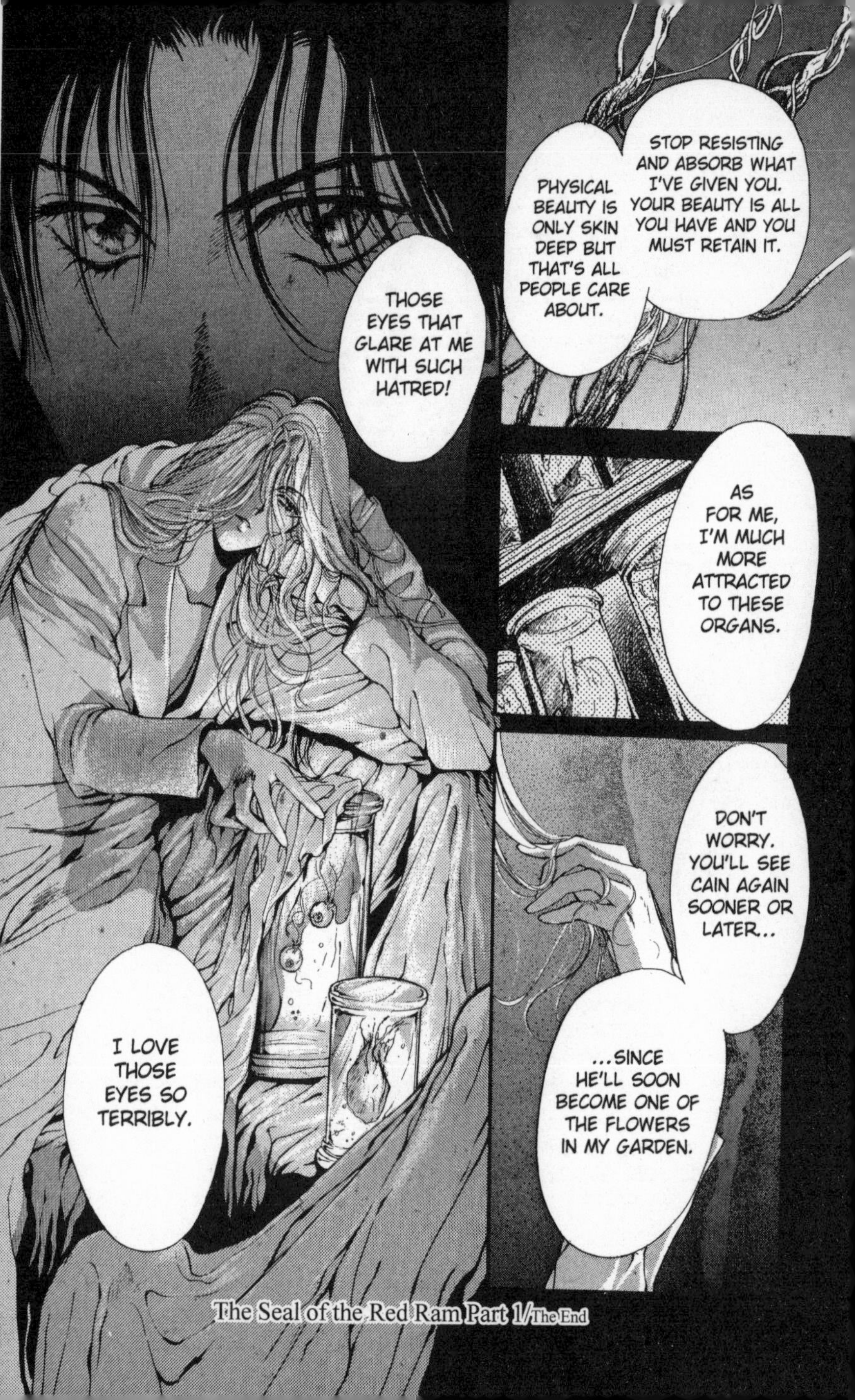
STOP RESISTING AND ABSORB WHAT I'VE GIVEN YOU. YOUR BEAUTY IS ALL YOU HAVE AND YOU MUST RETAIN IT.
PHYSICAL BEAUTY IS ONLY SKIN DEEP BUT THAT'S ALL PEOPLE CARE ABOUT.
AS FOR ME, I'M MUCH MORE ATTRACTED TO THESE ORGANS.
DON'T WORRY. YOU'LL SEE CAIN AGAIN SOONER OR LATER...
...SINCE HE'LL SOON BECOME ONE OF THE FLOWERS IN MY GARDEN.
THOSE EYES THAT GLARE AT ME WITH SUCH HATRED!
I LOVE THOSE EYES SO TERRIBLY.
The Seal of the Red Ram Part 1/The End

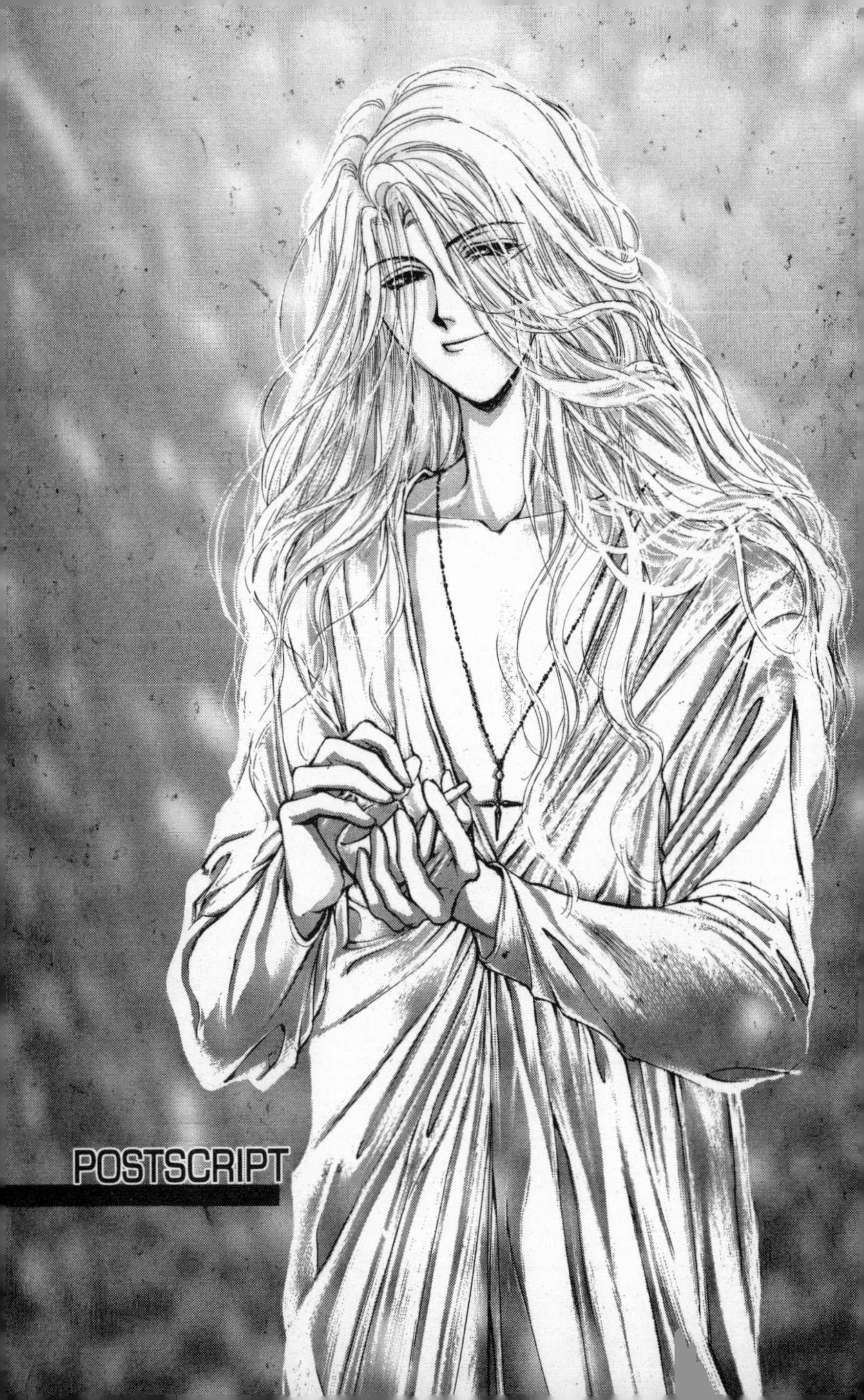
POSTSCRIPT

Hello. Here's my usual postscript. Just for your information, the person on the previous page is indeed Dr. Disraeli. His hair has grown much longer since *Earl Cain Series 3: Kafka*. He must be a real lech. (He certainly looks like one.) The doctor has a feminine face because his looks take after his mother. You will be learning a lot more about his past in coming episodes...probably...hopefully... but I can't promise... Like Cain, he may also be much younger than he looks. (Many readers say Riff looks younger than what he is. As for me, I like a man of 27 or 28 years old.) Some of you have pointed out that Disraeli talks like a pervert; well, I'd say he is a perv! He finds eyes, organs and blood erotic, talks to these organs as they float in jars of formaldehyde, and dreams of one day being preserved in formaldehyde himself. He gives each of the organs he collects a name like Josephine or Constancia. He also says things to them like, "Hi, you look beautiful today." No, I'm kidding. He doesn't name his organs. By the way, he doesn't seem to be interested in bones and brains because they don't hold any erotic appeal for him. (Please don't assume I share these tastes with Disraeli! I'm the sort of person who'd feel sick if she saw such things.) I sometimes feel so embarrassed about writing a gory story like this one that I almost feel dizzy. I wrote this somewhere else earlier, but I am really embarrassed to be drawing kiss scenes, gay scenes and so on. (Why don't I stop doing it then, right?) But I will not.)

Um, here's another correction to make: The error is found only in the first printing of "Shounen no Fuka Suru Oto (The Sound of a Boy Hatching)"*. On page 37, in the second to the last panel from the bottom, Mary Weather says, "10 years ago..." Please ignore the phrase, "10 years ago". She can't be referring to something that happened 10 years ago since she is only 10 years old. (It is corrected in the second printing.) Also, in the episode of "Tsurareta Otoko (The Hanged Man)", a maid says, "Alegra fell in love with Cain's father ten years ago before she disappeared. Then Cain's father left to look for her." However, this story is not true. I guess this was a story told to the servants to explain the father's disappearance. If I may add another correction, the phrase, "the culprit has come", in the first panel on page 34 should not be there. So please ignore it!

Thank you for the tape, the info, the cool-looking image tape, the dubbed tape of 1.3.5 and the Valentine Day's gifts (I was happy to receive them. I love white roses and soaps. I love you for being such a faithful reader and for writing me such sweet fan letters.) Meow.—

This is Jizabel when he was a teenager. The depiction of Dr. Disraeli in kimono in the postscript of the "Kafka" episode was well received (?!). Some said he looked like a courtesan and others thought he looked like the young proprietor of a kimono shop.

These letters on the bottom are so small...

NOTE: THESE ERRORS WERE NOT INCLUDED IN THE SHOJO BEAT EDITION OF THE SOUND OF A BOY HATCHING. THE PHRASE ON PG. 37 WAS "WHEN I FINALLY FOUND HER..." INSTEAD OF "IO YEARS AGO..." AND THE EXTRA PHRASE ABOUT THE CULPRIT ON PG. 34 DID NOT RUN. THE STORY ABOUT ALEGRA FALLING IN LOVE WITH ALEXIS IO YEARS AGO IS IN THE VIZ EDITION ON PG. 26. BUT SINCE IT IS A RUMOR TOLD BY THE SERVANTS, WE LEFT IT INTACT EVEN THOUGH IT MAY NOT PROVE TO BE TRUE LATER. --ED.

SHE LOVES HER BROTHER BLINDLY.

Report: "I Had the Audacity to Have a Book Signing (in Kashiwa City)"

I seriously worried that no one would come, but many people turned up.♥ (I assume it was mainly because they weren't required to obtain numbered tickets beforehand, but could just walk in.) However, I was in terrible condition that day: I hadn't had enough sleep due to a busy work schedule, and I was suffering with a cold. In the taxi on the way home from there, I almost threw up. —~ Kashiwa City is very far away from Tokyo where I live. ◍◍ During the signing, I felt even sicker because of the fumes from the marker I was using. On top of that, I wasn't used to book signings so I didn't do a very good job.¹¹ More than anything, I felt bad for those fans who had come such a long way and had to wait such a long time to have their books signed. My special thanks go to those who brought me gifts (especially the cat stuff- you know me very well!). Also many thanks to those who gave me music tapes and that fan publication- the pictures in the publication are very pretty!♬ I was happily surprised to learn that some of you loved Dr. Disraeli. Thank you also to those who cried when they saw me♥ (I was so surprised!♥). And thanks to the several male fans who turned up. Thank you all so much for coming to my book signing! ♥♥

My apologies to those fans who came all the way from really far places because I was only able to talk to you very briefly...♪

By the time the event was over, I had been given so many bouquets that I didn't know how to take them all home.♥ I was truly touched that some of you brought me salmon-pink tulips. Thanks! —♥♥ Every one of the bouquets was so beautiful that I was nearly speechless.§ That night, I went to bed surrounded by those flowers (like a corpse in a coffin?!◍) My office is normally so bare that I'll never forget those days when your flowers adorned it.¶ Well then, I'll talk to you next time when The Seal of the Red Ram Part 2 is out,♥ which is SOON!!*

untranslated?

*NOTE: THE CAIN SAGA 4, PART 2: THE SEAL OF THE RED RAM WILL BE ON SHELVES JUNE 2007! --ED.

RED RAM xxx

"Fairy Tale at 13 O'clock"

A twisted, crooked mechanical wind-up doll plots a rebellion
Against a spiral staircase that keeps twisting upward forever

Jade and amber and onyx

Cruel Alice and her friends are fixated on a mermaid's lifeless,
limp wings
And an angel's glass scales [note: as in fish scales.]
They wait at the shore of an ocean of cellophane where a sea
pig sleeps

A nightmare painted with beautiful, violent colors leaves a jet
black music box with a broken lock in an attic
And drips sin onto the pale sole of a boy engrossed in forbidden
daydreams.
It crouches
And cruelly plucks out the sickeningly sharp, opaque splinter.

Mother Goose of 13 o'clock. Labyrinth of time. Getting lost.
The door will never open, but no one notices.

Jareth*

Creator: Kaori Yuki

Date of Birth: December 18

Blood Type: B

Major Works: *Angel Sanctuary*
and *Godchild*

Kaori Yuki was born in Tokyo and started drawing at a very early age. Following her debut work *Natsufuku no Erie* (Ellie in Summer Clothes) in the Japanese magazine *Bessatsu Hana to Yume* (1987), she wrote a compelling series of short stories: *Zankoku na Douwatachi* (Cruel Fairy Tales), *Neji* (Screw), and *Sareki Ōkoku* (Gravel Kingdom).

As proven by her best-selling series *Angel Sanctuary* and *Godchild*, her celebrated body of work has etched an indelible mark on the gothic comics genre. She likes mysteries and British films, and is a fan of the movie *Dead Poets Society* and the show *Twin Peaks*.

THE CAIN SAGA, vol. 4

The Seal of the Red Ram, Part 1
The Shojo Beat Manga Edition

STORY & ART BY **KAORI YUKI**

Translation/Akira Watanabe
Touch-up Art & Lettering/James Gaubatz
Design/Izumi Evers
Editor/Joel Enos

Managing Editor/Megan Bates
Editorial Director/Elizabeth Kawasaki
VP & Editor in Chief/Yumi Hoashi
Sr. Director of Acquisitions/Rika Inouye
Sr. VP of Marketing/Liza Coppola
Exec. VP of Sales & Marketing/John Easum
Publisher/Hyoe Narita

Published by VIZ Media, LLC
P.O. Box 77010
San Francisco, CA 94107

Shojo Beat Manga Edition
10 9 8 7 6 5 4 3 2 1
First printing, April 2007

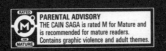

PARENTAL ADVISORY
THE CAIN SAGA is rated M for Mature and
is recommended for mature readers.
Contains graphic violence and adult themes.

store.viz.com

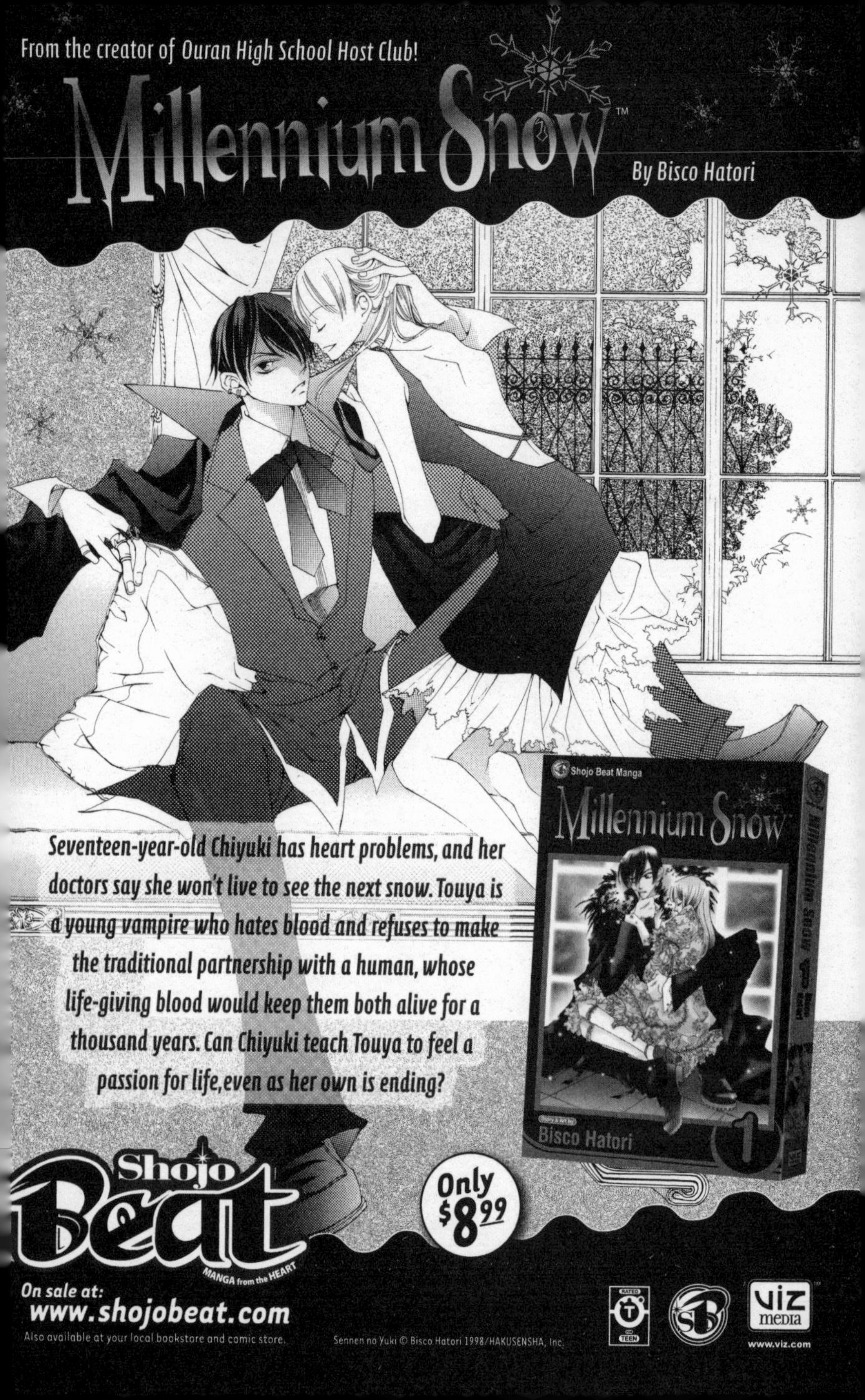
From the creator of Ouran High School Host Club!
Millennium Snow™
By Bisco Hatori
Shojo Beat Manga
Millennium Snow
Story & Art by
Bisco Hatori
1
Seventeen-year-old Chiyuki has heart problems, and her doctors say she won't live to see the next snow. Touya is a young vampire who hates blood and refuses to make the traditional partnership with a human, whose life-giving blood would keep them both alive for a thousand years. Can Chiyuki teach Touya to feel a passion for life,even as her own is ending?
Shojo Beat
MANGA from the HEART
Only $8.99
On sale at:
www.shojobeat.com
Also available at your local bookstore and comic store.
Sennen no Yuki © Bisco Hatori 1998/HAKUSENSHA, Inc.
RATED T TEEN
VIZ media
www.viz.com

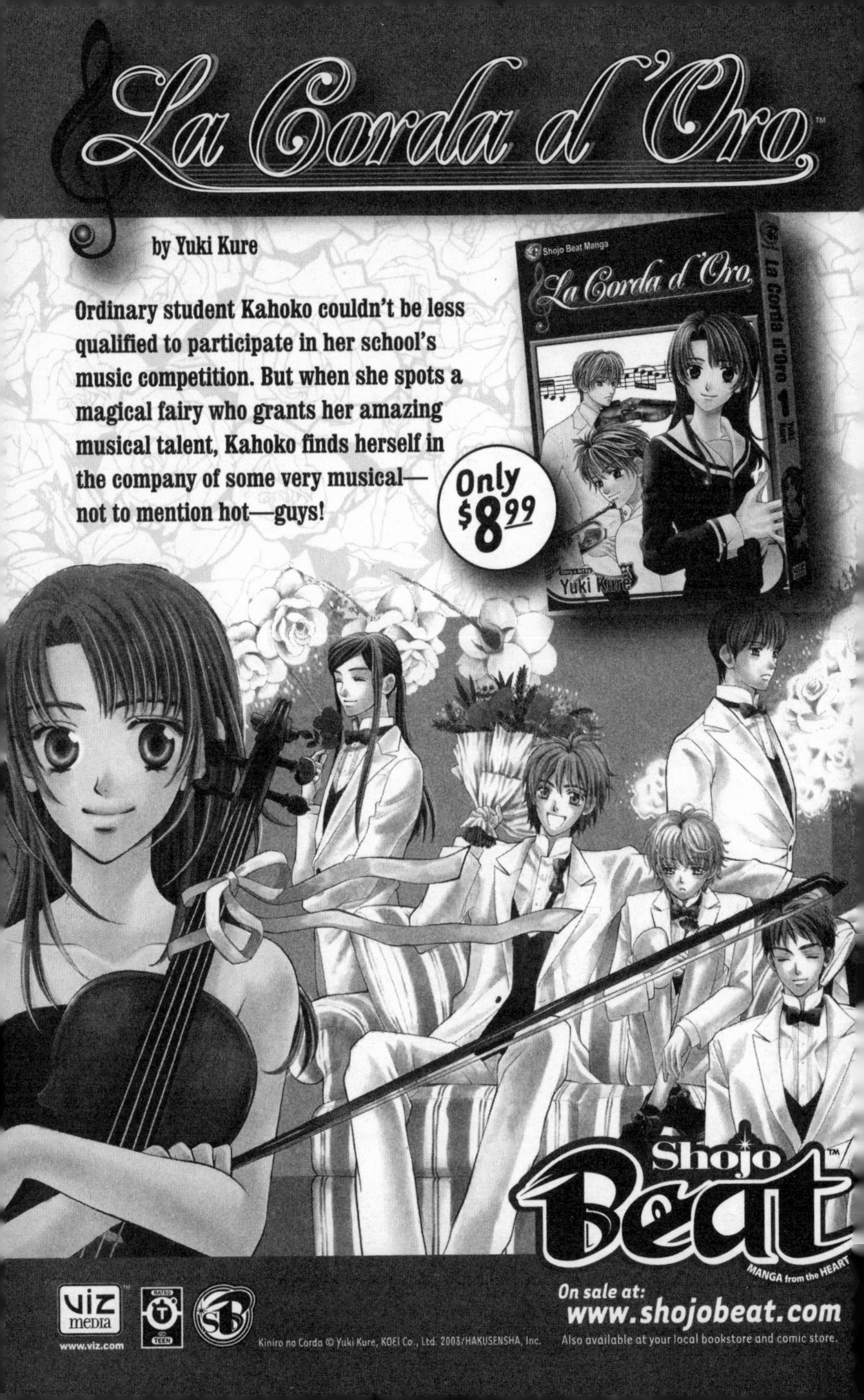

La Corda d'Oro™
by Yuki Kure
Ordinary student Kahoko couldn't be less qualified to participate in her school's music competition. But when she spots a magical fairy who grants her amazing musical talent, Kahoko finds herself in the company of some very musical—not to mention hot—guys!
Only $8.99
Shojo Beat Manga
La Corda d'Oro
La Corda d'Oro 1
Yuki Kure
Shojo Beat™
MANGA from the HEART
On sale at:
www.shojobeat.com
Also available at your local bookstore and comic store.
viz media
www.viz.com
RATED T TEEN
Kiniro no Corda © Yuki Kure, KOEI Co., Ltd. 2003/HAKUSENSHA, Inc.

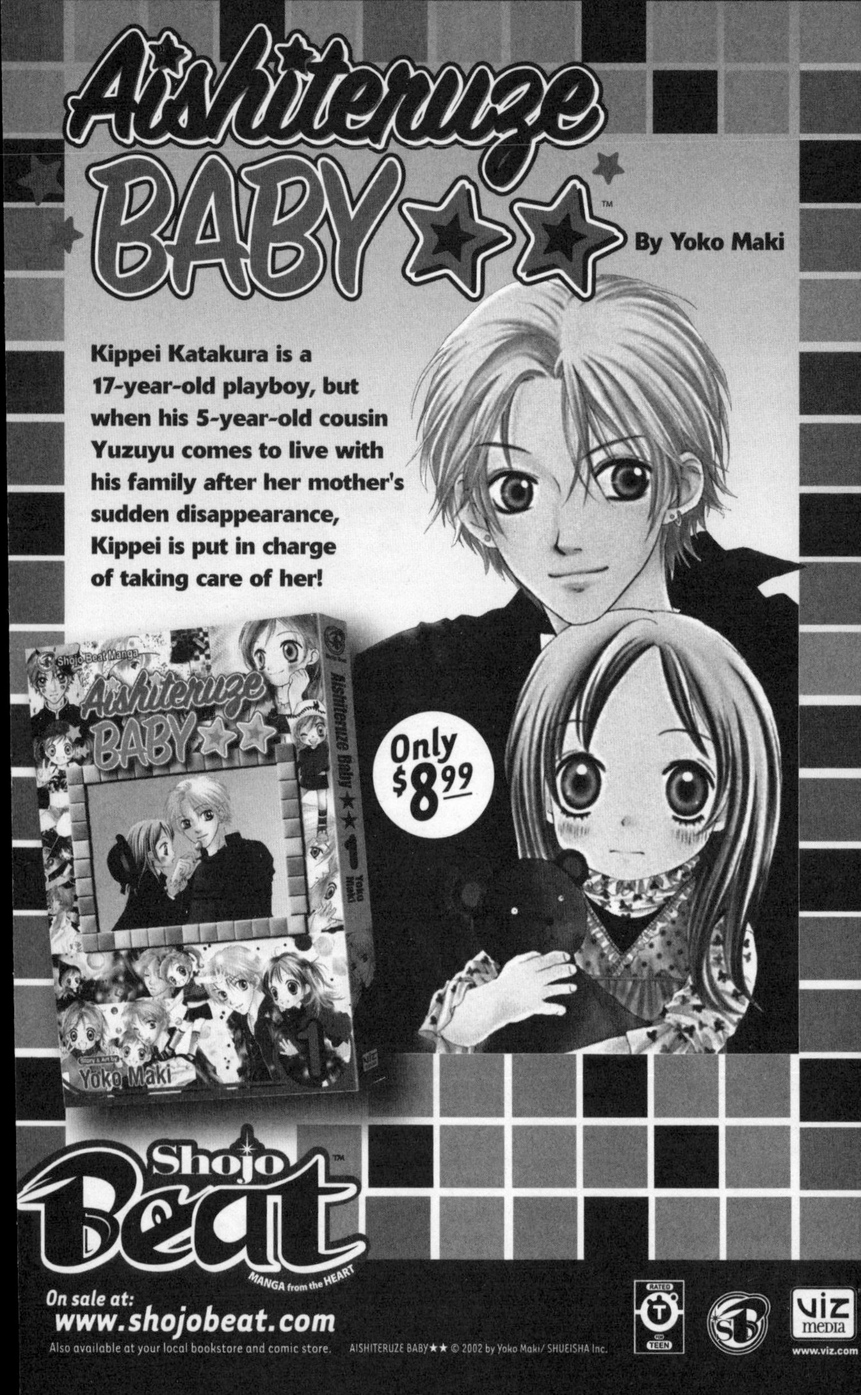
Aishiteruze BABY★★™
By Yoko Maki
Kippei Katakura is a 17-year-old playboy, but when his 5-year-old cousin Yuzuyu comes to live with his family after her mother's sudden disappearance, Kippei is put in charge of taking care of her!
Shojo Beat Manga
Aishiteruze BABY★★
Aishiteruze Baby ★★ 1 Yoko Maki
Story & Art by Yoko Maki
Only $8.99
Shojo Beat™
MANGA from the HEART
On sale at:
www.shojobeat.com
Also available at your local bookstore and comic store.
AISHITERUZE BABY★★ © 2002 by Yoko Maki/ SHUEISHA Inc.
RATED T FOR TEEN
VIZ media
www.viz.com

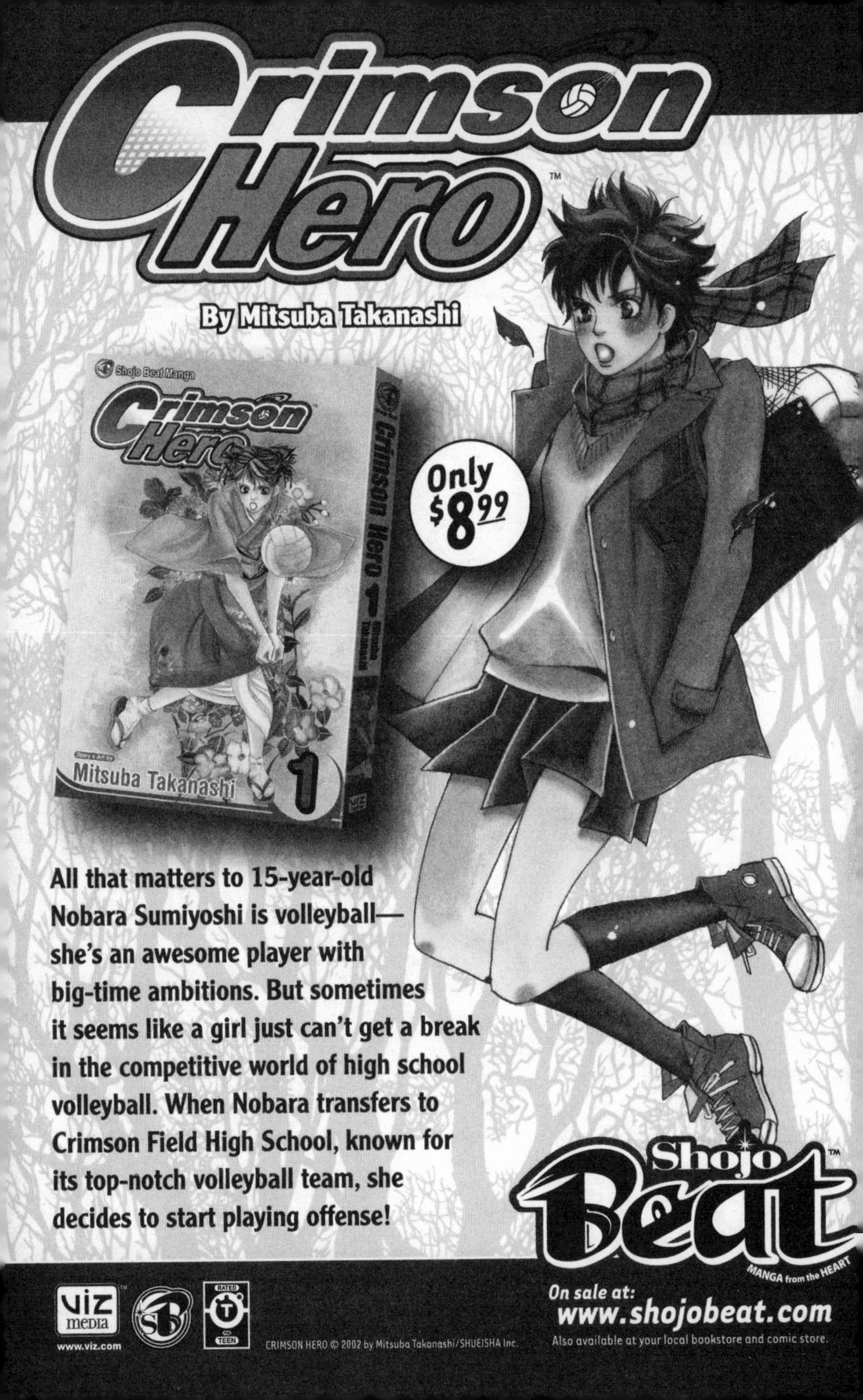
Crimson Hero™
By Mitsuba Takanashi
Shojo Beat Manga
Crimson Hero
Crimson Hero 1
Mitsuba Takanashi
Story & Art by
Mitsuba Takanashi
1
Only $8.99
All that matters to 15-year-old Nobara Sumiyoshi is volleyball—she's an awesome player with big-time ambitions. But sometimes it seems like a girl just can't get a break in the competitive world of high school volleyball. When Nobara transfers to Crimson Field High School, known for its top-notch volleyball team, she decides to start playing offense!
Shojo Beat™
MANGA from the HEART
On sale at:
www.shojobeat.com
Also available at your local bookstore and comic store.
viz media
www.viz.com
RATED T TEEN
CRIMSON HERO © 2002 by Mitsuba Takanashi/SHUEISHA Inc.

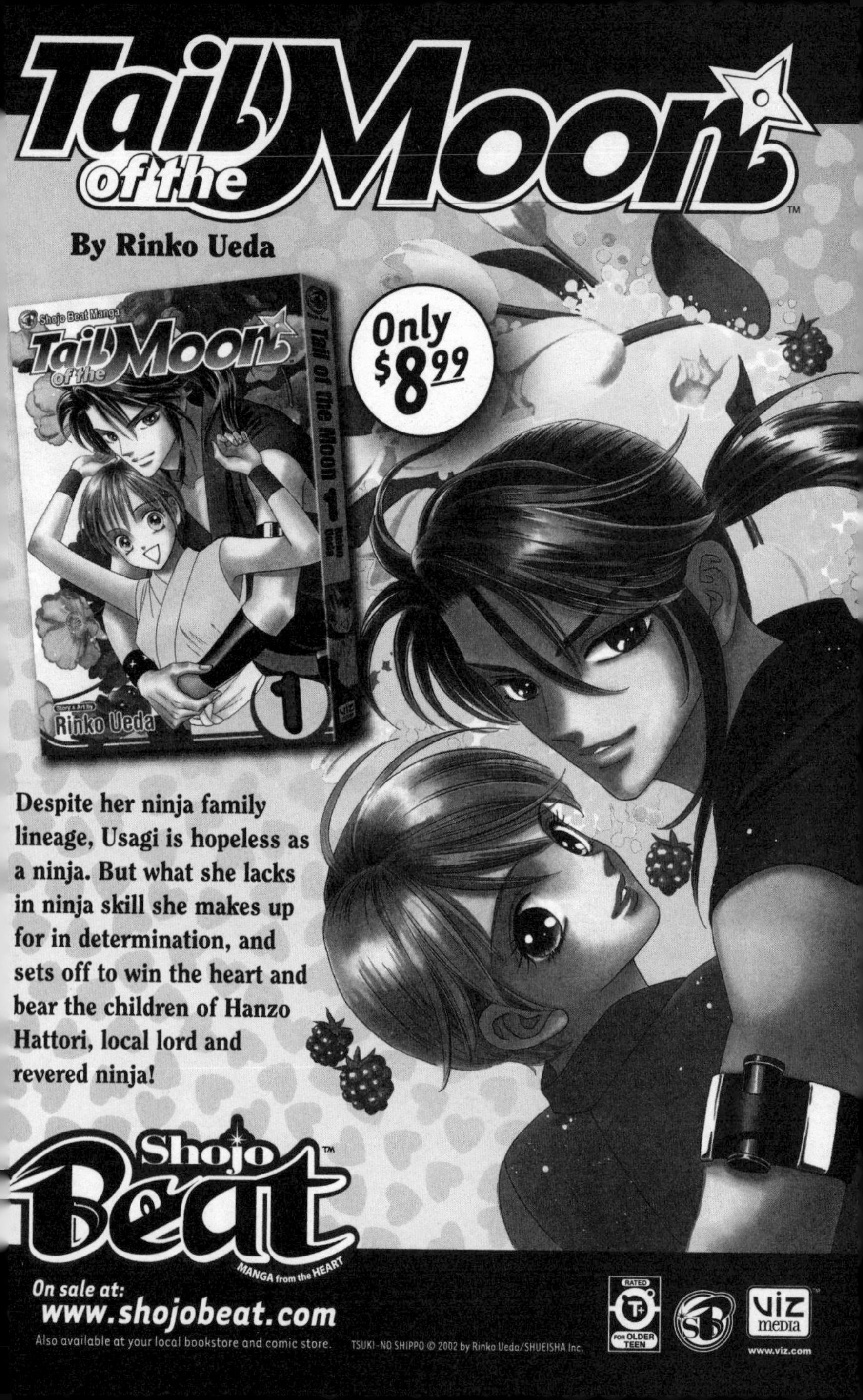

Tail of the Moon™
By Rinko Ueda
Shojo Beat Manga
Tail of the Moon
Story & Art by Rinko Ueda
1
Only $8.99
Despite her ninja family lineage, Usagi is hopeless as a ninja. But what she lacks in ninja skill she makes up for in determination, and sets off to win the heart and bear the children of Hanzo Hattori, local lord and revered ninja!
Shojo Beat™
MANGA from the HEART
On sale at:
www.shojobeat.com
Also available at your local bookstore and comic store.
TSUKI-NO SHIPPO © 2002 by Rinko Ueda/SHUEISHA Inc.
RATED T+ FOR OLDER TEEN
viz media
www.viz.com

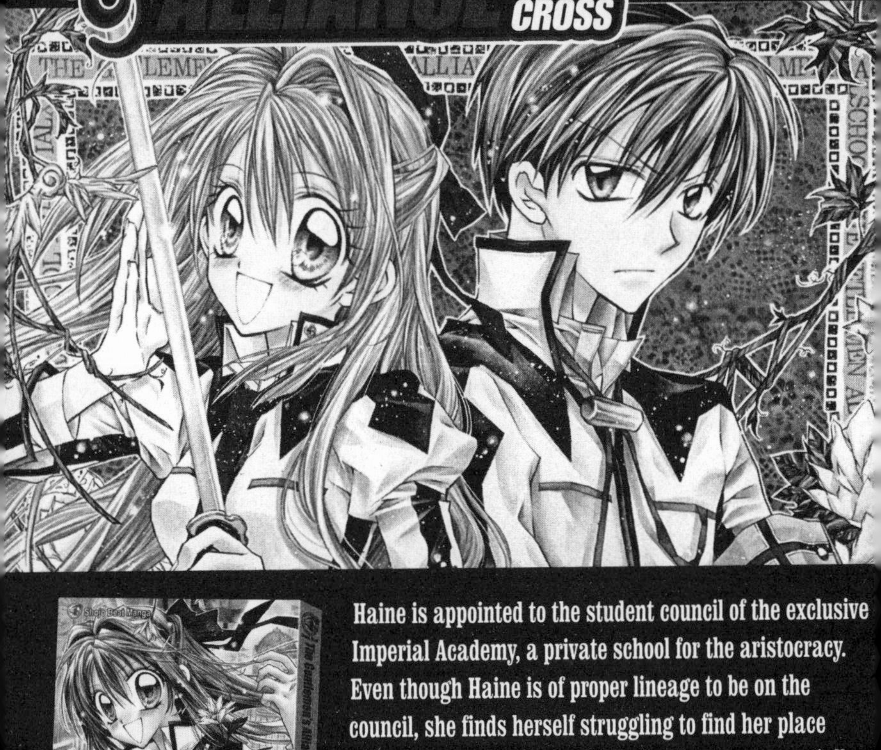

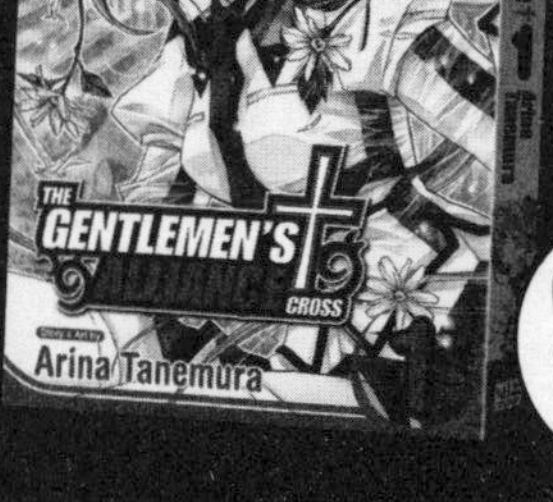
Shojo Beat Manga
The Gentlemen's Alliance†
THE GENTLEMEN'S ALLIANCE CROSS
Arina Tanemura

Tell us what you think about Shojo Beat Manga!

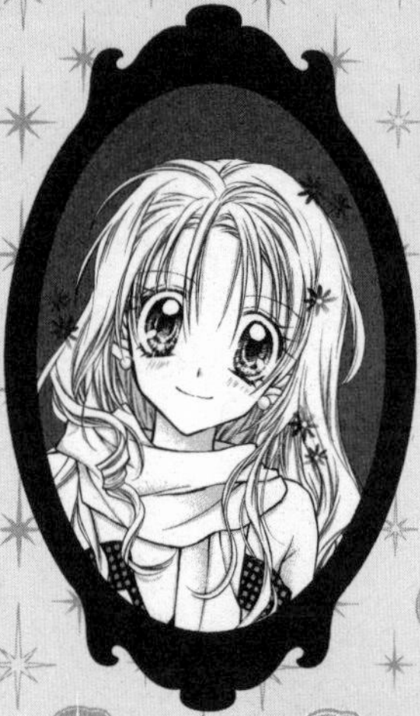

Our survey is now available online. Go to:

shojobeat.com/mangasurvey

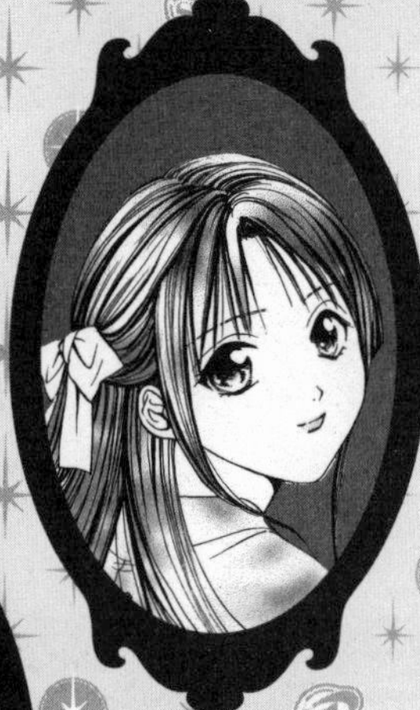

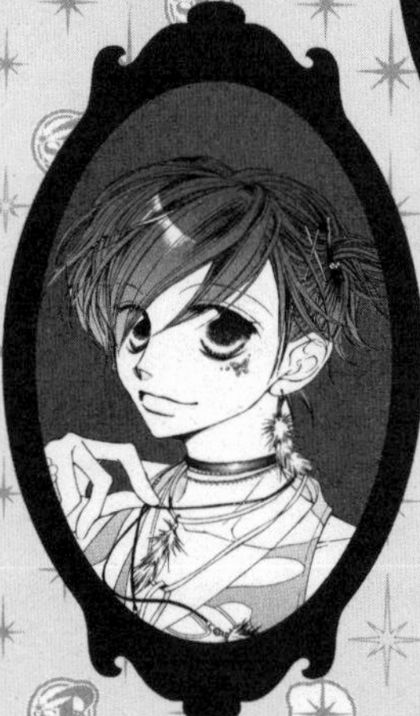

Help us make our product offerings better!

VIZ media

Shojo Beat MANGA from the HEART

THE REAL DRAMA BEGINS IN...

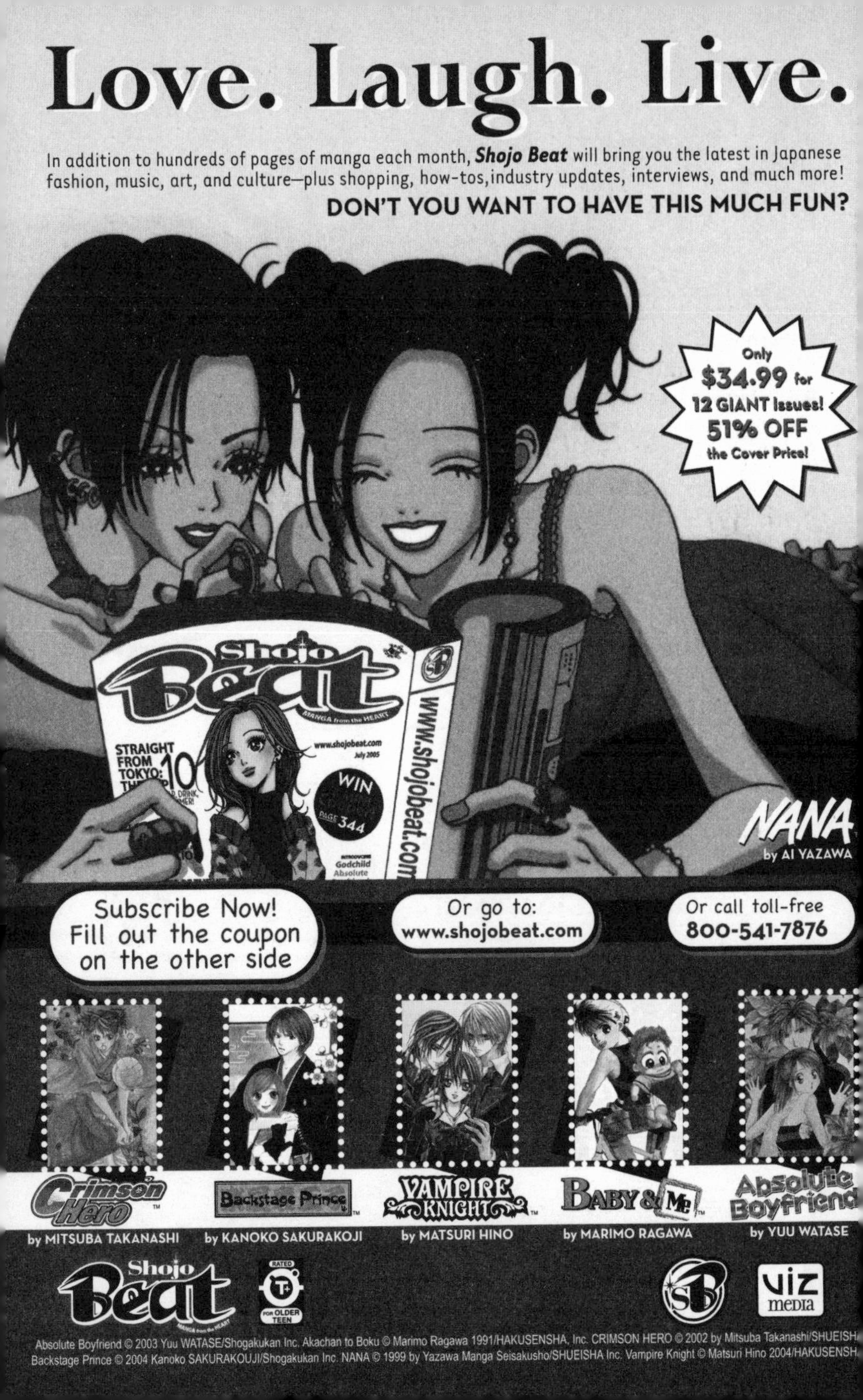
Love. Laugh. Live.
In addition to hundreds of pages of manga each month, Shojo Beat will bring you the latest in Japanese fashion, music, art, and culture—plus shopping, how-tos, industry updates, interviews, and much more!
DON'T YOU WANT TO HAVE THIS MUCH FUN?
Only $34.99 for 12 GIANT Issues! 51% OFF the Cover Price!
Shojo Beat
MANGA from the HEART
www.shojobeat.com
July 2005
STRAIGHT FROM TOKYO:
10
WIN
PAGE 344
Godchild
Absolute
www.shojobeat.com
NANA
by AI YAZAWA
Subscribe Now! Fill out the coupon on the other side
Or go to: www.shojobeat.com
Or call toll-free 800-541-7876
Crimson Hero
by MITSUBA TAKANASHI
Backstage Prince
by KANOKO SAKURAKOJI
VAMPIRE KNIGHT
by MATSURI HINO
BABY & Me
by MARIMO RAGAWA
Absolute Boyfriend
by YUU WATASE
Shojo Beat
RATED T+ FOR OLDER TEEN
viz media
Absolute Boyfriend © 2003 Yuu WATASE/Shogakukan Inc. Akachan to Boku © Marimo Ragawa 1991/HAKUSENSHA, Inc. CRIMSON HERO © 2002 by Mitsuba Takanashi/SHUEISH
Backstage Prince © 2004 Kanoko SAKURAKOUJI/Shogakukan Inc. NANA © 1999 by Yazawa Manga Seisakusho/SHUEISHA Inc. Vampire Knight © Matsuri Hino 2004/HAKUSENSH